Mastering Data Warehouse Design

Relational and Dimensional Techniques

Claudia Imhoff
Nicholas Galemmo
Jonathan G. Geiger

WILEY

Wiley Publishing, Inc.

Vice President and Executive Publisher: Robert Ipsen
Publisher: Joe Wikert
Executive Editor: Robert M. Elliott
Developmental Editor: Emilie Herman
Editorial Manager: Kathryn Malm
Managing Editor: Pamela M. Hanley
Text Design & Composition: Wiley Composition Services

This book is printed on acid-free paper. ⊛

Published by Wiley Publishing, Inc., Indianapolis, Indiana

Published simultaneously in Canada

For general information on our other products and services please contact our Customer Care Department within the United States at (800) 762-2974, outside the United States at (317) 572-3993 or fax (317) 572-4002.

Wiley also publishes its books in a variety of electronic formats. Some content that appears in print may not be available in electronic books.

ISBN: 0-471-32421-3

Printed in the United States of America

10 9 8 7 6 5 4 3

Claudia: For all their patience and understanding throughout the years, this book is dedicated to David and Jessica Imhoff.

Nick: To my wife Sarah, and children Amanda and Nick Galemmo, for their understanding over the many weekends I spent working on this book. Also to my college professor, Julius Archibald at the State University of New York at Plattsburgh for instilling in me the science and art of computing.

Jonathan: To my wife, Alma Joy, for her patience and understanding of the time spent writing this book, and to my children, Avi and Shana, who are embarking on their respective careers and of whom I am extremely proud.

CONTENTS

W e gratefully acknowledge the following individuals who directly or indirectly contributed to this book:

Greg Backhus – Helzberg Diamonds

William Baker – Microsoft Corporation

John Crawford – Merrill Lynch

David Gleason – Intelligent Solutions, Inc.

William H. Inmon – Inmon Associates, Inc.

Dr. Ralph S. Kimball- Kimball Associates

Lisa Loftis – Intelligent Solutions, Inc.

Bob Lokken – ProClarity Corporation

Anthony Marino – L'Oreal Corporation

Joyce Norris-Montanari – Intelligent Solutions, Inc.

Laura Reeves – StarSoft, Inc.

Ron Powell – *DM Review* Magazine

Kim Stannick – Teradata Corporation

Barbara von Halle – Knowledge Partners, Inc.

John Zachman – Zachman International, Inc.

We would also like to thank our editors, Bob Elliott, Pamela Hanley, and Emilie Herman, whose tireless prodding and assistance kept us honest and on schedule.

Claudia Imhoff, Ph.D. is the president and founder of Intelligent Solutions (www.IntelSols.com), a leading consultancy on CRM (Customer Relationship Management) and business intelligence technologies and strategies. She is a popular speaker and internationally recognized expert and serves as an advisor to many corporations, universities, and leading technology companies on these topics. She has coauthored five books and over 50 articles on these topics. She can be reached at CImhoff@IntelSols.com.

Nicholas Galemmo was an information architect at Nestlé USA. Nicholas has 27 years' experience as a practitioner and consultant involved in all aspects of application systems design and development within the manufacturing, distribution, education, military, health care, and financial industries. He has been actively involved in large-scale data warehousing and systems integration projects for the past 11 years. He has built numerous data warehouses, using both dimensional and relational architectures. He has published many articles and has presented at national conferences. This is his first book. Mr. Galemmo is now an independent consultant and can be reached at ngalemmo@yahoo.com.

Jonathan G. Geiger is executive vice president at Intelligent Solutions, Inc. Jonathan has been involved in many Corporate Information Factory and customer relationship management projects within the utility, telecommunications, manufacturing, education, chemical, financial, and retail industries. In his 30 years as a practitioner and consultant, Jonathan has managed or performed work in virtually every aspect of information management. He has authored or coauthored over 30 articles and two other books, presents frequently at national and international conferences, and teaches several public seminars. Mr. Geiger can be reached at JGeiger@IntelSols.com.

PART ONE

Concepts

We have found that an understanding of why a particular approach is being promoted helps us recognize its value and apply it. Therefore, we start this section with an introduction to the Corporate Information Factory (CIF). This proven and stable architecture includes two formal data stores for business intelligence, each with a specific role in the BI environment.

The first data store is the data warehouse. The major role of the data warehouse is to serve as a data repository that stores data from disparate sources, making it accessible to another set of data stores – the data marts. As the collection point, the most effective design approach for the data warehouse is based on an entity-relationship data model and the normalization techniques developed by Codd and Date in their seminal work throughout the 1970's, 80's and 90's for relational databases.

The major role of the data mart is to provide the business users with easy access to quality, integrated information. There are several types of data marts, and these are also described in Chapter 1. The most popular data mart is built to support online analytical processing, and the most effective design approach for it is the dimensional data model.

Continuing with the conceptual theme, we explain the importance of relational modeling techniques, introduce the different types of models that are needed, and provide a process for building a relational data model in Chapter 2. We also explain the relationship between the various data models used in constructing a solid foundation for any enterprise—the business, system, and technology data models—and how they share or inherit characteristics from each other.

CHAPTER 1

Introduction

W elcome to the first book that thoroughly describes the data modeling techniques used in constructing a multipurpose, stable, and sustainable data warehouse used to support business intelligence (BI). This chapter introduces the
data warehouse by describing the objectives of BI and the data warehouse and
by explaining how these fit into the overall Corporate Information Factory
(CIF) architecture. It discusses the iterative nature of the data warehouse construction and demonstrates the importance of the data warehouse data model
and the justification for the type of data model format suggested in this book.
We discuss why the format of the model should be based on relational design
techniques, illustrating the need to maximize nonredundancy, stability, and
maintainability. Another section of the chapter outlines the characteristics of a
maintainable data warehouse environment. The chapter ends with a discussion of the impact of this modeling approach on the ultimate delivery of the
data marts. This chapter sets up the reader to understand the rationale behind
the ensuing chapters, which describe in detail how to create the data warehouse data model.

Overview of Business Intelligence

BI, in the context of the data warehouse, is the ability of an enterprise to study
past behaviors and actions in order to understand where the organization has

been, determine its current situation, and predict or change what will happen in the future. BI has been maturing for more than 20 years. Let's briefly go over the past decade of this fascinating and innovative history.

You're probably familiar with the technology adoption curve. The first companies to adopt the new technology are called innovators. The next category is known as the early adopters, then there are members of the early majority, members of the late majority, and finally the laggards. The curve is a traditional bell curve, with exponential growth in the beginning and a slowdown in market growth occurring during the late majority period. When new technology is introduced, it is usually hard to get, expensive, and imperfect. Over time, its availability, cost, and features improve to the point where just about anyone can benefit from ownership. Cell phones are a good example of this. Once, only the innovators (doctors and lawyers?) carried them. The phones were big, heavy, and expensive. The service was spotty at best, and you got "dropped" a lot. Now, there are deals where you can obtain a cell phone for about $60, the service providers throw in $25 of airtime, and there are no monthly fees, and service is quite reliable.

Data warehousing is another good example of the adoption curve. In fact, if you haven't started your first data warehouse project, there has never been a better time. Executives today expect, and often get, most of the good, timely information they need to make informed decisions to lead their companies into the next decade. But this wasn't always the case.

Just a decade ago, these same executives sanctioned the development of executive information systems (EIS) to meet their needs. The concept behind EIS initiatives was sound—to provide executives with easily accessible key performance information in a timely manner. However, many of these systems fell short of their objectives, largely because the underlying architecture could not respond fast enough to the enterprise's changing environment. Another significant shortcoming of the early EIS days was the enormous effort required to provide the executives with the data they desired. Data acquisition or the extract, transform, and load (ETL) process is a complex set of activities whose sole purpose is to attain the most accurate and integrated data possible and make it accessible to the enterprise through the data warehouse or operational data store (ODS).

The entire process began as a manually intensive set of activities. Hard-coded "data suckers" were the only means of getting data out of the operational systems for access by business analysts. This is similar to the early days of telephony, when operators on skates had to connect your phone with the one you were calling by racing back and forth and manually plugging in the appropriate cords.

Fortunately, we have come a long way from those days, and the data warehouse industry has developed a plethora of tools and technologies to support the data acquisition process. Now, progress has allowed most of this process to be automated, as it has in today's telephony world. Also, similar to telephony advances, this process remains a difficult, if not temperamental and complicated, one. No two companies will ever have the same data acquisition activities or even the same set of problems. Today, most major corporations with significant data warehousing efforts rely heavily on their ETL tools for design, construction, and maintenance of their BI environments.

Another major change during the last decade is the introduction of tools and modeling techniques that bring the phrase "easy to use" to life. The dimensional modeling concepts developed by Dr. Ralph Kimball and others are largely responsible for the widespread use of multidimensional data marts to support online analytical processing.

In addition to multidimensional analyses, other sophisticated technologies have evolved to support data mining, statistical analysis, and exploration needs. Now mature BI environments require much more than star schemas—flat files, statistical subsets of unbiased data, normalized data structures, in addition to star schemas, are all significant data requirements that must be supported by your data warehouse.

Of course, we shouldn't underestimate the impact of the Internet on data warehousing. The Internet helped remove the mystique of the computer. Executives use the Internet in their daily lives and are no longer wary of touching the keyboard. The end-user tool vendors recognized the impact of the Internet, and most of them seized upon that realization: to design their interface such that it replicated some of the look-and-feel features of the popular Internet browsers and search engines. The sophistication—and simplicity—of these tools has led to a widespread use of BI by business analysts and executives.

Another important event taking place in the last few years is the transformation from technology chasing the business to the business demanding technology. In the early days of BI, the information technology (IT) group recognized its value and tried to sell its merits to the business community. In some unfortunate cases, the IT folks set out to build a data warehouse with the hope that the business community would use it. Today, the value of a sophisticated decision support environment is widely recognized throughout the business. As an example, an effective customer relationship management program could not exist without strategic (data warehouse with associated marts) and a tactical (operational data store and oper mart) decision-making capabilities. (See Figure 1.1)

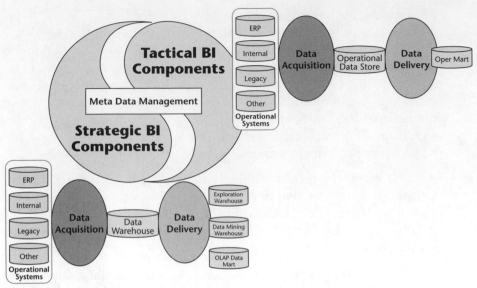

Figure 1.1 Strategic and tactical portions of a BI environment.

BI Architecture

One of the most significant developments during the last 10 years has been the introduction of a widely accepted architecture to support all BI technological demands. This architecture recognized that the EIS approach had several major flaws, the most significant of which was that the EIS data structures were often fed directly from source systems, resulting in a very complex data acquisition environment that required significant human and computer resources to maintain. The Corporate Information Factory (CIF) (see Figure 1.2), the architecture used in most decision support environments today, addressed that deficiency by segregating data into five major databases (operational systems, data warehouse, operational data store, data marts, and oper marts) and incorporating processes to effectively and efficiently move data from the source systems to the business users.

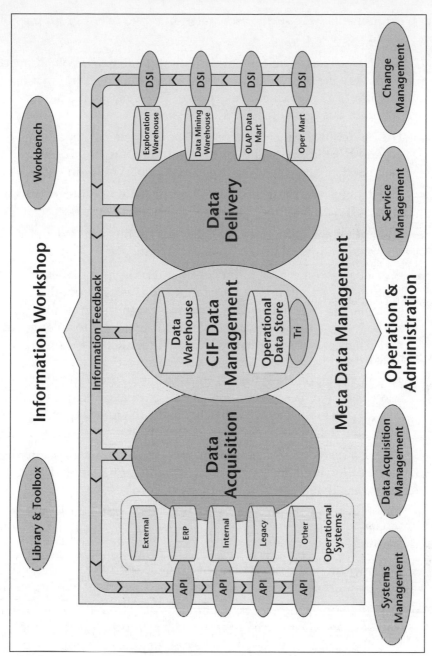

Figure 1.2   The Corporate Information Factory.

These components were further separated into two major groupings of components and processes:

- *Getting data in* consists of the processes and databases involved in acquiring data from the operational systems, integrating it, cleaning it up, and putting it into a database for easy usage. The components of the CIF that are found in this function:

  - The operational system databases (source systems) contain the data used to run the day-to-day business of the company. These are still the major source of data for the decision support environment.

  - The data warehouse is a collection or repository of integrated, detailed, historical data to support strategic decision-making.

  - The operational data store is a collection of integrated, detailed, current data to support tactical decision making.

  - Data acquisition is a set of processes and programs that extracts data for the data warehouse and operational data store from the operational systems. The data acquisition programs perform the cleansing as well as the integration of the data and transformation into an enterprise format. This enterprise format reflects an integrated set of enterprise business rules that usually causes the data acquisition layer to be the most complex component in the CIF. In addition to programs that transform and clean up data, the data acquisition layer also includes audit and control processes and programs to ensure the integrity of the data as it enters the data warehouse or operational data store.

- *Getting information out* consists of the processes and databases involved in delivering BI to the ultimate business consumer or analyst. The components of the CIF that are found in this function:

  - The data marts are derivatives from the data warehouse used to provide the business community with access to various types of strategic analysis.

  - The oper marts are derivatives of the ODS used to provide the business community with dimensional access to current operational data.

  - Data delivery is the process that moves data from the data warehouse into data and oper marts. Like the data acquisition layer, it manipulates the data as it moves it. In the case of data delivery, however, the origin is the data warehouse or ODS, which already contains high-quality, integrated data that conforms to the enterprise business rules.

The CIF didn't just happen. In the beginning, it consisted of the data warehouse and sets of lightly summarized and highly summarized data—initially a collection of the historical data needed to support strategic decisions. Over time, it spawned the operational data store with a focus on the tactical decision support requirements as well. The lightly and highly summarized sets of data evolved into what we now know are data marts.

Let's look at the CIF in action. Customer Relationship Management (CRM) is a highly popular initiative that needs the components for tactical information (operational systems, operational data store, and oper marts) and for strategic information (data warehouse and various types of data marts). Certainly this technology is necessary for CRM, but CRM requires more than just the technology—it also requires alignment of the business strategy, corporate culture and organization, and customer information in addition to technology to provide long-term value to both the customer and the organization. An architecture such as that provided by the CIF fits very well within the CRM environment, and each component has a specific design and function within this architecture. We describe each component in more detail later in this chapter.

CRM is a popular application of the data warehouse and operational data store but there are many other applications. For example, the enterprise resource planning (ERP) vendors such as SAP, Oracle, and PeopleSoft have embraced data warehousing and augmented their tool suites to provide the needed capabilities. Many software vendors are now offering various plug-ins containing generic analytical applications such as profitability or key performance indicator (KPI) analyses. We will cover the components of the CIF in far greater detail in the following sections of this chapter.

The evolution of data warehousing has been critical in helping companies better serve their customers and improve their profitability. It took a combination of technological changes and a sustainable architecture. The tools for building this environment have certainly come a long way. They are quite sophisticated and offer great benefit in the design, implementation, maintenance, and access to critical corporate data. The CIF architecture capitalizes on these technology and tool innovations. It creates an environment that segregates data into five distinct stores, each of which has a key role in providing the business community with the right information at the right time, in the right place, and in the right form. So, if you're a data warehousing late majority or even a laggard, take heart. It was worth the wait.

What Is a Data Warehouse?

Before we get started with the actual description of the modeling techniques, we need to make sure that all of us are on the same page in terms of what we mean by a data warehouse, its role and purpose in BI, and the architectural components that support its construction and usage.

Role and Purpose of the Data Warehouse

As we see in the first section of this chapter, the overall BI architecture has evolved considerably over the past decade. From simple reporting and EIS systems to multidimensional analyses to statistical and data mining requirements to exploration capabilities, and now the introduction of customizable analytical applications, these technologies are part of a robust and mature BI environment. See Figure 1.3 for the general timeframe for each of these technological advances.

Given these important but significantly different technologies and data format requirements, it should be obvious that a repository of quality, trusted data in a flexible, reusable format must be the starting point to support and maintain any BI environment. The data warehouse has been a part of the BI architecture from the very beginning. Different methodologies and data warehouse gurus have given this component various names such as:

A staging area.　A variation on the data warehouse is the "back office" staging area where data from the operational systems is first brought together. It is an informally designed and maintained grouping of data whose only purpose is to feed multidimensional data marts.

The information warehouse.　This was an early name for the data warehouse used by IBM and other vendors. It was not as clearly defined as the staging area and, in many cases, encompassed not only the repository of historical data but also the various data marts in its definition.

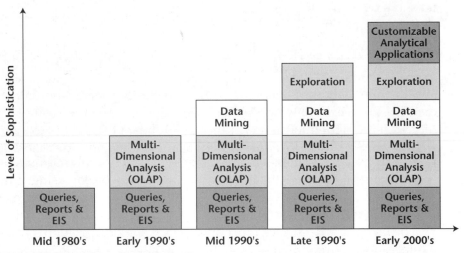

Figure 1.3　Evolving BI technologies.

The data warehouse environment must align varying skill sets, functionality, and technologies. Therefore it must be designed with two ideas in mind. First, it must be at the proper level of grain, or detail, to satisfy all the data marts. That is, it must contain the least common denominator of detailed data to supply aggregated, summarized marts as well as transaction-level exploration and mining warehouses.

Second, its design must not compromise the ability to use the various technologies for the data marts. The design must accommodate multidimensional marts as well as statistical, mining, and exploration warehouses. In addition, it must accommodate the new analytical applications being offered and be prepared to support any new technology coming down the pike. Thus the schemas it must support consist of star schemas, flat files, statistical subsets of normalized data, and whatever the future brings to BI. Given these goals, let's look at how the data warehouse fits into a comprehensive architecture supporting this mature BI environment.

The Corporate Information Factory

The Corporate Information Factory (CIF) is a widely accepted conceptual architecture that describes and categorizes the information stores used to operate and manage a successful and robust BI infrastructure. These information stores support three high-level organizational processes:

- *Business operations* are concerned with the ongoing day-to-day operations of the business. It is within this function that we find the operational transaction-processing systems and external data. These systems help run the business, and they are usually highly automated. The processes that support this function are fairly static, and they change only in quantum leaps. That is, the operational processes remain constant from day to day, and only change through a conscious effort by the company.

- *Business intelligence* is concerned with the ongoing search for a better understanding of the company, of its products, and of its customers. Whereas business operations processes are static, business intelligence includes processes that are constantly evolving, in addition to static processes. These processes can change as business analysts and knowledge workers explore the information available to them, using that information to help them develop new products, measure customer retention, evaluate potential new markets, and perform countless other tasks. The business intelligence function supports the organization's strategic decision-making process.

■ *Business management* is the function in which the knowledge and new insights developed in business intelligence are institutionalized and introduced into the daily business operations throughout the enterprise. Business management encompasses the tactical decisions that an organization makes as it carries out its strategies.

Taken as a whole, the CIF can be used to identify all of the information management activities that an organization conducts. The operational systems continue to be the backbone of the enterprise, running the day-to-day business. The data warehouse collects the integrated, historical data supporting customer analysis and segmentation, and the data marts provide the business community with the capabilities to perform these analyses. The operational data store and associated oper marts support the near-real-time capture of integrated customer information and the management of actions to provide personalized customer service.

Let's examine each component of the CIF in a bit more detail.

Operational Systems

Operational systems are the ones supporting the day-to-day activities of the enterprise. They are focused on processing transactions, ranging from order entry to billing to human resources transactions. In a typical organization, the operational systems use a wide variety of technologies and architectures, and they may include some vendor-packaged systems in addition to in-house custom-developed software. Operational systems are static by nature; they change only in response to an intentional change in business policies or processes, or for technical reasons, such as system maintenance or performance tuning.

These operational systems are the source of most of the electronically maintained data within the CIF. Because these systems support time-sensitive real-time transaction processing, they have usually been optimized for performance and transaction throughput. Data in the operational systems environment may be duplicated across several systems, and is often not synchronized. These operational systems represent the first application of business rules to an organization's data, and the quality of data in the operational systems has a direct impact on the quality of all other information used in the organization.

Data Acquisition

Many companies are tempted to skip the crucial step of truly integrating their data, choosing instead to deploy a series of uncoordinated, unintegrated data marts. But without the single set of business rule transformations that the data acquisition layer contains, these companies end up building isolated, user- or department-specific data marts. These marts often cannot be combined to produce valid information, and cannot be shared across the enterprise. The net effect of skipping a single, integrated data acquisition layer is to foster the uncontrolled proliferation of silos of analytical data.

Data Warehouse

The universally accepted definition of a data warehouse developed by Bill Inmon in the 1980s is "a subject-oriented, integrated, time variant and non-volatile collection of data used in strategic decision making"[1]. The data warehouse acts as the central point of data integration—the first step toward turning data into information. Due to this enterprise focus, it serves the following purposes.

First, it delivers a common view of enterprise data, regardless of how it may later be used by the consumers. Since it is the common view of data for the business consumers, it supports the flexibility in how the data is later interpreted (analyzed). The data warehouse produces a stable source of historical information that is constant, consistent, and reliable for any consumer.

Second, because the enterprise as a whole has an enormous need for historical information, the data warehouse can grow to huge proportions (20 to 100 terabytes or more!). The design is set up from the beginning to accommodate the growth of this information in the most efficient manner using the enterprise's business rules for use throughout the enterprise.

Finally, the data warehouse is set up to supply data for any form of analytical technology within the business community. That is, many data marts can be created from the data contained in the data warehouse rather than each data mart serving as its own producer and consumer of data.

Operational Data Store

The operational data store (ODS) is used for tactical decision making, whereas the data warehouse supports strategic decisions. It has some characteristics that are similar to those of the data warehouse but is dramatically different in other aspects:

- It is subject oriented like a data warehouse.
- Its data is fully integrated like a data warehouse.

[1]Building the Data Warehouse, Third Edition by W.H. Inmon, Wiley Publishing, Inc., 2001.

- Its data is current—or as current as technology will allow. This is a significant difference from the historical nature of the data warehouse. The ODS has minimal history and shows the state of the entity as close to real time as feasible.

- Its data is volatile or updatable. This too is a significant departure from the static data warehouse. The ODS is like a transaction-processing system in that, when new data flows into the ODS, the fields affected are overwritten or updated with the new information. Other than an audit trail, no history of the previous contents is retained.

- Its data is almost entirely detailed with a small amount of dynamic aggregation or summarization. The ODS is most often designed to contain the transaction-level data, that is, the lowest level of detail for the subject area.

The ODS is the source of near-real-time, accurate, integrated data about customers, products, inventory, and so on. It is accessible from anywhere in the corporation and is not application specific. There are four classes of ODS commonly used; each has distinct characteristics and usage, but the most significant difference among them is the frequency of updating, ranging from daily to almost real time (subminute latency). Unlike a data warehouse, in which very little reporting is done against the warehouse itself (reporting is pushed out to the data marts), business users frequently access an ODS directly.

Data Delivery

Data delivery is generally limited to operations such as aggregation of data, filtering by specific dimensions or business requirements, reformatting data to ease end-user access or to support specific BI access software tools, and finally delivery or transmittal of data across the organization. The data delivery infrastructure remains fairly static in a mature CIF environment; however, the data requirements of the data marts evolve rapidly to keep pace with changing business information needs. This means that the data delivery layer must be flexible enough to keep pace with these demands.

Data Marts

Data marts are a subset of data warehouse data and are where most of the analytical activities in the BI environment take place. The data in each data mart is usually tailored for a particular capability or function, such as product profitability analysis, KPI analyses, customer demographic analyses, and so on. Each specific data mart is not necessarily valid for other uses. All varieties of data marts have universal and unique characteristics. The universal ones are that they contain a subset of data warehouse data, they may be physically co-located with the data warehouse or on their own separate platform, and they range in size from a few megabytes to multiple gigabytes to terabytes! To maximize your data warehousing ROI, you need to embrace and implement data warehouse architectures that enable this full spectrum of analysis.

Meta Data Management

Meta data management is the set of processes the collect, manage, and deploy meta data throughout the CIF. The scope of meta data managed by these processes includes three categories. *Technical* meta data describes the physical structures in the CIF and the detailed processes that move and transform data in the environment. *Business* meta data describes the data structures, data elements, business rules, and business usage of data in the CIF. Finally, *Administrative* meta data describes the operation of the CIF, including audit trails, performance metrics, data quality metrics, and other statistical meta data.

Information Feedback

Information feedback is the sharing mechanism that allows intelligence and knowledge gathered through the usage of the Corporate Information Factory to be shared with other data stores, as appropriate. It is the use of information feedback that identifies an organization as a true "learning organization." Examples of information feedback include:

- Pulling derived measures such as new budget targets from data marts and feeding them back to the data warehouse where they will be stored for historical analysis.
- Transmitting data that has been updated in an operational data store (through the use of a Transactional Interface) to appropriate operational systems, so that those data stores can reflect the new data.
- Feeding the results of analyses, such as a customer's segment classification and life time value score, back to the operational systems or ODS.

Information Workshop

The information workshop is the set of tools available to business users to help them use the resources of the Corporate Information Factory. The information workshop typically provides a way to organize and categorize the data and other resources in the CIF, so that users can find and use those resources. This is the mechanism that promotes the sharing and reuse of analysis across the organization. In some companies, this concept is manifested as an intranet portal, which organizes information resources and puts them at business users' fingertips. We classify the components of the information workshop as the library, toolbox, and workbench.

The library and toolbox usually represent the organization's first attempts to create an information workshop. The library component provides a directory of the resources and data available in the CIF, organized in a way that makes sense to business users. This directory is much like a library, in that there is a standard taxonomy for categorizing and ordering information components. This taxonomy is often based on organizational structures or high-level business processes. The toolbox is the collection of reusable components (for example, analytical reports) that business users can share, in order to leverage work and analysis performed by others in the enterprise. Together, these two concepts constitute a basic version of the information workshop capability.

More mature CIF organizations support the information workshop concept through the use of integrated information workbenches. In the workbench, meta data, data, and analysis tools are organized around business functions and tasks. The workbench dispenses with the rigid taxonomy of the library and toolbox, and replaces it with a task-oriented or workflow interface that supports business users in their jobs.

Operations and Administration

Operation and administration include the crucial support and infrastructure functions that are necessary for a growing, sustainable Corporate Information Factory. In early CIF implementations, many companies did not recognize how important these functions were, and they were often left out during CIF planning and development. The operation and administration functions include CIF Data Management, Systems Management, Data Acquisition Management, Service Management, and Change Management. Each of these functions contains a set of procedures and policies for maintaining and enhancing these critically important processes.

The Multipurpose Nature of the Data Warehouse

Hopefully by now, you have a good understanding of the role the data warehouse plays in your BI environment. It not only serves as the integration point for your operational data, it must also serve as the distribution point of this data into the hands of the various business users. If the data warehouse is to act as a stable and permanent repository of historical data for use in your strategic BI applications, it should have the following characteristics:

It should be enterprise focused. The data warehouse should be the starting point for all data marts and analytical applications; thus, it will be used by multiple departments, maybe even multiple companies or subdivisions.

A difficult but mandatory part of any data warehouse design team's activities must be the resolution of conflicting data elements and definitions. The participation by the business community is also obligatory.

Its design should be as resilient to change as possible.   Since the data warehouse is used to store massive, detailed, strategic data over multiple years, it is very undesirable to unload the data, redesign the database, and then reload the data. To avoid this, you should think in terms of a process-independent, application-independent, and BI technology-independent data model. The goal is to create a data model that can easily accommodate new data elements as they are discovered and needed without having to redesign the existing data elements or data model.

It should be designed to load massive amounts of data in very short amounts of time.   The data warehouse database design must be created with a minimum of redundancy or duplicated attributes or entities. Most databases have bulk load utilities that include a range of features and functions that can help optimize this process. These include parallelization options, loading data by block, and native application program interfaces (APIs). They may mean that you must turn off indexing, and they may require flat files. However, it is important to note that a poorly or ineffectively designed database cannot be overcome even with the best load utilities.

It should be designed for optimal data extraction processing by the data delivery programs.   Remember that the ultimate goal for the data warehouse is to feed the plethora of data marts that are then used by the business community. Therefore, the data warehouse must be well documented so that data delivery teams can easily create their data delivery programs. The quality of the data, its lineage, any calculations or derivations, and its meaning should all be clearly documented.

Its data should be in a format that supports any and all possible BI analyses in any and all technologies.   It should contain the least common denominator level of detailed data in a format that supports all manner of BI technologies. And it must be designed without bias or any particular department's utilization only in mind.

Types of Data Marts Supported

Today, we have a plethora of technologies supporting different analytical needs—Online Analytical Processing (OLAP), exploration, data mining and statistical data marts, and now customizable analytical applications. The unique characteristics come from the specificity of the technology supporting each type of data mart:

OLAP data mart. These data marts are designed to support generalized multidimensional analysis, using OLAP software tools. The data mart is designed using the star schema technique or proprietary "hypercube" technology. The star schema or multidimensional database management system (MD DBMS) is great for supporting multidimensional analysis in data marts that have known, stable requirements, fairly predictable queries with reasonable response times, and recurring reports. These analyses may include sales analysis, product profitability analysis, human resources headcount distribution tracking, or channel sales analysis.

Exploration warehouse. While most common data marts are designed to support specific types of analysis and reporting, the exploration warehouse is built to provide exploratory or true "ad hoc" navigation through data. After the business explorers make a useful discovery, that analysis may be formalized through the creation of another form of data mart (such as an OLAP one), so that others may benefit from it over time. New technologies have greatly improved the ability to explore data and to create a prototype quickly and efficiently. These include token, encoded vector, and bitmap technologies.

Data-mining or statistical warehouse. The data-mining or statistical warehouse is a specialized data mart designed to give researchers and analysts the ability to delve into the known and unknown relationships of data and events without having preconceived notions of those relationships. It is a safe haven for people to perform queries and apply mining and statistical algorithms to data, without having to worry about disabling the production data warehouse or receiving biased data such as that contained in multidimensional designs (in which only known, documented relationships are constructed).

Customizable analytical applications. These new additions permit inexpensive and effective customization of generic applications. These "canned" applications meet a high percentage of every company's generic needs yet can be customized for the remaining specific functionality. They require that you think in terms of variety and customization through flexibility and quick responsiveness.

Types of BI Technologies Supported

The reality is that database structures for data marts vary across a spectrum from normalized to denormalized to flat files of transactions. The ideal situation is to craft the data mart schemas *after* the requirements are established. Unfortunately, the database structure/solution is often selected *before* the specific business needs are known. Those of us in the data warehouse consulting business have witnessed development teams debating star versus normalized designs before even starting business analysis. For whatever reason, architects and data modelers latch onto a particular design technique—perhaps through comfort with a particular technique or ignorance of other techniques—and force all data marts to have that one type of design. This is similar to the person who is an expert with a hammer—everything he or she sees resembles a nail.

Our recommendation for data mart designs is that the schemas should be based on the usage of the data and the type of information requested. There are no absolutes, of course, but we feel that the best design to support all the types of data marts will be one that does not preestablish or predetermine the data relationships. An important caveat here is that the data warehouse that feeds the marts will be required to support any and all forms of analysis—not just multidimensional forms.

To determine the best database design for your business requirements and ensuing data mart, we recommend that you develop a simple matrix that plots the volatility of the data against a type of database design required, similar to the one in Figure 1.4. Such a matrix allows designers, architects, and database administrators (DBAs) to view where the overall requirements lie in terms of the physical database drivers, that is, volatility, latency, multiple subject areas, and so on, and the analytical vehicle that will supply the information (via the scenarios that were developed), for example, repetitive delivery, ad hoc reports, production reports, algorithmic analysis, and so on.

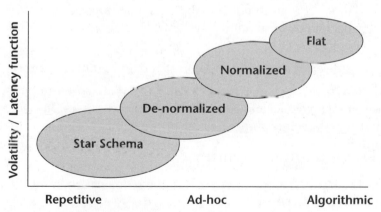

Figure 1.4 Business requirements—data mart design matrix.

Characteristics of a Maintainable Data Warehouse Environment

With this as a background, what does a solid, maintainable data warehouse data model look like? What are the characteristics that should be considered when designing any data warehouse, whether for a company just beginning its BI initiative or for a company having a sophisticated set of technologies and users, whether the company has only one BI access tool today or has a plethora of BI technologies available?

The methodology for building a BI environment is iterative in nature. We are fortunate today to have many excellent books devoted to describing this methodology. (See the "Recommended Reading" section at the end of this book.) In a nutshell, here are the steps:

1. First, select and document the business problem to be solved with a business intelligence capability (data mart of some sort).

2. Gather as many of the requirements as you can. These will be further refined in the next step.

3. Determine the appropriate end-user technology to support the solution (OLAP, mining, exploration, analytical application, and so on).

4. Build a prototype of the data mart to test its functionality with the business users, redesigning it as necessary.

5. Develop the data warehouse data model, based on the user requirements and the business data model.

6. Map the data mart requirements to the data warehouse data model and ultimately back to the operational systems, themselves.

7. Generate the code to perform the ETL and data delivery processes. Be sure to include error detection and correction and audit trail procedures in these processes.

8. Test the data warehouse and data mart creation processes. Measure the data quality parameters and create the appropriate meta data for the environment.

9. Upon acceptance, move the first iteration of the data warehouse and the data mart into production, train the rest of the business community, and start planning for the next iteration.

WARNING

Nowhere do we recommend that you build an entire data warehouse containing all the strategic enterprise data you will ever need before building the first analytical capability (data mart). Each successive business problem solved by another data mart implementation will add the growing set of data serving as the foundation in your data warehouse. Eventually, the amount of data that must be added to the data warehouse to support a new data mart will be negligible because most of it will already be present in the data warehouse.

Since you will not know how large the data warehouse will ultimately be, nor do you know all of the BI technologies that will eventually be brought to bear upon strategic problems in your enterprise, you must make some educated assumptions and plan accordingly. You can assume that the warehouse will become one of the largest databases found in your enterprise. It is not unusual for the data warehouse size to start out in the low gigabyte range and then grow fairly rapidly to hundreds of gigabytes, terabytes, and some now predict pedabytes. So, regardless of where you are in your BI life cycle—just starting or several years into building the environment—the relational databases are still the best choice for your database management system (DBMS). They have the advantage of being very conducive to nonredundant, efficient database design. In addition, their deployment for the data warehouse means you can use all the sophisticated and useful characteristics of a relational DBMS:

- **Access to the data by most any tool (data modeling, ETL, meta data, and BI access).**   All use SQL on the relational database.
- **Scalability in terms of the size of data being stored.**   The relational databases are still superior in terms of storing massive amounts of data.
- **Parallelism for efficient and extremely fast processing of data.**   The relational databases excel at this function
- **Utilities such as bulk loaders, defragmentation, and reorganization capabilities, performance monitors, backup and recovery functions, and index wizards.**   Again, the relational databases are ideal for supporting a repository of strategic data.

There may come a time when the proprietary multidimensional databases (MOLAP) can effectively compete with their relational cousins, but that is not the situation currently.

The Data Warehouse Data Model

Given that we recommend a relational DBMS for your data warehouse, what should the characteristics of the data model for that structure look like? Again, let's look at some assumptions before going into the characteristics of the model:

- The data warehouse is assumed to have an enterprise focus at its heart. This means that the data contained in it does not have a bias toward one department or one part of the enterprise over another. Therefore, the ultimate BI capabilities may require further processing (for example, the use of a data mart) to "customize" them for a specific group, but the starting material (data) can be used by all.

- As a corollary to the above assumption, it is assumed that the data within data warehouse does not violate any business rules established by the enterprise. The data model for the data warehouse must demonstrate adherence to these underlying rules through its form and documentation.

- The data warehouse must be loaded with new data as quickly and efficiently as possible. Batch windows, if they exist at all, are becoming smaller and smaller. The bulk of the work to get data into a data warehouse must occur in the ETL process, leaving minimal time to load the data.

- The data warehouse must be set up from the beginning to support multiple BI technologies—even if they are not known at the time of the first data mart project. Biasing the data warehouse toward one technology, such as multidimensional analyses, effectively eliminates the ability to satisfy other needs such as mining and statistical analyses.

- The data warehouse must gracefully accommodate change in its data and data structures. Given that we do not have all of the requirements or known uses of the strategic data in the warehouse from the very beginning, we can be assured that changes will happen as we build onto the existing data warehouse foundation.

With these assumptions in mind, let's look at the characteristics of the ideal data warehouse data model.

Nonredundant

To accommodate the limited load cycles and the massive amount of data that most data warehouses must have, the data model for the data warehouse should contain a minimum amount of redundancy. Redundancy adds a tremendous burden to the load utilities and to the designers who must worry about ensuring that all redundant data elements and entities get the correct data at the correct time. The more redundancy you introduce to your data warehouse data model, the more complex you make the ultimate process of "getting data in."

This does not mean that redundancy is not ever found in the data warehouse. In Chapter 4, we describe when and why some redundancy is introduced into the data warehouse. The key though is that redundancy is controlled and managed with forethought.

Stable

As mentioned earlier, we build the data warehouse in an iterative fashion, which has the benefit of getting a data mart created quickly but runs the risk of missing or misstating significant business rules or data elements. These would be determined or highlighted as more and more data marts came online. It is inevitable that change will happen to the data warehouse and its data model.

It is well known that what changes most often in any enterprise are its processes, applications, and technology. If we create a data model dependent upon any of these three factors, we can be assured of a major overhaul when one of the three changes. Therefore, as designers, we must use a data-modeling technique that mitigates this problem as much as possible yet captures the all-important business rules of the enterprise. The best data-modeling technique for this mitigation is to create a process-, application-, and technology-independent data model.

On the other hand, since change is inevitable, we must be prepared to accommodate newly discovered entities or attributes as new BI capabilities and data marts are created. Again, the designer of the data warehouse must use a modeling technique that can easily incorporate a new change without someone's having to redesign the existing elements and entities already implemented. This model is called a system model, and will be described in Chapter 3 in more detail.

Consistent

Perhaps the most essential characteristic of any data warehouse data model is the consistency it brings to the business for its most important asset—its data. The data models contain all the meta data (definitions, physical characteristics, aliases, business rules, data owners and stewards, domains, roles, and so on) that is critically important to the ultimate understanding of the business users of what they are analyzing. The data model creation process must reconcile outstanding issues, data discrepancies, and conflicts before any ETL processing or data mapping can occur.

Flexible in Terms of the Ultimate Data Usage

The single most important purpose for the data warehouse is to serve as a solid, reliable, consistent foundation of data for any and all BI capabilities. It should be clear by now that, regardless of what your first BI capability is, you must be able to serve all business requirements regardless of their technologies. Therefore, the data warehouse data model must remain application and technology independent, thus making it ideal to support any application or technology.

On the other hand, the model must uphold the business rules established for the organization, and that means that the data model must be more than simply flat files. Flat files, while a useful base to create star schemas, data mining, and exploration subsets of data, do not enforce, or even document, any known business rules. As the designer, you must go one step further and create a real data model with the real business rules, domains, cardinalities, and optionalities specified. Otherwise, subsequent usage of the data could be mishandled, and violations in business rules could occur.

The Codd and Date Premise

Given all of the above characteristics of a good data warehouse data model, we submit that the best data-modeling technique you can use is one based on the original relational database design—the entity-relationship diagram (ERD) developed by Chris Date and Ted Codd. The ERD is a proven and reliable data-modeling approach with straightforward rules of construction. The normalization rules discussed in Chapter 3 yield a stable, consistent data model that upholds the policies and rules of engagement established by the enterprise, while lending a tremendous amount of flexibility in how the data is later analyzed by the data marts. The resulting database is the most efficient in terms of storage and data loading as well. It is, however, not perfect, as we will see in the next section.

While we certainly feel that this approach is elegant in the extreme, more importantly, this data-modeling technique upholds all of the features and characteristics we specified for a sustainable, flexible, maintainable, and understandable data warehouse environment.

The resultant data model for your data warehouse is translatable, using any technology, into a database design that is:

Reliable across the business.   It contains no contradictions in the way that data elements or entities are named, related to each other, or documented.

Sharable across the enterprise.   The data warehouse resulting from the implementation of this data model can be accessed by multiple data delivery processes and users from anywhere in the enterprise

Flexible in the types of data marts it supports. The resulting database will not bias your BI environment in one direction or another. All technological opportunities will still be available to you and your enterprise.

Correct across the business. The data warehouse data model will provide an accurate and faithful representation of the way information is used in the business.

Adaptable to changes. The resulting database will be able to accommodate new elements and entities, while maintaining the integrity of the implemented ones.

Impact on Data Mart Creation

Now that we have described the characteristics of a solid data warehouse data model and have recommended an ERD or normalized (in the sense of Date and Codd) approach, let's look at the ramifications that decision will have on our overall BI environment.

The most common applications that use the data warehouse data are multidimensional ones—at least today. The dimensions used in the star schemas correlate roughly to the subject areas developed in the subject area model—order, customer, product, market segment—and time. To answer the questions, "How many orders for what products did we get in the Northeast section from January to June this year?" would take a significant amount of effort if we were to use the data warehouse as the source of data for that query. It would require a rather large join across several big entities (Order, Order Line Item, Product, Market Segment, with the restriction of the timeframe in the SQL statement). This is not a pretty or particularly welcomed situation for the average business user who is distantly familiar with SQL.

So, what we can see about this situation is that data warehouse access will have to be restricted and used by only those business users who are very sophisticated in database design and SQL. If an enterprise has good exploration and mining technology, it may choose to cut off all access to the data warehouse, thus requiring all business users to access an OLAP mart, or exploration or data mining warehouse instead.

Is this a problem? Not really. All BI environments must have "back room" capabilities of one sort or another. It is in the back room that we perform the difficult tasks of integration, data hygiene, error correction and detection, transformation, and the audit and control mechanisms to ensure the quality of the strategic data anyway. Therefore, all BI environments have this "closed off to the public" section of their environment. We have simply taken it one step further and said that this section should be formally modeled, created, and maintained.

In the data-mart-only world, the data delivery processes, described earlier, must take on not only the burden of ensuring the proper delivery of the information to the right mart at the right time but must also take on the entire set of ETL tasks found in the data acquisition processing over and over again. Given this situation, it should be obvious that the data delivery processes can be simplified greatly if all they have to worry about is extracting the data they specifically need from a consistent, quality source (the data warehouse), format it into that required by the data mart technology (star schema, flat file, normalized subset, and so on), and deliver the data to the data mart environment for uploading.

As another benefit to constructing the data warehouse from a solid, ERD-based data model, you get a very nice set of reusable data entities and elements. In a data-mart-only environment, each mart must carry all the detailed data it requires within its database. Unless the two data marts share common conformed dimensions, integrating the two may be difficult, or even impossible. Imagine if a repository of detailed data existed that the data delivery processes could extract from and the BI access tools could access, if they needed to, at any time without having to replicate the data over and over! That is another significant benefit the data warehouse brings to your BI environment.

Summary

There are several BI methodologies and consultants who will tell you that you do not need a data warehouse, that the combination of all the data marts together creates the "data warehouse," or at least a virtual one, or that really, all the business really wants is just a standalone data mart. We find all of these approaches to be seriously lacking in sustainability and sophistication. This book takes a "best practices" approach to creating a data warehouse. The best practices we use are a set of recommendations that tells designers what actions they should take or avoid, thus maximizing the success of their overall efforts. These recommendations are based on the years of experience in the field, participation in many data warehouse projects, and the observation of many successful and maintainable data warehouse environments. Clearly, no one method is perfect, nor should one be followed blindly without thought being given to the specific situation. You should understand what works best in your environment and then apply these rules as you see fit, altering them as changes and new situations arise.

In spite of this caveat, this book is filled with useful and valuable information, guidelines, and hints. In the following chapters, we will describe the data models needed in more detail, go over the construction of the data warehouse data model step by step, and discuss deployment issues and problems you may encounter along the way to creating a sustainable and maintainable business intelligence environment. By the end of the book, you should be fully qualified to begin constructing your BI environment armed with the best design techniques possible for your data warehouse.

CHAPTER 2

Fundamental Relational Concepts

Every data-modeling technique has its own set of terms, definitions, and techniques. This vernacular permits us to understand complex and difficult concepts and to use them to design complex databases. This book applies relational data-modeling techniques for developing the data warehouse data model. To that end, this chapter introduces the terms and terminology of relational data modeling. It then continues with an overview of normalization techniques and the rules for the different normalization levels (for example, first, second, and third normal form) and the purpose for each. Sample data models will be given, showing the progression of normalization. The chapter ends with a discussion of normalization of the data model and the associated benefits.

Before we get into the various types of data models we use in creating a data warehouse, it is necessary to first understand why a data model is important and the various types of data models you will create in developing your BI environment.

Why Do You Need a Data Model?

A model is an abstraction or representation of a subject that looks or behaves like all or part of the original. Examples include a concept car and a model of a building. All models have a common set of objectives. They are designed to help people envision how the parts fit together, help people understand how to use or apply the final product, reduce the development risk, and ensure that the people building the product and those requesting it have the same expectations. Let's look more closely at these benefits:

- A model reduces overall risk by ensuring that the requirements of the final product will be satisfactorily met. By examining a "mock-up" of the ultimate product, the intended users can make a reasonable determination of whether the product will indeed fulfill their needs and objectives.

- A model helps the developers envision how the final product will interface with other systems or functions. The level of effort needed to create the interfaces and their feasibility can be reasonably estimated if a detailed model is created. (In the case of a data warehouse, these interfaces include the data acquisition and the data delivery programs, where and when to perform data cleansing, audits, data maintenance processes, and so on.)

- A model helps all the people involved understand how to relate to the ultimate product and how it will pertain to their work function. The model also helps the developers understand the skills needed by the ultimate audience and what training needs to occur to ensure proper usage of the product.

- Finally a model ensures that the people building the product and those requesting it have the same expectations about the ultimate outcome of the effort. By examining the model, the potential for a missed opportunity is greatly reduced, and the belief and trust by all parties that the ultimate product will be satisfactory is greatly enhanced.

We feel that a model is so important, especially when undertaking a set of projects as complex as building a business intelligence (BI) environment, that we recommend a project be halted or delayed until the justification for a solid set of models is made, signed off on, and funded.

Relational Data-Modeling Objects

Now that we understand the need for a model, let's turn our attention to a specific type of model—the data model. Before describing the various levels of models, we need to come up with a common set of terms for use in describing these models.

NOTE
This book is not intended to replace the many significant and authoritative books written on generic data modeling; rather this section should only serve as a refresher on some of the more significant terms we will use throughout the book. If more detail is needed, please refer to the wealth of data-modeling books at your disposal and listed in the "Recommended Reading" section in this book.

Subject

The first term to describe is a *subject*. You will see us refer to a subject-oriented data warehouse and a subject area model. In both cases, the term subject refers to a data subject or a major category of data relevant to the business. A subject area is the subset of the enterprise's data and consists of related entities and relationships. Customers, Sales, and Products are examples of subject areas.

Entity

An *entity* is generally defined as a person, place, thing, concept, or event in which the enterprise has both the interest and the capability to capture and store information. An entity is unique within the data model. For the third normal form data model, there is one and only one entry representing that entity. In entity-relationship diagrams (ERD) or logical data modeling in the classical Codd and Date sense, there are four types of entities from which to build logical or business data models and data warehouse models (see Figure 2.1).

- A *Primary or Fundamental Entity* is defined as an entity that does not depend on any other entity for its existence. Generally each subject area is represented by a primary entity that has the same name (except that the subject area name is pluralized and the entity name is singular), such as Customer, Sale, and Product. These entities are a grouping of dependent data occurring singularly.

- A *Subtype Entity* is a logical division or category of a parent (supertype) entity. Examples of subtypes for the Customer entity are Retail Customer and Wholesale Customer. The subtypes always inherit the characteristics, or attributes and relationships, of the parent entity; that is, the Retail Customer will inherit any attributes that describe the more generic parent entity, Customer (for example, Customer ID, Customer Name), as well as relationships such as "Customer acquires Product."

- An *Attributive or Characteristic Entity* is an entity whose existence depends on another entity. It is created to handle a group of data that could occur multiple times for each instance of its parent entity. Customer Address is an attributive entity of Customer since each customer may have multiple addresses.

- An *Associative or Intersection Entity* is an entity that is dependent upon two or more entities for its existence, and that records data at the point of intersection. Order is an associative entity. Its key is composed of the keys of the two parent entities—Customer and Item—and a qualifier such as Date. Attributes that could be retained include the Quantity of the Item and Purchase Date.

With these four types of entities, we have all we will need in terms of components to create the business and data warehouse data models. We describe these models in the next section of this chapter and go through the steps to create them in Chapters 3 and 4.

Element or Attribute

An element or attribute is the lowest level of information relating to any entity. It models a specific piece of information or a property of a specific entity. Elements or attributes serve several purposes within an entity.

- A primary key serves to uniquely identify the entity and is used in the physical database to locate a record for storage or access. Examples include Customer ID for the Customer entity and Item ID for the Item entity.

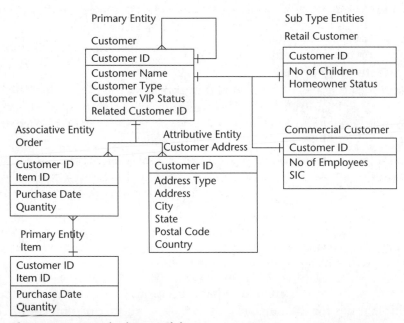

Figure 2.1 Sample data model.

NOTE

The key may be a single element or it may consist of multiple elements that are combined, in which case it is called a concatenated key. Finally, primary keys may or may not have meaning or intelligence. Care must be taken with intelligent primary keys. For example, an Account Code that also depicts geographic area or department is both confusing and erroneous in this data model. See the sidebar for further rules for good keys.

- A foreign key is a key that exists because of a parent-child relationship between a pair of entities. The foreign key in the child entity is the primary key in the parent entity and links the two entities together. For example, the Customer ID of the Customer entity is also found in the Order entity, relating the two.

- A nonkey element or attribute is not needed to uniquely identify the entity but is used to further describe or characterize information about the entity. Examples of nonkey elements or attributes are Customer Name, Customer Type, Item Color, and Item Quantity.

Characteristics of a Good Key

The following are characteristics of "well-behaved" keys—those keys that are maintainable and sustainable over the lifetime of the operational system and therefore, the data warehouse:

- ◆ The key is not null over the scope of integration. It is imperative that there can never be a situation or event that could cause a null key.

- ◆ The key is unique over the scope of integration. It is also imperative that there can never be a situation where duplicate keys could be generated.

- ◆ The key is unique by design not by circumstance. Key generation has been carefully thought out and tested under all circumstances.

- ◆ The key is persistent over time. This is mandatory in the data warehouse environment where data has a very long lifetime.

- ◆ The key is in a manageable format, that is, there is no undue overhead produced in the creation or maintenance of the key structures. It consists of straightforward integers or character strings, no embedded symbols or odd characters.

- ◆ The key should not contain embedded intelligence but rather is a generic string. (It may be created based on some intelligence but, once created, the intelligence embedded in the key is never used.)

Relationships

A *relationship* documents the business rule associating two entities together. The relationship is used to describe how the two entities are naturally linked to each other. Customer places Order and Order is for Items are examples of relationships in Figure 2.1.

There are different characteristics of relationships used in documenting the business rules of the enterprise:

- *Cardinality* denotes the maximum number of occurrences of one entity that can be related to another entity. Usually these are expressed as "one" or "many." In Figure 2.1, a Customer has many addresses (Bill-to, Ship-to) and every address belongs to one customer.

- *Optionality or modality* indicates whether an entity occurrence must participate in a relationship. This characteristic tells you the minimum number (zero or optional) of occurrences in the relationship.

There are also different types of relationships:

- An *identifying relationship* is one in which the primary key of the parent entity becomes a part of the primary key of the child entity.

- A *nonidentifying relationship* is one in which the primary key of the parent entity becomes a nonkey attribute of the child entity. An example of this type of relationship is a recursive relationship, that is, a situation in which an entity is related to itself. Customers who are related to other customers (for example, subsidiaries of corporations and families or households) are examples of recursive relationships. These are used to denote an entity occurrence that is related to another entity occurrence of the same entity.

See Figure 2.2 for more on these types of relationships. The components of a relationship in a data model consist of a verb phrase denoting the business rule (places, has, contains), the cardinality, and the modality or optionality of the relationship.

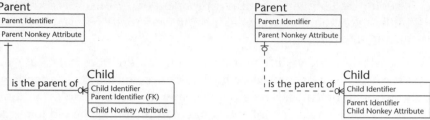

Figure 2.2   Identifying and nonidentifying relationships.

Types of Data Models

A *data model* is an abstraction or representation of the data in a given environment. It is a collection and a subsequent verification and communication method to fully document the data requirements used in the creation of accurate, effective, and efficient physical databases. The data model consists of entities, attributes, and relationships. Within the complete data model, appropriate meta data, such as definitions and physical characteristics, is defined for each of these.

As we stated earlier, we feel that the data models you create for your BI environment are critical to the overall success of your initiative as well as the long-term maintenance and sustainability of the environment.

If the data model is so important, why isn't it always developed? There are a number of reasons for this:

- **It's not easy.**   Creating the data model takes significant effort from the IT technical staff and business community. Data modelers must be either hired or internal resources trained in the disciplines of data modeling.

- **It requires discipline and tools.**   Once the techniques for data modeling are learned, they must be applied with conformity and compliance. The enterprise must create a set of documents detailing the standards it will use in the creation of its data models. Examples of these are naming standards, conflict resolution procedures, data steward rules and responsibilities (see Chapter 3 for more on this topic), and meta data capture and maintenance procedures.

■ **It requires significant business involvement.**   A company's data model must—repeat—must have business community involvement. We are, after all, designing the critical component of the business community's ultimate competitive weapon. It is for them that we are creating this vast wealth of information.

■ **It postpones the visible work.**   Data modeling does not create tangible products that can be used by the business community. The models provide the technical staff creating the environment with information about the business environment and some requirements. The old joke goes something like this: "Start coding—I'll go find out what they want."

■ **It requires a broad view.**   The data model for the BI environment must encompass the entire enterprise. It will be used to create the ultimate decision-making components—the data marts—for all strategic analysis. Therefore, it must have a multidepartment and multiprocess perspective.

■ **The benefits of a data model are often not realized with the first project.** The real productivity comes in its reuse and its enterprise perspective.

Having said all this, what is the impact of not developing a data model?

■ It becomes very difficult to extract desired data. It is easy to implement something that either misses the users' expectations or only partially satisfies them.

■ Significant effort is spent on interfaces that generally provide little or no business value.

■ The environment's complexity increases significantly. When there is no data model to serve as a roadmap, it becomes difficult, if not impossible, to know what you already have in your data warehouse and what needs to be added.

■ It virtually guarantees lack of data integration because you cannot visualize how things fit together. Data warehouse development will not be effective and efficient, and may not even be feasible.

■ One of the most significant drawbacks is that, without a data model, data will not be effectively managed as an asset.

Now, having explained the need for data models, what are the types of data models will you need for your data warehouse implementation? Figure 2.3 shows the types of data models we recommend and the interaction between the models. The following sections describe the different data models necessary for a complete, successful, and maintainable BI environment. It is important to note the two-way arrows. The arrows pointing to the next lower level of models indicate that the characteristics (basic entities, attributes, and relationships) are inherited from the upper model. This ensures that we are all singing from the same sheet of music in terms of format, definition, and business rules. The upward-pointing arrows indicate that changes constantly occur as we implement these models into reality and that the changes must be reflected or incorporated into the preceding models for them to remain viable.

Subject Area Model

Subject areas are major groupings of things[1] of interest to the enterprise. These things of interest are eventually depicted in entities. The typical enterprise has between 15 and 20 subject areas. One of the beauties of a subject area model is that it can be developed very quickly (typically within a few days). The initial model serves as a blueprint for the business data model, and refinements in the subject area model should be expected. One of the reasons that the subject area model can be developed quickly is that there are some subjects that are common to many organizations, and a company embarking on the development of a subject area model can begin with these.

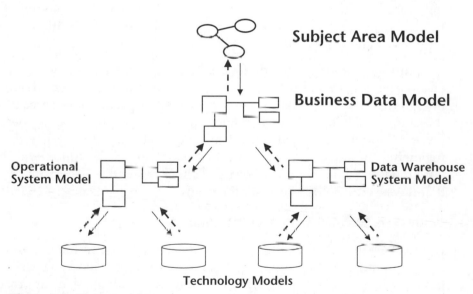

Figure 2.3 Data model types.

[1]In this context, "things" refers to physical items, concepts, events, people, and places.

These subject areas conform to standards governing the subject area model:

- Subject area names are plural nouns.
- Definitions apply implicitly to the past, present, and future.
- Subject areas are at approximately the same level of abstraction.
- Definitions are structured so that the subject areas are mutually exclusive.

Subject Area Model Benefits

Regardless of how quickly the subject area model can be developed, the effort should only be undertaken if there are benefits to be gained. Following are some of the major benefits provided by the subject area model.

Guide the Business Data Model Development

The business data model is the detailed model used to guide the development of the operational systems and the data warehouse. By doing so, it helps the data warehouse accomplish one of its major generic objectives—data consistency. Often, there are several people working on the business data model. One application of the subject area model is to divide the workload by subject area. In this manner, each person becomes an expert for a particular area such as Customers, Products, and Sales. The modelers sometimes address business functions, and hence each person's work could involve multiple subject areas. By establishing a primary person for each subject area, duplication of effort is minimized and coordination is improved.

Even if the workload is not divided by person, the subject area model helps ensure consistency and avoid redundancy. When a modeler identifies the need for a new entity, the modeler determines the appropriate subject area based on the definition. Before actually creating the new entity, the modeler need only review the entities in that subject area (typically less than 30) rather than reviewing the hundreds of entities that may exist in the full model. Armed with that information, the modeler can either create the new entity or ensure that the existing entity addresses the needs.

Guide Data Warehouse Project Selection

Companies often contemplate multiple data warehouse initiatives and struggle with both grouping the requirements into projects and with establishing the priorities. The subject area model provides a high-level approach for grouping projects based on the data they encompass. This information should be considered along with the business priority, technical difficulty, availability of people, and so on in establishing the final project sequence. Chapter 3 will cover this in more detail.

Guide Data Warehouse Development Projects

Subject matter experts often exist based on the data that is being addressed. For example, someone in the chief financial officer's organization would be the expert for "Financials"; someone in the Human Resources Department would be the expert for "Human Resources"; people from Sales, Marketing, and Customer Service would provide the expertise for "Customers." Understanding the subject areas being addressed helps the project team identify the business representatives that need to be involved. Also, data master files (for example, Customer Master File, Product Master File) tend to contain data related to specific subjects.

Business Data Model

The business data model is another type of model. It is an abstraction or representation of the data in a given business environment, and it provides the benefits cited for any model. It helps people envision how the information in the business relates to other information in the business ("how the parts fit together"). Products that apply the business data model include operational systems, data warehouse, and data mart databases, and the model provides the meta data (or information about the data) for these databases to help people understand how to use or apply the final product. The business data model reduces the development risk by ensuring that all the systems implemented correctly reflect the business environment. Finally, when it is used to guide development efforts, it provides a basis to confirm the developers' interpretation of the business information relationships to ensure that the key stakeholders share a common set of expectations.

Business Data Model Benefits

The business data model provides a consistent and stable view of the business information and business information relationships. It can be used as a basis for recognizing, evaluating, and responding to business changes. Specific benefits of the data model for data warehousing efforts follow.

Scope Definition

Every project should include a scope definition as one of its first steps, and data warehouse projects are no exception. If a business data model already exists, it can be used to convey the information that will be addressed by the resultant data warehouse. A section of the scope document should be devoted to listing the entities that will be included within the data warehouse; another section should be devoted to listing the entities that someone could reasonably expect to be included in the data warehouse but which have been excluded.

The explicit statement of the entities that are included and excluded ensures that there are no surprises with respect to the content of the data warehouse.

The list of entities is useful for identifying the needed subject matter experts and for identifying the potential source systems that will be needed. Additionally, this list can be used to help in estimating the project. A number of activities (for example, data warehouse model development, data transformation logic) are dependent on the number of data elements. Using the data entities (and attributes if available) as a starting point provides the project manager with a basis for estimating the effort. For example, the formula for developing the data warehouse model may consist of the number of entities and attributes[2] multiplied by the number of hours for each. The result can then be adjusted based on anticipated complexity, available documentation, an so on. While the formula for the first data warehouse effort may be very rough, if data is maintained on the actual effort, the formula can be refined, and the reliability of the estimates can be improved in future implementations.

Integration Foundation

In designing any enterprise's data model, the designer will immediately run into situations where homonyms (entities or attributes that have the same name but mean very different things) and synonyms (entities or attributes that have different names but mean exactly the same thing) are encountered. In Figure 2.4, the designer may see that the General Ledger and the Order Entry systems both have an attribute called "Account Number." Are these the same? Probably not! One is used to denote the field used for various financial accounts, and the other is used to denote the customer's account with the organization. Similarly, in Figure 2.5, the Order Entry and Billing systems have attributes called Account Number and Customer ID, respectively. Are these the same? The answer is probably yes.

In the data model being created, the designer must identify those attributes that are homonyms and ensure that they have distinctly different names. (If the naming convention for attributes recommended in this chapter is used, there will be no homonyms in the new models.) By the same token, an attribute must be represented once and only once in the model so the designer must reconcile the synonyms as well and represent each attribute by a single

---

[2]If the number of attributes is not known, an anticipated average number of attributes per entity can be used.

name. Thus, the data model is used to manage redundant entities and attributes rendering the "universal" name for each instance, reducing the redundancy in the environment. The data model is also very useful for clearing up confusing and misleading names for entities and attributes in the homonym situation as well. Ensuring that all entities and attributes have unique names guarantees that the enterprise as a whole will not make erroneous assumptions, which lead to bad decisions, about the data.

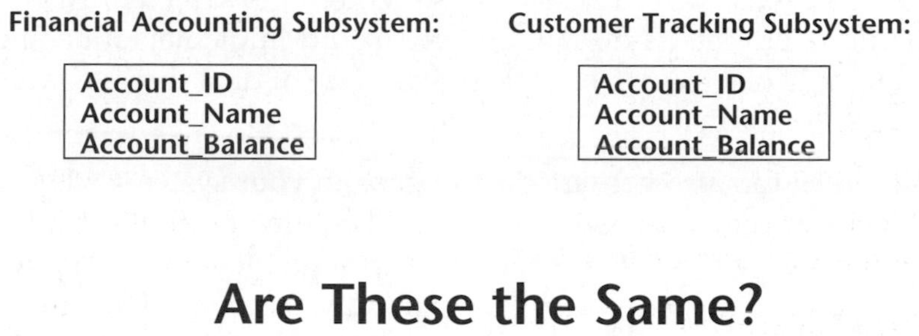

Financial Accounting Subsystem: **Customer Tracking Subsystem:**

| Account_ID |
| Account_Name |
| Account_Balance |

| Account_ID |
| Account_Name |
| Account_Balance |

Are These the Same?

Figure 2.4   Homonyms.

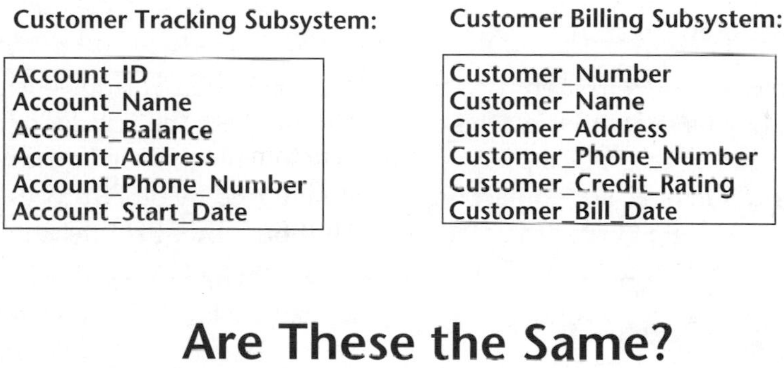

Customer Tracking Subsystem: **Customer Billing Subsystem:**

| Account_ID |
| Account_Name |
| Account_Balance |
| Account_Address |
| Account_Phone_Number |
| Account_Start_Date |

| Customer_Number |
| Customer_Name |
| Customer_Address |
| Customer_Phone_Number |
| Customer_Credit_Rating |
| Customer_Bill_Date |

Are These the Same?

Figure 2.5   Synonyms.

Multiple Project Coordination

A data warehouse program consists of multiple data warehouse implementation projects, and sometimes several of these are managed simultaneously. When multiple teams are working on the data warehouse, the subject area model can be used to initially identify where the projects overlap and gaps that will remain following completion of the projects.

The business data model is then used to establish where the projects overlap to fine-tune what data each project will use. Where the same entity is used by more than one project, its design, definition, and implementation should be assigned to only one team. Changes to that piece of data discovered by other projects can be coordinated by that team.

The data model can also help to identify gaps in your systems where entities and attributes are not addressed at all. Are all entities, attributes, and relationships created somewhere? If not, you have a real problem in your systems. Are they updated or used somewhere else within the systems? If so, do you have the right interfaces between systems to handle the flow of created data? Finally, are they deleted or disposed of somewhere in your systems? The creation of a matrix based upon the crossing of your data model with your systems' processes will give you a sound basis from which to answer these questions.

Dependency Identification

The data model helps to identify dependencies between various entities and attributes. In this fashion, it can be used to help assess the impact of change. When you change or create a process, you must be able to answer the question of whether it will have any impact on sets of data used by other processes. The data model can help ensure that dependent entities and attributes are considered in the design or implementation of new or changed systems.

Redundancy Management

The business data model strives to remove all redundancies. Entities, attributes, and relationships appear only once in this model unless they are used as foreign keys into other entities. By creating this model, you can immediately see overlaps and conflicts that must be resolved, as well as redundancies that must be removed, before going forward. The normalization rules specified in the "Relational Modeling Guidelines" section are designed to ensure a nonredundant data model.

There are many reasons to introduce redundancy back into system and technology data models; the most common one is to improve the performance of queries or requests for data. It is important to understand where and why any redundancy is introduced, and it is through the data model that redundancy can be controlled, thought out ahead of time, and examined for its impact on the overall design.

Change Management

Data models also serve as your best way to document changes to entities, attributes, and relationships. As systems are created, we may discover new business rules in effect and the need for additional entities and attributes. As these changes are documented in the technology and system data models (see Figure 2.3), these changes must be enforced all the way back up the data model chain—to the business data model and maybe even to the subject area diagram itself. Without solid change control over all levels of the data models, it should be clear that chaos will quickly take over and all the benefits of the data models will be lost.

System Model

The next level of data models in Figure 2.3 consists of the set of system models. A system model is a collection of the information being addressed by a specific system or function such as a billing system, data warehouse, or data mart. The system model is an electronic representation of the information needed by that system. It is independent of any specific technology or DBMS environment. For example, the billing system and data warehouse system models will most likely not have every scrap of data of interest to the enterprise found in them. Because the system model is developed from the business data model, it must, by default, be consistent with that model. See Chapter 4 for more detail on the construction of the data warehouse system model.

It is also important to note that there will be more than one system model. Each system or database that we construct will have its own unique system model denoting the specific data requirements for that system or the function it supports. Alternatively, there typically is only one system model per system. That is, there is only one system model for the data warehouse, one for the billing system, and so on. We may choose to physically implement many versions of the system model (see the next section on technology model) but still have only one system model from which to implement the actual system(s).

Technology Model

The last model to be developed is a technology model. This model is a collection of the specific information being addressed by a particular system and implemented on a specific platform. Now, we must consider all of the technology that is brought to bear on this database including:

Hardware.   Your choice of platform means that you must consider the sizes of the individual data files according to your platform technology and notate these specifications in the technology model.

Database management system (DBMS). The DBMS chosen for your data warehouse will have a great impact upon the ultimate design of your database. You must make the following determinations:

- **Amount of denormalization.** Some DBMS environments will perform better with minimal or no denormalization; others will require significant denormalization to achieve good performance.

- **Materialized views.** Depending on the DBMS technology you use, you may create materialized views or virtual data marts to speed up query performance.

- **Partitioning strategy.** You should use partitioning to speed up the loading of data into the data warehouse and delivery to the data marts. You have two choices—either horizontal or vertical partitioning. Chapter 5 discusses this topic in more detail.

- **Indexing strategy.** There are many choices, depending on the DBMS you use. Bitmap, encoded vector, sparse, hashing, clustered, and join indexes are some of the possibilities.

- **Referential integrity.** Bounded (the DBMS binds the referential integrity for you—you can't load a child until the parent is loaded) and unbounded (you load the data in a staging area to programmatically check for integrity and then load it into the data warehouse) are two possibilities. You must make sure that time is one of the qualifiers.

- **Data delivery technology.** How you deliver the data from the data warehouse into the various data marts will have an impact on the design of the database. Considerations include whether the data is delivered via a portal or through a managed query process.

- **Security.** Many times the data warehouse contains highly sensitive data. You may choose to invoke security at the DBMS level by physically separating this data from the rest, or you can use views or stored procedures to ensure security. If the data is extremely sensitive, you may choose to use encryption techniques to secure the data.

The technology model must be consistent with the governing system model. That is, it inherits its basic requirements from its system model. Likewise, any changes in the fundamental entities, attributes, and relationships discovered as the technology model is implemented must be reflected back up the chain of models as shown in Figure 2.3 (upward arrows).

Just as there are many system models—one per system—there may be multiple technology models for a single system model. For example, you may choose to implement subsets of the enterprise data warehouse in physically separate instances. You may choose to implement data by subject area—for example, using a physically different instance for customer, product, and order.

Or you may choose to separate subsets of data by geographic area—one warehouse for North America, another for Europe, and a third for Asia. Each of these physical instances will have its own technology model that is based upon the system model and modified according to the technology upon which you implement.

Relational Data-Modeling Guidelines

Data modeling is a very abstract process, and not all IT professionals have the qualifications to create a solid model. Data modelers require the ability to conceptualize intangible notions about what the business requires to perform its business and what its rules are in doing business. Also, data modeling is nondeterministic—there is *one* right way to create a data model. There are *many* wrong ways.

A common concern in data modeling is the amount of change that occurs. As we learn more and more about the enterprise, this knowledge will be reflected in changes to the existing data models. Data modelers must not see this aspect as a threat but rather be prepared for change and embrace it as a good sign—a sign that the model is, in fact, more insightful and that it more closely resembles the enterprise as a whole.

Data modelers must adhere to a set of principles or rules in creating the various data models. It is recommended that you establish these "ground rules" before you start your modeling exercise to avoid confusion and emotional arguments later on. Any deviation from these rules should be documented and the reasons for the exception noted. Any mitigating or future actions that reduce or eliminate the exception later on should be documented as well.

Finally, data modeling also requires judgment calls even when the reasons for the judgment are not clear or cannot be documented. When faced with this situation, the data modeler should revisit the three guidelines described in the next section. If adding or deleting something from the model improves its utility or ability to be communicated, then it should be done.

It is the goal of this book to ensure that you have the strong foundation and footing you need to deal with these issues before you begin your data warehouse design. Let's start with a set of guidelines garnered from the many years of data modeling we have performed.

Guidelines and Best Practices

The goal of any data model is to completely and accurately reflect the data requirements and business rules for handling that data so that the business can perform its functions effectively. To that end, we believe that there are three guidelines that should be followed when designing your data models:

Communication tool. The data models should be used as a communication tool between the business community and the IT staff and within the IT staff. Data requirements must be well documented and understood by all involved, must be business-oriented, and must consist of the appropriate level of detail. The data model should be used to communicate the business community's view of the enterprise's data to the technical people implementing their systems. When developing these models, the objectives must always be clarity and precision. When adding information to a data model, the modeler should ask whether the addition adds to clarity or subtracts from it.

Level of granularity. The data models should reflect the "lowest common denominator" of information that the enterprise uses. Aggregated, derived, or summarized data elements should be decomposed to their basic parts, and unnecessary redundancy or duplication of data elements should be removed. When we "denormalize" the model by adding back aggregations, derivations, or summarization according to usage and performance objectives, we know precisely what elements went into each of these components. In other words, the data should be as detailed as necessary to understand its nature and ultimate usage. While the ultimate technology model may have significant aggregations, summarizations, and derivations in it, these will be connected back to the ultimate details through the data modeling documentation.

Business orientation. It is paramount that the models represent the enterprise's view of itself without physical constraints. We strive always to model what the business wants to be rather than model what the business is forced to be because of its existing systems, technologies, or databases. Projects that are not grounded in what the business community wants are usually doomed to fail. Generally, we miss the boat with our business community because we cut corners in the belief that we already know what the results of analysis will be (the "if we build it, they will come" belief).

These guidelines should always be at the forefront of the modeler's mind when he or she commences the modeling process. Whenever questions or judgment calls come into play, the modeler should fall back to these guidelines to determine whether the resolution adds or detracts to the overall usability of the models.

With these in mind, let's look at some of the best practices in data modeling:

Business users' involvement. It must be understood up front that the business community must set aside time and resources to help create the various data models; data modeling is not just a technical exercise for IT people. If the business community cannot find the time, refuses to participate, or basically declares that IT should "divine" what data they need, it is the wise project manager who pulls the plug on the project. Data modeling in a business community vacuum is a waste of time, resources, and effort, and is highly likely to fail. Furthermore, the sooner the business community gets involved, the better. As a first step, you must identify who within the business community should be involved. These people may or may not be willing to participate. If they are openly resistant, you may need to perform some education, carry out actions to mitigate their fears, or seek another resource. Typical participants are sponsoring executives, managers with subject matter expertise, and business analysts.

Interviews and facilitated sessions. One of the most common ways to get a lot of information in a short amount of time is to perform interviews and use facilitated sessions. The interviews typically obtain information from one or two people at a time. More depth information can be obtained from these sessions. The facilitated sessions are usually for 5 to 10 attendees and are used to get general direction and consensus, or even for educational purposes. The documentation from these sessions is verified and added to the bank of information that contributes to the data models.

Validation. The proposed data model is then verified by either immediate feedback from the interviews or facilitated sessions, or by formal walkthroughs. It may be that you focus on just the verification of the business rules and constraints rather than the actual data model itself with some of the business community members. With others though, you should verify that the actual data model structures and relationships are appropriate.

Data model maintenance. Because change becomes a common feature in any modeling effort, you should be prepared to handle these occurrences. Change management should be formalized by documented procedures that have check-in and check-out processes, formal requests for changes, and processes to resolve conflicts.

Know when "enough is enough." Perhaps the most important practice any data modeler should learn is when to say the model is good enough. Because we are designing an abstract, debatable structure, it is very easy for the data modeler to find him- or herself in "analysis paralysis." When is the data model finished? Never! Therefore it is mandatory that the modeler make the difficult determination that the model is sufficient to support the needs of the function being implemented, knowing that changes will happen and that he or she is prepared to handle them at a later date.

Normalization

Normalization is a method for ensuring that the data model meets the objectives of accuracy, consistency, simplicity, nonredundancy, and stability. It is a physical database design technique that applies mathematical rules to the relational technology to identify and reduce insertion, update, or deletion anomalies. The mantra we use to get to third normal form is that all attributes must depend *on the key, the whole key, and nothing but the key*—to put it simply.

Fundamentally this means that normalization is a way of ensuring that the attributes are in the proper entity and that the design is efficient and effective for a relational DBMS. We will walk through the steps to get to this data model design in the next sections of this chapter. Normalization has these characteristics as well:

- Verification of the structural correctness and consistency of the data model
- Independence from any physical constraints
- Minimization of storage space requirement by eliminating the storage of data in multiple places

Finally, normalization:

- Removes data inconsistencies since data is stored only once, thus eliminating the possibility of conflicting data
- Diminishes insertion, updating, and deletion anomalies because data is stored only once
- Increases the data structure stability because attributes are positioned in entities based on their intrinsic properties rather than on specific application requirements

Normalization of the Relational Data Model

Normalization is very useful for the business data model because:

- It does not instruct any physical processing direction, thus making the business model a good starting place for all applications and databases.
- It reduces aggregated, summarized, or derived elements to their basic components, ensuring that no hidden processes are contained in the data model.
- It prevents all duplicated or redundant occurrences of attributes and entities.

The system and technology models inherit their characteristics from the business data model and so start out as a fully normalized data model. However, denormalized attributes will be designed into these data models for a variety of reasons, as described in Chapters 3 and 4, and it is important to recognize where and when the denormalization occurs and to document the reasons for that denormalization. Uncontrolled redundancy or denormalization will result in a chaotic and nonperforming database design.

Normalization should be undertaken during the business data model design. However, it is important to note that you should not alter the business rules just to follow strict normalization rules. That is, do not create objects just to satisfy normalization.

First Normal Form

First normal form (1NF) takes the data model to the first step described in our mantra—the attribute is dependent on the key. This requires two conditions—that every entity have a primary key that uniquely identifies it and that the entity contain no repeating or multivalued groups. Each attribute should be at its lowest level of detail and have a unique meaning and name. 1NF is the basis for all other normalization techniques. Figure 2.6 shows the conversion of our model to 1NF.

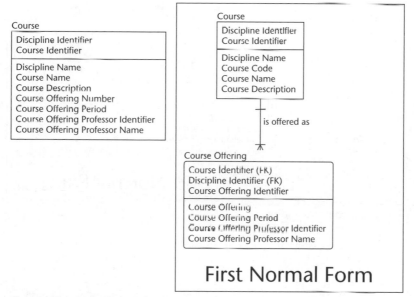

Figure 2.6 First normal form.

In Figure 2.6, we see that the Course entity contains the attributes that deal with a specific offering of the course rather than the generic course itself (Course Offering, Period, Professor Identifier, and Professor Name). These attributes are not dependent on the Course entity key for their existence, and therefore should be put into their own entity (Course Offering).

Second Normal Form

Second normal form (2NF) takes the model to the next level of refinement according to our mantra—the attributes must be dependent on the whole key. To attain 2NF, the entity must be in 1NF and every nonprimary attribute must be dependent on the entire primary key for its existence. 2NF further reduces possible redundancy in the data model by removing attributes that are dependent on part of the key and placing them in their own entity. Notice that Discipline Name was only dependent on the Discipline Identifier. If this remains in the model, then Discipline Identifier and Name must be repeated for every course. By placing these in their own entity, they are stored only once. Figure 2.7 shows the conversion of our model to 2NF.

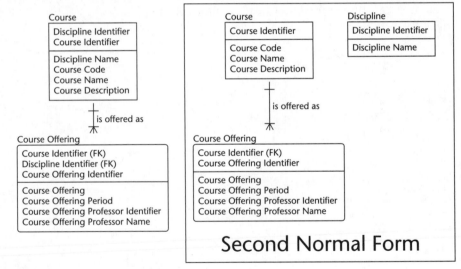

Figure 2.7 Second normal form.

Third Normal Form

Third normal form (3NF) takes the data model to the last level of improvement referred to in our mantra—the attribute must be dependent on nothing but the key. To attain 3NF, the entity must be in 2NF, and the nonkey fields must be dependent on only the primary key, and not on any other attribute in the entity, for their existence. This removes any transitive dependencies in which the nonkey attributes depend on not only the primary key but also on other nonkey attributes. Figure 2.8 shows the conversion of our model to 3NF.

In Figure 2.8, notice that Course Offering Professor and Course Offering Professor Name are recurring attributes. Neither the Professor Name or the Professor Identifier depend on the Course Offering. Therefore, we remove these attributes from the Course Offering entity and place them in their own entity, titled Professor. At this point, the data model is in 3NF in which all attributes are dependent on the key, the whole key, and nothing but the key.

Your business data model should be presented in 3NF at a minimum. At this point, it is ready for use in any of your technological implementations—operational systems such as billing, order entry, or general ledger (G/L); business intelligence such as the data warehouse and data marts; or any other environment such as the operational data store.

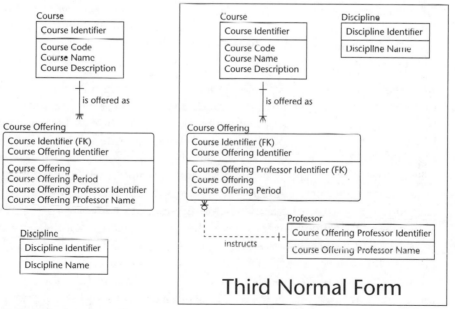

Figure 2.8 Third normal form.

Other Normalization Levels

We usually stop with 3NF when we design the business model for organizations. However, you should be aware of other levels of normalization and their benefits to determine if 3NF will be sufficient for your organization. There are several good data-modeling books that discuss the merits of Boyce/Codd and fourth and fifth normal forms. We will not discuss these further in this book.

WARNING

▬▬▬▬ **We caution you against overzealous usage of these normalization techniques. In other words, don't overnormalize your models. You should balance the consideration of business meanings with structural consistency. You should always base your model on business concepts first, then apply the normalization techniques to verify the structural integrity and consistency.**

Summary

We have discussed in this chapter the fact that data models are essential for managing data as a corporate asset. Without the set of data models described here, the business users and technical staff creating systems cannot develop a comprehensive and precise representation of information structures, business rules, and relationships among the data. This can only be accomplished when the databases are designed with the concept of reusability, consistency, and integration in mind and with rigorous of compliance to the modeling techniques contained in this chapter.

We covered the need for various data models, starting with a subject area diagram, and migrating to a business data model, the system, and the technology models—each one defining a different level of abstraction and transformation—ultimately leading to a coordinated and fully integrated database schema. We see that the subject area diagram can be developed very quickly, usually within a few days. The full business data model will take a bit longer and, when fully developed, contains the business rules for the entire enterprise and can be used by all applications, including the data warehouse. It is important to note here that if your organization does not have either of these models, we recommend that you create an enterprise-wide subject area diagram but focus on only the subject area(s) needed for your data warehouse for the business data model. You will continue to fill out the business and data warehouse data models as new areas are needed in the data warehouse but should not get sidetracked into trying to create the entire business data model before you generate your first data warehouse subject area. See Chapter 4 for more information on this.

There are three important guidelines to follow in developing any of the models we discuss. These are to remember that the data model is a communication tool, that it contains the lowest common denominator of detail, and that it reflects a solid business orientation. When confronted with difficult decisions, these three guidelines should rule the day.

We also learned in this chapter about normalization and its benefits for database design. Our recommendation is to develop your business data model in 3NF. In 3NF, attributes are dependent:

1NF.   On the key, accomplished by removing repeating groups

2NF.   The whole key, accomplished by removing attributes dependent on part of the key

3NF.   Nothing but the key, accomplished by removing attributes dependent on nonkey attributes

We warn against overzealous normalization and analysis paralysis. At the end of the day, the key is to get a set of models that is fully integrated, consistent, and reusable. These models produce stable and maintainable databases (or a subset of them) quickly so that work can proceed on providing timely business deliverables from the data warehouse.

PART TWO

Model Development

The data warehouse should represent the enterprise perspective of the data, and that perspective starts with the subject area and business data models. Using a fictitious company, we provide a step-by-step process to develop these two models in Chapter 3. Then using the business data model as the starting point, Chapter 4 develops the data warehouse data model using eight sequential transformation steps. The following four chapters delve into specific aspects of the data warehouse data model and include case studies demonstrating the principles. These case studies primarily use two company scenarios to develop the business case. The first is the General Omnificent Shopping Haven (GOSH). GOSH is a national department store chain with designs to expand internationally. The second is The Delicious Food Company (DFC). DFC is a large consumer packaged goods manufacturer that produces a wide range of food products, from powders and canned goods to dairy products, frozen dinners, and ice cream.

The data warehouse integrates data from multiple sources and stores the integrated form of that data for a long period of time. The keys that are used in each source system may have uniquely identified records within each system, but they may not be appropriate for the data warehouse. In Chapter 5, we review the problems posed by key structures in the operational systems and how these should be addressed in the data warehouse data model.

One of the distinguishing characteristics of the data warehouse is its historical perspective. In Chapter 6, we explain the importance of modeling the calendar in the data warehouse and different approaches for maintaining the historical perspective in this data model. These approaches help us deal with the unusual nature of the data warehouse, that is, it is used to capture snapshots of the data over time.

Chapters 7 and 8 delve into modeling two types of data frequently stored in the data warehouse – hierarchies and transactions. The design of the data warehouse reflects a compromise. It recognizes both the structure of the source systems (typically relational) and the structure of the popular dimensional data marts. The treatment of the hierarchies and transactions provides techniques for striking the right balance.

We close this part of the book with a chapter on the steps needed to ensure that the data warehouse performs well. In Chapter 9, we describe what is needed to optimize the physical data warehouse schema.

CHAPTER 3

Understanding the Business Model

All application systems, as well as the data warehouse, contain information based on the data used by the company. The business data model represents that data and is the foundation for all systems' models, including the data warehouse model. In Chapter 2, we described how a third normal form model provides data consistency and restricts data redundancy. As we will present in this chapter, the business model is a third normal form model. Since one of the objectives of the data warehouse is to provide a consistent view of the facts and figures for the enterprise, it is important to start with a model that meets those criteria; therefore, the business model is used as the foundation for the data warehouse model. Building the data warehouse model consists of transforming the business data model using eight well-defined steps, and this is covered in Chapter 4.

A fully developed business data model may contain hundreds of entities. A subject area model, which defines the major groupings of information, is a good way to manage these entities by providing a logical approach for grouping the entities. This chapter begins by describing the subject area model, with particular emphasis on how it helps ensure consistency and manage redundancy in the data warehouse model. We then outline the business data model, its relationship to the subject area model, and the steps required to develop it. A common complaint about the business data model is that it is esoteric and of limited practical value. The section on the business data model dispels these concerns and demonstrates that this model is a means of describing the business in a shorthand notation (that is, rectangles and lines) that facilitates the subsequent development of supporting application systems. It provides a high-level description of the process for building the subject area model and business data model. Complete books have been written on this subject alone, and they should be consulted for additional information. We've included some of our favorite books on this topic in the "Recommended Reading" section of this book.

This is a "how to" book on data warehouse modeling. Throughout Parts Two and Three of the book, the modeling concepts will be demonstrated using practical scenarios. We use a business scenario to demonstrate the modeling activities, and it is described at the beginning of this the chapter.

Business Scenario

We use a business scenario of an automobile manufacturer to develop the subject area model and business data model in this chapter and the data warehouse data model in Chapter 4. Following the description of the business scenario, we will dive into the subject area model.

Our automotive manufacturing firm is named Zenith Automobile Company (ZAC). ZAC was founded in 1935, and manufactures two makes of automobile—Zeniths and the higher-end luxury Tuxedos. Each of these makes have models that describe the type of car, and each model has three series available. The models are described in Table 3.1, and the series are described in Table 3.2.

Table 3.1   Car Models

MAKE	MODEL NAME	TARGET GROUP	DESCRIPTION
Zenith	Zipster	The young at heart (and age)	The Zipster is a sporty, subcompact-class car with a small price tag, excellent gas mileage, and limited options. This is the low-end offering in the Zenith line of cars.
Zenith	Zombie	Older, retired drivers with a limited income	The Zombie is a compact-sized, four-door automobile, noted for its economical upkeep and good gas mileage.
Zenith	Zoo	Families with small children	The Zoo is a four-door, mid-size car. The car is moderately priced and has good gas mileage.

Table 3.1   *(continued)*

MAKE	MODEL NAME	TARGET GROUP	DESCRIPTION
Zenith	Zoom	Sports car enthusiast of modest means seeking excitement	The Zoom is a moderately expensive, big-engine performance car that offers quick response, agile handling, and fast acceleration.
Zenith	Zeppelin	Luxury minded individual	The Zeppelin is the top-of-the-line Zenith car offering unsurpassed quality and features. It is a four door, full-sized model.
Tuxedo	Topsail	Young professionals	The Topsail is a mid-sized, two-door sedan equipped with a full complement of luxury features, including leather seats, an eight-way power-adjustable seat, a tilt steering wheel, and a high-tech car alarm.
Tuxedo	Tiara	The truly discriminating, sophisticated driver	The Tiara is a full-sized four-door sedan that is the top of the line Tuxedo automobile and is priced accordingly. It has many of the same features found in the Topsail but offers every conceivable luxury, including seat and outside mirror heaters.
Tuxedo	Thunderbolt	Wealthy sports car enthusiasts	The Thunderbolt marks an acknowledged milestone in sports cars. It combines all the breathtaking performance of a thoroughbred with the ease of operation, comfort, and reliability of a passenger car.

All of ZAC's cars are sold through dealers throughout the United States. Dealers are independent entities, but to retain their right to serve as ZAC dealers, they are governed by ZAC's rules. One of those rules requires them to submit monthly financial statements. The dealers are located within sales areas, which are grouped into sales territories, which are grouped into sales regions. Allocations are made at the sales area level, and incentive programs are developed by ZAC corporate.

Table 3.2 Car Series

MAKE	SERIES NAME	ACRONYM	DESCRIPTION
Zenith	No Frills	NF	This is the base level containing no upgrades. Base level consists of vinyl seats, low-end carpeting, smaller engines, manual transmissions, and three paint colors.
Zenith	Some Frills	SF	This is the next level and comes with upgraded fabric for the interior seats, moderately upgraded carpet, automatic transmission, larger engines, tinted windows, radio, five paint colors including metallic colors, and so on.
Zenith	Executive Frills	EF	The cars in this series come with leather interior, high-quality carpet, automatic transmission, larger engines, air conditioning, tinted windows, cruise control, power windows and locks, radio/tape player, eight paint colors including metallic colors, and so on. This series is not available for the Zipster or the Zombie.
Tuxedo	Pricey Frills	PF	Cars in this series come with leather interior, radio/tape deck, air conditioning, optional automatic transmission, cruise control, power windows and door lock, and keyless entry system.
Tuxedo	Decadent Frills	DF	Cars in this series come with all the features for the CF Series plus tinted windows, antitheft car alarm, moon roof, and radio/tape player/CD player with eight speakers.
Tuxedo	Truly Decadent Frills	TDF	Cars in this series have all the features listed for the PF Series plus power-operated moon roof, advanced sound system and insulation, automatic climate control system, dual illuminated vanity mirrors, and heated front seats.

Over the years, ZAC has developed a myriad of systems on mainframes, minicomputers, and even PCs. It built and/or bought other automobile manufacturing facilities, which resulted in even more disparate systems and databases.

Currently, it has IBM 3090s, DEC VAXs, Tandems, Suns, and HPs, plus PCs and Macintoshes. Their data is spread out in DB2, VSAM and Enscribe files, Non-stop SQL, RDB, Oracle, Sybase, and Informix. End users have tools such as Paradox, Rbase, Microsoft Access, and Lotus Notes. Needless to say, the data is spread out in hundreds of disparate databases throughout the company, with many in inaccessible formats.

ZAC is just beginning an information engineering effort to reengineer its business. The first project the reengineering effort highlighted as critical to the survival of the company is a data warehouse containing information about its dealers' car sales. The subject areas it has identified for this warehouse are Automobiles and Dealers, with less emphasis on Incentive Programs and Sales Organizations.

The impetus for the data warehouse is the fact that the data from these subject areas is not easily obtained today, causing opportunities to be lost, money to be wasted, and high-level executives to be uneasy about the direction and health of their company and their automotive sales. Based on interviews with key stakeholders, the ZAC decided to undertake development of a data warehouse and a set of data marts that could answer the following questions:

- What is the monthly sales trend in terms of quantity and dollar amounts sold of each make, model, series, and color (MMSC) for a specific dealer, by each sales area, sales territory, and sales region, for each state and for each metropolitan statistical area (MSA)?

- What is the pattern in the monthly quantity of inventory by MMSC for each dealer, by each sales area, sales territory, sales region, and MSA?

- How does the monthly quantity and dollars of sold automobiles by MMSC having a particular emissions type—by Dealer, Factory, Sales Area, Sales Territory, and Sales Region— compare with the same time frame last year and the year before?

- What is the trend in monthly actual sales (dollars and quantities) of MMSC for each dealer, sales area, sales territory, and sales region compared to their objectives? Users require this information both by monthly totals and cumulative year to date (YTD).

- What is the history (two-year comparisons) of the monthly quantity of units sold by MMSC and associated dollar amounts by retail versus wholesale dealers?

- What are the monthly dollar sales and quantities by MMSC this year to date as compared to the same time last year for each dealer?

- What is the monthly trend in sales dollars and quantities by MMSC for particular types of incentive programs, by dealer, sales area, sales territory, sales region, and MSA?

- What is the monthly trend in the average time it takes a dealer to sell a particular MMSC (called velocity and equal to the number of days from when a dealer receives the car to the date it is sold) by sales area, sales territory, sales region, and MSA?

- What was the monthly average selling price of an MMSC for each dealer, sales area, sales territory, sales region, and MSA?

- How many days was a dealer placed on credit hold for this month only and for the entire year? In addition, what was the total number of months in the past two years that the dealer was put on credit hold?

- Compare monthly sales dollars and quantities from the last body style (body style is make + model) to the current body style for each sales region? Body styles change every four years.

Subject Area Model

A data warehouse is organized by subject area, so it is only natural that the methodology for a data warehouse data model should begin with the subject area model. The subject-orientation of the data warehouse distinguishes it from a traditional application system. In the traditional operational system, although the data model should begin with a subject area model, this step is often omitted. Since the operational system is oriented toward specific business functions and processes, its design needs to emphasize the efficiency with which it can process the related transactions. Its model, therefore, is adjusted to emphasize the transaction-processing capabilities, with the processes that use it greatly influencing the data's organization. With the data warehouse, the subject orientation remains at the core of the physical database design. The core business processes are depicted in the source operational systems and with the data marts that people use to obtain data from the data warehouse, but the core data warehouse design remains subject oriented.

As we indicated in Chapter 2, subject areas are major groupings of physical items, concepts, people, places, and events of interest to the enterprise. We also indicated that the subject area model can be developed very quickly. An organization developing its first subject area model can benefit from work performed by others so that it doesn't need to start from scratch. There are many subject areas that are common across industries; virtually all organizations have customers, suppliers, products, and facilities. These are candidates for subject areas. A good point at which to start, as explained later in this chapter, is a generic model, such as the one shown in Table 3.3.

Table 3.3 Common Subject Areas

SUBJECT AREA	DEFINITION	EXAMPLES	REMARKS
Business Environment	Conditions, external to the company, which affect its business activities	•Regulation •Competition •License	These are often not implemented in a data warehouse.
Communications	Messages and the media used to transmit the messages	•Advertisement •Audience •Web Site Content	These often pertain to marketing activities, though they can apply to internal and other communications.
Customers[1]	People and organizations who acquire and/or use the company's products	•Customer •Prospect •Consumer	The definition provides for capturing potential customers (prospects) and for distinguishing between parties who buy the product and those who use it.
External Organizations[1]	Organizations, except Customers and Suppliers, external to the company	•Competitor •Partner •Regulator	The exclusion of Customers and Suppliers is consistent with the subject areas' being mutually exclusive.
Equipment	Movable machinery, devices, and tools and their integrated components	•Computer •Vehicle •Crane	Software that is integral to equipment is included within this subject area; other software is included within the Information subject area.
Facilities	Real estate and structures and their integrated components	•Real Estate •Building •Mountain	Integrated components (for example, an alarm system within a building) are often included as part of the facility unless a company is specifically interested in those components.

(continued)

Table 3.3 *(continued)*

SUBJECT AREA	DEFINITION	EXAMPLES	REMARKS
Financials	Information about money that is received, retained, expended, or tracked by the company	•Money •Receivable •Payable	
Human Resources[1]	Individuals who perform work for the company and the formal and informal organizations to which they belong	•Employee •Contractor •Position	Includes prospective (for example, applicants) and former (for example, retirees) employees. Some companies prefer to establish the organizational structure within a separate subject area.
Information	Facts and information about facts and the mechanisms that manage them	•Application System •Database •Meta Data	This includes the information about the company's computing environment, and also includes nonelectronic information.
Locations	Geographical points or areas	•Geopolitical Boundary •Country •Address	This can be expanded to include electronic locations such as email addresses and phone numbers.
Materials	Goods and services that are used or consumed by the company or that are included in a piece of equipment, facility, or product	•Chemical •Fuel •Supply	Sometimes, a product is used as a component of another product. When this is the case, a relationship between the relevant entities will be indicated in the business data model.
Products	Goods and related services that the company or its competitors provide or make available to Customers	•Product •Service •Advice	Competitor items that the company does not provide are often included to facilitate monitoring these and to support future decisions.

Table 3.3 *(continued)*

SUBJECT AREA	DEFINITION	EXAMPLES	REMARKS
Sales	Transactions that shift the ownership or control of a product from the Company to a Customer	•Sales Transaction •Sales Transaction Detail •Credit Memo	Sales is actually an associative subject area in that it is the intersection of the Customer, Store, Product, and so on. Some companies may choose to include the entities related to sales within one of those subject areas instead.
Suppliers[1]	Legal entities that provide the company with goods and services	•Broker •Manufacturer •Supplier	In the case of a contractor, the person doing the work is included in Human Resources, and the company that provides that person is included in Suppliers.

[1] Another approach is to create "Parties" as a subject area in lieu of Customers, External Organizations, Human Resources, and Suppliers. While Parties may be a useful concept to avoid duplication in a physical implementation, distinguishing among the major parties (for example, Customers, External Organizations, Human Resources, and Suppliers) improves comprehension and usage of the subject area model.

As a further aid, we recommend that you consider characteristics specific to your industry. The next section describes considerations for organizations in specific industries embarking on development of a subject area model.

Considerations for Specific Industries

Each industry has characteristics that are common to companies within that industry. By understanding these distinctions, the process of creating the subject area model can be further simplified. Some examples follow.

Retail Industry Considerations

Special considerations for building the subject area model in the retail industry are:

- Within the retail industry, major emphasis is often placed on the sales organization hierarchy. Companies in this industry would, therefore, tend to separate the Human Resources subject area as described in Table 3.3 into two subject areas: Human Resources and Internal Organizations.

- While facilities are certainly of interest to retailers, one particular facility, the Store, is often of major interest. As a result, stores are sometimes distinguished as a separate subject area.

- Retailers typically don't create products and often refer to what they sell as Items. This would replace the Products subject area, with the definition adjusted accordingly.

Manufacturing Industry Considerations

Special considerations for building the subject area model in the manufacturing industry are:

- Within the manufacturing industry, the manufacturing facilities are of particular interest, so these are often distinguished within a separate subject area.

- Waste is often produced as part of the manufacturing process, and there are laws that govern the waste. Waste is sometimes isolated as a separate subject area.

Utility Industry Considerations

Special considerations for building the subject area model in the utility industry are:

- Within the utility industry, power-producing facilities (for example, power plants) are of particular interest, and these may be distinguished into separate subject areas.

- The electrical network or gas pipeline consists of both physical and logical components. The physical components consist of the actual wires, switches, pipes, valves, and so on; the logical components consist of the load-carrying capacity, network topology, and so forth. These are sometimes split into two subject areas with Equipment addressing the physical components and Networks addressing the logical components.

Property and Casualty Insurance Industry Considerations

Special considerations for building the subject area model in the property and casualty insurance industry are:

- The property and casualty insurance industry typically deals with premiums, policies, and claims. Each of these is usually treated as a separate subject area.

- In the Financials subject area, these companies also need to deal with reserves, and due to the importance of the reserves, they could be treated in a separate subject area.

- The definition of customer needs to be adjusted to incorporate the concept of the party that owns an insurance policy and the party that may benefit from a claim. In some respects, this is similar to the concept of the customer who buys a product and the consumer who uses it.

Petroleum Industry Considerations

A special consideration for building the subject area model in the petroleum industry is that wells and refineries could be described as facilities, but due to their significance within this industry, each deserves to be its own subject area.

Health Industry Considerations

Special considerations for building the subject area model in the health industry are:

- There are several types of suppliers in the health industry, including the healthcare facility, the physician, the pharmacist, and so on. Consideration needs to be given to each of these to determine their positioning in the subject area model.

- In some companies within the health industry, the only customer of interest is the patient, and the Customers subject area would then be named Patients.

Subject Area Model Development Process

As stated earlier in this chapter, the subject area model can be developed in a matter of days. There are three major ways of developing the subject area model:

- Closed room
- Interviews
- Facilitated sessions

In each of the methods, you have the option of either starting from a clean slate or using a generic model as the starting point. Both approaches are valid, and the selection depends on the participants' preferences and background. The three major methods are summarized in Table 3.4. We recommend that the third approach—the use of facilitated sessions—be used if feasible. We explain why in the sections that follow.

Closed Room Development

Closed room development entails the modelers working on their own with little or no involvement by business representatives. It is in keeping with a philosophy that the modeling expertise is the most important skill needed in developing the subject area model. It further presumes that the modeler understands the business. When this approach is used, the modeler develops the subject area model based on his or her perceptions of the business. The process that the modeler typically uses consists of trying to group the enterprise's information into 15–20 major groupings, each of which would be a subject area. Once this is done, the modeler would create a definition for each one and would ensure that all of the definitions are mutually exclusive.

Table 3.4 Subject Area Model Development Options

METHOD	DESCRIPTION	ADVANTAGES	DISADVANTAGES
Closed Room	Data modeler(s) develop the subject area model in a vacuum, based on information they have, and then submit it for approval.	•Modelers understand the process. •A model can be developed quickly.	•Modelers may not possess sufficient business knowledge. •The business has no sense of ownership.
Interviews	Key business representatives are interviewed individually, and the modelers use this information to create the model. The result is then submitted for approval.	•Each person has the opportunity to contribute to the model. •Contributors possess the business knowledge. •Some business ownership is obtained.	•Individual interviews take more time. •While business knowledge is obtained, consensus isn't built.

Table 3.4   *(continued)*

METHOD	DESCRIPTION	ADVANTAGES	DISADVANTAGES
Facilitated Sessions	A facilitator leads a group of business representatives in the development of the subject area model.	•Contributors possess the business knowledge. •Business ownership is generated. •Consensus is developed through the interaction.	•Scheduling the required participants may be difficult.

This approach is generally not recommended. The modeler rarely, if ever, fully understands the entire business sufficiently to create a durable subject area model. There are some aspects of the model that are more art than science. For example, the modeler needs to decide whether to keep Human Resources as a single subject area or to create a Human Resources Subject Area for the employees, contractors, applicants, and so on, and a separate Internal Organizations Subject Area for the positions, organizational hierarchy, job classifications, and so on. Either approach is correct from a modeling perspective, as long as the definitions reflect the scope of the subject area. The decision is often based on people's preferences and it is important that the modeler not be the one to make this decision. When a model developed using this approach is subsequently presented for review, the business representatives are prone to treat this as another information technology exercise, thus making it difficult to garner support for it.

There are circumstances under which this approach is necessary. If the modeler cannot get sufficient business support to create the model, then the choice becomes whether to use this approach or to have no model. When this situation exists, it is better to have a model that is likely to be close than to have no model at all. The modeler should fully expect that adjustments will be needed and should continuously try to gain constructive business criticism of the model. While work on the subject area model can proceed with minimal business support, if the business support is not forthcoming when work on the business data model begins, serious consideration should be given to halting the project.

Development through Interviews

Interviews provide an excellent means of obtaining information from individual business representatives. The first challenge in setting up the interviews is determining who needs to participate. Since the subject area model represents the entire enterprise, a good place to start is the organizational chart. The modeler should interview people who represent the major departments in the enterprise either by their current position or by virtue of their previous positions. A reasonable representation of the enterprise should be available by interviewing 10–15 people. Each of these people should be asked to describe the high-level workflow in his or her area. Using this information, the interviewer should try to identify the major groupings of information of interest to each person and the interactions among them. A sample interview is provided in the "Interview with the Sales Executive" sidebar.

Interview with the Sales Executive

Following is the beginning of a sample interview:

Interviewer: Good morning, Jim (vice president of sales). I appreciate your taking time from your busy schedule to speak with me this morning. (The interviewer would then briefly explain the purpose of the interview and the importance of getting information from Jim's perspective.)

Interviewer: Please describe the sales process to me at a high level.

Sales VP: Our customers come into our store and look around. They select items that they would like and then place them in a cart. At the checkout counter, the items they've selected are electronically scanned. The terminal alerts the salesperson to promotional items, then the salesperson asks the customer about his or her interest in these. The salesperson also tries to obtain the customer's phone number. If it is already in our database, the salesperson confirms the customer's name and address; if it is a new one, the salesperson tries to get the customer's name and address and enters them into our database. We've been successful in obtaining information to identify about 70 percent of our customers. The customer then leaves the store.

Interviewer: Based on our discussion, I've identified the following major things of interest: customers, stores, salespeople, sales transactions, and items. Is that correct?

Sales VP: We gain a lot of value from having the promotional information available to our salespeople. I think that's important, too.

Interviewer: Thanks, I missed that one. Let's take a look at the relationships among these things. The customer comes into the store—can customers buy the items elsewhere?

Sales VP: Not at this time, but we're considering establishing an electronic commerce facility.

Interviewer: Are all the customers individual consumers, or are some considered representatives of organizations?

Sales VP: Our customers may be either consumers or representatives of businesses.

Interviewer: Is there any difference in the treatment of the two types of customers?

(Interview continues with the interviewer delving further into items based on the answers received.)

One of the major products of the interview should be a set of subject areas and definitions from that person's perspective. The information obtained will help create the subject area model and will also provide information for the business data model. By delving further within this interview, we make better use of the business representatives' time. When we subsequently work on the business data model, we can start with the information we obtained from these interviews and then focus on confirmation and refinement.

TIP

Go to an interview prepared with a set of questions, but don't expect to use them all. The questions provide a good checklist for ensuring that key points are covered; however, a good interviewer adjusts the interview to reflect the information being provided and the way that it is provided.

Once the interviews are completed, the modeler needs to consolidate the information. It is possible that the modeler will receive conflicting information, and these conflicts need to be resolved. Sometimes, the resolution may be one of using the most generalized case, but at other times, a discussion to clarify the differences may be needed.

The resultant subject area model should be provided to each of the interviewees for verification. Depending upon the person's position and technical disposition, the verification may be conducted through a brief discussion rather than through submission of the model for review.

Development through Facilitated Sessions

The approach that the authors have found to be the most effective and efficient is the use of facilitated sessions. These sessions involve representatives of the various business areas, just as the interviews do. The significant difference is that the people are interacting with each other instead of providing individual contributions. While it is sometimes difficult to get the people together, when this is accomplished, the product is completed very quickly and reflects compromises with which the business representatives agree. The major steps in the process are preparation, one or two facilitated sessions, work between the facilitated sessions, and follow-on work. If the group is starting from a clean slate, two facilitated sessions will be needed; if the group is using a starter model, it may be possible to complete the effort in one session.

Preparation

Preparation consists of selecting and inviting the participants and making the logistical arrangements. The preparation should be performed at least one to two weeks before the session. One of the keys to a successful session is to ensure that the participants understand the purpose, the process, and their role. These should be described in the invitation letter.

First Facilitated Session

The agenda for the first session should include the following items:

Introductions.   The participants introduce themselves, and the session objectives are reviewed.

Education.   Education is provided on the relevant concepts and on the process.

Brainstorming.   Brainstorming is used to develop a list of potential subject areas.

Refinement.   The list of potential subject areas is reviewed and refined to arrive at the set of subject areas.

Conclusion.   The session results are reviewed, and assignments for definition creation are made.

This agenda presumes that the group will be starting with a clean slate. If the group starts with a generic or industry model, the following agenda would apply:

Introductions.   The participants introduce themselves, and the session objectives are reviewed.

Education.   Education is provided on the relevant concepts, on the process, and on the starter model.

Review and refinement of subject areas.   The subject areas in the starter model are reviewed, and a set of subject areas is derived. Definitions for those subject areas are then reviewed and refined.

Refinement.   The list of potential subject areas is reviewed and refined to arrive at the set of subject areas.

A critical part of the agenda for the first session is education. During the educational portion of the meeting, the facilitator explains what a subject area is, how it should be identified and defined, and why the resultant model is beneficial. The processes (for example, brainstorming) to be employed are also described along with the rules for the facilitated session.

TIP

If some members of the group understand the concepts and others don't, consider having an educational session before the actual facilitated session. This provides the attendees with a choice and does not force people who know the topic to attend redundant education.

The remainder of this section presumes that the group is not beginning with a starter model.

Following the educational session, the group engages in a brainstorming session to identify potential subject areas. In a brainstorming session, all contributions are recorded, without any discussion. It is, therefore, not uncommon for people to identify reports, processes, functions, entities, attributes, organizations, and so on, in addition to real subject areas. Figure 3.1 shows the potential result of such a brainstorming session for an automobile manufacturer such as the Zenith Automobile Company. If you look closely at the flip charts, you'll see that most of the second sheet and part of the third sheet deviated into too great a level of detail. When this happens, the facilitator should remind the group of the definition of a subject area.

POTENTIAL SUBJECT AREAS - PAGE 1	POTENTIAL SUBJECT AREAS - PAGE 2
• CUSTOMERS • PRODUCTS • CARS • DEALERS • WAREHOUSES • DISTRIBUTION CTRS • CONSUMER • PAINT • VARIANCE REPORT • MARKETING • DISPLAY CASE	• SALES ORDER • CASH REGISTER • SALES REGION • DELIVERY TRUCK • EMPLOYEES • COMPETITORS • REGULATORS • GENERAL LEDGER • CREDIT CARD • LOAN • PROMOTIONS

POTENTIAL SUBJECT AREAS - PAGE 3	POTENTIAL SUBJECT AREAS - PAGE 4
• ADVERTISEMENT • CONTRACTOR • WARRANTY • SERVICE POLICY • SALES TRANSACTIONS • SUPPLIER • MANUFACTURERS • PARTS • PACKAGES • LOANER CARS • SALES ANALYSIS RPT	• PROSPECTS • ITEMS • MOTORS • USED CARS • WASTE • SUPPLIES • DEALER

Figure 3.1   Result of brainstorming session.

The next step in the process is to examine the contributed items and exclude items that are not potential subject areas. Each item is discussed and, if it does not conform to the definition of a potential subject area, it is removed and possibly replaced by something that conveys the concept and could conform to the definition of a subject area. When this process is over, there will be fewer subject areas on the list, as shown in Figure 3.2. Some of the transformation actions that took place follow:

■ ITEMS and PRODUCTS were determined to be the same thing and AUTOMOBILES was selected as the term to be used since all the products and items were driven by the automobiles. Further, these were found to encompass CARS, PAINT, LUXURY CAR, PARTS, PACKAGES, MOTORS, USED CARS.

■ CUSTOMER and CONSUMER were determined to be the same thing and CUSTOMERS was selected as the term to be used. PROSPECTS was absorbed into this area.

■ VARIANCE REPORT and SALES ANALYSIS REPORT were determined to be reports and eliminated.

- MARKETING was determined to be a function and was eliminated. During the discussion, ADVERTISEMENTS and PROMOTIONS were added.

- CREDIT CARD and LOAN were grouped into PAYMENT METHODS.

- EMPLOYEES and CONTRACTOR were combined into HUMAN RESOURCES.

- DEALERSHIPS and DEALERS were deemed to be the same, and DEALERS was chosen as the subject area.

The resultant list should consist solely of data groupings, but some may be more significant than others. Next, the group is asked to look at the list and try to group items together. For example, WAREHOUSES, DISTRIBUTION CENTERS, and FACTORIES are shown in Figure 3.2. WAREHOUSES and DISTRIBUTION CENTERS could be grouped into a potential subject area of FACILITIES, with FACTORIES also established as a subject area. When this process is over, the most likely candidates for the subject areas will have been identified, as shown in Figure 3.3.

POTENTIAL SUBJECT AREAS - PAGE 1	POTENTIAL SUBJECT AREAS - PAGE 2
• CUSTOMERS • PRODUCTS • ~~CARS~~ • ~~DEALERSHIPS~~ • WAREHOUSES • DISTRIBUTION CTRS • ~~CONSUMER~~ • ~~PAINT~~ • ~~VARIANCE REPORT~~ • ~~MARKETING~~ • DISPLAY CASE	• SALES ORDER • CASH REGISTER • SALES REGION • DELIVERY TRUCK • ~~EMPLOYEES~~ • COMPETITORS • FACTORY • GENERAL LEDGER • ~~CREDIT CARD~~ • ~~LOAN~~ • SHOWROOM

POTENTIAL SUBJECT AREAS - PAGE 3	POTENTIAL SUBJECT AREAS - PAGE 4
• ~~LUXURY CAR~~ • ~~CONTRACTOR~~ • WARRANTY • SERVICE POLICY • SALES TRANSACTION • SUPPLIER • MANUFACTURERS • ~~PARTS~~ • ~~PACKAGES~~ • LOANER CARS • ~~SALES ANALYSIS RPT~~	• ~~PROSPECTS~~ • ~~ITEMS~~ • ~~MOTORS~~ • USED ~~CARS~~ • WASTE • SUPPLIES • DEALER • ADVERTISEMENTS • PROMOTIONS • PAYMENT METHODS • HUMAN RESOURCES

Figure 3.2 Result of refinement process.

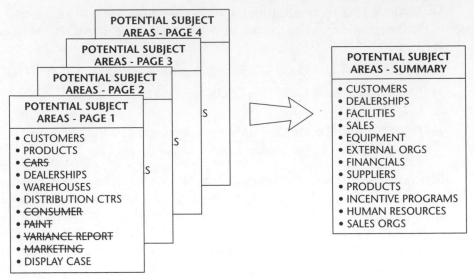

Figure 3.3 Result of reduction process.

This virtually completes the first facilitated session. In preparation for the next session, each subject area should be assigned to two people. Each of these people should draft a definition for the subject area and should identify at least three entities that would be included within it. (Some people may be responsible for more than one subject area.) The work should be completed shortly following the meeting and submitted to the facilitator. The group should be advised that on the intervening day, the facilitator uses this information and information from subject area model templates (if available) to provide a starting point for the second session.

Consolidation and Preparation for Second Facilitated Session

During the period (potentially as little as one day) between the two facilitated sessions, the facilitator reviews the definitions and sample entities and uses these to create the defined list of subject areas that will be used in the second facilitated session. The facilitator should create a document that shows the contributions provided, along with a recommendation. For example, for the subject area of Customers, the following contributions could have been made:

Contribution 1.   "Customers are people who buy or are considering buying our items." Sample entities are Customer, Wholesaler, and Prospect.

Contribution 2.   "Customers are organizations that acquire our items for their internal consumption." Sample entities are Customer, Customer Subsidiary, and Purchasing Agent.

The subject area template information (previously shown in Table 3.3) provides a definition of Customers as "People and organizations who acquire and/or use the company's products," and provides Customer, Prospect, and Consumer as sample entities. Using this information, the facilitator could include the information for CUSTOMERS shown in Table 3.5. Similar information would be provided for each of the subject areas.

Second Facilitated Session

The agenda for the second session should include the following items:

Review.   The results of the first session and the work performed since then are reviewed.

Refinement.   The subject areas and their definitions are reviewed and refined.

Relationships.   Major relationships between pairs of subject areas are created.

Conclusion.   The model is reviewed, unresolved issues are discussed, and follow-up actions are defined.

Table 3.5 Potential Subject Area: CUSTOMER

POTENTIAL DEFINITIONS	RECOMMENDED DEFINITION	SAMPLE ENTITIES	COMMENTS
•Customers are people who buy or are considering buying our products. •Customers are organizations that acquire our items for their internal consumption. •People and organizations who acquire and/or use the company's products	People or organizations who acquire the Company's items	•Consumer •Customer •~~Customer Purchasing Agent~~ •Prospect	•Some customers lease our items, hence acquire is more appropriate than buy. •"Considering buying" is left out since all definitions imply past, present, and future. •Customer Purchasing Agent is not used since this is part of Human Resources.

The success of the second session is highly dependent on each of the participants completing his or her assignment on time and on the facilitator compiling a document that reflects the input received and best practices. A limit should be placed on the discussion time for each subject area. If the subject area is not resolved by the end of the allotted time, the responsibility to complete the remaining work should be assigned to a member of the team. Often, the remaining work will consist of refining the wording (but not the meaning) of the definition.

After all of the subject areas have been discussed, the major relationships among the subject areas are identified and the resultant subject area diagram is drawn. This step is the least critical one in the process because the subject area relationships can be derived naturally from the business data model as it is developed. A critical final step of the second facilitated session is the development of the issues list and action plan.

Follow-on Work

The issues list and action plan are important products of the second facilitated session, since they provide a means of ensuring that the follow-on work is completed. The issues list contains questions that were raised during the session that need to be resolved. Each item should include the name of the person responsible and the due date. The action plan summarizes the remaining steps for the subject area model. Often, the product of the session can be applied immediately to support development of the business data model, with refinements being completed over time based on their priority.

Subject Area Model Benefits

Regardless of how quickly the subject area model can be developed, the effort should be undertaken only if there are benefits to be gained. Three major benefits were cited in Chapter 2:

- The subject area model guides the business data model development.
- It influences data warehouse project selection.
- It guides data warehouse development projects.

The subject area model is a tool that helps the modeler organize his or her work and helps multiple teams working on data warehouse projects recognize areas of overlap. The sidebar shows how the subject area model can be used to assist in data warehouse project definition and selection.

Data Warehouse Project Definition and Selection

Figure 3.4 shows the primary subject areas that are needed to answer the business questions for the Zenith Automobile Company.

QUESTION	SUBJECT AREA					
	AUTO-MOBILES	CUSTOMERS	DEALERS	FACTORIES	INCENTIVE PROGRAMS	SALES ORGS
1						
2						
3						
4						
5						
6						
7						
8						
9						
10						
11						

Figure 3.4 Mapping requirements to subject areas.

Using the information in Figure 3.4, a logical implementation sequence would be to develop the Automobiles, Dealers, and Sales Organizations subject areas first since virtually all the questions are dependent on them. Factories or Incentive Programs could be developed next, followed by the remaining one of those two. For the business questions posed, no information about Customers and Suppliers is needed.

Even if the business considered question 3 or 7 to be the most significant, they should not be addressed first. The reason for this conclusion is that in order to answer those questions, you still need information for the other three subject areas.

This is an example of the iterative development approach whereby the data warehouse is built in increments, with an eye toward the final deliverable.

Subject Area Model for Zenith Automobile Company

A potential subject area model for the Zenith Automobile Company is provided in Figure 3.5. Only the subject areas needed to answer the business questions and Customers are shown.

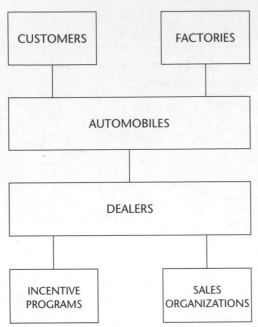

Figure 3.5 Zenith Automobile Company partial subject area.

Definitions for each subject area follow:

- *Automobiles* are the vehicles and associated parts manufactured by Zenith Automobile Company and sold through its dealers.

- *Customers* are the parties that acquire automobiles and associated parts from Dealers.

- *Dealers* are agencies authorized to sell Zenith Automobile Company automobiles and associated parts.

- *Factories* are the facilities in which Zenith Automobile Company manufactures its automobiles and parts.

- *Incentive Programs* are financial considerations designed to foster the sale of automobiles.

- *Sales Organizations* are the groupings of Dealers for which information is of interest.

Figure 3.6 provides a potential subject area model for a retail company. This model is provided as a reference point for some of the case studies used in Chapters 5–8.

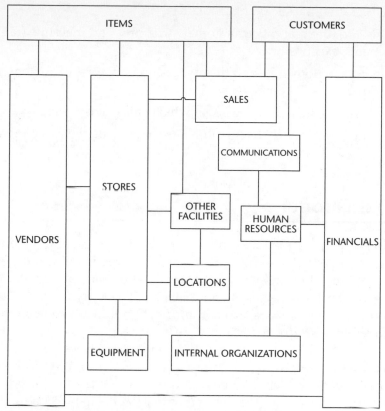

Figure 3.6 Retail subject area model starter.

Sample definitions for each of the subject areas follow.

- *Communications* are messages and the media used to transmit the messages.

- *Customers* are people and organizations who acquire and/or use the company's items.

- *Equipment* is movable machinery, devices, and tools and their integrated components.

- *Human Resources* are individuals who perform work for the company.

- *Financials* is information about money that is received, retained, expended, or tracked by the company.

- *Internal Organizations* are formal and informal groups to which Human Resources belong.

- *Items* are goods and services that the company or its competitors provide or make available to Customers.

- *Locations* are geographic points and areas.

- *Other Facilities* are real estate and other structures and their integrated components, except stores.

- *Sales* are transactions that shift the ownership or control of an item from the Company to a Customer.

- *Stores* are places, including kiosks, at which Sales take place.

- *Vendors* are legal entities that manufacture or provide the company with items.

Business Data Model

As we explained in Chapter 2, a model is an abstraction or representation of a subject that looks or behaves like all or part of the original. The business data model is one type of model, and it is an abstraction or representation of the data in a given business environment. It helps people envision how the information in the business relates to other information in the business ("how the parts fit together"). Products that apply the business data model include application systems, the data warehouse, and data mart databases. In addition, the model provides the meta data (or information about the data) for these databases to help people understand how to use or apply the final product. The subject area model provides the foundation for the business data model, and that model reduces the development risk by ensuring that the application system correctly reflects the business environment.

Business Data Development Process

If a business data model does not exist, as is assumed in this section, then a portion of it should be developed prior to embarking on the data warehouse data model development. The process for developing the business data model cannot be described without first defining the participants. In the ideal world, the data stewards and the data modelers develop the business data model jointly.

Most companies do not have formal data stewardship programs, and the business community (and sometimes the information technology community) may not see any value in developing the business data model. After all, it delays producing the code! The benefits of the business data model were presented in Chapter 2, but in the absence of formal data stewards, the data modeler needs to identify the key business representatives with the necessary knowledge and the authority to make decisions concerning the data definitions and relationships. These are often called "subject matter experts" or

SMEs (pronounced "smeeze"). Once these people are identified, the modeler needs to obtain their commitment to participate in the modeling activities. This is no small chore, and often compromises need to be made. For example, the SMEs may be willing to answer questions and review progress, but may not be willing to participate in the modeling sessions. After the modeler understands the level of participation, he or she should evaluate the risk of the reduced SME involvement to the accuracy and completeness of the model. Then, the modeler should adjust his or her effort estimate and schedule if there is a significant difference between the SMEs' committed level of involvement and the level that was assumed when the plan was created.

Development of a complete business data model can take 6 to 12 months, with no tangible business deliverable being provided during that timeframe. While this may be the theoretically correct approach, it is rarely a practical one. We recommend using the following approach:

1. Identify the subject area(s) from which data is needed for the project iteration.

2. Identify the entities of interest within the affected subject area(s) and establish the identifiers.

3. Determine the relationships between pairs of entities.

4. Add attributes.

5. Confirm the model's structure.

6. Confirm the model's content.

The remainder of this section describes these six activities.

Identify Relevant Subject Areas

The subject areas with information needed to answer the questions posed in the scenario described for are shown in Figure 3.5. These are: Automobiles, Dealers, Factories, Incentive Programs, and Sales Organizations.

There are other subject areas in the subject area model, but these do not appear to be needed for the first few iterations of the data warehouse. This first application of the subject area model provides us with a quick way of limiting the scope of our work. We could further reduce our scope if we want to address only a few of the questions. For example, let's assume that the first iteration doesn't answer questions 3 and 7.

To answer these questions, we don't need any information from Factories and Incentive Programs, nor do we need information about Customers for any of the questions. Being able to exclude these subject areas is extremely important.

Customer data, for example, is one of the most difficult to obtain accurately. If the business is initially interested in sales statistics, then information about the specific customers can be excluded from the scope of the first iteration of the model. This avoids the need to gain a common definition of "customer" and to solve the integration issues that often exist with multiple customer files. (In the automotive industry, information about Customers requires cooperation from the Dealers.) It is important to remember that excluding a subject area has no bearing on its importance—it only has a bearing on the urgency of defining the business rules governing that area and hence the speed with which the next business deliverable of the data warehouse can be created, as shown in Figure 3.7. Similarly, in developing the details for the other subject areas, the focus should remain on the entities needed for the iteration being developed.

Figure 3.7 points out several benefits of using the subject areas to limit scope. First, the project can be subdivided into independent iterations, each of which is shorter than the full project. Second, the iterations can often overlap (if resources are available) to further shorten the elapsed time for completing the entire effort. For example, once the analysis and modeling are completed for the first iteration, these steps can begin for the second iteration, while the development for the first iteration proceeds. Some rework may be needed as additional iterations are pursued, but this can often be avoided through reasonable planning. The value of providing the business deliverables quicker is usually worth the risk.

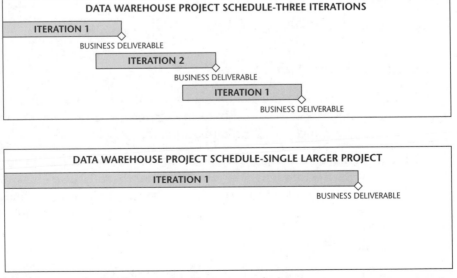

Figure 3.7 Schedule impact of subject area exclusion.

Identify Major Entities and Establish Identifiers

An entity is a person, place, thing, event, or concept of interest to a company and for which the company has the capability and willingness to capture information. Entities can often be uncovered by listening to a user describe the business, by reviewing descriptive documents for an area, and by interviewing subject matter experts. We concluded that information from three subject areas—Automobiles, Dealers, and Sales Organizations—is needed to address the first three questions. Let's examine Sales.

Potential entities should be developed through a brainstorming session, interviews, or analysis. The initial list should not be expected to be complete. As the model is developed, entities will be added to the list and some items initially inserted in the list may be eliminated, particularly for the first iteration of the data warehouse. Each of the entities needs to be defined, but before spending too much time on an entity, the modeler should quickly determine whether or not the entity is within the scope of the data warehouse iteration being pursued. The reason for this screening is obvious—defining an entity takes time and may involve a significant amount of discussion if there is any controversy. By waiting until an entity is needed, not only is time better spent, but the SMEs are also more inclined to work on the definition since they understand the importance of doing so.

Eventually, the model will be transformed into a physical database with each table in that database requiring a key to uniquely identify each instance. We therefore should designate an identifier for each entity that we will be modeling. Since this is a business model, we need not be concerned with the physical characteristics of the identifier; therefore, we can simply create a primary key attribute of "[Entity Name] Identifier" or "[Entity Name] Code" for each entity. The difference between Identifier and Code is described in the "Entity- and Attribute-Modeling Conventions" sidebar, which shows the entity-modeling conventions we've adopted. Most modeling tools generate foreign keys when the relationships dictate the need and, by including the identifier, our model will include the cascaded foreign keys. The "Entity- and Attribute-Modeling Conventions" sidebar summarizes the conventions we used to name and define entities and attributes. Table 3.6 presents the results of this activity for the entities of interest for the business questions that need to be answered.

Entity- and Attribute-Modeling Conventions

The rules for naming and defining entities and attributes should be established within each enterprise. Entities and attributes represent business-oriented views, and the naming conventions are not limited by physical constraints. Some of the conventions to consider are as follows.

Entity naming conventions include:

◆ Each entity should have a unique name.

◆ The entity name should be in title case (that is, all words except for prepositions and conjunctions are capitalized).

◆ Entity names should be composed of business-oriented terms:

▪ Use full, unabbreviated words.

▪ Use spaces between words.

▪ Use singular nouns.

▪ Avoid articles, prepositions, and conjunctions.

◆ The length of the name is not limited. (A good entity name would be Bill to Customer; a poor one would be BTC or Bill-to-Cust.)

Attribute naming conventions include:

◆ Attribute names should contain one or more prime words, zero or more modifiers, and one class word.

▪ The prime word describes the item. It is often the same as the name of the entity within which the attribute belongs.

▪ The qualifier is a further description of the item

▪ The class word (for example, amount, name) is a description of the type of item.

◆ Each attribute should have a unique name within an entity. If the same attribute, except for the prime word (for example, expiration date, status) is used in several entities, it should always have the same definition.

◆ The attribute name should be in title case.

◆ Each attribute name should be composed of business-oriented terms:

▪ Use full, unabbreviated words. The length of the name is not limited.

▪ Use spaces between words.

▪ Use singular nouns.

▪ Avoid articles, prepositions, and conjunctions such as "the" and "and."

Entity and attribute definition conventions include:

◆ **Definitions should use consistent formats.**

◆ **Definitions should be self-sufficient.**

◆ **Definitions should be clear and concise.**

◆ **Definitions should not be recursive. A word should not be used to define itself.**

◆ **Definitions should be business-oriented.**

◆ **Definitions should be mutually exclusive.**

◆ **Definitions should be independent of physical system constraints.**

Table 3.6   Entity Definitions.

ENTITY	DEFINITION	SUBJECT AREA
Allocated Automobile	The Allocated Automobile is one that has been assigned and paid for by a specific Dealer. It now becomes part of the Dealer's inventory and the Dealer assumes responsibility for the car and its ultimate sale to a Customer.	Automobiles
Automobile	The Automobile is the specific product produced by ZAC. There are two lines of automobiles: Zeniths and Tuxedos. Each line has several models to choose from, and each model has three series containing different features.	Automobiles
Automobile Status	Automobile Status indicates the automobile's stage within the product life cycle. Statuses are manufactured, in inventory, at the Dealer, sold to a Customer.	Automobiles
Color	The Color is the coloration that is used for the exterior of an Automobile.	Automobiles
Customer	A Customer is a person or business entity that acquires an Automobile.	Customers
Dealer	The Dealer is an independent business that chooses to sell ZAC cars. The Dealer must purchase the cars and then sell them to its customers. ZAC supports the dealers by running national ads, supplying sales brochures, providing sales incentive programs, and so on. The Dealer must, in turn, supply ZAC with its financial statements and agree to abide by ZAC's quality guidelines and service standards.	Dealers

(continued)

Table 3.6 *(continued)*

ENTITY	DEFINITION	SUBJECT AREA
Dealer Financial Statement	The Dealer Financial Statement is the required statement of financial information that the Dealer must supply to ZAC. This is ZAC's method of verifying the sales that the Dealer claims to have made. This is especially important for Incentive Program Sales where the Dealer receives an incentive for each sale.	Dealers
Dealer Objective	The Dealer Objective is the Dealer's estimate of the quantity of cars by MMSC that it will sell during the month. These figures are used to calculate the allocations of cars to Dealers by ZAC.	Dealers
Dealer on Credit Hold	If a Dealer does not pay for its allocated cars on time, it is placed on Credit Hold until such payment is received. While on Credit Hold, the Dealer cannot receive any more of its allocated cars.	Dealers
Emission Type	The Emission Type indicates the type of emissions equipment in the Automobile. Different states require different emissions equipment installed in the automobiles sold in their area—some are more stringent than others. The cost of the Automobile varies according to the complexity of the emissions equipment.	Automobiles
Factory	The Factory is the plant manufacturing the Automobile. This is sometimes referred to as the Source. Zenith automobiles are built in Asheville, NC; Cortez, CO; and Southington, CT. Tuxedo automobiles are made in Greenville, SC; Newark, OH; and Bremen, IN.	Factories
Incentive Program	The Incentive Program is offered by ZAC to its Dealers. The Program provides some form of rebate or reduction in an automobile's price so that the Dealer may offer this reduced price to the Customer, thus enhancing the Customer's purchase desire.	Incentive Programs
Incentive Program Participant	The Dealer may choose to participate in ZAC's Incentive Program. If it does, it can offer the incentives to its customers in order to enhance their purchasing desire.	Incentive Programs
Incentive Program Term	The Incentive Program Term is a term or condition under which the reduced price offered is valid.	Incentive Programs
Make	The Make is the company manufacturing the Automobile, for example, Zenith or Tuxedo.	Automobiles

Table 3.6 *(continued)*

ENTITY	DEFINITION	SUBJECT AREA
Metropolitan Statistical Area	The Metropolitan Statistical Area is assigned by the Federal Government and is based on statistically significant population groupings.	Dealers
Model	The Model is the type of Automobile manufactured and sold. Examples are the Zenith Zipster, Zenith Zoo, Tuxedo Tiara, and Tuxedo Thunderbolt.	Automobiles
MSA Zipcode	A listing of Zipcode within an MSA.	Dealers
Option	The Option is a feature added to a specific Automobile to enhance the car.	Automobiles
Option Package	The Option Package is the grouping of Options that are added to a specific Automobile. This is a convenient way of identifying a standard grouping of options.	Automobiles
Sales Area	The Sales Area is the lowest level of ZAC's sales force. The area is usually a large city, a group of smaller cities, or a geographic area.	Sales Organizations
Sales Manager	The Sales Manager is the employee responsible for managing the sales area. (This is a subtype of Employee.)	Employees
Sales Region	The Sales Region is responsible for several Sales Territories. It is the highest level in the Sales Organization.	Sales Organizations
Sales Territory	The Sales Territory is responsible for several Sales Areas.	Sales Organizations
Series	The Series indicates the set of features that come with the Make and Model. For example, the Zenith Models come in the following series: NF (no frills), SF (some frills), MF (max frills). The Tuxedo Models come with these series: CF (costly frills), PF (pricey frills), DF (decadent frills), and TDF (truly decadent frills).	Automobiles
Sold Automobile	A Sold Automobile is now the property of the Customer purchasing it. The ownership transfers to the Customer or to the Customer's loaning institution.	Automobiles
Unallocated Automobile	The Unallocated Automobile is considered part of ZAC's inventory. It becomes assigned to a Dealer when it is allocated.	Automobiles
Warehouse	The Warehouse is the company-owned facility at which manufactured automobiles are stored prior to allocation and shipment to dealers.	Facilities

In the business model, we can provide an attribute for the description (and avoid having a reference entity for translating the code into the description). The code is needed only when we migrate to the data warehouse, where it is used either to ensure that only valid codes are used (domain constraints can also accomplish this) or to reduce the storage requirements. We create code—description entities—when we build the data warehouse model.

Define Relationships

A modeling tool is essential for developing and maintaining all data models. Some of the common tools on the market follow. There are advantages and disadvantages to each of the tools, but every one of them performs at least the basic modeling functions. The differences among the tools change with each release and hence are not described in this book.

Common data modeling tools include

- ERwin by Computer Associates
- ER Studio by Embarcadero
- Oracle Designer by Oracle
- Silverrun by Magna Solutions
- System Architect by Popkin
- Visio by Microsoft
- Warehouse Designer by Sybase

The relationships diagrammatically portray the business rules. Following is a partial set of business rules that need to be reflected in the business data model.

- An automobile is classified by make, model, series, and color.
- An automobile is manufactured in a factory.
- An option package contains one or more options, each of which may be included in several option packages.
- An automobile contains zero, one, or more option packages.
- An automobile is allocated to a dealer.
- An automobile is sold by a dealer.

These rules would be uncovered through discussions with appropriate subject matter experts. The next step in the process is to define the relationships between pairs of entities. Figure 3.8 shows the entities needed in the model to support these questions.

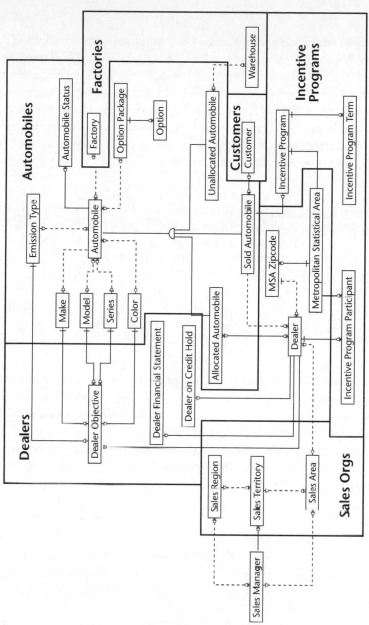

Figure 3.8 Entity-relationship diagram—entities.

An examination of the business data model reveals that the entities are grouped by subject area. This organization of the business data model is very helpful as more and more entities are added to the model.

TIP

Another source of information for the business data model is the database of an existing system. While this is a source, the modeler needs to recognize that the physical database used by a system reflects technical constraints and other (frequently undocumented) assumptions made by the person who designed it as well as erroneous or outdated business rules. It should, therefore, not be considered to *be* the business model, but it certainly can be used as input to the model. Any differences discovered in using a database from an existing system should be documented. These will be used when the transformation rules are developed.

Add Attributes

An attribute is a fact or discrete piece of information pertaining to an entity. One such attribute has already been included in the diagram—the identifier. At this point, additional attributes needed to answer the business questions of interest are added. For example, the questions involving the Store requested information on the store's age. Based on that requirement, the store inception date should be added as an attribute.

TIP

In the business model, information that changes with time should be tied to calendar dates whenever possible. For example, instead of store age, the date the store was opened or last renovated should be shown. In the data warehouse model, we have options on whether to store just the date of birth or both the date of birth and the age. If we're doing analysis based on a range of ages, we may choose to store the age range in the mart. (If we choose this option, we will need to include logic for updating the age range unless the mart is rebuilt with each load cycle.)

The difficulty with a data warehouse data model is anticipating the attributes that business users will eventually want. Since the business data model is being built primarily to support the warehouse, that problem manifests itself at this point. Part of the reason for the difficulty is that the business users truly do not know everything they need. They will discover some of their needs as they use the environment. Some sources to consider in identifying the potential elements are existing reports, queries, and source system databases. This area is discussed more thoroughly in Chapter 4 as part of the first step of creating the data warehouse data model.

The "Entity- and Attribute-Modeling Conventions" sidebar summarizes the conventions we used to name and define attributes. Figure 3.9 shows the expanded model, with the attributes included. As was the case with the entities, we should expect additions, deletions, and changes as the model continues to evolve.

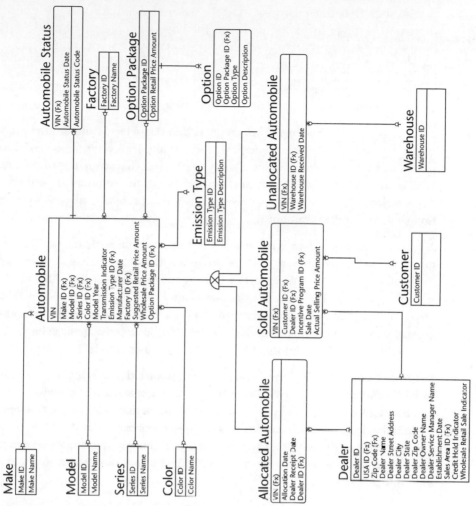

Figure 3.9 Entity-relationship diagram—entities and attributes.

The model in Figure 3.9 reflects attributes that, from a business perspective, appear to fit within the designated entities for the Automobiles Subject Area. (Some entities from other subject areas are included in the diagram to provide a more complete picture.)

Confirm Model Structure

The business data model should be presented in what is known as "third normal form." The third normal form was described in Chapter 2. By way of summary, in the third normal form, each attribute is dependent on the key of the entity in which it appears, on the whole key, and on nothing but the key.

Remember that the business model does not need to provide good performance. It is never implemented. It is the basis of subsequent models that may be used for a data warehouse, an operational system, or data marts. For that usage, the third normal form provides the greatest degree of flexibility and stability and ensures the greatest degree of consistency.

TIP

A purist view of the business data model is that it is a third normal form model that is concerned only with the logical (and not physical) view. Several of the data-modeling tools store information about the physical characteristics of the table for each entity and about the physical characteristics of the column for each attribute. The theoretician would address these only when the model is applied for an application such as the data warehouse.

A more practical approach is to include some information pertaining to the physical model in the business model. The reason for this is that several applications will use the business model, and they start by copying the relevant section of the model. If more than one application needs the same entity, then each is forced to establish the physical characteristics such as datatype for the resultant table and its columns. This creates duplicate effort and introduces a potential for inconsistency. A better approach is to create some of this information within the business model in the modeling tool.

The use of domain definitions is another technique that experienced modelers use to minimize work and provide flexibility. The domain feature of the modeling tool can be used to define valid values, data types, nullability, and so on. One application of domains is to establish one for each unique combination of these, then instead of defining each of the physical characteristics of a column, it is merely assigned to a domain. In addition to reducing the workload, this provides the flexibility to accommodate future changes.

Confirm Model Content

The last, and possibly most important, step in developing the business data model is to verify its content. This is accomplished through a discussion with business representatives. The techniques used vary. In meeting with the business users, the modeler must remember that the model is a means to an end. It is a technique for describing the business in a way that facilitates the development of systems and data warehouses. Some business representatives may be both willing and able to review the actual model. With others, the modeler may need to ask questions in plain English that verify the business rules and definitions. For example, the modeler may need to conduct an interview in which he or she confirms the relationships by asking the business representative if each of the business rules that the relationships represents is valid.

Summary

The subject area model is inherent in the foundation of the data warehouse, since the warehouse itself is "subject oriented." The subject area model provides a good way of organizing the business data model. The subject area model identifies the 15–25 major groupings of significance to the company, with each one mutually exclusive of the others. The subject area model can be created in a few days, using facilitated sessions. The first of two facilitated sessions includes education on the relevant concepts, brainstorming a list of potential subject areas, and refinement of the list. Preliminary definitions are developed prior to the second meeting, at which the results of the first session and the work performed since then are reviewed, the subject areas and their definitions are reviewed and refined, major relationships are added to the model, and the model is reviewed. Unresolved issues and follow-up actions may also be identified.

This business data model is the foundation of everything that follows. Significant errors can have a cascading effect, so it is very important to verify both the structure and the content of the model. The business data model describes the information of importance to an enterprise and how pieces of information are related to each other. It is completely independent of any organizational, functional, or technological considerations. It therefore provides a solid foundation for designing the database for any application system, including a data warehouse. A complete business data model is complex and can easily require a year to complete. Instead of developing a complete business data model, the data warehouse modeler should create only those portions of the model that are needed to support the business questions being asked.

Within the scope of the business questions being asked, the business data model is developed by identifying the subject areas from which data is needed, identifying and defining the major entities, establishing the relationships between pairs of entities, adding attributes, conforming to the third normal form, and confirming the content of the model.

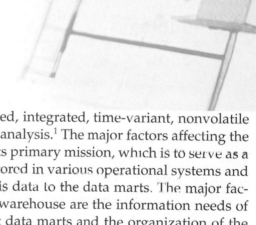

CHAPTER 4

Developing the Model

The data warehouse is a subject-oriented, integrated, time-variant, nonvolatile collection of data to support strategic analysis.[1] The major factors affecting the design of the data warehouse reflect its primary mission, which is to serve as a collection point for the needed data stored in various operational systems and as a distribution point for sending this data to the data marts. The major factors affecting the content of the data warehouse are the information needs of the people who will use the resultant data marts and the organization of the data in the source systems. Unlike the source systems that are built to support business processes, the data warehouse model needs to reflect the business relationships of the information, independent of the business processes and organization.

As explained earlier in the book, the relational model, based on a third-normal form model that depicts the business relationships, best meets the needs for storage of data in the data warehouse. The third normal form model, in its pure form, however, is not the best structure for the data warehouse. Using the third normal form model for the data warehouse is analogous to selecting any screwdriver for the job. Just as the screwdriver should be based on the size of the screw being driven, the third normal form model needs to be adjusted to meet the data warehouse needs. The business scenario used to develop the data warehouse data model is the Zenith Automobile Company that we introduced

---

[1] See *Building the Data Warehouse,* 2nd Edition, by W. H. Inmon, Wiley Publishing, Inc., 2000.

in Chapter 3. Using that scenario, we begin this chapter by explaining an eight-step methodology for transforming the third normal form model into the data warehouse model.

This chapter details the process of building a data warehouse model using entity-relationship modeling techniques. The process starts with the business data model and applies eight steps to arrive at a model that is optimized to meet the objectives of the data warehouse. The specific information requirements will be identified, and these will be used as the basis for developing the data warehouse model. Some of the issues to be addressed include selecting the data elements of interest, handling historical requirements, ensuring data consistency, and creating merged tables that can facilitate data delivery to the data marts. Some additional changes to improve the performance of the model are then provided.

Methodology

The data warehouse system data model is developed by applying an eight-step transformation process to the business data model. The eight steps are:

1. Select the data of interest.
2. Add time to the key.
3. Add derived data.
4. Determine granularity level.
5. Summarize data.
6. Merge entities.
7. Create arrays.
8. Segregate data.

The eight steps can be grouped into two categories. The first four steps deal primarily with business-related issues. Data elements are selected based on the business requirements for the project, time is added to the key to accommodate the historical perspective, derived data is created for consistency, and the level of granularity is determined to ensure that data exists to address the business needs. Once these steps are completed, the data warehouse should be capable of meeting the business objectives, though we can still do much to improve its performance in data delivery.

The second set of steps deals primarily with the performance issues. Summaries are created to improve the data delivery process performance, entities are merged to reduce the need to join data that is commonly used together, arrays are created to facilitate creation of data marts that need cross-tab analysis, and data is segregated based on stability (to reduce the number of rows added to the data warehouse) and usage (to reduce the need to join data to satisfy queries. These steps help organize the data to meet performance objectives in loading data into the data warehouse, minimizing storage requirements, and delivering the data to the data marts.

Once these basic steps are completed, additional tuning activities such as further denormalization and partitioning may also be applied.

Step 1: Select the Data of Interest

The first step in developing the data warehouse is to select the data of interest. There are two major reasons for making this the first step. First, it places the purpose and business objectives of the data warehouse project in the foreground. All decisions made concerning the data warehouse model consider the business purpose and objectives. Second, this step confines the scope of the data warehouse model to just that needed in the project. Since this step is designed to serve as a funnel and eliminate consideration of data elements that are not needed in the data warehouse, it only makes sense to perform it before additional work is performed on those elements.

Inputs

The business data model is only one of the inputs for Step 1. Other inputs include the project scope document, information requirements, prototypes, existing reports and queries, and the system or physical models of the systems expected to be sources to the data warehouse. The modeler needs to recognize that despite best intentions, not all of the information requirements can be defined in advance.

One of the advantages using a relational model for the data warehouse and of segregating the data warehouse from the data marts is that this facilitates incorporation of subsequently discovered information requirements without having a deleterious effect on the data marts already in production. The data warehouse model, and hence in the physical data warehouse, will evolve as additional needs are discovered. Since the business community is not directly accessing the data, changes in the data warehouse can be made without affecting users who do not need the changed data, as shown in Figure 4.1.

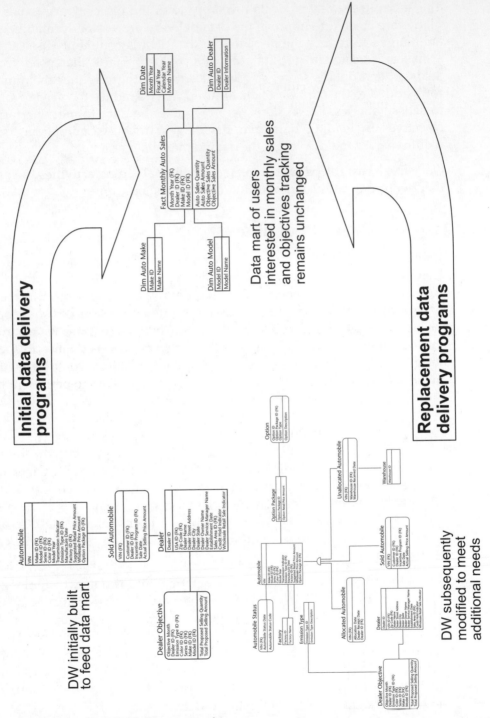

Figure 4.1 Benefit of data segregation.

Business Data Model

A fully developed business data model provides an ideal inventory of the available data elements. The fully developed business data model usually contains hundreds, and possibly thousands, of data elements. The development team needs to quickly cull the elements to only those that must be included in this iteration of the data warehouse. When a business data model does not exist and the development team creates the business data model for the scope of the project, virtually all of the elements in that model are included in the data warehouse model. Since only the data elements considered necessary for the project were included in the business data model, the scope containment was performed by restricting the elements included in the business data model.

Figure 4.2 depicts the business data model for the Zenith Automobile Company at the entity level.

Scope Document

The scope document sets the expectations for this iteration of the data warehouse. In addition to other information, it includes a section that identifies the data to be included, and may also include a section that delineates the data that is excluded from the iteration. In a way, this is a precursor to Step 1 in that the only data that needs to be considered in the model transformation is that data that could be considered to be within scope based on the level of detail contained in the scope document. The 11 business questions for the Zenith Automobile Company provide the needed information to scope the content of the data warehouse. Figure 4.3 shows how the scope document can quickly be used to narrow the entities that are addressed by the project.

Information Requirements

Information requirements constitute the third set of inputs. There are several sources for the information requirements. Since the data warehouse should be aligned with the ultimate business goals, a review of available corporate planning documents and the annual report may prove useful. Facilitated sessions and interviews with business executives, analysts, and end users provide a major source of information requirements. These sessions are designed to get the business community to identify the specific business questions to be answered and the data elements that are needed to answer those questions. The data analyst should avoid asking the business person, "What do you want in the data warehouse?" Virtually all business users have a common answer to this question—everything!

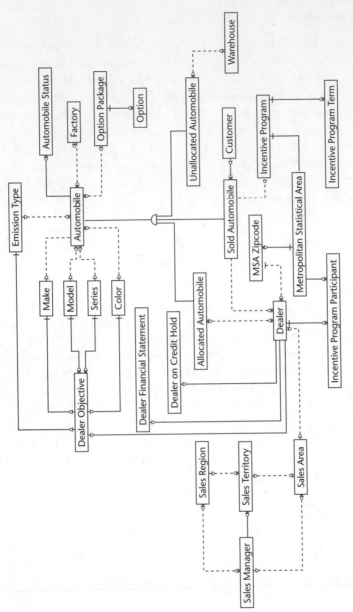

Figure 4.2 ZAC business data model.

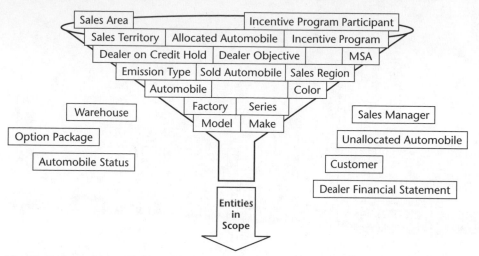

Figure 4.3   Reducing the entities to be considered.

Instead, the interview should focus on the business questions to be answered, how the data will be used, and on the specific data elements needed to answer those questions. These data-gathering meetings provide a starting point of people's perceptions concerning the data that will need to be available. The resultant information gets combined with information requirements gathered from other sources. In working with the business analysts and users requiring dimensional analysis, it is often useful to depict both the data warehouse content and the data marts that will be generated. The business representatives may find it easier to visualize their needs and to think out of the box by looking at the data navigation possibilities portrayed by the star schema. (The data mart model need not be refined at this point unless it is used to generate a prototype.)

The attribute-level section of the business data model for the Automobiles subject area is shown in Figure 4.4. Table 4.1 lists the attributes available within this subject area and the decision concerning their inclusion or exclusion in the data warehouse. The decision in Table 4.1 is based solely on the known business questions. In the section dealing with selection criteria, we identify additional factors that should be considered in making the decision. (Some entities from other subject areas are included in the diagram to help visualize the links to those subject areas. These are excluded from Table 4.1.)

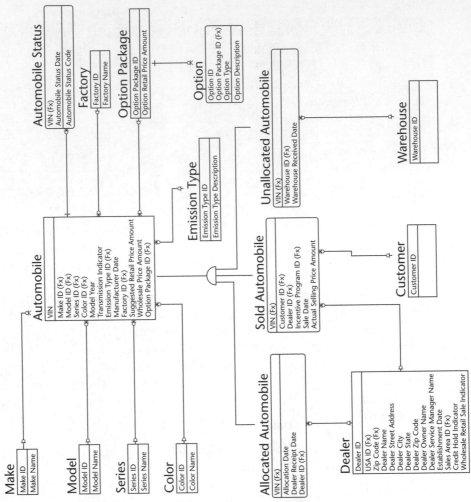

Figure 4.4   Automobiles subject area.

Table 4.1   Attribute Exclusion

ENTITY	ATTRIBUTE	DECISION	RATIONALE
Automobile	VIN	Retain	Needed as a key and to establish relationships
Automobile	Model Year	Retain	Needed to answer one or more questions
Automobile	Transmission Indicator	Omit	Not needed to answer any question
Automobile	Manufacture Date	Omit	Not needed to answer any question

Table 4.1 (continued)

ENTITY	ATTRIBUTE	DECISION	RATIONALE
Automobile	Suggested Retail Price Amount	Omit	Not needed to answer any question
Automobile	Wholesale Price Amount	Omit	Not needed to answer any question
Make	Make ID	Retain	Needed as a key and to establish relationships
Make	Make Name	Retain	Needed to provide descriptive label
Model	Model ID	Retain	Needed as a key and to establish relationships
Model	Model Name	Retain	Needed to provide descriptive label
Series	Series ID	Retain	Needed as a key and to establish relationships
Series	Series Name	Retain	Needed to provide descriptive label
Color	Color ID	Retain	Needed as a key and to establish relationships
Color	Color Name	Retain	Needed to provide descriptive label
Automobile Status	Automobile Status Date	Omit	Not needed to answer any question
Automobile Status	Automobile Status Code	Omit	Not needed to answer any question
Option Package	Option Package ID	Omit	Not needed to answer any question
Option Package	Option Retail Price Amount	Omit	Not needed to answer any question
Option	Option ID	Omit	Not needed to answer any question
Option	Option Type	Omit	Not needed to answer any question
Option	Option Description	Omit	Not needed to answer any question
Emission Type	Emission Type ID	Retain	Needed as a key and to establish relationships
Emission Type	Emission Type Description	Retain	Needed to provide descriptive label

(continued)

Table 4.1 *(continued)*

ENTITY	ATTRIBUTE	DECISION	RATIONALE
Allocated	Allocation Date Automobile	Omit	Not needed to answer any question
Allocated Automobile	Dealer Receipt Date key and to establish relationships	Retain	Needed as a key and to establish relationships
Sold Automobile	Sale Date key and to establish relationships	Retain	Needed as a key and to establish relationships
Sold Automobile	Actual Selling Price key and to establish relationships		
Unallocated Automobile	Warehouse Received Date	Omit	Not needed to answer any question

Existing Reports and Queries

Existing reports and queries provide another source of information requirements, but these need to be used carefully. Just because a report is regularly produced and distributed does not mean that anyone uses it. Some reports were created to meet a specific need that no longer exists, but no one bothered to delete the report from the production schedule. Similarly, even if a report is used, it may contain some data that is not used. Data may be unused either because it was included "just in case," but was never actually needed, or because it was needed when the report was created, but circumstances changed. So, even though an existing report contains extraneous data, its users may have deemed to be more expedient to leave the data in rather than try to justify the programming changes needed to generate a more streamlined report.

Prototype

Possibly the most effective way to identify the required data elements is by creating a prototype of the ultimate product. In the section dealing with information requirements, we indicated that a star schema may be drawn to help users visualize how they will receive the data. The prototype consists of deploying this design with actual data so that the users can verify its adequacy. A properly developed and managed prototype helps business users visualize the end result and enables them to better articulate the information needs.

The prototype exercise consists of more than just providing the user with access to the mart and waiting for a reaction. A properly managed prototype exercise requires constant interaction between the data warehouse designer and the user and the incorporation of appropriate revisions to the design based on the feedback. Another critical aspect of a well-managed prototype is knowing when to stop. Remember, the objective of the prototype is to refine the requirements—not to provide an early production deliverable.

Source Data

Information about the anticipated data warehouse sources also provides useful information for selecting the data elements. The source system data structures provide information about how the data is physically stored within the systems used for day-to-day operation. These provide a checklist, and if a user has not requested data elements that are stored with other data elements of interest, the data analyst should consider asking additional questions to ensure that the additional elements are not needed. Once the elements that are needed are determined, the elements to be included can be selected. The next section introduces additional considerations that have an impact on this decision.

Selection Process

The selection of the data elements for actual inclusion is not a simple process. Consider the first business question: "What is the monthly sales trend in quantity and dollar amounts sold for each Make, Model, Series, and Color (MMSC) for a specific dealer, by each Sales Area, Sales Territory, and Sales Region, for each state and for each Metropolitan Statistical Area (MSA)?" The question requests "sales trends," which implies that some information from the sales transaction, summarized on a monthly basis, is needed. Having 50–100 data elements about a sales transaction is not uncommon, and if the only information the user wanted was sales quantity and sales amount, there could be a significant amount of excess data in the data warehouse. Data elements in the operational system basically fall into three groupings. One group (for example, date, sales quantity, sales amount) consists of elements that are definitely needed, a second group (for example, record update date and time,) consists of data elements that are definitely not needed, and a third group (for example, time of sale, special discounts, promotional allowances, sales tax amount) consists of elements that might be needed. It is the third group that requires the most attention. The question that should be asked about each element is, "Is it reasonable to expect that this element is needed for strategic analysis?"

For many data elements, there is no definitive answer to this question. Three major considerations are the use of the data for calculating a derived element, the classification of the data as transactional or reference, and the structure of the source data.

Use of Data Element for a Derived Field

Often, users require a derived field, such as net sales amount, but do not require each of the elements that was used to calculate the derived field.[2] As a general rule, we recommend that any element that is used in calculating a derived field be included in the data warehouse. (It need not be included in any data mart.) There are two major reasons for including the element. First, the algorithm used to calculate the needed element may change, and by retaining the individual components, the derived field can be recalculated for both current views and historical views if needed. Second, business users often drill down to the data used to calculate a needed field when they are analyzing results, particularly if the value of the derived element is unexpected. Even though this need is not identified initially, we should anticipate it.

Classification of Data as Transactional or Reference

Within the data warehouse, we are often interested in transactions reflect activity over a period of time, sometimes spanning several years. We need to recognize that users often can't anticipate all of the data that they need from these transactions, and we're then faced with deciding whether or not to bring additional elements into the data warehouse. As a general rule, with transactional data, if we are in doubt, we should bring it in. There are three major reasons for this, all of which deal with what it would take to retrieve the data should we later discover we need it:

- **The transaction may be purged from the source system.**   The data warehouse retains history beyond what is retained in the operational system. If the need for the data element is discovered after the data is purged from the source system, it can never be recovered.

- **The transactions occur over time.**   If the need for the data element is discovered months or years after the initial construction of the data warehouse, recovery of the data will require navigation through all the transactions that transpired during the intervening time. This can be a very significant effort, and complications may be introduced due to changes in reference data and the resultant complexities involved in ensuring referential integrity.

- **Transactional data integration is generally simple.**   Unlike reference data, such as customer data that may be gathered from multiple sources, individual transactions originate at only one place. Integration of transactional data entails adding transactions from multiple files and not merging of information within each transaction. This characteristic results in a simpler process, and hence the impact on the development project is minimized.

---

[2] The creation of derived fields is explained in Step 3 of the data warehouse data model development process.

The major disadvantage of bringing in the questionable elements is the volume of data. If there are millions of transactions and dozens of questionable fields, the data warehouse tables will grow unnecessarily. An approach that some companies use is "triage," in which all of the transactions from the source system are extracted and retained in an archived, offline, file. With this approach, when an element subsequently needs to be recovered, we have a more readily accessible source. Figure 4.5 shows how this approach can be pursued.

Reference data is different. Often, even if we later discover that we need a data element that we did not initially obtain, we find that the need to recover history is limited. For example, if we later discover that we need the date a dealership was established, we can simply start extracting it from the current record. Therefore, with reference data, if you are in doubt about including an element, we recommend leaning towards excluding it. (The triage approach can also be pursued with reference data if desired.)

Source Data Structure

The structure of the source data is another factor that should be considered. If most of the columns from a source table are required, then serious consideration should be given to including all of the elements. That approach simplifies the extraction, transformation, and load process. Mitigating factors to adding an element include perceptions concerning agreement on its definition and the quality of the actual data. (If there is significant disagreement on the definition or if the data quality is inadequate, then the analysis time and subsequent data acquisition process development are lengthened.) If only a few of the columns from a source table are needed, the tendency should be to exclude the remaining columns.

Keep in mind that the source data structure was designed based on operational needs, and tables often contain denormalized data. For example, the sales transaction in the operational system could contain the item description and the customer name. This data should not be obtained from the transaction table—it should be obtained from the reference table—unless the operational system provides users with the ability to override the standard reference data.

The first step in creating the data warehouse model is complex, and it requires extensive business user involvement. The tendency of some data warehouse teams is to skip this step and just include all columns from any table that is used to provide data. Reasons for skipping this step include a perception that it will be easier to simply bring in all the data. That temptation should be avoided due to the development, load, storage, and performance impacts:

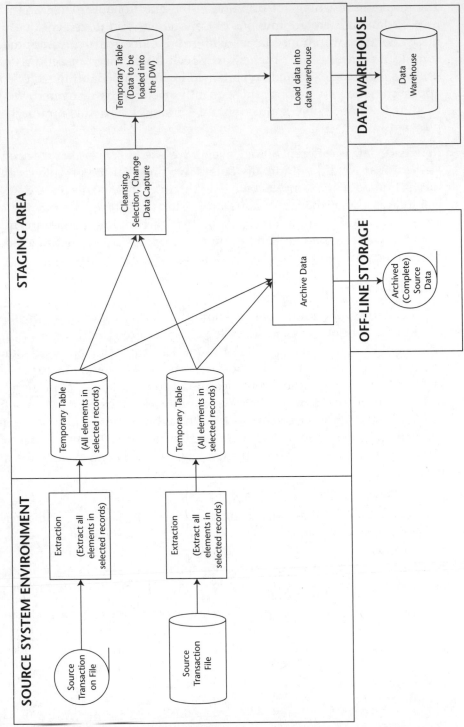

Figure 4.5 Archiving questionable data.

Development impact.   Each data element included in the data warehouse model must be understood. It must be defined. Its quality must be ascertained, and appropriate cleansing logic needs to be developed. If there are multiple potential sources, integration rules need to be established and subsequently coded. If it is a simple item (for example, sales tax amount), then these steps may be fairly simple. If it is a complex or controversial item, these steps may require extensive discussions and compromises. If it is unlikely that the element will ever be needed, then the development team should not waste its time.

Load impact.   Each data element needs to be loaded into the data warehouse. Sometimes the processing window is tight and the inclusion of the additional elements adds to the required processing time.

Storage impact.   Each data element is stored in the data warehouse and, to make matters worse, its history is stored. The stored data requires additional disk space and also adds to the backup and recovery processing times.

Performance impact.   Inclusion of the additional data elements widens the rows of the tables and, if the elements are textual, the rows may be substantially widened. The increased table size could have a substantial impact on the performance of some load processing as well as the delivery of the data to the data marts.

With the completion of the first step, the basic scope of the data warehouse data model for this iteration is established, and the model should contain all the elements needed to support the business questions being asked.

TIP

The data modeler needs to always keep in mind the objectives and scope of the data warehouse and user these to guide all actions. The first step is one of the most critical in that regard since it has a significant impact on the data warehouse project's duration and the eventual data warehouse operating cost and performance.

Step 2: Add Time to the Key

The business data model is a "point-in-time" model. That is, the model portrays the business at the present. The data warehouse data model, on the other hand, is an "over-time" model. An "over-time" model portrays an enterprise with a historical perspective. Since the data warehouse is time variant (that is, it has a historical perspective or a series of snapshots), this is the type of model that is appropriate for the data warehouse. The historical perspective is another reason for the use of an E-R model for the data warehouse. In an E-R model, the historical perspective is achieved for each entity of interest by merely adding time to the key of the entity. The model responds well to this addition, and since its objective is not ease of use by an end user, we need not concern ourselves with the potential complexity of queries. We gain an advantage in that we can easily create a dimension with the most recent view of a hierarchy or one with the historical view, based on the user's needs.

With a dimensional model, several entities may be compressed into one to represent a hierarchy. When we add the time aspect to the key of this dimension, we create a "slowly changing dimension," and a new row is created whenever any data for any of the levels of the hierarchy changes. Since a compound key for each dimensional is not advisable due to the impact on the length of the key of the fact table, a surrogate key is then used to gain a unique identifier for each row. While this can correctly represent the data, when we force a slowly changing dimension unnecessarily, we needlessly complicate queries for the users who require only the current view of the hierarchy. Remember, the primary objective of the data mart design and of the dimensional model is to make access easier for the end user.

The second step in developing the data warehouse data model adds the time component (for example, date and possibly time) to the key of each entity to provide the historical perspective, as shown in Figure 4.6. (For our data warehouse, we chose to take monthly snapshots, and hence the key is "Month Year.")

As the second step in the transformation process, it also reshapes the model. In addition to requiring a time component in the key of each entity, the inclusion of history also changes some relationships from one-to-many to many-to-many, as shown in Figure 4.7. On the left side of Figure 4.7, we depict the business rule that at a point in time a Sales Territory has many Sales Areas, and that a Sales Area belongs to a single Sales Territory. In the data warehouse, we add the time component for each of these two entities, as shown in the right side of Figure 4.7. We may go through a period of time in which there are no changes to these two entities, but during which a Sales Area is transferred from one Sales Territory to another. The resultant many-to-many relationship is resolved with an associative entity that contains the effective date as part of its key. (Other ways of handling this situation are explained later in this section.)

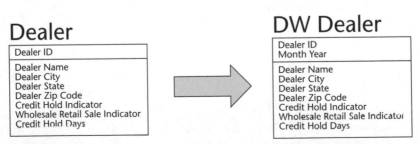

Figure 4.6 Adding the time component to the key.

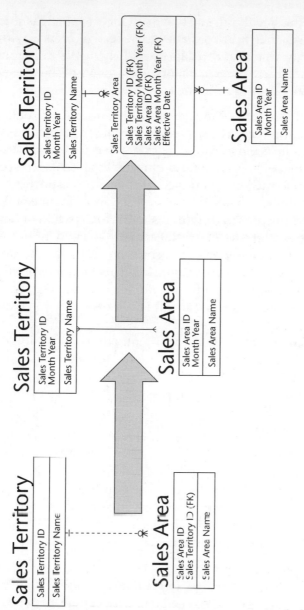

Figure 4.7 Relationship transformation.

Some entities may have attributes that can never change. While the theory dictates that the time component should be added to the key of every entity, if the data can never change, there can't be any history, and hence there is an exception to the rule. In Figure 4.8, we have the entity for Automobile. Within this entity, the only attributes of interest are the VIN, the identifiers for the Make,

Model, Series, Color, Emission Type, and Factory. Once a vehicle is manufactured, none of these can change from a business perspective. Hence, within the data warehouse, the only way that the data would change is if there were a data entry problem. If we are to retain a history of all views of the automobile, then the time component needs to be in the key; otherwise, it is unnecessary.

The time component of the entities can take one of two forms. For data that is a snapshot (for example, number of customers or inventory level), the addition to the key is a point in time, such as a date. For data that pertains to a span of time (for example, number of new customers or number of items received into inventory), the addition to the key is a period of time. The distinction is very important and is sometimes overlooked. As Figure 4.8 shows, some of the data in the table on the left is for a point in time and some is for a period of time. The date shown in the key (February, for example) actually has two meanings, and therefore violates basic data-modeling rules. For some of the data, it means a particular date in February and, for other data, it means the full month of February. In the data warehouse, two entities would be created, as shown on the right of Figure 4.8. Meta data is needed to explain the specific meaning, and additional care must be taken to ensure that even within each of the two resultant entities, the definition of the date is consistent. For example, it would be inappropriate to use February to mean a fiscal month for some data and a calendar month for other data within the same entity.

One of the practical challenges facing the data warehouse team is capturing each historical occurrence of interest and the associated date or time of the occurrence. When the source system does not capture the date or time of a change, it limits our ability to capture each occurrence of history in the data warehouse. If the source system product file has no date, the best that the data warehouse can do is reflect an effective date equivalent to the date that data was extracted from the system. If a more precise date is needed, then an extraction process that could normally have been executed monthly may need to be executed on a daily or weekly basis. For some data, even a daily extraction won't be sufficient.

If multiple changes can be made during a single day and each change must be captured, then a log file may need to be used or modifications may be needed in the source system. When this occurs, the data warehouse team should ensure that the business community understands the cost of capturing the data and that the business value is sufficient. The team must further ensure that the model definitions accurately reflect the nature of the history. If the source system needs to be changed, then a separate project should be initiated; the data warehouse team should not absorb that effort into its project.

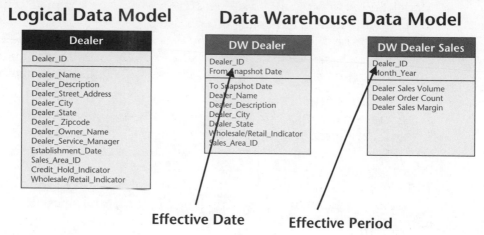

Figure 4.8 Forms of the time component.

Capturing Historical Data

Adding a time component to the key enables a distinct record to be created each time a new snapshot is taken and each time data for a new period is captured. Inclusion of this time component has a significant design implication. Since the entity may be the parent in some one-to-many relationships, the generated foreign key would now include the time component. This has a number of nasty results, as shown in the first situation in Figure 4.9. It generates a new occurrence for every child, even if no data in the child entity changed. This happens because there is a change in the content of the time component of the foreign key. This condition is compounded if an entity is the child of several parent entities. Each of the parents generates a foreign key with its governing time period. This happens regardless of whether or not the change in the parent creates any change in the child.

There are five potential approaches that can be chosen, as shown in Figure 4.9:

- Generate the dual foreign key, as previously described.
- Generate a serial key in the parent entity for each occurrence and store the identifier and time component as a nonkey attribute within the entity. This scenario reduces the number of attributes generated as foreign keys but still generates a new instance of the child each time there is a change in a parent entity.
- Programmatically enforce referential integrity rather than using the DBMS to enforce it, and only enforce referential integrity for the identifier. This approach requires additional programming effort to ensure referential integrity. (In the figure, the date is made into a nonkey attribute.)

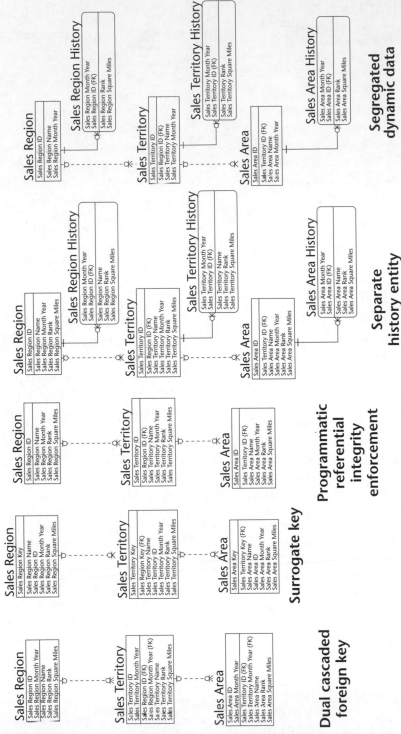

Figure 4.9 Approaches for reflecting historical perspective.

- Segregate the data into an entity that contains the history and another entity that only contains the current data. The relationships would only emanate from the table with the current data, and hence would not include the time component. The referential integrity for the historical data would be programmatically enforced by virtue of records being created as copies of records in the current data entity.

- Maintain the base entity with only data elements that can never change, and create an attributive entity with the attributes that could change over time. This approach enables the key of the base entity to consist solely of the identifier, and since the attributive entity has no children, the date component of the key does not cascade. (In the figure, the presumption is that the name never changes, but that the rank and square miles do.)

Any of these approaches is viable, and the modeler may choose different approaches within the same data warehouse. The volatility of the data would be a major consideration, with a tendency to use the fourth or fifth option as the data volatility increases. The third approach is the easiest from a data-modeling perspective; it does require programmatic enforcement of referential integrity. We recommend using the third or fourth approach as your default choice. Another consideration is whether or not the entity is part of a hierarchy, and that is explained further in the next section.

Capturing Historical Relationships

Relationships also change over time. The result of these changes is the creation of a many-to-many relationship. Within a third normal form model, predictable hierarchies are represented by a series of entities with successive one-to-many relationships, as shown on the left in Figure 4.9. In that figure, a Sales Region contains one or more Sales Territories, and each Sales Territory contains one or more Sales Areas. While this may be true at a particular point in time, the historical perspective requires the model to handle situations in which a Sales Area may be moved from one Sales Territory to another and a Sales Territory may be moved from one Sales Region to another. This condition can be handled in one of two ways.

One way is to insert an associative entity to resolve the many-to-many relationship. This approach is useful if the historical information about the individual entities is handled by the fourth approach described in the previous section, and the fourth scenario described in Figure 4.9 is expanded to include the associative entities on the right portion of Figure 4.7. The left portion of Figure 4.9 shows a different method. In this case, the cascading of the date from the parent entity to the child entity may be done either to reflect a change in the data of the parent or to reflect a change in the relationship. In other words, when a Sales Area is reassigned to a different Sales Territory, a new record is generated for the Sales Area, with the only change being the time component of the foreign key generated by the relationship.

The approach to be taken for capturing historical relationships is dependent on two primary factors. One factor is the number of levels in the hierarchies. As the number of hierarchies increases, preference should be given to using the associative entity since a change in the highest level of the hierarchy generates a new entity for each subservient level. The second factor is the relative stability of the entity data versus the relationship data. If the entity data (for example, Sales Area description) is more stable than the relationship (for example, Sales Territory to which the Sales Area is assigned), then preference should be given to using the associative entity since few changes in the base entities would be needed. If the relationship data is more stable, then preference should be given to cascading the foreign key since the instances of cascading keys are minimized.

Dimensional Model Considerations

In the E-R model, each occurrence of history of interest can be captured and readily related to the business item of interest. In a dimensional model, the handling of history depends on whether it relates to the transaction (with key information stored in the fact table) or the reference data (stored in the dimension table). Changes to reference data were discussed earlier; any change of interest to the data of or relationship within a hierarchy covered by a dimension table requires another entry and creates a slowly changing dimension.

For transaction data, the impact differs depending upon how the data is stored. If the data is stored in a transaction table with a key of transaction identifier, the dimensional model and E-R model are equivalent. The transaction table conforms to rules for E-R modeling since it has a key that uniquely identifies the transaction. A second component of the key can be added to indicate the date of the view of the transaction. In a dimensional model, when data is stored this way, we need to go through another step of creating a fact table prior to making the data accessible to the user. If the data is already stored in a fact table, the complexity depends on whether or not any of the keys change. If we are merely changing the order quantity, none of the keys change, and hence we can provide a second (or, if the business rules dictate) a replacement row. If we are substituting a different item for delivery, then the key to the fact table actually changes since it includes a reference to the item being ordered. Handling this type of change is more complex in a dimensional model. When the E-R model is built first, we can use it to generate the appropriate dimensional model in the data mart based on each user group's need for data.

Step 3: Add Derived Data

The third step in developing the data warehouse model is to add derived data. Derived data is data that results from performing a mathematical operation on one or more other data elements. Derived data is incorporated into the data warehouse model for two major reasons—to ensure consistency, and to improve data delivery performance. The reason that this step is third is the business impact—to ensure consistency; performance benefits are secondary. (If not for the business impact, this would be one of the performance related steps.) One of the common objectives of a data warehouse is to provide data in a way so that everyone has the same facts—and the same understanding of those facts. A field such as "net sales amount" can have any number of meanings. Items that may be included or excluded in the definition include special discounts, employee discounts, and sales tax. If a sales representative is held accountable for meeting a sales goal, it is extremely important that everyone understands what is included and excluded in the calculation.

Another example of a derived field is data that is in the date entity. Many businesses, such as manufacturers and retailers, for example, are very concerned with the Christmas shopping season. While it ends on the same date (December 24) each year, the beginning of the season varies since it starts on the Friday after Thanksgiving. A derived field of "Christmas Season Indicator" included in the date table ensures that every sale can quickly be classified as being in or out of that season, and that year-to-year comparisons can be made simply without needing to look up the specific dates for the season start each year.

The number of days in the month is another field that could have multiple meanings and this number is often used as a divisor in calculations. The most obvious question is whether or not to include Saturdays and Sundays. Similarly, inclusion or exclusion of holidays is also an option. Exclusion of holidays presents yet another question—which holidays are excluded? Further, if the company is global, is the inclusion of a holiday dependent on the country? It may turn out that several derived data elements are needed.

In the Zenith Automobile Company example, we are interested in the number of days that a dealer is placed on "credit hold." If a Dealer goes on credit hold on December 20, 2002 and is removed from credit hold on January 6, 2003, the number of days can vary between 0 and 18, depending on the criteria for including or excluding days, as shown in Figure 4.10. The considerations include:

- Is the first day excluded?
- Is the last day excluded?
- Are Saturdays excluded?

- Are Sundays excluded?
- Are holidays excluded? If so, what are the holidays?
- Are factory shutdown days excluded? If so, what are they?

By adding an attribute of Credit Days Quantity to the Dealer entity (which also has the month as part of its key), everyone will be using the same definition.

When it comes to derived data, the complexity lies in the business definition or calculation much more so than in the technical solution. The business representatives must agree on the derivation, and this may require extensive discussions, particularly if people require more customized calculations. In an article written in *ComputerWorld* in October 1997, Tom Davenport observed that, as the importance of a term increases, the number of opinions on its meaning increases and, to compound the problem, those opinions will be more strongly held. The third step of creating the data warehouse model resolves those definitional differences for derived data by explicitly stating the calculation. If the formula for a derived attribute is controversial, the modeler may choose to put a placeholder in the model (that is, create the attribute) and address the formula as a non-critical-path activity since the definition of the attribute is unlikely to have a significant impact on the structure of the model. There may be an impact on the datatype, since the precision of the value may be in question, but that is addressed in the technology model.

DECEMBER 2002						
S	M	T	W	T	F	S
1	2	3	4	5	6	7
8	9	10	11	12	13	14
15	16	17	18	19	20	21
22	23	24	25	26	27	28
29	30	31				

JANUARY 2003						
S	M	T	W	T	F	S
			1	2	3	4
5	6	7	8	9	10	11
12	13	14	15	16	17	18
19	20	21	22	23	24	25
26	27	28	29	30	31	

Figure 4.10 Derived data—number of days.

Creating a derived field does not usually save disk space since each of the components used in the calculation may still be stored, as noted in Step 1. Using derived data improves data delivery performance at the expense of load performance. When a derived field used in multiple data marts, calculating it during the load process reduces the burden on the data delivery process. Since most end-user access to data is done at the data mart level, another approach is to either calculate it during the data delivery process that builds the data marts or to calculate it in the end-user tool. If the derived field is needed to ensure consistency, preference should be given to storing it in the data warehouse. There are two major reasons for this. First, if the data is needed in several data marts, the derivation calculation is only performed once. The second reason is of great significance if end users can build their own data marts. By including the derived data in the data warehouse, even when construction of the marts is distributed, all users retain the same definitions and derivation algorithms.

Step 4: Determine Granularity Level

The fourth step in developing the data warehouse model is to adjust the granularity, or level of detail, of the data warehouse. The granularity level is significant from a business, technical, and project perspective. From a business perspective, it dictates the potential capability and flexibility of the data warehouse, regardless of the initially deployed functions. Without a subsequent change to the granularity level, the warehouse will never be able to answer questions that require details below the adopted level. From a technical perspective, it is one of the major determinants of the data warehouse size and hence has a significant impact on its operating cost and performance. From a project perspective, the granularity level affects the amount of work that the project team will need to perform to create the data warehouse since as the granularity level gets into greater and greater levels of detail, the project team needs to deal with more data attributes and their relationships. Additionally, if the granularity level increases sufficiently, a relatively small data warehouse may become extremely large, and this requires additional technical considerations.

Some people have a tendency to establish the level of granularity based on the questions being asked. If this is done for a retail store for which the business users only requested information on hourly sales, then we would be collecting and summarizing data for each hour. We would never, however, be in a position to answer questions concerning individual sales transactions, and would not be able to perform shopping basket analysis to determine what products sell with other products. On the other hand, if we choose to capture data at the sales transaction level, we would have significantly more data in the warehouse.

There are several factors that affect the level of granularity of data in the warehouse:

Current business need. The primary determining factor should be the business need. At a minimum, the level of granularity must be sufficient to provide answers to each and every business question being addressed within the scope of the data warehouse iteration. Providing a greater level of granularity adds to the cost of the warehouse and the development project and, if the business does not need the details, the increased costs add no business value.

Anticipated business need. The future business needs should also be considered. A common scenario is for the initial data warehouse implementation to focus on monthly data, with an intention to eventually obtain daily data. If only monthly data is captured, the company may never be able to obtain the daily granularity that is subsequently requested. Therefore, if the interview process reveals a need for daily data at some point in the future, it should be considered in the data warehouse design. The key word in the previous sentence is "considered" —before including the extra detail, the business representatives should be consulted to ensure that they perceive a future business value. As we described in Step 1, an alternate approach is to build the data warehouse for the data we know we need, but to build and extract data to accommodate future requirements.

Extended business need. Within any industry, there are many data warehouses already in production. Another determining factor for the level of granularity is to get information about the level of granularity that is typical for your industry. For example, in the retail industry, while there are a lot of questions that can be answered with data accumulated at an hourly interval, retailers often maintain data at the transactional level for other analyses. However, just because others in the industry capture a particular granularity level does not mean that it should be captured but the modeler and business representative should consider this in making the decision.

Data mining need. While the business people may not ask questions that require a display of detailed data, some data mining requests require significant details. For example, if the business would like to know which products sell with other products, analysis of individual transactions is needed.

Derived data need. Derived data uses other data elements in the calculation. Unless there is a substantial increase in cost and development time, the chosen granularity level should accommodate storing all of the elements used to derive other data elements.

Operational system granularity.   Another factor that affects the granularity of the data stored in the warehouse is the level of detail available in the operational source systems. Simply put, if the source system doesn't have it, the data warehouse can't get it. This seems rather obvious, but there are intricacies that need to be considered. For example, when there are multiple source systems for the same data, it's possible that the level of granularity among these systems varies. One system may contain each transaction, while another may only contain monthly results. The data warehouse team needs to determine whether to pull data at the lowest common level so that all the data merges well together, or to pull data from each system based on its available granularity so that the most data is available. If we only pull data at the lowest common denominator level, then we would only receive monthly data and would lose the details that are available within other systems. If we load data from each source based on its granularity level, then care must be taken in using the data. Since the end users are not directly accessing the data warehouse, they are shielded from some of the differences by the way that the data marts are designed and loaded for them. The meta data provided with the data marts needs to explicitly explain the data that is included or excluded. This is another advantage of segregating the functionality of the data warehouse and the data marts.

Data acquisition performance.   The level of granularity may (or may not) significantly impact the data acquisition performance. Even if the data warehouse granularity is summarized to a weekly level, the extract process may still need to include the individual transactions since that's the way the data is stored in the source systems, and it may be easier to obtain data in that manner. During the data acquisition process, the appropriate granularity would be created for the data warehouse. If there is a significant difference in the data volume, the load process is impacted by the level of granularity, since that determines what needs to be brought into the data warehouse.

Storage cost.   The level of granularity has a significant impact on cost. If a retailer has 1,000 stores and the average store has 1,500 sales transactions per day, each of which involves 10 items, a transaction-detail-level data warehouse would store 15,000,000 rows per day. If an average of 1,000 different products were sold in a store each day, a data warehouse that has a granularity level of store, product and day would have 1,000,000 rows per day.

Administration.   The inclusion of additional detail in the data warehouse impacts the data warehouse administration activities as well. The production data warehouse needs to be periodically backed up and, if there is more detail, the backup routines require more time. Further, if the detailed data is only needed for 13 months, after which data could be at a higher level of granularity, then the archival process needs to deal with periodically purging some of the data from the data warehouse so that the data is not retained online.

This fourth step needs to be performed in conjunction with the first step—selecting the data of interest. That first step becomes increasingly important when a greater (that is, more detailed) granularity level is needed. For a retail company with 1,000,000 transactions per day, each attribute that is retained is multiplied by that number and the ramifications of retaining the extraneous data elements become severe.

The fourth step is the last step that is a requirement to ensure that the data warehouse meets the business needs. The remaining steps are all important but, even if they are not performed, the data warehouse should be able to meet the business needs. These next steps are all designed to either reduce the cost or improve the performance of the overall data warehouse environment.

If the data warehouse is relatively small, the data warehouse developers should consider moving forward with creation of the first data mart after completing only the first four steps. While the data delivery process performance may not be optimal, enough of the data warehouse will have been created to deliver the needed business information, and the users can gain experience while the performance-related improvements are being developed. Based on the data delivery process performance, the appropriate steps from the last four could then be pursued.

Step 5: Summarize Data

The fifth step in developing the data warehouse model is to create summarized data. The creation of the summarized data may not save disk space—it's possible that the details that are used to create the summaries will continue to be maintained. It will, however, improve the performance of the data delivery process. The most common summarization criterion is time since data in the warehouse typically represents either a point in time (for example, the number of items in inventory at the end of the day) or a period of time (for example, the quantity of an item sold during a day). Some of the benefits that summarized data provides include reductions in the online storage requirements (details may be stored in alternate storage devices), standardization of analysis, and improved data delivery performance. The five types of summaries are simple cumulations, rolling summaries, simple direct files, continuous files, and vertical summaries.

Summaries for Period of Time Data

Simple cumulations and rolling summaries apply to data that pertains to a period of time. Simple cumulations represent the summation of data over one of its attributes, such as time. For example, a daily sales summary provides a summary of all sales for the day across the common ways that people access it. If people often need to have sales quantity and amounts by day, salesperson, store, and product, the summary table in Figure 4.11 could be provided to ease the burden of processing on the data delivery process.

A rolling summary provides sales information for a consistent period of time. For example, a rolling weekly summary provides the sales information for the previous week, with the 7-day period varying in its end date, as shown in Figure 4.12.

Sales Transactions

Date	Product	Quantity	Sales $
Jan 2	A	6	$3.00
Jan 2	B	7	$7.00
Jan 2	A	8	$4.00
Jan 2	B	4	$4.00
Jan 3	A	4	$2.00
Jan 3	A	7	$3.50
Jan 3	A	8	$4.00
Jan 3	B	5	$5.00
Jan 4	A	8	$4.00
Jan 4	A	9	$4.50
Jan 4	A	8	$4.00
Jan 7	B	8	$8.00
Jan 7	B	9	$9.00
Jan 8	A	8	$4.00
Jan 8	A	8	$4.00
Jan 8	B	9	$9.00
Jan 9	A	6	$3.00
Jan 9	B	7	$7.00
Jan 9	A	8	$4.00
Jan 10	B	4	$4.00
Jan 10	A	4	$2.00
Jan 10	A	7	$3.50
Jan 10	A	8	$4.00
Jan 11	B	5	$5.00
Jan 11	A	8	$4.00
Jan 11	A	9	$4.50
Jan 14	A	8	$4.00
Jan 14	B	8	$8.00
Jan 14	B	9	$9.00
Jan 14	A	8	$4.00
Jan 14	A	8	$4.00
Jan 14	A	9	$4.50

Daily Sales

Date	Product	Quantity	Sales $
Jan 2	A	14	$7.00
Jan 2	B	11	$11.00
Jan 3	A	19	$9.50
Jan 3	B	5	$5.00
Jan 4	A	27	$13.50
Jan 7	B	17	$17.00
Jan 8	A	16	$8.00
Jan 8	B	9	$9.00
Jan 9	A	14	$7.00
Jan 9	B	7	$7.00
Jan 10	A	19	$9.50
Jan 10	B	4	$4.00
Jan 11	A	17	$8.50
Jan 11	B	5	$5.00
Jan 14	A	33	$16.50
Jan 14	B	17	$17.00

Figure 4.11 Simple cumulation.

Daily Sales

Date	Product	Quantity	Sales $
Jan 2	A	14	$7.00
Jan 2	B	11	$11.00
Jan 3	A	19	$9.50
Jan 3	B	5	$5.00
Jan 4	A	27	$13.50
Jan 7	B	17	$17.00
Jan 8	A	16	$8.00
Jan 8	B	9	$9.00
Jan 9	A	14	$7.00
Jan 9	B	7	$7.00
Jan 10	A	19	$9.50
Jan 10	B	4	$4.00
Jan 11	A	17	$8.50
Jan 11	B	5	$5.00
Jan 14	A	33	$16.50
Jan 14	B	17	$17.00

Rolling Seven-Day Summary

Start Date	End Date	Product	Quantity	Sales $
Jan 1	Jan 7	A	60	$30.00
Jan 1	Jan 7	B	33	$33.00
Jan 2	Jan 8	A	76	$38.00
Jan 2	Jan 8	B	42	$42.00
Jan 3	Jan 9	A	76	$38.00
Jan 3	Jan 9	B	42	$42.00
Jan 4	Jan 10	A	76	$38.00
Jan 4	Jan 10	B	37	$37.00
Jan 5	Jan 11	A	66	$33.00
Jan 5	Jan 11	B	42	$42.00
Jan 6	Jan 12	A	66	$33.00
Jan 6	Jan 12	B	42	$42.00
Jan 7	Jan 13	A	66	$33.00
Jan 7	Jan 13	B	42	$42.00
Jan 8	Jan 14	A	99	$49.50
Jan 8	Jan 14	B	42	$42.00

Figure 4.12   Rolling summary.

Summaries for Snapshot Data

The simple direct summary and continuous summary apply to snapshot data or data that is episodic, or pertains to a point in time. The simple direct file, shown on the top-right of Figure 4.13, provides the value of the data of interest at regular time intervals. The continuous file, shown on the bottom-right of Figure 4.13, generates a new record only when a value changes. Factors to consider for selecting between these two types of summaries are the data volatility and the usage pattern. For data that is destined to eventually migrate to a data mart that provides monthly information, the continuous file is a good candidate if the data is relatively stable. With the continuous file, there will be fewer records generated, but the data delivery algorithm will need to determine the month based on the effective (and possibly expiration) date. With the simple direct file, a new record is generated for each instance each and every month. For stable data, this creates extraneous records. If the data mart needs only a current view of the data in the dimension, then the continuous summary facilitates the data delivery process since the most current occurrence is used, and if the data is not very volatile and only the updated records are transferred, less data is delivered. If a slowly changing dimension is used with the periodicity of the direct summary, then the delivery process merely pulls the data for the period during each load cycle.

Operational System Snapshot

January Customer Address

Customer Name	Address
Brown, Murphy	99 Starstruck Lane
Leary, Timothy	100 High St.
Monster, Cookie	12 Muppet Rd.
Picard, Jean-Luc	2001 Celestial Way

February Customer Address

Customer Name	Address
Alden, John	42 Pocahontas St.
Brown, Murphy	92 Quayle Circle
Leary, Timothy	100 High St.
Monster, Cookie	12 Muppet Rd.
Picard, Jean-Luc	2001 Celestial Way

Customer Address: Simple Direct Summary

Month	Customer Name	Address
Jan	Brown, Murphy	99 Starstruck Lane
Jan	Leary, Timothy	100 High St.
Jan	Monster, Cookie	12 Muppet Rd.
Jan	Picard, Jean-Luc	2001 Celestial Way
Feb	Alden, John	42 Pocahontas St.
Feb	Brown, Murphy	92 Quayle Circle
Feb	Leary, Timothy	100 High St.
Feb	Monster, Cookie	12 Muppet Rd.
Feb	Picard, Jean-Luc	2001 Celestial Way

Customer Address: Continuous Summary

Customer Name	Address	Date
Alden, John	42 Pocahontas St.	Feb-Pres
Brown, Murphy	99 Starstruck Lane	Jan-Jan
Brown, Murphy	92 Quayle Circle	Feb-Pres
Leary, Timothy	100 High St.	Jan-Pres
Monster, Cookie	12 Muppet Rd.	Jan-Pres
Picard, Jean-Luc	2001 Celestial Way	Jan-Pres

Figure 4.13 Snapshot data summaries.

Vertical Summary

The last type of summarization—vertical summary—applies to both point in time and period of time data. For a dealer, point in time data would pertain to the inventory at the end of the month or the total number of customers, while period of time data applies to the sales during the month or the customers added during the month. In an E-R model, it would be a mistake to combine these into a single entity. If "month" is used as the key for the vertical summary and all of these elements are included in the entity, month has two meanings—a day in the month, and the entire month. If we separate the data into two tables, then the key for each table has only a single definition within its context.

Even though point-in-time and period-of-time data should not be mixed in a single vertical summary entity in the data warehouse, it is permissible to combine the data into a single fact table in the data mart. The data mart is built to provide ease of use and, since users often create calculations that combine the two types of data, (for example, sales revenue per customer for the month), it is appropriate to place them together. In Figure 4.14, we combined sales information with inventory information into a single fact table. The meta data should clarify that, within the fact table, month is used to represent either the entire period for activity data such as sales, and the last day of the period (for example) for the snapshot information such as inventory level.

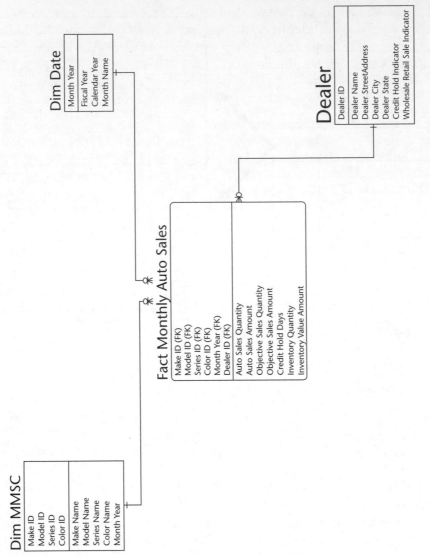

Figure 4.14 Combining vertical summaries in data mart.

Data summaries are not always useful and care must be taken to ensure that the summaries do not provide misleading results. Executives often view sales data for the month by different parameters, such as sales region and product line. Data that is summarized with month, sales region identifier, and product line identifier as the key is only useful if the executives want to view data as it existed during that month. When executives want to view data over time to monitor trends, this form of summarization does not provide useful results if dealers frequently move from one sales region to another and if products are frequently reclassified. Instead, the summary table in the data warehouse should be based on the month, dealer identifier, and product identifier, which is the stable set of identifiers for the data. The hierarchies are maintained through relationships and not built into the reference data tables. During the data delivery process, the data could be migrated using either the historical hierarchical structure through a slowly changing dimension or the existing hierarchical structure by taking the current view of the hierarchy.

Recasting data is a process for relating historical data to a changed hierarchical structure. We are often asked whether or not data should be recast in the data warehouse. The answer is no! There should never be a need to recast the data in the warehouse. The transaction is related to the lowest level of the hierarchy, and the hierarchical relationships are maintained independently of the transaction. Hence, the data can be delivered to the data mart using the current (or historical) view of the hierarchy without making any change in the data warehouse's content. The recasting is done to help people look at data—the history itself does not change.

A last comment on data summaries is a reminder that summarization is a process. Like all other processes, it uses an algorithm and that algorithm must be documented within the meta data.

Step 6: Merge Entities

The sixth step in developing the data warehouse model is to merge entities by combining two or more entities into one. The original entities may still be retained. Merging the entities improves the data delivery process performance by reducing the number of joins, and also enhances consistency. Merging entities is a form of denormalizing data and, in its ultimate form, it entails the creation of conformed dimensions for subsequent use in the data marts, as described later in this section.

The following criteria should exist before deciding to merge entities: The entities share a common key, data from the merged entities is often used together, and the insertion pattern is similar. The first condition is a prerequisite—if the data cannot be tied to the same key, it cannot be merged into a common entity since in an E-R model, all data within an entity depends on the key. The third condition addresses the load performance and storage. When the data is merged into a single entity, any time there is a change in any attribute, a new row is generated. If the insertion pattern for two sets of data is such that they are rarely updated at the same time, additional rows will be created. The second condition is the reason that data is merged in the first place—by having data that is used together in the same entity, a join is avoided during the delivery of data to the data mart. Our basis for determining data that is used together in building the data marts is information we gather from the business community concerning its anticipated use.

Within the data warehouse, it is important to note that the base entities are often preserved even if the data is merged into another table. The base entities preserve business rules that could be lost if only a merged entity is retained. For example, a product may have multiple hierarchies and, due to data delivery considerations, these may be merged into a single entity. Each of the hierarchies, however, is based on a particular set of business rules, and these rules are lost if the base entities are not retained.

Conformed dimensions are a special type of merged entities, as shown in Figure 4.15. In Figure 4.15, we chose not to bring the keys of the Territory and Region into the conformed dimension since the business user doesn't use these. The data marts often use a star schema design and, within this design, the dimension tables frequently contain hierarchies. If a particular dimension is needed by more than one data mart, then creating a version of it within the data warehouse facilitates delivery of data to the marts. Each mart needing the data can merely copy the conformed dimension table from the data warehouse. The merged entity within the data warehouse resembles a slowly changing dimension. This characteristic can be hidden from the data mart if only a current view is needed in a specific mart, thereby making access easier for the business community.

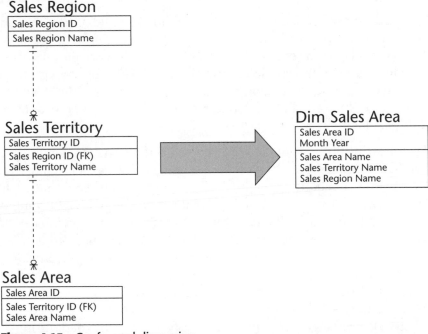

Figure 4.15 Conformed dimension.

Step 7: Create Arrays

The seventh step in developing the data warehouse model is to create arrays. This step is rarely used but, when needed, it can significantly improve population of the data marts. Within the traditional business data model, repeating groups are represented by an attributive entity. For example, for accounts receivable information, if information is captured in each of five groupings (for example, current, 1–30 days past due, 31–60 days past due, 61–90 days past due, and over 90 days past due), this is an attributive entity. This could also be represented as an array, as shown in the right part of that figure. Since the objective of the data warehouse that the array is satisfying is to improve data delivery, this approach only makes sense if the data mart contains an array. In addition to the above example, another instance occurs when the business people want to look at data for the current week and data for each of the preceding 4 weeks in their analysis. Figure 4.16 shows a summary table with the week's sales for each store and item on the left and the array on the right. The arrays are useful if all of the following conditions exist:

- The number of occurrences is relatively small. In the example cited above, there are five occurrences. Creating an array for sales at each of 50 regions would be inappropriate.

- The occurrences are frequently used together. In the example, when accounts receivable analysis is performed, people often look at the amount in each of the five categories together.

- The number of occurrences is predictable. In the example, there are always exactly five occurrences.

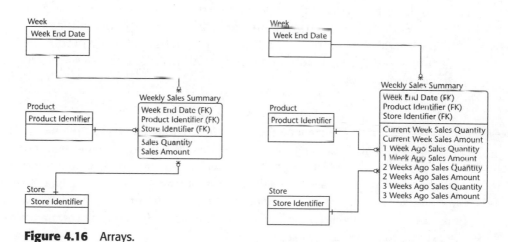

Figure 4.16 Arrays.

- The pattern of insertion and deletion is stable. In the example, all of the data is updated at the same time. Having an array of quarterly sales data would be inappropriate since the data for each of the quarters is inserted at a different time. In keeping with the data warehouse philosophy of inserting rows for data changes, there would actually be four rows by the end of the year, with null values in several of the rows for data that did not exist when the row was created.

Step 8: Segregate Data

The eighth step in developing the data warehouse model is to segregate data based on stability and usage. The operational systems and business data models do not generally maintain historical views of data, but the data warehouse does. This means that each time any attribute in an entity changes in value, a new row is generated. If different data elements change at different intervals, rows will be generated even if only one element changes, because all updates to the data warehouse are through row insertions.

This last transformation step recognizes that data in the operational environment changes at different times, and therefore groups data into sets based on insertion patterns. If taken to the extreme, a separate entity would be created for each piece of data. That approach will maximize the efficiency of the data acquisition process and result in some disk space savings. The first sentence of this section indicated that the segregation is based on two aspects—stability (or volatility) and usage. The second factor—usage—considers how the data is retrieved (that is, how it is delivered to the data mart) from the data warehouse. If data that is commonly used together is placed in separate tables, the data delivery process that accesses the data generates a join among the tables that contain the required elements, and this places a performance penalty on data retrieval. Therefore, in this last transformation step, the modeler needs to consider both the way data is received and the way it is subsequently delivered to data marts.

The preceding steps define a methodology for creating the data warehouse data model. Like all methodologies, there are occasions under which it is appropriate to bend the rules. When this is being contemplated, the data modeler needs to carefully consider the risks and then take the appropriate action. For example, the second step entails adding a component of time to the key of every entity. Based on the business requirements, it may be more appropriate to fully refresh certain tables if referential integrity can be met.

Summary

The application of entity relationship modeling techniques to the data warehouse provides the modeler with the ability to appropriately reflect the business rules, while incorporating the role of the data warehouse as a collection point for strategic data and the distribution point for data destined directly or indirectly (that is, through data marts) to the business users. The methodology for creating the data warehouse model consists of two sets of steps, as shown in Table 4.2. The first four steps focus on ensuring that the data warehouse model meets the business needs, while the second set of steps focuses on balancing factors that affect data warehouse performance.

Table 4.2 Eight Transformation Steps

STEP	ACTION	OBJECTIVE	ACTION
1	Select data of interest	Contain scope, reduce load time, reduce storage requirements	Determine data elements to be included in the model and consider archiving other data that might be needed in the future
2	Add time to the key	Accommodate history	Add time component to key and resolve resultant changes in the relationships due to conversion of the model from a "point-in-time" model to an "over-time" model
3	Add derived data	Ensure business consistency and improve data delivery process performance	Calculate and store elements that are commonly used or that require consistent algorithms
4	Adjust granularity	Ensure that the data warehouse has the right level of detail	Determine the desired level of detail, balancing the business needs and the performance and cost implications
5	Summarize	Facilitate data delivery	Summarize based on use of the data in the data marts
6	Merge	Improve data delivery performance	Merge data that is frequently used together into a single table if it depends on the same key and has a common insertion pattern

(continued)

Table 4.2 *(continued)*

STEP	ACTION	OBJECTIVE	ACTION
7	Create arrays	Improve data delivery performance	Create arrays in lieu of attributive entities if the appropriate conditions are met
8	Segregate	Balance data acquisition and data delivery performance by splitting entities	Determine insertion patterns and segregate data accordingly if the query performance will not significantly degrade

This chapter described the creation of the data warehouse model. The next chapter delves into the key structure and the changes that may be needed to keys inherited from the source systems to ensure that the key in the data warehouse is persistent over time and unique regardless of the source of the data.

CHAPTER 5

Creating and Maintaining Keys

The data warehouse contains information, gathered from disparate systems, that needs to be retained for a long period of time. These conditions complicate the task of creating and maintaining a unique key in the data warehouse. First, the key created in the data warehouse needs to be capable of being mapped to each and every one of the source systems with the relevant data, and second, the key must be unique and stable over time.

This chapter begins with a description of the business environment that creates the challenges to key creation, using "customer" as an example, and then describes how the challenge is resolved in the business data model. While the business data model is not actually implemented, the data warehouse technology data model (which is based on the business model) is, and it benefits from the integration achieved in the business data model. The modelers must also begin considering the integration implications of the key to ensure that each customer's key remains unique over the span of integration. Three options for establishing and maintaining a unique key in the data warehouse are presented along with the examples and the advantages and disadvantages of each. In general, the surrogate key is the ideal choice within the data warehouse.

We close this chapter with a discussion of the data delivery and data mart implications. The decision on the key structure to be used needs to consider the delivery of data to the data mart, the user access to the data in the marts, and the potential support of drill-through capabilities.

Business Scenario

Companies endeavoring to implement customer relationship programs have recognized that they need to have a complete view of each of their customers. When they attempt to obtain that view, they encounter many difficulties, including:

- The definition of customer is inconsistent among business units.
- The definition of customer is inconsistent among the operational systems.
- The customer's identifier in each of the company's systems is different.
- The customer's identifier in the data file bought from an outside party differs from any identifier used in the company's systems.
- The sold-to customer, bill-to customer, and ship-to customer are separately stored.
- The customer's subsidiaries are not linked to the parent customer.

Each of these situations exists because the company does not have a process in place that uniquely identifies its customers from a business or systems perspective. The data warehouse and operational data store are designed to provide an enterprise view of the data, and hence the process for building these components of the Corporate Information Factory needs to address these problems. Each of these situations affects the key structure within the Corporate Information Factory and the processes we must follow to ensure that each customer is uniquely identified. Let's tackle these situations one at a time so that we understand their impact on the data model. We start with the business data model implications because it represents the business view, and information from it is replicated in the other models, including the data warehouse model. Hence, from a Corporate Information Factory perspective, if we don't tackle it at the business model level, we still end up addressing the issue for the data warehouse model.

Inconsistent Business Definition of Customer

In most companies, business units adopt definitions for terms that best meet their purposes. This leads to confusion and complicates our ability to uniquely identify each customer. Table 5.1 provides definitions for customer that different business units may have.

Table 5.1 Business Definition for Customer

BUSINESS UNIT	POTENTIAL DEFINITION	IMPLICATION
Marketing	Any party that might or does buy our product	Includes prospects
Customer Service	A party that owns our product and has an existing service agreement	Includes only customers that we need to support
Sales	Any party that buys our product	This is typically the sold-to or bill-to customer; it excludes the ship-to customer
Commercial Sales	A company that buys our product	Restricted to commercial sales
Manufacturing	Companies that buy directly from us	Excludes retail sales and restricted to commercial sales

In the business data model, we need to create an entity for "customer," and that entity can have one, and only one, definition. To create the data model, either we need to get each unit to modify its definition so that it fits with the enterprise definition or we need to recognize that we are really dealing with more than one entity. A good technique is to conduct a facilitated session with representatives of each of the units to identify the types of customers that are significant and the definitions for each. The results of such a session could yield a comprehensive definition of customer that includes parties that might buy our product as well as those who do buy the product. Each of the types of customers would be subtypes of "Customer," as shown in Figure 5.1.

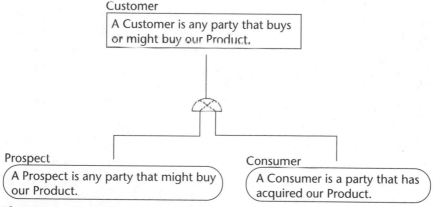

Figure 5.1 Enterprise perspective of customer.

As we will see subsequently in this chapter, resolving this issue in the business data model makes building the data warehouse data model easier.

Inconsistent System Definition of Customer

Operational systems are often built to support specific processes or to meet individual business unit needs. Traditionally, many have been product-focused (and not customer-focused), and this magnifies the problem with respect to consistent customer definitions. When the business definitions differ, these differences often find their way into the operational systems. It is, therefore, not uncommon to have a situation such as the one depicted in Figure 5.2.

These types of differences in the operational system definitions do not impact the business data model since that model is independent of any computer applications and already reflects the consolidation of the business definitions causing this problem.

There is another set of operational system definition differences that is more subtle. These are the definitions that are implicit because of the way data is processed by the system in contrast to the explicit definition that is documented. The attributes and relationships in Figure 5.2 imply that a Customer must be an individual, despite the definition for customer that states that it may be "any party." Furthermore, since the Customer (and not the Consumer) is linked to a sale, this relationship is inherited by the Prospect, thus violating the business definition of a prospect.

These differences exist for a number of reasons. First and foremost, they exist because the operational system was developed without the use of a governing business model. Any operational system that applies sound data management techniques and applies a business model to its design will be consistent with the business data model. Second, differences could exist because of special circumstances that need to be handled. For example, the system changed to meet a business need, but the definitions were not updated to reflect the changes. The third reason this situation could exist is that a programmer did not fully understand the overall system design and chose an approach for a system change that was inappropriate. When this situation exists, there may be downstream implications as well when other applications try to use the data.

Typically, these differences are uncovered during the source system analysis performed in the development of the data warehouse. The sidebar provides information about conducting source system analysis. It is important to understand the way the operational systems actually work, as these often depict the *real* business definitions and business rules since the company uses the systems to perform its operational activities. If the differences in the operational systems violate the business rules found in the business model, then the business model needs to be reviewed and potentially changed. If the differences only affect data-processing activities, then these need to be considered in building the data warehouse data model and the transformation maps.

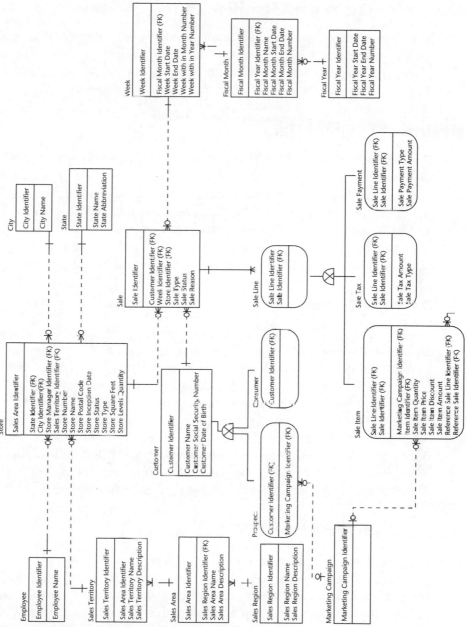

Figure 5.2   Operational system definitions.

Since one of the roles of the data warehouse is to store historical data from disparate systems, the data warehouse data model needs to consider the definitions in the source systems, and we will address the data warehouse design implications in the next major section.

Inconsistent Customer Identifier among Systems

Inconsistent customer identifiers among systems often prevent a company from recognizing that information about the same customer is stored in multiple places. This is not a business data modeling issue—it is a data integration issue that affects the data warehouse data model, and is addressed in that section.

Inclusion of External Data

Companies often need to import external data. Examples include credit-rating information used to assess the risk of providing a customer with credit, and demographic information to be used in planning marketing campaigns. External data needs to be treated the same as any other operational information, and it should be reflected in the business data model. There are two basic types of external data relating to customers: (1) data that is at a customer level, and (2) data that is grouped by a set of characteristics of the customers.

Data at a Customer Level

Integrating external data collected at the customer level is similar to integrating data from any internal operational source. The problem is still one of merging customer information that is identified inconsistently across the source systems. In the case of external data, we're also faced with another challenge—the data we receive may pertain to more than just our customers (for example, it may apply to all buyers of a particular type of product), and not all of our customers are included (for example, it may include sales in only one of our regions). If the data applies to more than just our customers, then the definition of the customer in the business model needs to reflect the definition of the data in the external file unless we can apply a filter to include only our customers.

Data Grouped by Customer Characteristics

External data is sometimes collected based on customer characteristics rather than individual customers. For example, we may receive information based on the age, income level, marital status, postal code, and residence type of customers. A common approach for handling this is to create a Customer Segment entity that is related to the Customer, as shown in Figure 5.3.

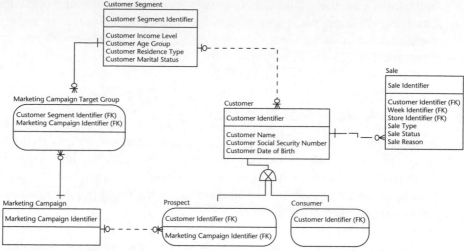

Figure 5.3 Customer segment.

Each customer is assigned to a Customer Segment based on the values for that customer in each of the characteristics used to identify the customer segment. In our example, we may segment customers of a particular income level and age bracket. Many marketing campaigns target customer segments rather than specific prospects. Once the segment is identified, then it can also be used to identify a target group for a marketing campaign. (In the model, an associative entity is used to resolve the many-to-many relationship that exists between Marketing Campaign and Customer Segment.)

Customers Uniquely Identified Based on Role

Sometimes, customers in the source system are uniquely identified based on their role. For example, the information about one customer who is both a ship-to customer and a bill-to customer may be retained in two tables, with the customer identifiers in these tables being different, as shown on the left side of Figure 5.4.

When the tables are structured in that manner, with the identifier for the Ship-to Customer and Bill-to Customer being independently assigned, it is difficult, and potentially impossible, to recognize instances in which the Ship-to Customer and Bill-to Customer are either the same Customer or are related to a common Parent Customer. If the enterprise is interested in having information about these relationships, the business data model (and subsequently the data warehouse data model) needs to contain the information about the relationship. This is typically handled by establishing each role as a subtype of the master entity. Once that is done, we reset the identifiers to be independent of the role. This results in the relationship shown on the right side of Figure 5.4, in which the Customer has two relationships to the sale, and the foreign key generated by each indicates the type of relationship.

Customer Hierarchy Not Depicted

Information about customers is not restricted to the company that is directly involved in the sale. It is often important to recognize how customers are related to each other so that, if several customers are subsidiaries of one corporation, we have a good understanding of the value of the whole corporation. There are services, such as Dunn & Bradstreet (D&B), that provide this type of information. Wholly owned subsidiaries are relatively simple to handle since these can be represented by a one-to-many relationship, as shown on the left side of Figure 5.5. (The relationship should be nonidentifying to provide flexibility for mergers and acquisitions.) Partially owned subsidiaries are more difficult. In this case, the model needs to handle a many-to-many relationship, which is resolved with the associative entity on the right side of Figure 5.5. More significantly, the modeler needs to consider the downstream impact and capture the associated business rules. Essentially, decisions need to be made concerning the parent company that gets credit for a sale and the portion of that sale allocated to that company.

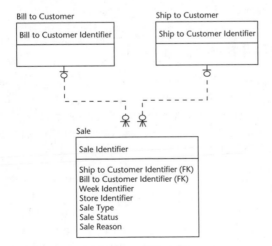
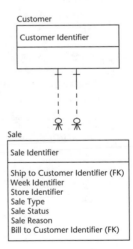

Figure 5.4   Role-based identifiers.

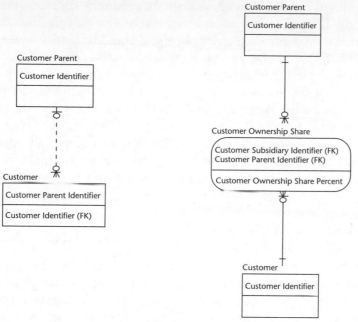

Figure 5.5 Customer hierarchy.

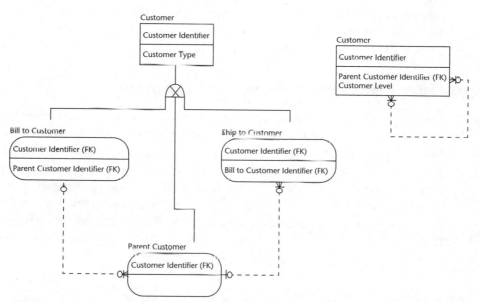

Figure 5.6 Multilevel hierarchy options.

Figure 5.5 handles the simplistic case—when the hierarchy consists of only two levels. Often, the hierarchy consists of more levels. The way this is handled is dependent on the predictability of the levels. If the number of levels is predictable and constant, then the business model can either depict each level or present the hierarchy in the form of a recursive relationship, as shown in Figure 5.6. If the number of levels is not predictable or constant, then the only solution is a recursive relationship. When a recursive relationship is used in the business model, the hierarchy will eventually need to be clarified to create the physical schema. If the model shows multiple distinct levels, then each of these needs to be defined, and the definitions of the various levels need to differ from each other. A complete discussion of hierarchies is covered in Chapter 7.

Data Warehouse System Model

In the day-to-day running of the company, information is typically viewed in terms of the individual sales transaction life cycle, and the lack of integrated customer information does not prevent making the sale, invoicing the customer, or collecting the payment. When the company tries to consolidate all the sales for each of its customers, the lack of integrated customer information becomes a problem. In the data warehouse, we expect to be able to see all of the sales transactions for each customer, so we need to tackle the problem head on. We therefore need to deal with the definitional differences, the lack of unique keys, and the other situations previously described.

Inconsistent Business Definition of Customer

The inconsistent business definition of Customer was resolved during the creation of the business data model. When we build the data warehouse model, we need to select the data elements of interest (Step 1 of the transformation process). If our business questions only deal with sales, and not potential sales, using the entities described in Figure 5.1, we would ignore data for prospects and only consider the data related to "Consumer." Similarly, in selecting the attributes for the Consumer, we would choose the ones needed to address the business questions being addressed, as explained in Chapter 4 (Step 1 of the transformation process).

Inconsistent System Definition of Customer

The data warehouse system model needs to provide a practical target environment for data that is in the operational systems. When the definition of the customer differs among systems, then the data warehouse system model needs to be structured so that it can receive all of the legitimate definitions, while maintaining an enterprise perspective of the data. Since the warehouse is oriented to the enterprise perspective, the model typically is not affected because of the definitional differences among the systems unless they reflect previously undocumented business rules. In that case, the business model incorporates the business rules, and the data warehouse model inherits them. Often, the system differences are handled in the transformation logic and in the staging area. For example, if the one operational system considers a customer to include prospects and another system does not, then in the transformation logic, we could apply appropriate rules to segregate the consumers and prospects in the data warehouse.

Inconsistent Customer Identifier among Systems

Inconsistent customer identifiers among systems cause most of the key integration problems. Inconsistent customer identifiers among systems mean that the key structure differs from system to system, and therefore, collecting data for a customer from multiple systems is a challenge. A similar problem exists if a system either reuses keys or cannot guarantee that the same customer exists only once in the data file. In the data warehouse model, we simply identify the key as "Customer Identifier." In the data warehouse technology model, which transforms into the physical schema, we need to determine how the key is structured. Three options are described in the section dealing with that model, which follows. When the customer identifiers among the systems vary, most data warehouse modelers lean towards creating a surrogate key.

Absorption of External Data

When the external data is at the customer level, then the data warehouse model issues are the same as those discussed in the previous section for the business data model. For external data based on a set of characteristics of the customer, the business data model includes a single entity representing the Customer Segment. Each of the attributes in that entity represents a characteristic, and a discrete set of values exists for each of these. Within the data warehouse, these discrete values are typically stored in individual code entities, as shown in Figure 5.7.

Customers Uniquely Identified Based on Role

The business data model resolved this issue by providing information about the relationship. This resolution is transferred directly to the data warehouse model.

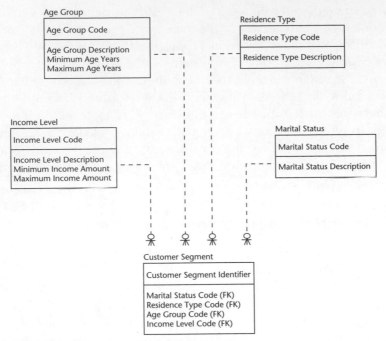

Figure 5.7 Segment characteristics.

Customer Hierarchy Not Depicted

The business data model resolved this issue by including the hierarchy (if the number of levels is predictable or consistent) or by deploying a recursive relationship. The business model is concerned with a complete picture of the hierarchy. Often, for decision support, we are only interested in specific layers of the customer hierarchy. For example, even if we depict four layers in the business data model, the data warehouse model may only need to depict the top and bottom layer. Hence, the data warehouse model is more likely to have an exploded structure than a recursive structure.

Data Warehouse Technology Model

The data warehouse technology model, which is used to generate the physical schema, needs to consider the structure of the key. We have three basic options to consider:

- Use the key from existing system(s)
- Use the key from a recognized standard
- Create a surrogate key

Key from the System of Record

In the simplest situation, we can actually use the key from an existing system. For this to be practical, the system must have a key structure that can accommodate data that is derived from other sources. This happens when there is one recognized primary source of record for the data, such as an ERP system. Some of the needed characteristics of that file follow.

That file should include every customer of interest to the company. There may be other files with information about customers, but each customer should at least exist in this file. It is important that we not be faced with creating a customer key in the data warehouse using that file's key structure, and hence we do not run the risk of the system creating the identical key at another time for a different customer.

Each customer can exist only once in the file. The business rules for the systems that add customers to this file must be such that they prevent a data entry person from inadvertently duplicating a customer within the file. If a customer can exist twice within the file, the key of at least one of these customers will need to change when we integrate the data.

The key cannot be reused. Some operational systems recycle keys. When this occurs, the same key can be used to identify different customers. The data warehouse stores historical information, and if the key is reused, the data warehouse will erroneously append the information to the customer that no longer exists in the source system instead of adding a new customer.

The key is not very long. While the length of the key is not necessarily a problem in the data warehouse, it does present a problem in the data mart. The delivery of data to the marts and the support of drill-through capabilities are enhanced if the warehouse and the mart share a common key structure. In dimensional data marts, the key of the fact table is a concatenation of the keys of the primary dimension tables. If the keys of the dimension tables are long, the key of the fact table becomes *very* long.

The key will not change. If you are leaning toward using the operational system's key in the data warehouse, you need to consider the lifespan of the operational system as compared to the lifespan of the data warehouse. If the company is even considering changing its operational system software, it is reasonable to expect that, at some time in the future, you may be faced with a reassignment of keys. While changing keys is a normal exercise when converting systems, it is a far more difficult and complex task in a data warehouse because of its historical nature. It is a task best avoided.

For reference data such as customer, product, or location, it is very rare for a file to exhibit all of these characteristics, and companies often find themselves choosing one of the other options. The requirements for transaction files (for example, sales, invoices) are slightly different. A company that has grown through acquisition may have multiple sales order systems, each of which creates a nonreusable key for the sales order that is unique within that system. This is consistent with the second and third conditions above, but not with the first. An option to consider in the data warehouse is using a compound key that includes a source system identifier. However, if you expect to be loading data from multiple independent systems as a matter of course, you should consider using surrogate keys to avoid potential problems as new systems and interfaces are encountered.

Dealing with Multiple Instances

It is not unusual to encounter cases where there are multiple instances of the same entity. This manifests itself in the database in such situations as the same customer appearing more than once under different customer numbers. While it is great to say on paper that such situations should be resolved and a single customer instance placed in the data warehouse, the reality is, to do so can involve enormous conflict and pain within an organization. Aside from the difficulty in actually trying to find and identify such duplicates, there may often be heated political battles among business areas and IT support groups as to whose problem it really is. Resolving these issues often involves process and system changes in the operational environment, something business areas may be unwilling to do, particularly if the problem only came up as a result of this "data warehouse thing" the company is building. After all, things have been running fine as they are. Why should they change?

From a data warehouse point of view, we know that as long as the keys are different, these will always be different customers. And, from a technical standpoint, this does not present a problem as far as loading and processing the data. However, it can have implications in the business analysis that results from such a situation. As a customer has different physical instances in the database, each instance may have differing attributes values, be assigned to different hierarchy structures, and have other data anomalies. It would be impossible to obtain a true picture of that customer.

A business case would need to be made to correct this situation. Action will depend on how the business perceives the value of a single, proper view of a customer and the costs involved in attaining and maintaining such a view. Doing so involves more than cross-referencing customer keys. Changes are required in the operational systems and processes to prevent such occurrences from happening in the future.

Key from a Recognized Standard

There are nationally and internationally recognized code and abbreviation standards. Examples of these include country codes and currency codes. Regardless of whether or not any of the systems in the company adopts these standards, the data warehouse can use the standard codes as the key to its code tables. The staging area would include a transformation table to translate the code used by the source system to that used in the data warehouse.

This option presumes there is a direct correlation between internal and the industry standard coding system. When such a correlation does not exist, the translation may introduce ambiguity and loss of information. In addition, it is common for end users to demand to see the operational system codes in the data warehouse. These are the codes they are most familiar with. If code reassignment does occur, you would most probably retain the original value for query and reporting purposes. This can be accomplished by providing attributes for both the internal and standard codes in the entity.

Surrogate Key

By far the most popular option is a surrogate key. A surrogate key is a substitute key. It is usually an arbitrary numeric value assigned by the load process or the database system. The advantage of the surrogate key is that it can be structured so that it is always unique throughout the span of integration for the data warehouse. When using surrogate primary keys, the term "natural key" is used to refer to the original source system key. The natural key serves as the alternate key for the entity. All foreign key references to that entity are through the surrogate key.

Surrogate keys fit all the requirements of a perfect key. They are unique, unambiguous, and never change. In addition, surrogate keys provide a number of advantages in the physical database:

The surrogate key is small.   Surrogate keys are usually arbitrary sequentially assigned integers. Databases that support binary data types can store such numbers in 4 bytes. This compactness reduces overall database size and, more importantly, results in smaller, more efficient indexes.

A surrogate key eliminates compound keys.   The primary key for a table is always a single column. Joins and maintenance of indexes for single column keys are generally more efficient than compound keys.

Surrogate keys share the same physical data characteristics.   The fact that all surrogate keys are the same data type comes in handy when a foreign key reference is role based or nonspecific. This will be discussed in greater detail in subsequent chapters.

A surrogate key is stable.   Its value and format will never change. This is a big advantage when you must interface multiple independent systems or when the source system is changed. The business key is reduced to alternate key status and only resides in the reference table. Only the surrogate key is propagated to other tables as a foreign key. If you have a new interface that requires some change to the physical attributes or contents of the business key, you only need to change the reference table that holds the value. The foreign key references remain unchanged.

The assignment process ensures referential integrity.   When setting the value of a foreign key, the process must find the surrogate key value by locating the target row in the target table using the natural key.

Assigning Surrogate Keys

If you are using surrogate keys as the primary keys of your reference tables, your load processes into the data warehouse must implement logic to assign these keys as well as locate surrogate key values for use as the foreign key.

When used as a primary key, the table should have the primary key column as well as an alternate, business key. The latter, called the natural key, serves as the row identifier from the business point of view. The natural key is usually the primary key from the source system. It may also include a source system identifier column to qualify business key values where the data is sourced from multiple systems and there is a danger of duplicate key values.

The actual surrogate key value is always numeric. It is an arbitrary unique value carried on each row. Some database systems provide data types that automatically generate unique numeric values in a column. Other database systems provide sequence counters that can be used to perform the same function. Also, almost every ETL tool provides sequence generators for this purpose as well.

As you will see later in this book, there is some advantage to controlling the generation of these surrogate key values. In fact, you may wish to use a single number sequence to generate surrogate keys for all tables that need them. As such, database features that automatically generate keys for a table is a less desirable feature since it is unable to create key values that are mutually exclusive across tables. The lack of mutually exclusive values complicates the delivery of table unions to data marts, a technique commonly used to support hierarchical reporting in a dimensional model.

We recommend that surrogate key sequences be generated in the ETL process and that a few sequences be used as possible to allow for mutually exclusive values across reference tables that may need to be unioned when delivered to a data mart. In fact, most data warehouse applications can function with a single surrogate key sequence. We do not recommend applying surrogate key assignment to transactional data tables. In a dimensional mart, the transactional data is delivered to fact tables that do not have surrogate primary keys. The primary key to a fact table is always a combination of one or more of its foreign keys. Within the data warehouse, a transaction table's primary key would consist of a combination of surrogate foreign keys and source system values, such as line numbers.

The process of assigning surrogate foreign keys will ensure referential integrity within the data warehouse. This can be used to your advantage to speed data loading by disabling redundant foreign key reference checking by the database system. The basic process to assign a surrogate foreign key to incoming data is to locate the row in the referenced table using the natural key value and selecting the primary surrogate key. This value is then used to substitute the business key in the incoming data.

If the lookup cannot find a row using the business key, you have a problem with referential integrity. There are two techniques to handle this problem. One technique is to reject the incoming data row and produce an exception report. The other technique is to create a new row in the reference table using the business key from the incoming data as the natural key. The new surrogate key value would be used as the foreign key for the incoming data, which is then processed and loaded into the data warehouse. The reference table row generated in this manner would be identified as one being generated to resolve an error so the transaction data can appear in an exception report.

Both techniques have their merits and which to use will depend on your business requirements and policies. If a common problem is that data feeds sometimes go out of sync, and reference data comes in after the transaction data, then the latter technique has significant advantages. It allows the transaction to flow into the data warehouse and, at the same time, reserves a place for the reference data once it arrives. When the reference data is loaded, it would find a row already in place. It could then update that row with the missing data.

The act of performing the surrogate key lookup should not have a significant impact on your data load process times. If you are using an ETL tool, almost all tools provide a means to preload such cross-references into memory. If you do not use an ETL tool, a database technique to use is to create a compound index of the natural key and the surrogate key, then tune the database to cache this index in memory. This would result in very fast lookup response from the database.

Dimensional Data Mart Implications

In general, it is most desirable to maintain the same key in the data warehouse and the data marts. The data delivery process is simplified, since it does not need to generate keys; drill-through is simplified since the key used in the data mart is used to drill through to the data warehouse. However, it is not always possible to maintain the same key structure because of the different techniques used to create the models. An entity is not equivalent to a dimension. The rules of entity relationship modeling and normalization are vastly different from the rules of dimensional modeling. When both are performed correctly, the same modeling task can result in widely different schemas. The disparity can be so great that one is unrecognizable by the other, yet both would be capable of providing the same information.

Differences in a Dimensional Model

In Chapter 2, we reviewed the basic concepts of relational modeling. An entity typically represents an identifiable business object, such as a Customer, Warehouse, Product, or Order. An entity contains attributes that describe the entity and establish its primary key. Attributive entities provide additional detail about a primary entity, such as Order Line and Warehouse Inventory. The structure of these entities, their relationships and their attributes closely resemble their actual structure in the business. In a dimensional model, this is not the case. A basic dimensional model is made up of two classes of objects: dimensions and facts. A fact contains measures and dimension foreign keys. A measure is usually a numeric value and represents the magnitude of an action that has occurred in the business. For example, in the case of a Sales Fact Table, the measures would represent items such as quantity sold and the value of the sale. The dimension foreign keys associated with the measures define the context of the measures by referencing the appropriate dimension rows. A dimension is a collection of attributes. Note that the term attribute as used in dimensional modeling only refers to columns in a dimension table, whereas in relational modeling the term attribute is more generic. In relational modeling terms, both dimensional attributes and measures would be considered attributes. While it is common to have dimensions that represent business objects, it is not always the case. For example, a typical dimensional model may not contain dimensions for transactional entities such as an Order. Instead, there may be a number of dimensions that contain attributes that describe various aspects of an Order, such as Payment Terms, Shipping Method, and so forth. The foreign keys in the order fact table would provide the association between these dimensions so that through these relationships you have a complete picture of the order.

Figure 5.8 shows an example of this disparity. On the left side is a typical normalized representation of a sales order. There is an Order entity to describe information about the order document and an Order Line entity to describe information about the order line. Both entities contain attributes to describe the order and its status. On the right side is an Order Status dimension. This dimension describes unique combinations of status code values encountered on an order and its lines. It includes attributes that appear in both the Order and Order Line entities in the entity model. When the sales order fact row is loaded, its foreign key is set to reference the appropriate combination of status codes in the Order Status dimension.

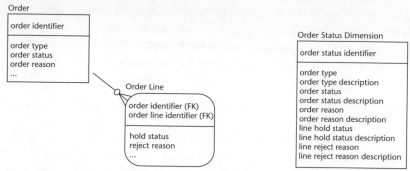

Figure 5.8 Differences between entity-relation and dimensional models.

The whole point of the dimensional design is to simplify and speed queries. For example, let's say that the user is performing an analysis based on a specific order reason against a database that contains 5 million orders. In a relational model, the query would need to locate the orders with that order reason, then join to the order lines. If there were 1 million orders with that specific reason, the database system will need to do a lot of work to find all the lines. On the other hand, the Order Status dimension would only contain unique combinations of status codes. Attributes in such dimensions are usually chosen based on the level of correlation between the values, so that a typical dimension like this may only contain 100 or 200 rows, of which only 25 may contain the reason code of interest. The database is only required to look up 25 foreign keys in the fact table to locate all the order fact rows.

Maintaining Dimensional Conformance

One challenge in fielding dimensional models from a purely relational data warehouse is to provide a consistent foreign key reference between fact tables and dimensions. There are two sides to this challenge: First, it is usually desirable to update existing data marts rather than performing a complete refresh. Therefore, foreign keys provided in a delivery must be consistent with the existing dimensional keys in the target data mart. Second, the dimensional keys used in one data mart should be consistent with the same dimension used in other data marts. This latter requirement is known as dimensional conformance. This simply means that the value of a foreign key in one fact table means the same thing as the same value of the same foreign key in another fact table. Maintaining conformance allows you to create joins across fact tables, allowing for unanticipated data analysis without the need to field additional data marts.

To achieve dimensional conformance you must maintain the dimension tables within the data warehouse itself, in addition to the base relational representation. (See Step 6 in Chapter 4.) In cases where the Customer entity is the same as the Customer dimension, this is easy to do. Simply use the surrogate key of the Customer entity or store the dimensional surrogate key as an attribute in the Customer entity. In the case of minidimensions, such as the one shown in Figure 5.8, or any other dimension that has no direct entity relationship, you will need to maintain the dimension table within the data warehouse.

While dimensional maintenance can be performed as part of the delivery process, it is more useful to do this work up front during the load process. Assigning and storing dimensional foreign keys in your transactional data during the load allows you to use those keys to support detailed drill-through from the data marts. This allows you to field smaller summarized data marts and use the data warehouse to supply highly detailed information on an as-needed basis. It also has the advantage of focusing dimensional key assignment on new or changed data, doing the assignment only once and simplifying the delivery processes by having the foreign keys readily available in the tables being extracted. This approach is not without risk. First, it can slow down the loading process. Second, as new dimensions created, you would be required to rework the schema and load processes to maintain the dimension and store the new dimensional foreign keys. However, even if you do not plan to permit drill-through into the data warehouse, we believe that addressing dimensional key assignment during the loading process streamlines the delivery process and ensures key consistency across data marts. This is a long-term benefit that outweighs the additional complexity in the loading process.

Table 5.2 Physical Key Structures

OPTION	ADVANTAGES	DISADVANTAGES	APPLICABILITY
Source System Key	Familiarity	If the key is long, it may generate performance problems downstream.	Single, recognized source that contains some data for each instance
Recognized Standard Key	Recognized standard exists.	Structure to accommodate integration	Applies for a few code tables
Surrogate Key	Can be generated by DBMS.	May cause additional joins for retrieval of the business key	Applicable for virtually any situation except date and situations for which users generally use the data's key for retrieval

Summary

The data warehouse key structure needs to be viewed at two levels: a business perspective and a technical perspective. From a business perspective, the key is an identifier that distinguishes each instantiation of an entity. To achieve this purpose, the modeler needs to pay careful attention to the definition of the equivalent entity (or table) in each business area and in each contributing system. It is only through such analysis that the business and data warehouse models can establish entity structures and their respective identifiers to provide the enterprise perspective.

From a technical perspective, the key needs to be unique over the span of integration and time addressed by the data warehouse. The key should not be used for anything other than establishing a unique record and relating it to other records. Using the value of the key or a portion of it to mean something should always be avoided. Several options exist, such as using the key from the source system, using an accepted standard, and using a surrogate key. Table 5.2 summarizes the three options and provides recommendations for when each best fits.

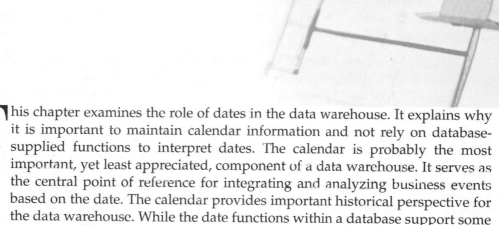

CHAPTER 6

Modeling the Calendar

This chapter examines the role of dates in the data warehouse. It explains why it is important to maintain calendar information and not rely on database-supplied functions to interpret dates. The calendar is probably the most important, yet least appreciated, component of a data warehouse. It serves as the central point of reference for integrating and analyzing business events based on the date. The calendar provides important historical perspective for the data warehouse. While the date functions within a database support some analyses, most businesses use more than one calendar in their operations. In addition to the Gregorian calendar, we often see references to a fiscal calendar, a planning calendar, and other specialized calendars that may be unique based on the analyses being performed.

In this chapter, we will examine the types of calendars used in business, and the implications that these have on the data warehouse. These case studies will explore the following types of calendars:

- Simple fiscal calendar
- Location-specific calendar
- Multilingual-calendar
- Multiple-fiscal calendars
- Seasonal calendars

We start with a description of the different types of calendars and incorporate these into the business data model, which is the basis of the data warehouse (as well as system and technology) models. Using case studies, we then describe how the data warehouse data model needs to be developed for each scenario. Recognizing that data warehouse design decisions affect the delivery of data to the data marts, we then provide information on the data mart design implications for each of the case studies.

Calendars in Business

Businesses use a variety of calendars. The purpose of a calendar is to relate dates for a particular application. In business, in addition to the standard (Gregorian) calendar, there's a fiscal calendar that is used for accounting and financial management purposes. In addition, some companies have other calendars based on business needs. These include billing-cycle calendars, factory calendars, and others.

Each of these calendars serves a specific purpose and needs to be referenced in a specific business context to be meaningful. The data warehouse must support each of the appropriate calendars and ensure that when data is presented for analysis, it is done within the context of the correct calendar. In this section, we will examine the business calendars from three perspectives: the types of calendars, the critical elements within these calendars, and the implications for conglomerates and companies that operate globally or in many locations.

Calendar Types

The Gregorian calendar is generally accepted as the basis for establishing dates for business activities. Within some countries, other calendars are used, and we will describe how to handle these in the section dealing with companies that have a global presence. Within the context of this book, we will use the Gregorian calendar as the foundation for all of the other calendars being discussed. Figure 6.1 shows how we would model the Gregorian calendar in the business model.

Figure 6.1 is fairly simplistic. Each date is composed of a year, a month, and a day within the month, each through a foreign key relationship. In addition, each date can be related to one of the seven days of the week.

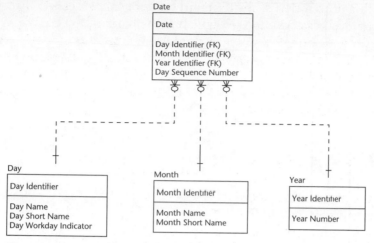

Figure 6.1 Calendar in the business model.

The Fiscal Calendar

The fiscal calendar is the clock that drives financial reporting and accounting practices within the business. This calendar is made up of a fiscal year that contains four fiscal quarters, each of which contain three fiscal months, which are sometimes called fiscal periods. The fiscal months each contain individual dates, and some fiscal calendars group these into fiscal weeks.

As Figure 6.2 shows, the first quarter in the fiscal calendar does not necessarily correspond to the first quarter in the Gregorian calendar. Further, the calendar date of July 3 may actually fall in the fiscal month of June if the fiscal month of July begins on July 3. The date is the element that is shared between the Gregorian and fiscal calendar, as shown in Figure 6.3, which adds the fiscal calendar to the business data model.

The start and end of the fiscal calendar is up to the individual company. Many companies choose to use January 1 as the start date and December 31 as the end date. A company that has significant activity during a particular period may choose to end its year shortly after that period. For example, a retailer may choose to use January 31 as the end of its fiscal year to reflect post Christmas sales, and a university may choose to use August 31 as the end of its fiscal year to correspond to the end of its academic year.

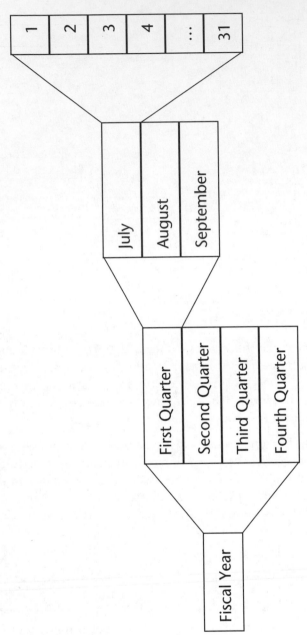

Figure 6.2 Fiscal calendar.

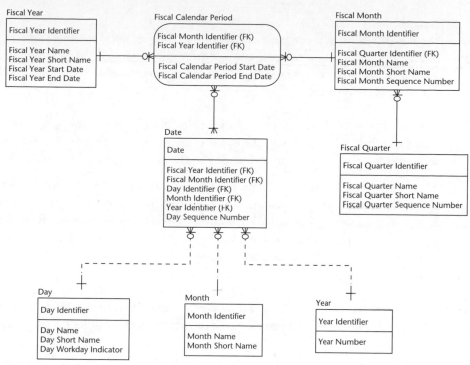

Figure 6.3 Fiscal calendar in the business data model.

The 4-5-4 Fiscal Calendar

In the retail industry, sales comparisons are often made on a week-to-week basis. When weekly results are rolled up to months, these comparisons lose some meaning because the weeks would need to be split. Retail companies have solved this problem by adopting a "4-5-4 calendar" for fiscal analysis and reporting. With a potential exception of the year end, this calendar establishes all of its periods based on 7-day periods ending on a particular day of the week, such as Friday. Each quarter contains 13 weeks, and these are allocated to the 3 months within the quarter, with the first month containing 4 weeks, the second month containing 5 weeks, and the third month containing 4 weeks.

The 4-5-4 fiscal calendar is very well suited for analyses performed by week or by quarter; it is not well suited for comparing one month to another since a third of the months are 25 percent longer than the other months. When monthly analyses are performed, they need to compensate for the differing length of the months.

NOTE

The day of the week a company chooses for ending its fiscal week is sometimes related to its marketing campaigns. Food stores, for example, have promotions that span from Thursday to Wednesday. These often correspond to their fiscal week, which ends on Wednesday.

Four quarters, each consisting of 13 weeks, consume 364 days, and a calendar year contains 365 or 366 days. Options typically employed to address this problem are to anchor the first and last day of the fiscal year and to float these dates.

Most companies using the 4-5-4 fiscal calendar anchor their fiscal year within the Gregorian calendar using, for example, January 1 as the first day and December 31 as the last day. Within this calendar, there will be 52 weeks in the year, though the first and last weeks of the year are either short or long, depending on the day of the week on which the year starts.

NOTE

A 4-5-4 fiscal calendar contains two weeks (the first and last) that differ in length from other weeks. Analyses that compare weekly results must consider these differences.

A modified version of a 4-5-4 fiscal calendar entails a week-centric approach. This method identifies one day of the week as the last day of the week, and does not make any adjustments for the end of the year. The month in which that day falls determines the fiscal month to which the week is assigned. For example, if Friday is the last day of the week, and August 2 falls on a Friday, then the week of July 27 through August 2 would be considered to be the first week of the August fiscal month. This method eliminates the calendar shift problem of a strict 4-5-4 calendar, but the number of weeks in a year as well as in any fiscal month can vary from year to year.

In the modified version of the 4-5-4 fiscal calendar, the number of weeks in each month is not predictable since the month with 5 weeks is not always the second month of the quarter. Similarly, some years will have 52 weeks, while others will have 53 weeks. If the accuracy of year-to-year comparisons needs to be better than 98 percent, then this discrepancy must be taken into account. For strategic analyses that can tolerate a small margin of error, the difference could be ignored.

Figure 6.4 incorporates the fiscal week into the fiscal calendar. The model includes separate relationships between the date to the fiscal week and the date to the fiscal month. Companies using the 4-5-4 calendar often relate sales revenues to the fiscal week, and other financial data such as depreciation and other expenses to the fiscal month. By maintaining the separate relationships, data can be related in the appropriate manner based on the specific data element.

With data-modeling tools that support it, the relationship should be shown as an "exclusive or" relationship, meaning that one of the two relationships applies to each data instance.

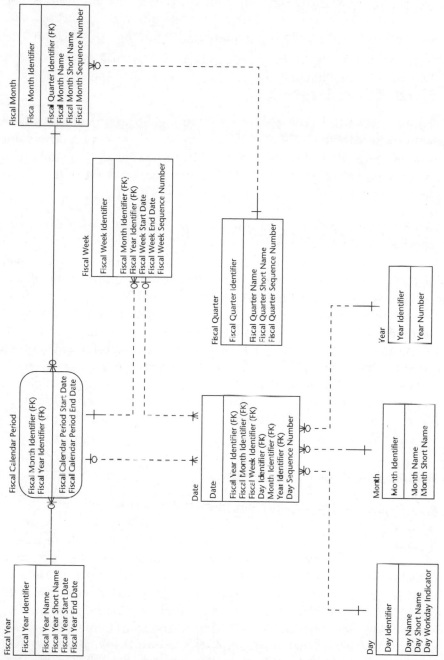

Figure 6.4 Week-centric fiscal calendar.

Thirteen-Month Fiscal Calendar

Another week-centric calendar is the 13-month fiscal calendar. This calendar divides the fiscal year into 13 months, each consisting of 4 weeks. This structure facilitates month-to-month comparisons, since all months consist of exactly 4 weeks, but does not accommodate quarterly reporting. Due to the prevalence of quarterly financial reporting requirements, this type of calendar is rarely used.

Other Fiscal Calendars

There are other fiscal calendars that are unique to a particular business. All of the calendars define a fiscal year, and most define fiscal quarters and fiscal months. Regardless of the structure of the fiscal calendar, the data warehouse must support structures that provide both a fiscal and a traditional (for example, Gregorian) calendar view of the business's data.

The Billing Cycle Calendar

Many companies, such as utilities and credit card companies, have events that are tied to a billing cycle. For example, in an utility company, the meter may be read 2 days prior to billing, the payment may be due 14 days after billing, charges may be subject to interest payments 30 days after billing, and the account may go into the arrears 60 days after billing. The formula, in terms of the number of days (be they business days or calendar days), is constant. Given a billing date, the businessperson can readily anticipate when certain events take place. Further, in these businesses, there is a typical payment pattern that is based on the billing date. Given a billing date and the amount being billed, financial planners can make cash flow projections using information stored in the data warehouse.

The Factory Calendar

A factory calendar is a specialized calendar and was initially developed to schedule and plan production in a factory. Factory calendars are typically based on workdays and shifts. Each day in a factory calendar represents a day of production. Nonproduction days are excluded. In the past, the calendar was organized by "cycles" of anywhere from 100 to 1000 days. These cycles were used in production scheduling and planning to ease calculation of future dates. For example, if a production shop floor routing requires materials to be sent off-site for specialized work and the turn-around time is 15 working days, material that enters that production step on day 183 will be expected back on the floor on day 198. Modern computer systems have eliminated the need to maintain calendars on these terms, allowing the user to see April 18, 2002 instead of day 198, and yet internally, such systems continue to count days based on working and nonworking days. By their very nature, factory calendars are localized. That is, each production facility may have its own factory calendar to reflect the workdays and shifts within that facility.

Whether you are developing your data warehouse for a manufacturer or not, the idea of tracking workdays has wide applicability when performing analysis for a variety of businesses. The concept of the factory calendar has been expanded in modern usage to provide a calendar for consistently measuring the number of workdays between two events, such as the beginning and end of a promotional period, and for facilitating data access for an equal number of workdays regardless of the elapsed calendar days. The premise behind the factory calendar was to homogenize the timeline so that day calculations could be done using simple arithmetic. This homogeneity is also important when performing year-over-year and month-over-month analysis. If you have a sales force that works Monday through Friday and you need to compare this month's performance to date against last month's, it makes sense to count the same number of selling days in each month; otherwise, the comparison can be skewed depending on where the weekend falls in relation to the start of the month. This concept will be discussed at length in the next section.

Calendar Elements

An effective calendar entity can significantly improve people's ability to perform analysis over time. There are three fundamental concepts that facilitate the analysis:

- The day of the week, particularly in Retail businesses
- Accounting for nonworking days to provide meaningful comparative analysis and elapsed-time calculations
- Defining time periods of interest, such as holiday seasons, for analysis

Day of the Week

The day of the week is probably the most commonly recognized special day for performing date-oriented analyses. Often the day of the week is used to distinguish between workdays and nonworkdays. A workday indicator in the Day of the Week entity in Figure 6.1 shows whether it is a regularly scheduled workday, and this can be used to facilitate analysis.

A company's revenue cycle is also sometimes dependent on the day of the week. Some retailers have a heavier daily sales volume during weekend days, while other retailers may have a lower volume during the weekend, particularly if they have shorter hours. Sales on Mondays may be consistently higher than sales on other days for some companies. The relationship between the Day of the Week and the Date in Figure 6.1 facilitates analysis based on the day of the week.

NOTE Some sales cycles are also dependent on the day of the month. For example, commercial sales may be higher at the beginning of the month than at the end of the month. Inclusion of a day sequence number in the Date entity in Figure 6.1 can help analysts who need to use that information.

Holidays

Holidays impact two areas: your organization's business practices and your customers' ability to do business with you. In the first case, holidays (or more generically, nonworkdays) are established by internal business policies and impact company holiday schedules, store hours, plant closings, and other events. Within the Date entity in Figure 6.1, we've included a workday indicator within the Day of the Week entity and a Holiday Indicator within the Date entity. With this information, analysis based on workdays is facilitated. In addition, the use of a Workday Sequence Number helps in comparing results during the first 10 workdays of two months. As Figure 6.5 shows, in June 2006, the 10th workday occurs on the 14th, while the 10th workday in July 2006 will not occur until the 17th.

WARNING Analysts should be careful with the criteria used to perform month-to-month analysis. For example, in companies that are heavily oriented toward commercial sales or sales through distribution channels, it may be very appropriate to make comparisons based on the number of business days in the month since these are the days in which purchasing agents typically make buying decisions. In companies that are oriented toward retail sales, it would be more appropriate to make comparisons based on the number of days that the stores are open.

June 2006						
S	M	T	W	T	F	S
				1	2	3
4	5	6	7	8	9	10
11	12	13	14	15	16	17
18	19	20	21	22	23	24
25	26	27	28	29	30	

July 2006						
S	M	T	W	T	F	S
						1
2	3	4	5	6	7	8
9	10	11	12	13	14	15
16	17	18	19	20	21	22
23	24	25	26	27	28	29
30	31					

Figure 6.5 Workday comparisons.

The effect that holidays have on your customers is a much different matter. The greatest impact is seen in the retail business, in which holidays and other events can have a significant impact on comparative statistics. For example, it makes no sense to directly compare January sales against December sales if 25 percent (or more) of your sales for the year occur in the weeks leading up to Christmas. External calendars influence businesses in many different ways. Children's clothing and tourism have cycles influenced by the school calendar. Candy sales are influenced by events such as Easter and Halloween. Firework sales are influenced by special events such as Independence Day and New Year's Day. When performing analyses of sales that are influenced by such events, it is important for the data warehouse to provide the means to apply the necessary context to the data as the data migrates to the marts. Without such context, direct comparison of the numbers can be misleading, which may lead to bad decisions.

These are predictable business sales cycles. Hence information about these can be included in the business data model and cascaded to the data warehouse model. Attributes can be included (as shown in Figure 6.5) in the Date entity to indicate special periods to which the date belongs. If there are a small number of such periods, then each could be accommodated by a separate attribute; if the number of periods is large, then the periods could be classified into logical groupings and the attributes could indicate the group(s) to which the date belongs.

Holiday Season

The holiday season, which begins on the day following Thanksgiving and ends on Christmas Day (December 25), is of special interest in retailing. An indicator for this season is very useful since the beginning date varies each year. With an indicator, an analyst comparing Holiday Season sales for 3 years can simply select dates based on the value of the indicator.

The holiday season impact cascades beyond just sales during the holiday season since companies need to ensure that the products are available at that time. To prepare for the large sales volume, there are preceding periods that affect product planning and production. Sometimes it is meaningful to track these as well. For example, large inventory levels following the peak-selling season are not healthy, but it is very appropriate (and in fact essential) to have high inventory levels immediately preceding the peak selling season. One way of handling this is to include a derived field that represents the number of days before the peak selling season. The analyst can use that information to qualify analysis of data for the inventory levels, production schedules, and so on.

Company holiday information is easily obtained from the Human Resources Department within your organization. The challenge is that such information may not be readily available from an existing application. You may find that the only source for a list of nonworking days is from memos and other such documents. In such cases, it would become necessary to implement a data entry application to collect and maintain this data for the warehouse. From a technical standpoint, it is a very simple, low-volume application. However, finding a department to support this data may be difficult. Usually, the holiday schedule is published by the Human Resources Department so it would be the most likely candidate to maintain this information in the application. In most cases, initial warehouse implementations often do not support the Human Resources Department, and the Human Resources Department is typically out of the loop when discussing warehouse requirements. So, it is common that, when asked, the Human Resources Department may decline to assume that responsibility. Do not be surprised if the responsibility for maintaining this data within the data warehouse falls on the data warehouse support staff.

Seasons

In addition to holidays and other events, seasons play an important role in influencing business activity. In the context of this discussion, it is best to look at a season is its most generic form. A season is defined as any time period of significance. What this means depends on what is significant to your business. If you are in sporting goods, then the baseball season is significant. If you manufacture watercraft, then summer is important. Carried to a logical conclusion, a seasonal calendar can be used in a data warehouse to provide context to any date or range of dates. Figures 6.15 and 6.16, later in this chapter, show an example of a seasonal calendar model.

The advantage of a seasonal calendar is that it formalizes a process that allows the end user to surround any period of time with a special context. It recognizes the fact that the impact on business is not the event itself, but rather the days, weeks, or months preceding or following that event. It also facilitates year-to-year analysis based on seasons that are important to the business, similar to the holiday season previously described. The concept of the season acknowledges the fact that, as a data warehouse designer, you cannot anticipate every conceivable avenue of analysis. A seasonal calendar structure puts that control in the hands of the end user. Creating a seasonal calendar will be discussed later in this chapter.

Dealing with Missing Information

The data warehouse will have a column for each data element, including a column for dates into the future, and the data to populate this column may not initially be available. Therefore, these columns may be null at first (if your database standards permit this). When the data becomes available, a new row is added to the data warehouse with values in these columns. From a purely theoretical point of view, the old row is also retained. To simplify the structure of the data warehouse, companies sometimes choose not to keep history of that nature, in which case the previous row containing data for that date is deleted.

Calendar Time Span

A major application of the calendar is to provide a time context to business activity. At a minimum, the calendar should cover the historical and current activity time period maintained in the warehouse. From a practical standpoint, it should cover the planning horizon (for example, the future time span for which a forecast or quota that is used in strategic analysis may be created), which is often several years into the future.

Some industries, such as banking, may require much longer timeframes in their calendar to cover maturity dates of bonds, mortgages, and other financial instruments. As you will see later in this section, there is a lot of information about a date that a calendar entity can include. It may not be possible to gather all the necessary information for dates 10, 20, or 30 years into the future. This should not be of great concern. There is no requirement that all columns for all dates be populated immediately. If the data is not available, then a null condition or a value indicating that the data is not available may be used. When this is done, the metadata should explain the meaning of the field content.

Time and the Data Warehouse

Time can be an important aspect of analysis, depending on your business. In retail, identifying busy and slow parts of the day can aid in better work scheduling. In logistics, analysis of delay patterns at pickup and delivery points can help improve scheduling and resource utilization. This section will examine the use of time in the data warehouse.

The Nature of Time

A common mistake in data warehouse design is to treat date and time together. This is understandable because it is common for people and the business to consider them as one and the same. This natural tendency can result in very undesirable effects in the data warehouse.

If we develop the business model (such as the one shown in Figure 6.3) with the understanding that the Date attribute represents a specific Gregorian date, then all other entities that refer to the Date entity have a foreign key that represents a specific Gregorian date. An attribute that represents both the date and time cannot be used as a foreign key since it represents a point in time rather than a date. To avoid this conflict, the model should represent date and time of day as separate attributes. Doing so will help clarify the model and avoid potential implementation issues.

Standardizing Time

An aspect of time is that it is different from place to place. While it is 3:33 P.M. on June 2 in New York, it is 1:03 A.M. on June 3 in Calcutta. When you are designing the data warehouse, you will need to take into account which time is important for the business: a common standard time, the local time, or both. A traditional retail chain is most likely interested in the local time because it represents time from the customer's perspective. Whereas a telecommunications company needs both, local time to analyze customer patterns and rates, and a common standard time to analyze network traffic.

If there is a requirement for a common standard time, you must store the local time and date as well as the standard time and date in the data warehouse. There are some basic reasons for this. If you only stored one date and time, it would be very difficult to reliably calculate the other, particularly in historical analysis. Around the world, the recording of time has more to do with politics than it does with science. It is up to government authorities in each country to decide what time they will keep and how they will keep it. At the time of this writing, there are 37 different standard time zones. This number increases if you take into account those that observe daylight savings time and those who don't.

Storing Time

Receiving time values from different systems can be problematic as each system may provide time at different levels of precision. Two decisions you need to arrive for the data warehouse is what degree of precision is useful and how will the time value be stored. The level of precision will depend on your business. In most cases, hour and minute are sufficient. However, some industries—such as telecommunications and banking—require more precise values.

When storing time, there are three approaches. One method is to store time as you would expect to display it, for example, as a four-digit number where the first two digits are the hour and the last two digits are the minute. A second method is to express the time as the number of minutes or seconds since the beginning of the day. The first method is useful when displaying time, while the second is more useful for calculating elapsed time. Both methods are useful for sorting. Both methods need to be supplemented with functions to accommodate their particular shortcoming.

A third approach is to store a discrete time value using one of the other two methods and to store a full date/time value in the databases native format. This is redundant, as you would be storing a discrete date, discrete time, and a continuous timestamp. The latter value will allow you to use native database functions to manipulate and measure time, while the discrete values provide useful keys for analysis. This approach provides the greatest flexibility and utility.

Of course, there is another class of date/time attributes that is used internally for audit and control purposes. The values of these attributes would never be used for business analysis and would not be made available to the user community at large. These values should be stored as timestamps in the native database format. No effort should be made to store them as discrete date and time values as such values are only useful for business analysis.

If your source is Web-based transactions, it is fairly easy to do. Web transmissions are time stamped with the local time as well as Zulu (UMT or Greenwich Mean Time) time. Otherwise, you need to check your source systems to determine what time is collected. If a standard time is not recorded, it may be worthwhile investigating modifications to the transactional system to collect this information.

If all else fails, there are services that can provide worldwide time zone information on a subscription basis. The data will typically contain ISO country and region coding, the offset from Zulu time, and the dates that daylight savings time is observed. These services will provide periodic updates, so you do not need to worry about regulatory changes. The challenge will be to associate your locations with the ISO country and regional-coding standard. Also, it is not certain that the ISO codes will be specific enough to differentiate between sections of states. Therefore, initial use of such data may require some analysis and manual effort to assign the ISO codes to your locations in order to correlate them with the time zone data. A search for "time" at www.google.com will locate such services as well as a wealth of information about time zones.

In addition, the observation dates will vary from country to country. The job would be easier if it were a national decision, but it is not. In the United States for example, it is up to the States and Tribal Nations, not the Federal government, to establish time rules. For example, Arizona does not observe daylight savings time, whereas the Navajo Indian Reservation in Arizona does observe daylight savings time. In other cases, time zones go through States, following a river, mountain crest, or keeping true to the longitude. To avoid getting bogged down in legislative and geographic minutia, it is better to capture both times at the time of the transaction.

Data Warehouse System Model

The previous section described the business characteristics of the calendar, including the various types, elements, and time spans. In this section, we describe the impact on both the system and technology representations of the data warehouse. Before getting into the case studies, we introduce the concept of keys as they apply to the calendar. This material expands on the material provided in Chapter 5.

As you will see throughout the remainder of this chapter, the use of entity-relationship modeling concepts for the data warehouse provides the designer with significant flexibility. Properly structured, we preserve the primary mission of the warehouse as a focal point for collecting data and for subsequently distributing it to the data marts.

Date Keys

Within the data warehouse, data is related to the calendar by foreign keys to the calendar entity's primary key. Transaction dates—such as enrollment date, order date, or invoice date—would be associated to the calendar in this manner. Other dates, such as birth dates, that have no relationship to business activity, are usually stored as dates with no relationship to the calendar.

As discussed in Chapter 4, the date is one of the few attributes that has a known, reliable set of unique values. We can also assume that, at least in our lifetime, there will not be a change in the calendar system so there is no danger that management will decide to renumber the dates. A date has all the trappings of a perfect key. Whether or not to use a surrogate key for the calendar table will depend on your particular preferences and policies. One could have a policy that all keys for all tables should contain surrogate keys. That is fine because it certainly removes any question as to the nature of a table's primary key. The other issues to consider are why you may want a surrogate key for the calendar and how you plan to deal with bad dates. The surrogate key section in Chapter 5 discusses different strategies to deal with erroneous reference data. Review that discussion before you decide.

The entity will also have multiple alternate natural key attributes depending on how dates are represented in the source systems. One attribute may be the date in the native database format; unless you are using a surrogate primary key, this attribute would serve as the primary key. Additional attributes could contain the dates stored in the format used by incoming data feeds. For example, if one of the data sources contains dates stored as an eight-character CCYYMMDD field, you should include an attribute in the date entity with the date in that format to ease interfacing the external system with the data warehouse. By storing the date in these different formats, your data warehouse load interfaces can locate the appropriate date row without having to use date format conversion functions. This avoids potential problems should the date being received be an invalid one. If you store a single natural key, usually a date in the database's native format, you will be faced with developing code to validate and cleanse the date prior to using it to lookup the primary key. Failure to do this properly will cause an exception from the database system during the load. Such an exception will cause the load process to abort and require some late-night troubleshooting and delays in publishing the warehouse data. As the data warehouse grows and new system interfaces are encountered, it is not unusual to discover new date formats. Adding new attributes to the entity easily accommodates these new formats.

Case Study: Simple Fiscal Calendar

Our consumer packaged goods company, Delicious Foods Company (DFC), is implementing its data warehouse in phases over many years. The initial phases will concentrate on sales, revenue, and customer fulfillment. All sales and revenue reporting is tied to the fiscal calendar. The company uses a modified 4-5-4 calendar, where the fiscal year always begins on January 1 and ends on December 31.

The company has the following business rules for its calendar:

- The fiscal year begins January 1.
- The fiscal year ends December 31.
- There are always 52 fiscal weeks in the year.
- The week begins on Monday and ends on Sunday.
- If the year begins on a Monday, Tuesday, or Wednesday, the first week of the year ends on the first Sunday of the year, otherwise it ends on the second Sunday of the year.
- The last week of the year is week 52 and always ends on December 31.
- Each quarter has 3 fiscal months consisting of 4 weeks, 5 weeks, and 4 weeks (4-5-4), respectively.
- Workdays are Monday through Friday, except holidays. Activity on Saturday or Sunday is treated as the same workday as the preceding Friday unless that Saturday and/or Sunday is in a different fiscal year, that is, the Friday in question fell on December 30 or December 31. Activity on a holiday is counted in the preceding business day.

Year	Month	Day	Period_ID
2002	1	27	1
2002	2	24	2
2002	3	31	3
2002	4	28	4
2002	5	26	5
2002	6	30	6
2002	7	28	7
2002	9	1	8
2002	9	29	9
2002	10	27	10
2002	12	1	11
2002	12	31	12

Figure 6.6 Fiscal calendar data feed.

The company would like the calendar to support both fiscal and Gregorian calendars. It should support reporting by day, month, and year as well as fiscal week, fiscal month, fiscal quarter, and fiscal year. Year-to-date versus last-year-to-date and fiscal-month-to-date versus last-year-fiscal-month-to-date comparisons must use the working day of the fiscal month as the point of comparison. For example, if the current date is the 15th workday of the fiscal month, then last year's numbers must be those for the period through the 15th workday of last year's fiscal month. However, if the current date is the last day of the fiscal month, the comparison should include all days of last year's fiscal month regardless of the number of workdays. The company has a standard holiday list that is produced annually by the Human Resources Department. Days on this list are considered nonworkdays.

The company's operational system can provide a data feed that defines a fiscal year by providing 12 records containing the calendar date for the end of each fiscal month. Figure 6.6 shows an example of a typical data feed that defines the fiscal calendar for 2002. The incoming data contains four fields, the year, month, and day (which specifies the last day of the fiscal month), and the fiscal month number.

Based on the business models discussed earlier, this section discusses how the technical model is implemented within the data warehouse.

Analysis

It is not unusual for an operational system to provide insignificant data surrounding fiscal calendars. The concern on the operational side is to ensure that transactions are posted to the proper fiscal month. It is not concerned with workdays or other aspects of the date. Fortunately, most calendar information can be generated algorithmically, with no other input than the date itself. With the exception of the holiday list from Human Resources, the entire calendar can be generated without additional data feeds.

The Human Resources Department's holiday list may be published as a memo. This means that someone's annual task will be to enter the dates into the data warehouse for processing. This duty almost always falls on the data warehouse team to perform. To avoid potential errors, a process should be in place to collect the new dates in a file or a staging table. A report of these dates can be generated and sent to a designated business user for validation. After validation, the list of dates can then be applied to the data warehouse.

At DFC, the next year's holiday schedule is published in November. Since the calendar data is generated years in advance to accommodate orders with future delivery dates and sales planning data, this data may be much too late to incorporate into next year's calendar. Therefore, the holiday load process will need to adjust workdays in the calendar.

A Simple Calendar Model

This case has very basic requirements for the calendar. Figure 6.4 shows the basic business model to support these requirements. What follows is a discussion of the technical model in the data warehouse. In the sections that follow, we will examine a number of techniques to provide additional functionality to support the load and delivery processes.

Extending the Date Table

The Date table contains one row per day for the time span appropriate to your needs. Usually, this time span is all the previous years of transactional data retained in the warehouse plus at least 2 years into the future to support planning and budgets. The physical model has been extended to include columns representing the date in a number of different formats. These columns serve as natural or reference keys to the table. The sample model in Figure 6.7 shows three examples of this. The Date column represents the date in the native database format. The Date CYMD column contains the date as a string in CCYYMMDD format, while Date YYDDD is an integer column with the date stored in Julian format. Your table may contain more or less than this, depending on the number of different formats in which you receive in your data interfaces.

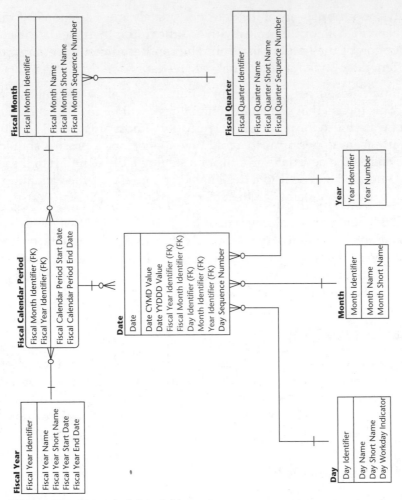

Figure 6.7 Extended date table.

The remainder of the physical model follows the business models shown in Figure 6.3. However, the model, while complete, presents a number of challenges when it becomes necessary to deliver data to the data marts and other external systems. The business requires that there be a number of derived values, such as number of workdays in the fiscal period, same day last year, and so forth. While the model will allow for this, such derivations can require significant processing, slowing down the delivery process. Since our objective is to provide this data in an efficient manner, further refinement of the physical model is necessary.

Chapter 4 discusses the process involved in refining the model. The calendar data is one area where this process can be applied to its fullest to achieve significant processing efficiencies. The reason for that is we are dealing with a small, stable data set. There is very little cost to fully denormalize this data set, yet doing so will greatly reduce the cost of using it. We will discuss this next.

Denormalizing the Calendar

The basic calendar is delivered to the data marts as a single denormalized table. Figure 6.8 shows an example of the Calendar dimension as it may appear in a data mart. As is typical with dimension tables, there is a significant amount of data redundancy and derived values. The purpose of which is to improve query performance and ensure consistency of derived values across queries. The same need exists within the data warehouse to support the delivery of calendar information. If delivery was based solely on the instantiation of the normalized business model, calculation of some of the derivations from normalized tables will require significant processing. Furthermore, each delivery process would have to derive the values itself, unnecessarily extending the development and testing process.

Calendar

Date
Same Day Last Fiscal Year Date (FK)
Same Day Last Fiscal Month Date (FK)
Day Identifier
Day Name
Day Short Name
Day Workday Indicator
Month Identifier
Month Name
Month Short Name
Year Identifier
Year Number
Fiscal Month Identifier
Fiscal Month Start Date
Fiscal Month End Date
Fiscal Month Name
Fiscal Month Short Name
Fiscal Month Sequence Number
Fiscal Quarter Identifier
Fiscal Quarter Name
Fiscal Quarter Short Name
Fiscal Quarter Sequence Number
Fiscal Week Identifier
Fiscal Week Start Date
Fiscal Week End Date
Fiscal Week Sequence Number
Fiscal Year Identifier
Fiscal Year Name
Fiscal Year Short Name
Fiscal Year Start Date
Fiscal Year End Date
Workday Indicator
Workday of Week
Workday of Month
Workday of Fiscal Month
Workday of Year
Workday of Fiscal Year
Workday Count
Workdays in Week
Workdays in Month
Workdays in Fiscal Month
Workdays in Year
Workdays in Fiscal Year
Last Day of Month Indicator
Last Day of Fiscal Month Indicator
Last Day of Year Indicator
Last Day of Fiscal Year Indicator

Figure 6.8 Denormalized calendar table.

Alternate Date Formats

Your Date table should contain additional columns for alternate date formats, such as the Julian date, YYMMDD text date, and so forth. At minimum, there should be one column for each date format you expect to receive in your external data feeds. These columns should be populated as part of the table creation process.

Creating alternate indexes on these columns allows the ETL process to locate the proper date row and primary key value using the native format received in the data feed. This combines both date format conversion and date validation into a single step, simplifying the ETL process and error-trapping procedures.

Due to the processing required to derive some of the data values, we recommend that you implement the denormalized calendar structure in the data warehouse. These tables would exist in addition to the normalized tables outlined in the business model. While redundant, the denormalized structures are solely dependent on an internal delivery process to generate the tables after updates are applied to the normalized tables. Creating the tables in this manner will not introduce data inconsistencies that may sometimes occur where redundant data exists. Also, since calendars are very small tables, data storage should not be an issue.

The denormalized tables should then be used as the source of calendar data for all delivery processes. In the case of delivery to dimensional data marts, the tables can be moved en masse without the need for modification. When delivering information to other environments, such as flat file extracts, you should join to the denormalized tables to retrieve the necessary data.

Table 6.1 explains the derived columns in the denormalized Calendar table. You may add or exclude columns to suit your business requirements. The primary objective of these columns is to eliminate or reduce the logic necessary during data delivery. Columns such as Last Day of Month Indicator are good examples of that. Providing such attributes allows the delivery process to be unfettered by business rules, workdays, and leap years.

Ensuring Key Conformance

When generating denormalized tables in the data warehouse to support the data delivery process, it is important that the primary key value remain consistent after repeated updates or regenerations of this data.

Within dimensional data marts, the fact tables store the key value as a foreign key to the dimension table. If the regeneration process reassigns primary key values, these foreign key references are not longer value when the denormalized data is used to update the mart's dimension table. This destroys the referential integrity of the data and would require reloading the fact data with the proper foreign keys. Such a situation should be avoided.

Table 6.1 Calendar Table Derived Columns

CALENDAR COLUMN	DESCRIPTION
Workday Indicator	This is a true/false value, indicating if the day is a workday.
Workday of Week	This is the number of the workday in the week, with the first workday in the week being 1; the second, 2; and so on.
Workday of Month, Workday of Fiscal Month	This is the number of the workday in the month or fiscal month. This value is typically used for month-over-month or year-over-year comparisons. To compare a month-to-date total for this day to a month-to-date total from last year, you would include all days in last year's month where the Workday of Month is less than or equal to this date's number of workdays.
Workday of Year, Workday of Fiscal Year	This is the number of workdays in the year or fiscal year. This is useful when performing year-to-date comparisons of actuals and projections. This value divided into the total number of workdays in the year will give you the percentage of the year completed.
Workday Count	This is a running count of workdays, in chronological order, from the beginning of the calendar. This value is used to determine the number of workdays between any two dates.
Workdays in...	This is the number of workdays in the current week, month, fiscal month, year, and fiscal year. This value can be used to calculate percentage of completion for the time period and for printing the expected duration in a report (that is, day 8 of 25).
Last Day of Month Indicator	A true/false value set to true for the last day of the month. Business rules should determine how this gets set. For example, if the month ends on a Sunday, it may be that Friday, Saturday, and Sunday are considered the "last day" if both Saturday and Sunday are nonworkdays.

(continued)

Table 6.1 *(continued)*

CALENDAR COLUMN	DESCRIPTION
Last Day of Fiscal Month Indicator, Last Day of Year Indicator, Last Day of Fiscal Year Indicator	A true/false value set to true for the last day of the fiscal month, year, and fiscal year. Again, your business rules would determine how this flag is set.
Same Day Last Fiscal Month Date, Same Day Last Fiscal Year Date	These are recursive foreign keys pointing to rows for the same day in the last fiscal period and the same day in the last fiscal year, respectively. These keys would take into account any business rules to determine what day it really is. For example, it may be the same calendar day or the same workday. You can add other such keys as necessary to support data analysis requirements.

Case Study: A Location Specific Calendar

Our food store chain, General Omnificent Shopping Haven (GOSH), uses a week-centric 4-5-4 calendar as their fiscal calendar. The chain also maintains different working schedules for each store, each distribution center, and the corporate offices. When performing store analysis, it is not only interested in the days of operation, but the hours as well. These schedules can vary widely from store to store due to local regulations, the season, and market conditions. The operational system maintains this data as a series of schedules with each store being assigned a schedule for a specified time period. Changes may occur to the schedule as well as the schedule assignment for the store being changed. The distribution centers are maintained in the same manner as the stores. The corporate office holiday schedule comes from a memo sent by Human Resources.

The company would like the analysis of comparative store sales to take into account days and hours of operation. They also wish to profile sales by time of day and day of the week. The time of day of a sale is captured by the check-out system in both local and Zulu (GMT) time.

Analysis

This case differs from the previous case on two basic points: The fiscal calendar is different, the workday calendar varies by location, and hours of operation are part of the analysis requirements.

The model must accommodate the operation schedules and the assignment of those schedules to the locations (stores and distribution centers). Another consideration is maintaining a history of schedules so that past and future dates can be associated with the correct hours of operation. The operational system maintains a set of schedules. Schedules are assigned to locations bounded by effective and expiration dates. Those who maintain the schedules may effect a change in two different ways. They may alter the schedule, which affects all locations assigned to that schedule, or they may reassign a location to a different schedule. In both cases, changes have an effective date range associated with them. Typically, these dates are in the future.

The GOSH Calendar Model

The simple model shown in Figure 6.4 assumed a single fiscal calendar with a single set of nonworkdays applicable to the entire enterprise. However, in this case, this simple model is not sufficient. We will use the simple calendar model as a foundation to handle corporate needs and expand the model to support the location dependent schedules. All entities and attributes in the simple model remain in this model.

Figure 6.9 shows the additional entities required to support the location-specific schedules. The Schedule table contains the definition of each schedule. The Location Schedule entity defines the relationship between location and schedule. It has effective and expiration date attributes to record changes to the assignments.

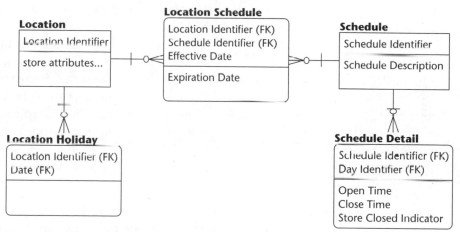

Figure 6.9 Location-specific schedules.

Delivering the Calendar

As discussed in the previous case study, it makes sense to store a denormalized physical model derived from the business model. So, in addition to the physical instantiation of the normalized business model, an internal delivery process should also create denormalized versions of the data within the data warehouse. In this case, where you have both a standard corporate calendar and local variations, it would be most efficient to produce two sets of tables. The first would be the corporate calendar that supports fiscal reporting, and the other would be location-specific work schedule using both the date and location as the primary key.

The new location-specific table is a copy of the basic calendar schema with additional attributes for the operating hours for the store. The content is adjusted according to the work schedule at the location. Many of the attributes, such as fiscal month are redundant, but this is not a significant issue due to the small size of these tables. The redundancy avoids the need for an additional join if certain attributes are needed when delivering location-specific data. If you are dealing with a very large number of locations, you may wish to remove the fiscal-calendar-related columns from the Location Calendar table. When delivering the data to the data marts, you have the option of delivering a single table, created by reintroducing the redundancy by joining the Calendar and Location Calendar tables, or to deliver two separate dimension tables. Figure 6.10 shows the structure of the denormalized tables.

As you can see, the Location Calendar table would have a compound primary key of location and date. This is not desirable in a dimensional data mart. Such a dimension would perform better in the data mart if there were a single simple primary key. In such cases it is best to create and store a surrogate primary key within the denormalized data warehouse table and use the location and date as an alternate key to support the data delivery process. Note that Figure 6.10 has been abbreviated to show the pertinent differences from the basic denormalized calendar shown in Figure 6.8. The content of these tables may vary depending on your business requirements. You may implement all columns in both tables or you may consider splitting the columns, placing common columns in the Calendar table and location-specific columns in the Location Calendar table. The latter is worth considering if you have a very large number of locations.

However, using a surrogate key in the Location Calendar table complicates the process of generating the table. As discussed in the previous case study, these denormalized tables are regenerated whenever updates are applied to the normalized calendar data. If these denormalized tables are delivered as dimension tables to data marts, it is important to maintain the same primary key values between generations of these tables. If the key values change, the new

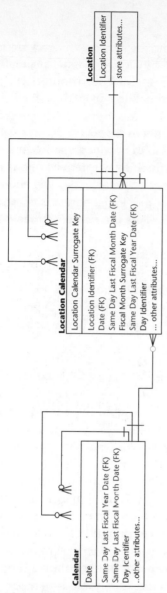

Figure 6.10 Denormalized location calendar tables.

keys would not be compatible with foreign keys contained in the mart's fact-tables, forcing you to completely reload the data marts each time the denormalized table is regenerated. While it is possible to reload, it is better to implement a process that maintains the key value. Such a process is not difficult to implement. Rather than rebuild the Location Calendar table, update existing rows and add new rows when necessary. The update will retain the same primary key value, ensuring historical integrity in the data marts.

Calendar Redundancy

Throughout this chapter, we recommend that you create both normalized and denormalized versions of the calendar structure in the data warehouse. We believe this is an expedient way to provide both simplified updating and efficient delivery of calendar data.

Depending on your business, you may be required to support complex calendar structures. Maintaining normalized calendar tables provides a simple means to apply changes that may have significant side effects on the derived calendar data. For example, changing a day from a workday to a nonworkday will alter the running workday counts for all days following that day. In the normalized version you do not store derived workday counts, so the update is a matter of changing an indicator on a single row.

A process to generate the denormalized calendar structures is required to deliver the calendar in a form usable by the data marts and other external systems. Since this process can be resource intensive due to the derivations required, it makes sense to store the results of the process in the data warehouse. In this way, the process is only run when the calendar changes, not every time you need to deliver the calendar.

Calendar delivery is sourced from the generated denormalized structures. This provides a direct means to pull the derived data without any additional calculations. This ensures data consistency across deliveries and significantly simplifies the delivery process. This approach provides a simpler, more consistent process at the cost of maintaining a few additional small tables.

Another consideration for the data marts is the fact that the Calendar and Location Calendar dimensions shown in Figure 6.10 are semantically different. If your data mart is to contain both location-specific detail and a summary by date, the location-specific fact table should have foreign keys to both the Calendar and Location Calendar dimensions. This will allow for dimensional conformance with the date summary fact table, which would contain a foreign key to the Calendar dimension and not the Location Calendar dimension. If you have split columns across the two dimension tables, then you must always deliver both dimensions to location-specific data marts and provide foreign keys to both in the fact tables.

Case Study: A Multilingual Calendar

With the advent of GOSH's expansion into Canada, management would like to add the ability to produce reports in French. Since the company also has future plans to expand into other countries, it is reasonable to assume that support for other languages will be required as well.

Analysis

There is a bit more to this request hidden below the surface when discussing a calendar. In addition to being able to support descriptive text in multiple languages, the manner in which dates are presented varies around the world. While MM/DD/YYYY is common in the United States, DD-MM-YYYY and YYYY-MM-DD are used elsewhere. Furthermore, the same language, in particular English, may be different in different parts of the world. Canada uses British English spellings, such as *colour*, instead of *color*.

Your business may decide that such differences are not important. However, in this example, we will assume that they are. In such cases, each variation is treated as a different language. Such treatment doesn't materially affect the model, but rather affects the level of maintenance required to support the languages.

Storing Multiple Languages

It is clear with GOSH's expansion plans that providing support for only one other language would be shortsighted as well as counterproductive. From a design-and-processing perspective, it is actually easier to handle an unlimited number of languages than a fixed number of languages. If the requirement is for only one or two other languages, one is tempted to simply add columns. For example, the row contains one column for English text, one column for French text, and one column for Spanish text. This horizontal arrangement is not very flexible and requires the user or query tool to consciously select a particular text.

Ideally, a multilingual implementation should be transparent to the end user. When logged in, the user should see text in his or her language of choice without any special action on the user's part. This is best accomplished by storing the texts vertically by placing different language versions in different rows. This is accomplished by adding a language code to the key of each of the text tables. Figure 6.11 shows the modified schema.

Handling Different Date Presentation Formats

As the scope of the data warehouse expands internationally, it is necessary to accommodate different date and number formats for each country. Ideally, the task of maintaining these formats should be handled in the data marts rather than the data warehouse. The first two approaches, database and query tool localization, rely on functionality of those software components to handle data presentation. The third approach, delivery localization, handles presentation formats in the data warehouse delivery process. There are a number of different approaches that can accomplish this.

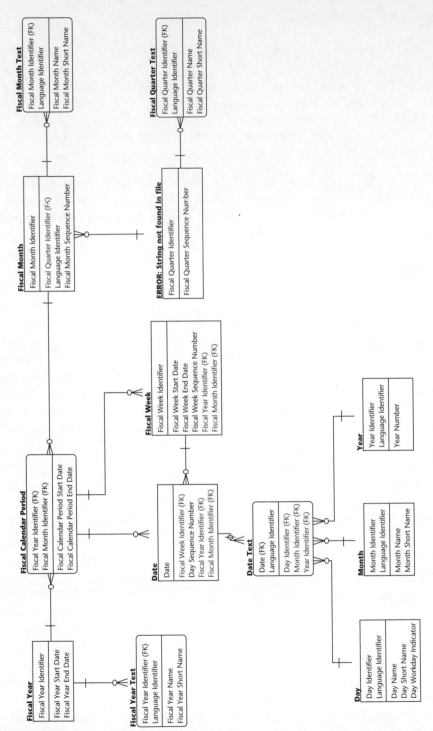

Figure 6.11 A multilingual calendar.

Database Localization

If the plan is to publish separate data marts for each target country, and that each of these marts would reside in its own database, you can rely on the database's own localization parameters. These parameters allow you to specify how the database should return date and numeric values. All databases support these parameters in some form, and this is the most practical method to implement localization. This approach would not require any special actions when publishing data to the data marts.

Query Tool Localization

Many query tools support similar localization parameters. The query tool retrieves the value from the database, then transforms the values to the presentation format you have defined for the target audience. This approach is necessary if you plan to support different target audiences though the same data mart database. Again, this approach does not require any special actions when delivering data to the data marts.

Delivery Localization

In this approach, you publish the date as a text column for display purposes. This circumvents any action by either the database or the query tool to format the date. This requires that the data warehouse contain definitions of the different date formats appropriate for the target audience. It has the advantage of providing central control as to how dates are presented, but it does so at the expense of adding additional complexity to the publication process. Furthermore, this approach cannot control how numeric values are displayed, because it is not practical to publish and store numeric values in text columns. This option is one of last resort, to be used only if the first two options are not available.

Every database has a function to covert a date column to a text string. These functions usually have two parameters, one being the date column to convert and the other being a format string or code number. Your data delivery process must then either be hard coded with the appropriate formatting information or be able to accept a parameter to define the desired format. The former approach requires separate publication processes for each target audience. This can lead to excessive development and maintenance effort. The latter is more flexible and can be integrated with the ability to publish in different languages. In the latter case, you can support the process by creating a table, keyed by language code, which contains the appropriate date formatting parameters. When you publish the data, the language code parameter passed to the process would also be used to control the date format.

> ## Eliminating Compound Primary Keys
>
> When delivering data to dimensional data marts, it is desirable to eliminate primary keys that consist of multiple columns, otherwise known as compound keys. Use of compound keys can degrade data mart performance, particularly when bitmap indexes are used in the fact tables. If dimensional delivery is supported by a denormalized table in the data warehouse, the compound primary key can be substituted with a single column surrogate primary key. The compound key columns would then be used to define an alternate key that would be used to maintain the data and in the delivery process to associate the table with other data warehouse tables.
>
> Defining and storing the surrogate primary key in the data warehouse allows the surrogate key value to remain consistent across delivery processes. Keeping a stable primary key value is critical to maintaining conformance across the data marts and ensuring referential integrity with historical fact data.

Delivering Multiple Languages

When delivering different languages to dimensional data marts, it is solely an issue of delivering dimensional data. All descriptive text attributes reside in dimension tables, not fact tables, in a properly designed star schema. Therefore, language is not an issue when delivering transactional data. This section examines the issues in delivering the calendar dimension. This approach is applicable to any dimension table that must support multiple languages. When supporting multiple languages, it is inevitable you will be faced with the challenge of delivery data in the user's language of choice as well as delivering multilingual data. We will examine each approach.

Monolingual Reporting

Delivering language-specific data does not mean delivering only one language, but rather that the delivered data structure only supports one language per user. The data warehouse should support a multilingual version of the denormalized table structure, as shown in Figure 6.7. To accommodate multiple languages, the primary key should be changed to include the Language Identifier. When delivering a language-specific version to a data mart, the Language Identifier column would be stripped from the primary key, providing a conforming date key across all data marts.

Combining Languages

To provide the ability to report in two or more languages within the same query, you need to publish the data with multiple languages in the same row. As shown in Figure 6.12, our calendar schema is expanded to hold both English and French descriptions.

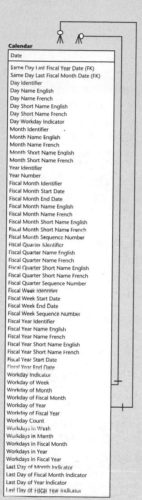

Figure 6.12   A multilingual calendar dimension.

Publishing information in this manner allows the user to select both languages at the same time, allowing the user to produce bilingual reports. This approach can be extended to handle additional languages; however, it would be unusual to require more than three for this type of situation.

(continued)

Combining Languages *(continued)*

We do not recommend that such tables be stored within the data warehouse, but rather that they be generated in the delivery process. Attempting to store different language combinations in the data warehouse can become an excessive maintenance burden. The simple join required to create combinations in the delivery process is not significant and does not justify such denormalization efforts to eliminate the join.

Creating a Multilingual Data Mart

If the mart needs to support different languages for different users, some database systems (such as Oracle) provide tricks to easily create transparent multilingual environments. In Oracle, a single database instance can support multiple schemas. It also allows you to create synonyms in one schema to reference a table in another schema.

As an example, let's say you need to create a data mart that must support both English and French users. Within Oracle you would create three schemas:

- One to hold non-language-sensitive data, such as fact tables
- One to hold English language dimension tables
- One to hold French language dimension tables

The dimension tables in both the English and French schemas would use the same table and column names and the same primary key values so they appear to be the same to the query tools. The language-sensitive schemas would also contain synonyms pointing to the fact and other tables in the common schema. The data delivery process would simply create two versions of the dimension tables, one in each language. User accounts would be established with either the English schema or the French schema as the default schema, based on the user's language preference. When the user logged into the database, the user would be presented with dimensional data in the language of choice.

Case Study: Multiple Fiscal Calendars

The Delicious Food Company (DFC) just announced the acquisition of a large ice cream manufacturer, Ice Cream Enterprises (ICE). It has announced plans to move the existing ice cream business over to ICE and operate ICE as a subsidiary. In subsequent meetings with management, it stated a new requirement to consolidate the revenue data of ICE into the current revenue reports.

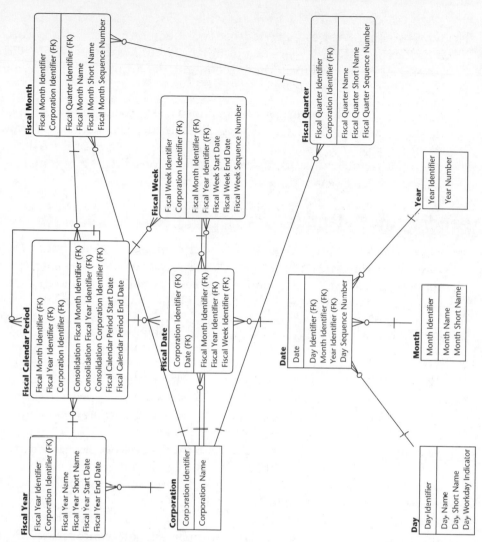

Figure 6.13 Supporting multiple fiscal calendars.

Consolidation would occur with data summarized by fiscal month. ICE operates under a calendar-based fiscal calendar with the fiscal year beginning July 1. Sales booked in a fiscal month by ICE will be reported in the DFC fiscal month designated by Accounting.

The data warehouse must support both calendars and will collect data from both corporations.

Analysis

DFC management has stated that the numbers will be consolidated by fiscal month. This is significant because DFC fiscal months, which operate on a 4-5-4 calendar, do not directly correlate with ICE's calendar, which uses calendar months as its fiscal month. Another consideration is that fiscal years do not match as well. DFC's year runs from January to December, while ICE's year runs from July to June. The Accounting department will determine the relationship between the two.

Use of fiscal months in this way is not unusual in consolidations. Consolidations based on transaction date are very difficult to reconcile since a transaction reported under one fiscal calendar can fall into one of two or three different fiscal months under another fiscal calendar. Consolidating summarized data makes it much easier to directly compare financial reports.

Expanding the Calendar

The basic change to the calendar business model, such as the one in Figure 6.4, is to create a Fiscal Date entity and add a Corporation Identifier to the related fiscal entities. The Fiscal Date entity assumes the relationships to the other fiscal entities, while the Date entity retains the Gregorian calendar relationships. The association between corporate fiscal periods is handled by a recursive relationship in the Fiscal Calendar Period entity. Figure 6.13 shows the revised model.

The revised structure is basically multiple independent calendars. As before, you are best served by creating denormalized tables to support the data delivery process. Figure 6.14 shows how this table would appear. In this example, surrogate keys are in the Calendar table. Date and Corporation Identifier serve as the alternate key. By using a surrogate key, you can use the table and key structure in data marts that support all the corporations. Each fact would be linked to the appropriate dimension row for the corporation involved. Even if your current requirements do not call for deliveries to multicorporate data marts, it is better to design for it up front. If you do not, and the requirement does become a reality, you will be faced with the time-consuming task of reloading data marts in order to maintain key conformance. Note that

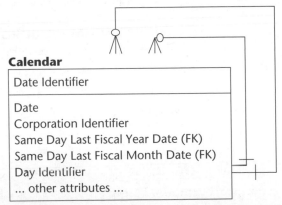

Figure 6.14 Denormalized multiple calendar table.

Figure 6.14 has been abbreviated to show the pertinent differences from the basic denormalized calendar shown in Figure 6.8. This Calendar would contain the same additional attributes shown in Figure 6.8.

Case Study: Seasonal Calendars

GOSH stores would like to plan and analyze sales more effectively. To do so, they wish to be able to report sales by season. Management wishes to have the ability to define any season it wishes as a period of contiguous days. The managers also wish to define seasons as they apply to any level of their store hierarchy. In other words, they wish to be able to vary a season's definition by store or region or have common seasons for all stores.

A season may repeat year over year. A repetition of a season is considered a different instance of the same season. In other words, an analysis of Christmas season would require obtaining data across specified years, all of which identified as belonging to the same season.

There is no existing mechanism in the current data warehouse design or elsewhere to create and maintain these definitions. Management desires that one be developed.

Analysis

Starting with the last point first, it is not uncommon to encounter situations where the data warehouse is asked to support data that is not available anywhere else. It is important to understand that sometimes a data warehouse effort goes beyond data collection and publication and into areas of data creation and maintenance. When such a situation occurs, it is to best to deal with it as a separate application effort. A common approach is to build an application to create and maintain the data separate from the data warehouse, then to treat this data as any other data source being collected into the data warehouse. This is more effort than creating an application that updates the data warehouse tables directly, but provides better control over the introduction of updated information into the data warehouse.

The seasonal calendar definition itself includes the following aspects:

- A season may be defined for a store or a collection of stores based on an existing store hierarchy.
- A season is a contiguous range of dates.
- The same season may be defined differently for different stores.
- A season may reoccur over time. Each repetition is considered a separate instance of the same season. GOSH will use the year the season starts to identify the particular instance.

Seasonal Calendar Structures

Figure 6.15 shows the entities that will support seasonal calendars. There are four entities:

- *Season* defines the names and other descriptive information about each season.
- *Season Schedule* holds the dates for the season.
- *Season Stores* is an associative entity to handle the many-to-many relationship between seasonal schedules and stores.
- The *Store entity* defines information about the stores.

The tolerance for many-to-many relationships between seasons and dates will depend upon their meaning to the business and how they are used. Certainly one could expand the season definitions to include product groupings or other criteria. Knowing sales of women's clothing during baseball season may not be a useful statistic, so such a relationship can be eliminated by further qualifying season definitions by product categories. However, this will probably not eliminate the many-to-many relationship and would limit avenues of analysis. Presuming that certain relationships do not exist prevents the discovery that correlations may, in fact, exist.

Delivering Seasonal Data

Seasonal data needs to be treated independently of the calendar information discussed earlier in this section. This is because any single day may belong to more than one season. Figure 6.16 shows an associative entity, Season Store Date, which should be created to support the delivery process. This entity enumerates the relationships and aids in handling the many-to-many joins that may result with overlapping seasons. Because of the many-to-many relationship that may occur, different delivery strategies are required depending on the delivery target.

If the target is a dimensional data mart, all that is probably necessary is to deliver a season dimension table and the association table as is. It would be up to the user to interpret the results of seasonal analysis with the understanding that sums across seasons are inaccurate due to the many-to-many relationship.

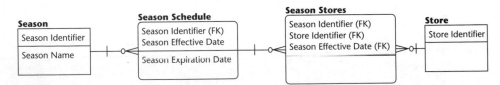

Figure 6.15　Seasonal structures.

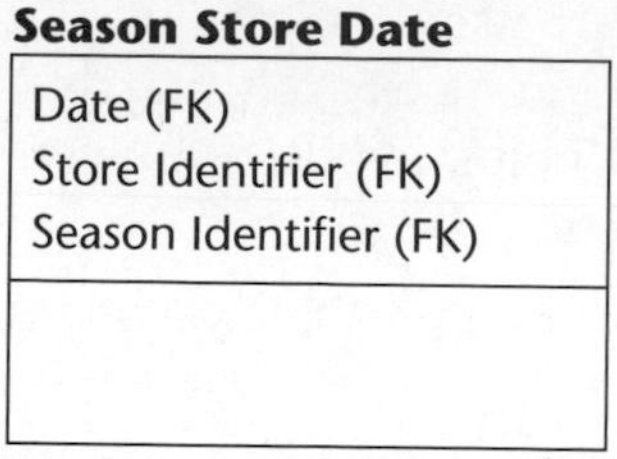

Season Store Date

Date (FK)
Store Identifier (FK)
Season Identifier (FK)

Figure 6.16 Season associations.

If the target is a flat file to an external system or analysis tool, the approach will depend on the business requirement. If the delivery is for a specific season, the many-to-many relationship is eliminated. If not, either the repetition of some data, such as sales, is tolerated or the process must perform some sort of allocation or priority assignment. If allocations or a priority assignment is required, and the delivery is performed frequently, it may make sense to create additional association tables to support these requirements. A process to generate such a table would include an allocation factor or limit the content of the association table to only contain one season association per day based on some business rule that determines its selection. Such a table can be generated when business requirements dictate and used by multiple delivery processes.

Summary

In this chapter, we examined various forms that calendar data can take in your data warehouse. We also introduced the concept of predelivery staging within the data warehouse by creating denormalized tables with precalculated derived values. This technique can significantly reduce the effort necessary to deliver information to external databases and systems. It is particularly useful for calendar data because of the complexity of the derivations and the stability of the data.

We also discussed when surrogate keys are mandatory to eliminate compound primary keys in a delivered dimensional table. These keys should be defined in the denormalized delivery staging table, and the update process for that table should be such that the surrogate key values are stable over time. A stable surrogate is critical to ensure referential integrity in the dimensional data marts.

Another important point is treating date and time of day as separate attributes in your system model, and subsequently, as separate columns in the technical model. Doing so does not diminish the information they represent, but does improve the utility of the attributes. Separating them changes an attribute that represents continuous values to two, each of which represents a quantifiable number of discrete values. This improves their usefulness as primary keys. Furthermore, the separation makes your model more explicit, clearly identifying where date or time of day appear. This helps avoid confusion during model review and data warehouse development.

CHAPTER 7

Modeling Hierarchies

The term "drill down" refers to the act of traversing a hierarchy from higher levels of aggregation to lower levels of detail. Hierarchies are an integral part of any business and a fundamental aspect of data warehousing. Proper collection and publication of hierarchical information and its integration with transactional data is paramount to a successful implementation.

In this chapter, we will look at the use of hierarchies in business and how to effectively model them in the data warehouse. First, we will take a look at the use of hierarchies in business and the different ways they can be represented in the business data model. The transition to the data warehouse model will be examined next. We will then examine the physical deployment options for the data warehouse, including the implications for the derivative data marts, using specific business cases.

Hierarchies in Business

As previously mentioned, hierarchies are integral parts of any business. They are used to define the chain of command, to organize material, products, and customers, and to perform planning, budgeting, and analysis. Without hierarchies, management reports would be overburdened in a morass of detail, making it difficult, if not impossible, to identify where the problems and opportunities lie. We truly would not be able to "see the forest for the trees."

Hierarchies are, for the most part, a natural outgrowth of the business process. As a business expands, it is natural to subdivide and arrange spans of control so that resources can be effectively managed and applied to the tasks at hand. For example, sales territories are defined and clustered under managers who, in turn, report to regional directors; products are grouped into product families, and customer ownership structures are also maintained.

An item may have multiple hierarchies. A product, for example, may have one hierarchy that is based on its physical characteristics and another that is based on its usage characteristics. In addition, there are relationships that appear to be hierarchical from a business perspective, but are not hierarchies in a third normal form model. A sales subgroup may have responsibility for a product, and that sales group may be part of a larger sales group. From a business perspective, this appears to be another hierarchy for product. From a modeling perspective, it is important to recognize that we have a sales responsibility hierarchy, which at its lowest level has a relationship to a product.

It is also common to see other hierarchies combined to perform analysis or generate reports. A commissioned sales force, for example, would have a sales hierarchy reflecting the personnel structure. In addition, the products may be divided into categories reflecting their commission rates. Finally, a third hierarchy may reflect commission multipliers based on volume or dollars sold. All three structures are combined to calculate and report commissions. From a business point of view, this may simply be referred to as the "commission structure" and viewed as a monolithic hierarchy. From a data warehouse modeling perspective, it is actually a combination of normal relationships and hierarchies, and it is up to the data warehouse modeler to detect and dissect such organizations to effectively implement their structures. Within derivative data marts, the relationships and hierarchies may be combined to facilitate business analysis.

Through multiple case studies, this chapter will examine the use of hierarchies in business. Each will present an analysis of the business terminology and its technical implications. Based on this analysis, one or more models will be provided to address the business requirements. But first, let us take a look at the nomenclature surrounding the various forms of hierarchy structures.

The Nature of Hierarchies

Related entities in a data warehouse often exhibit a "parent-child" relationship. In this type of relationship, one parent may have multiple children, and a child can belong to no more than one parent. For example, a person may be assigned to one department, and a department may have many people assigned to it. In this type of "parent-child" relationship, the parent and child do not necessarily have anything in common other than the fact that they are related.

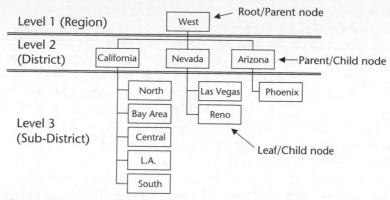

Figure 7.1   Simple hierarchy.

A hierarchy, sometimes called a tree, is a special type of a "parent-child" relationship. In a hierarchy, a child represents a lower level of detail, or granularity, of the parent. This creates a sense of ownership or control that the superior entity (parent) has over the inferior one (child). This section examines the characteristics of hierarchies you will encounter. In general, all hierarchies will fall into one of the categories outlined here.

Another bit of terminology worth mentioning is the set of names for various parts of a hierarchy. Each member in a hierarchy is called a "node." The topmost node in a hierarchy is called the "root node," and each of the bottommost nodes is a "leaf node." A "parent node" is a node that has children, and a "child node" is a node that has a parent. A parent (except a root node) may also be a child, and a child (except a leaf node) may also be a parent. Figure 7.1 shows such a hierarchy. This type of tree structure diagram is commonly called an inverted tree because the root is at the top and leafs are at the bottom. Tree structures and other methods are discussed later in this chapter.

Hierarchy Depth

The depth of a hierarchy refers to the number of generations or levels; that is, parent entities with children, those child entities with children, and so on. The maximum number of levels is the depth of the hierarchy. Figure 7.1 shows an example of a three-level hierarchy.

When it comes to depth, hierarchies fall into two categories: hierarchies of known depth and hierarchies of unknown depth. Most common to business are those of known depth. Sales hierarchies, organizational hierarchies, and product hierarchies are all typically of a known depth. In such hierarchies, the levels of the hierarchy usually have names, such as Region, District, Territory, and Area. The known depth refers to the number of levels between a root node and the leaf nodes. In the simplest (and fortunately most common) case, each level of the hierarchy must be traversed.

Hierarchies and Business Users

The word "hierarchy" means different things to different people. It is up to the analyst to discern what the business users mean when they call something a hierarchy. From a technical standpoint, a hierarchy refers to a strict parent-child relationship, where a child has one and only one parent. While a business user will certainly refer to such relationships as hierarchies or organizations, the business use of the term is far broader. The business user may, in fact, be referring to a collection of independent attributes that have been arranged in some order of precedence.

It is possible to transform a hierarchy into a collection of independent attributes and independent attributes into a hierarchy. This chapter will present some techniques to accomplish this. What you choose to do should be based on a solid understanding of what you are dealing with and what the business requirements demand.

A common example of a hierarchy of unknown depth is a bill of materials. This is a list of raw materials and subassemblies necessary to manufacture an item. At the top of the hierarchy is the finished item, for argument's sake a Boeing 777 aircraft. The next level down may be the major assemblies, such as the airframe, avionics, and cabin. It is reasonable to expect that the complete hierarchy for such a complex machine may exceed 40 to 50 levels deep, and, more than likely, these levels change as refinements in design and options are included or excluded from the manufacture. A major differentiator of this type of hierarchy is that each level does not have a unique description. For example, there may be several nested levels of assemblies and subassemblies, as shown in Figure 7.2.

Hierarchy Parentage

Most hierarchies used in business reporting are simple hierarchies. In a simple hierarchy, every child has one and only one parent. This is desirable for reporting because each child will be counted once in an aggregation. If the child had multiple parents, the same data would be seen under each parent. An example of a hierarchy in which a child can have multiple parents is a company that is partially owned by two companies.

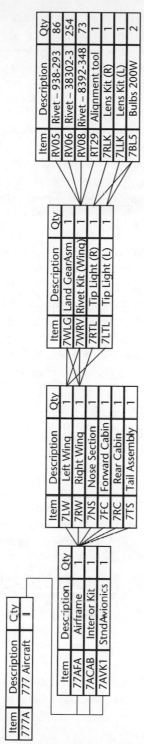

Figure 7.2 Bill of materials.

Our bill of materials is another example of a complex hierarchy. Each child node, representing a subassembly or part, may be used in many different assemblies, represented by the parent node. When a complex hierarchy is used in this type of application, including data about the child under many parents is a desirable trait.

Such complex hierarchies limit your options to represent them in the model. As we will discuss later in this chapter, such hierarchies are stored as recursive tree structures. While a basic recursive tree comprises parent-child relationships, the entity must be expanded to include attributes describing the child's contribution to the parent. These attributes usually contain percentages, so that if a child belongs to two or more parents you can use the percentages to allocate portions of a child's total to each parent. The difficulty and complexity involved in creating these allocation percentages will depend on your business and the availability of such information from your source systems. In the consumer packaged goods business, many different products may be packaged together into a single unit (a variety pack, for example). The business would want the revenue, cost, weight, and other measures allocated back to the respective profit centers based on the sale of the variety pack. Often, a simple unit count, as provided by a bill of materials, is not sufficient to perform such allocations. It may require three or more allocation factors, depending on the nature of the product. If such information is not available from the source system, you will be called upon to calculate these factors based on business rules. Such calculations should be performed when the hierarchy is loaded and the results stored in the data warehouse for use in future deliveries.

Allocation Factors

In this chapter, we discuss the use of factors to perform data allocations. A factor is a numeric value with which you multiply another value to obtain an allocated value. Factors are stored as fractional values. For example, 50 percent would be stored as 0.5.

When factors are used in a hierarchy to allocate contribution, the factors are multiplied as you traverse up the hierarchical relationship. For example, if A is the parent of B and B is the parent of C, and B contributes 50 percent of its revenue to A and C contributes 30 percent of its revenue to B, we can calculate C's revenue contribution to A by multiplying the two factors: 0.5 * 0.3 = 0.15. From this we know that C contributes 15 percent of its revenue to A.

When creating the physical schema, be sure you allocate sufficient decimal precision to factor columns to allow for multiplication of many fractional values.

Once the allocation factors are calculated and stored in the recursive tree structure, you can then apply the denormalization and flattening techniques described in this chapter. The flattened structure will contain a single set of allocation factors, calculated by multiplying, rather than summing, the factors from each level in the hierarchy.

Hierarchy Texture

A hierarchy's texture is another distinguishing characteristic. When discussing texture, a hierarchy is described as being balanced or ragged. An alternate term used for texture is sparsity; however, this term more accurately describes ragged hierarchies with a fixed number of levels where there are missing nodes at some levels. Not all ragged hierarchies will contain missing nodes. In this section, we will describe each form.

Balanced Hierarchies

Balanced hierarchies are full through all levels. By full, we mean that all leaves exist at the lowest level in the hierarchy, and every parent is one level removed from the child. For example, if you have a sales hierarchy made up of regions, districts, territories, and customers, then every region will have one or more districts, every district will have one or more territories, and every territory will have one or more customers.

Balanced hierarchies, also referred to as smooth hierarchies, are always of a known, fixed depth. Because of this, there are a number of different methods that can be used to represent balanced hierarchies in the data warehouse. The variety of choices available allows you to select the most effective structure for the business use at hand.

Ragged Hierarchies

Ragged hierarchies are hierarchies of varying depth. Take, for example, a sales hierarchy that divides the sales force and customers into regions, districts, and territories. Imagine that you also have one big customer that accounts for a sizable percentage of your business. So much so, in fact, that this customer has a sales group dedicated to it and the customer is treated as its own region. This customer would be the child of a region, with no relationship to a district or territory. In addition, since the business deals with both large and small customers, some of the large ones are handled at the district level. Since this hierarchy has a fixed number of levels, it may also be described as a sparse hierarchy because, in some cases, intermediate levels are missing.

Such a hierarchy would be considered a ragged hierarchy because the depth—the number of levels from the root to a leaf—is not the same. While the customer is always at the leaf level, the very large customers may appear one level down from the top of the hierarchy, while smaller customers may be at three or four levels from the top.

History

The historical nature of the data warehouse adds another consideration when it comes to hierarchies. Within a hierarchy, there are two aspects that may change over time. There may be changes in the entity itself, such as when information about a sales region changes, or there may be changes in the hierarchical relationships, such as when a sales district is assigned to a different sales region. The treatment in the data warehouse is affected by the relative frequency of the two types of historical changes. In Figure 7.3, we show the hierarchy with no history (point-in-time view), the hierarchy with either entity changes or relationship changes, and a merged table that could be created in addition to the base entity structures (as described in Step 6 in Chapter 4). The merged table becomes a conforming (slowly changing) dimension of the sales hierarchy, and it can be used to create either a slowly changing dimension or a current view dimension in a derivative data mart.

Summary of Hierarchy Types

We've described several types of hierarchies, and the data warehouse model must be capable of handling each and every one of these. The hierarchy types are:

- Balanced tree structure, in which the hierarchy has a consistent number of levels, each of which can be named, with each child having one parent at the level immediately above it.

- Variable depth tree structure, such as a bill of materials, in which the number of levels is inconsistent and in which each level cannot be named.

- Ragged tree structure, in which the hierarchy has a maximum number of levels, each of which can be named, with each child having a parent at a level not necessarily immediately above it.

- Complex tree structure, in which a child may have multiple parents.

- Multiple tree structures for the same leaf node.

We will now deal with each of these situations through case studies.

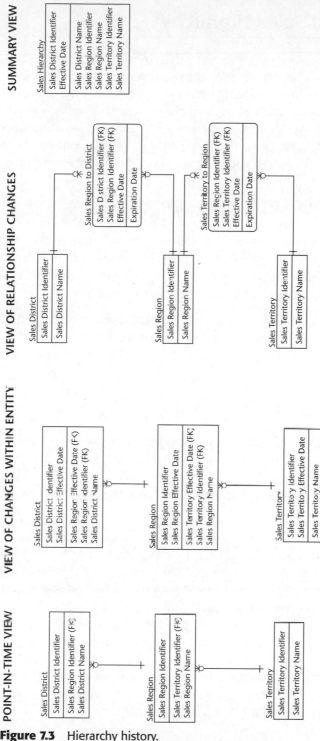

Figure 7.3 Hierarchy history.

Case Study: Retail Sales Hierarchy

Our retail chain operates stores around the country. The sales management organization has the country divided into four regions. Each region is further divided into districts, with a district manager overseeing a number of stores. Departments subdivide each store, which represent a collection of similar products, such as women's clothing, children's clothing, sporting goods, and so forth. The products assigned to a department are the same for every store. Because the sizes of the stores vary, not all stores have all departments.

The store hierarchy, regions, and districts, remains fairly stable. The organization is reviewed once a year to determine if regions and districts should be created or consolidated. Such changes always occur after the close of a fiscal quarter and are effective immediately. Other changes involve the opening or closing of stores, which can occur at any time. The design should also take into consideration management's plans to expand internationally. This may introduce a new level to the hierarchy at some time in the future.

Sales reports will be generated using the current hierarchy at the time of the sale. However, during the annual review, management would like to review proposed changes using the current active hierarchy and the planned future hierarchy.

Analysis of the Hierarchy

Figure 7.4 depicts the hierarchy as depicted by the business. At first glance, it appears it is a six-level hierarchy, consisting of corporation, region, district, store, department, and product. However, when this structure is defined in the business model shown in Figure 7.5, the true nature of the relationships becomes readily apparent.

The business model requires an associative entity, Store Department, to resolve the many-to-many relationship between stores and departments. The existence of this entity makes it clear that we are not dealing with a single hierarchy, but rather with two independent hierarchies. The first is the relationship between product and department, and the second, the store-district-region-corporation hierarchy. This associative entity is not part of the hierarchies. It is reasonable to expect that transactional data will reference a product and a store. The transaction itself is sufficient to associate the two hierarchies. However, the associative entity is useful to support analysis or data delivery functions that do not involve transactional data. For example, the data warehouse may need to deliver a list of all stores and their departments.

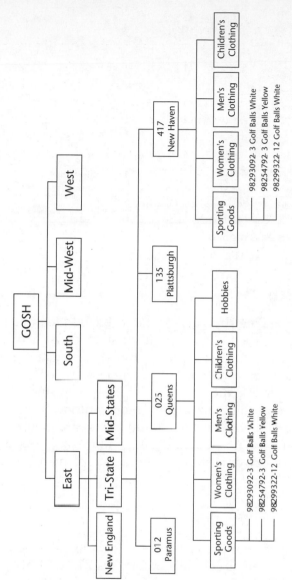

Figure 7.4 Sales hierarchy.

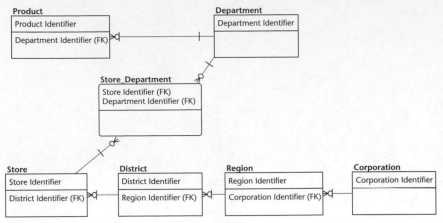

Figure 7.5 Sales hierarchy business model.

Implementing the Hierarchies

There are two basic physical data structures that may be used to implement a hierarchy: a recursive tree structure or a nonrecursive tree structure, also known as a flattened tree structure. A recursive tree data structure must be used for hierarchies of unknown depth, because that is the only structure capable of properly representing such a hierarchy. However, since this case deals with a hierarchy of known depth, there is more latitude. The flattened tree data structure is simpler to implement and much easier to query, making it the preferred structure for a data warehouse. We will use a flattened structure for this case. Recursive tree data structures will be presented later in this chapter.

Flattened Tree Hierarchy Structures

A flattened (tree) hierarchy is a simple structure that arranges the hierarchical elements horizontally, in different columns, rather than rows. This type of structure can only be used with hierarchies of known depth. A flattened hierarchy is modeled as a chain of normalized nested tables (3NF), as shown in Figure 7.6.

Third Normal Form Flattened Tree Hierarchy

Figure 7.6 shows the stores and product hierarchies as a series of normalized hierarchical tables related to the sale. This follows the business model depicted in Figure 7.5. The diagram includes the sales transaction entity as a point of reference to show how the hierarchies would be applied. The sales transaction would contain foreign keys referencing the product sold and the store where

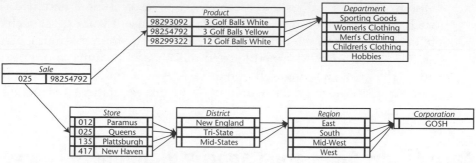

Figure 7.6   A 3NF flattened tree hierarchy.

the sale took place. The product entity has a foreign key to the department it is assigned to. The store has a foreign key to the assigned district, which, in turn, has a foreign key to its assigned region.

This type of structure is very easy to query using common SQL implementations. Each level of the hierarchy is directly accessible as columns, allowing the data to be sorted using attributes of the hierarchy entities. Also, the foreign key chain enforces strict traversal of the hierarchy.

There are also a number of limitations to this structure. A change to the hierarchy structure, such as the addition or removal of a level, will require both a change to the data and a change to the database schema. Because of the strict relationships enforced by the foreign key chain, inclusion of new hierarchy levels will force users to modify all standard reports that use the hierarchy. This structure cannot support a ragged hierarchy very well since the structure requires an entity at each level. To support a ragged structure, you would need to create empty entity rows specific to the particular branch of the tree so the path from leaf to root is correct. This can become a real challenge to maintain.

Figure 7.7 shows the effect of adding a new level, Country, to the hierarchy. A new entity is created and is placed between region and corporation in the foreign key chain. The corporation foreign key is removed from the region entity and replaced with a country foreign key. The country entity is linked to the corporation through the corporation foreign key.

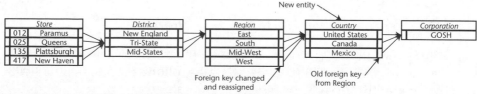

Figure 7.7   Altering a 3NF flattened tree hierarchy.

Due to the complexities that hierarchy changes present, a flattened structure such as this is not optimal for the data warehouse if you expect such changes to occur frequently enough to become an issue in your environment. A recursive tree structure, described later in this chapter, is much more flexible and adaptable to such changes. If you are able, you should implement a recursive tree structure in the data warehouse and deliver flattened structures to the data marts.

Case Study: Sales and Capacity Planning

Our packaged goods manufacturer produces a sales plan annually. This plan is reviewed and adjusted quarterly based on changes in market demands and requirements. The sales plan is used to plan production, warehouse capacity, and transportation requirements. The sales plan is based on three entities: the product, the customer, and time. In the operational system, the customer entity is subdivided by type. There are ship-to customers that represent delivery locations, sold-to customers that represent buyers, planning customers, and so forth. Monthly sales volumes are projected at various levels in the customer and product hierarchies. The company operates a number of distribution centers to support distribution channels based on product storage requirements (frozen, refrigerated, and ambient). Their customers are retail chains that have a number of delivery locations (ship-to customers), with each location specific to a distribution channel. In other words, the customer may have multiple locations to receive frozen goods and other locations to receive refrigerated and ambient goods. Each of these customer ship-to locations is assigned to a distribution channel and preferred distribution center that service it.

At the lowest level of the product hierarchy is the Stock Keeping Unit (SKU). This represents a specific variation of a standard product. These variations are simply packaging differences to accommodate special seasons and promotions, such as contests. The standard product and its variations each have a unique internal SKU, or material ID, but share a common retail Universal Product Code (UPC). In addition, there is commonality among standard products as well. The same chocolate bar may be produced in four different sizes. Each size is a different standard product, with a different UPC. The planners do most planning by product group, a collection of all sizes and variants of the same basic product, in order to project future revenues and promotion expenses. For certain products, they will also plan at the standard product level. No planning is performed at the SKU level; however, each SKU is assigned to a distribution channel based on its storage requirements. Figure 7.8 shows the product hierarchy.

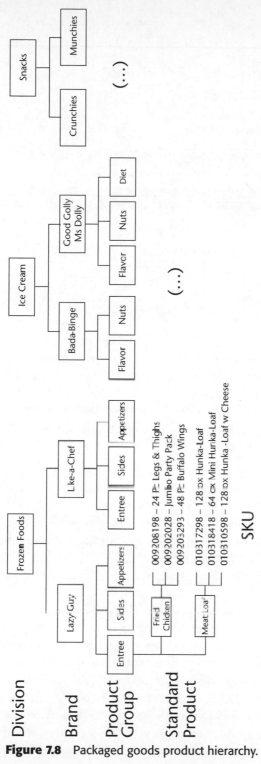

Figure 7.8 Packaged goods product hierarchy.

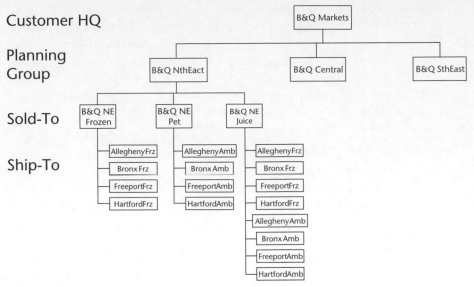

Figure 7.9 Packaged goods customer hierarchy.

The lowest level of the customer's distribution hierarchy is the ship-to-customer location. These are grouped under sold-to customers, which represent the customer's purchasing representatives. These are further grouped into planning customers, which is the lowest level at which sales plans are estimated. Figure 7.9 shows the full hierarchy. Capacity planning is handled by another system, which allocates to plants and distribution centers the sales plan based upon previous sales history.

The planners wish to use the data warehouse to support various levels of analysis. They wish to monitor the plan against actual sales in order to adjust both the sales and capacity plans to reflect recent experience. So that the comparisons are meaningful, the reports must reflect the hierarchies that were in effect at the time the plan was published. Both the product and customer are simple hierarchies. Each child has only one parent.

Analysis

There are a number of aspects to consider concerning how the hierarchies are to be used in this application. First, and most important, there is a need to compare values that are provided at different levels in the hierarchies: a sale, which is collected at the transaction level and is specific to a SKU, sold-to customer, and ship-to address; and the sales plan which is specified at a higher level in both the product and customer hierarchies. Second, the data warehouse will most likely be called on to provide sales history to the capacity-planning system. The feed would be required to tie the detailed history to the higher-level hierarchy entities where the planning has taken place. It may even be necessary to calculate the allocation percentages. Third, while planning is done at an intersection of the customer and product hierarchies, different user groups require the numbers to be reported using one side of the hierarchy tree. In the case study, the sales group is interested in reporting based on the customer sales hierarchy. It can be presumed that other groups have similar requirements using other hierarchies.

Because sales and the sales plan exist at different levels of detail, there are two options available for reporting sales against the sales plan. Either summarize the lower level data (sales) to the higher-level data (the sales plan) or allocate the sales plan to the sales data level. The business managers feel that allocating the sales plan to such a low level of detail is of no real value. Instead, there is a need to summarize the detailed sales data to match the level of the sales plan. The simple aggregation of the sales data to the sales plan should occur as part of the delivery process using the hierarchy to drive the aggregation. If, however, the decision is to allocate the sales plan to a lower level, you may wish to consider storing the allocations within the data warehouse. This decision would be based on the complexity of the allocation, the amount of data involved, how frequently the allocation needs to be performed, and the number of data marts or other applications requiring this allocation. If the allocation results are used frequently but are relatively stable, you may reduce delivery effort by storing the allocation results in the data warehouse. If the sales plan or the basis for allocations change almost as often as the need to delivery it, there would be little benefit to store the results. Instead, handle the allocation in the delivery process.

Further examination of the hierarchy provided by the business shows that the ship-to customer may be a child of more than one sold-to customer. The reason for this is simple. The sold-to customer represents a buyer within the customer's organization, while a ship-to customer is a physical location that receives the goods. In our example of B&Q Markets, buyers are organized by types of products that are shipped to many of the same locations, which are B&Q Market's distribution centers. With additional investigation, it is found that this sold-to/ship-to relationship is primarily for operational control and not necessary for analysis. In fact, when an order is processed, both the buyer (sold-to customer) and shipping destination (ship-to customer) are recorded in the system. Both will be received in the transactional data feed. From this, we determine that the ship-to customer is not needed in the hierarchy to analyze sales. However, there is a desire to produce customer lists without transactional data using the full hierarchy. Later, we will show how to use different parts of the hierarchy for different classes of queries. Another issue is the mention of the preferred distribution center assigned to each ship-to customer address. It is often the case that from a business point of view, users may think of this as being part of the "hierarchy." This is natural and should be expected.

However, it is up to you as the modeler to not confuse your design. The assigned distribution center is an independent attribute of the ship-to customer as these are assigned based on the geographic location of the delivery point regardless of the customer hierarchy structure. It is important to identify such cases and avoid attempts to include such attributes in a hierarchical structure.

Later discussions with the operational system support staff revealed the product hierarchy is maintained as a flattened structure, while the customer hierarchy is a recursive tree structure. In the next sections, we will discuss the most effective way to store these hierarchies. Another challenge we will examine is creating a data structure that will bridge data stored at different levels of summarization. In this case, tying detail sales data to the sales plan.

Figure 7.10 shows the complete business model representation of these entities. In the remainder of this section, we will examine how this model is implemented and used within the data warehouse. We will first look at the product hierarchy data feed and the processing issues it presents.

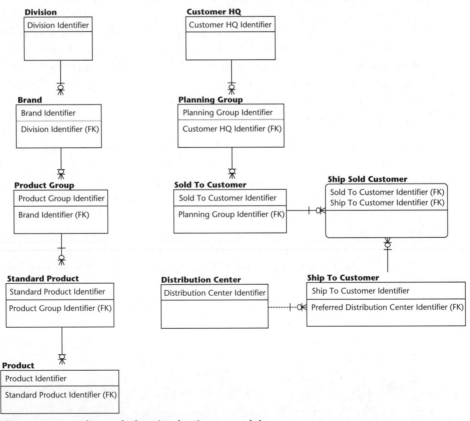

Figure 7.10 Sales and planning business model.

The Product Hierarchy

In this section, we will look at the issues involved in receiving a flattened (non-recursive) denormalized hierarchy from the operational system. Denormalized flat hierarchy structures, represented as a series of columns or a single column, do not inherently enforce any business rules that may exist. If the data is physically stored in this manner in the source system, it would be up to the source system's application logic or manual effort by those maintaining the data to enforce whatever hierarchy rules that exist. This can lead to incorrect data that can materially effect how the data warehouse should receive and store the data.

Storing the Product Hierarchy

The product hierarchy is received from the source system as a single column. The column's value contains formatted text where portions of the text represent different parts of the hierarchy. For this example, the division is stored in positions 1 to 2, the brand in positions 3 to 5, the product group in positions 6 to 9, and the standard product code in positions 10 to 14.

Receiving hierarchies in this manner from packaged software products is not unusual. Like the data warehouse, application software developers have the option to represent hierarchies as recursive trees or flattened structures. Those that implement them as flattened structures run into a problem with hierarchy depth. They wish to build flexibility into the application by allowing the end users the ability to define their own hierarchy, but how do you do that if the hierarchy must be of known depth to fit into the flat structure? Do you define a schema with some large number of columns, say 10, to allow a user to specify up to 10 levels in the hierarchy? What if the user needs 11? What if he or she only uses three? How does the application deal with the other columns?

A common solution is to simply provide one large text column. The user would then define the hierarchy levels and assign positions in this text field to hold the code value for each element of the hierarchy. This allows the end user to define as many levels as necessary, with the only restriction being the combined width of the code values. This is a good, workable solution for an application system, but a bad design for a data warehouse.

As a function of the extract, transform, and load process in the data warehouse, the column must be interpreted to derive meaning from it. This interpretation should be performed up front in the data load process to create a structure like the one shown in Figure 7.11. This, of course, fixes the structure to known entities and a known depth. By breaking the column into its components and defining entities for each component, you clarify the model and simplify the use of the data.

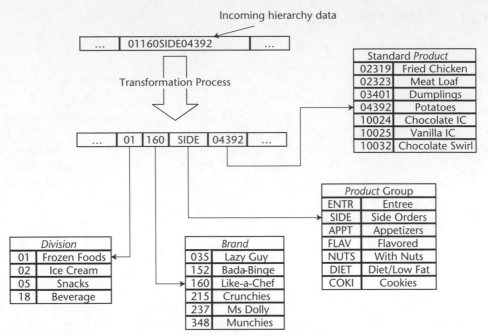

Figure 7.11 Transforming the flattened hierarchy column.

The resulting structure is in 2NF. This differs from the 3NF structure discussed earlier by the fact that the 2NF structure does not enforce true hierarchical relationships. In fact, each attribute in the hierarchy is independent of the others. In the sample data, product group codes are shared across brands. Since the model does not enforce relationships between the entities, there is no guarantee that a child has one and only one parent. Without this guarantee, we cannot generate the types of reports required by the business. We need to perform additional transformations of the data to convert the complex hierarchy into a simple hierarchy and store it in 3NF.

Simplifying Complex Hierarchies

In this example, we have seen that the danger of receiving a denormalized flattened hierarchy is there may be no guarantee that this is not a complex hierarchy. A complex hierarchy is one where a child may have multiple parents. As the product hierarchy in Figure 7.8 shows, common product groups are shared among different brands. For example, both Lazy Guy and Like-A-Chef brands have an Entrée product group. But, it is also true that leaves of this hierarchy, the products themselves, have unique SKUs and that the SKUs that are Lazy Guy entrees are mutually exclusive of SKUs that are Like-A-Chef entrees. So, what we have is an identity crisis, where two different product groups share the same identifier.

Retaining Ancestry

To avoid a complex hierarchy in this example, the Lazy Guy Entrée product group must have a different business key than the Like-A-Chef Entrée product group. Where such a key does not exist, it becomes the responsibility of the data warehouse process to create such a key. The easiest technique to do this is to prefix the code with the codes of its parents. This becomes the business key. As Figure 7.12 shows, each child becomes framed within the context of its ancestry. Conceptually, this makes the children dependent (as opposed to independent) entities.

As the figure shows, this is only necessary for the hierarchy entities. It is reasonable to expect that the SKU is unique and unambiguous. It is not necessary to create a new key for the SKU.

Here are some tips for use when building the 3NF tables:

- Use a surrogate key as the primary key. This will reduce the size of the key, particularly in foreign key references. Use the concatenated business key as an alternate key.

- Retain the original code value if they have business meaning and are unique within a source system. This is necessary to update attributes since the source system would provide such data using this value. Create an inversion index on this column, because duplicate values will exist. Updates should modify all rows with that value.

Interface Issues

A complex hierarchy raises specific issues that must be supported in the data feeds received by the data warehouse. The business case stated that most planning occurs by product group. Yet, if the code ENTR represents the Entrée product group, then the question becomes, "Which brand's product group?" Retaining ancestry in the key, as described in the previous section, will resolve the ambiguity in the data warehouse. However, the data feed for the sales plan must also provide the same ancestry data so that it properly identifies the proper product group.

Without the necessary ancestry information, it is not possible to properly associate the sale plan with sales. If, as is the case here, the planning system is separate from the operational system, you will need to verify that such information is available. How such information is provided will depend on the environment and may require some transformation before is can be loaded into the data warehouse. The simplest is to receive a clean concatenated key that matches the ancestry business key described earlier. Or, you may receive a SKU for one of the products in the group. In such a case, you would use the hierarchy keys defined for that SKU. Regardless of how it is received, it is critical that data feeds, which provide information related to a hierarchy, unambiguously reference that hierarchy.

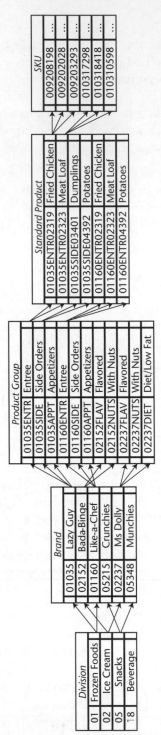

Figure 7.12 Adding ancestry to the business key.

Bridging Levels

An aspect of the reporting requirements is to summarize detailed sales data to the same level as the sales plan numbers. A table that matches the detail level keys with the hierarchy level keys can best handle this. Figure 7.13 shows an example. In this example, there is a sales plan for the Side Dish product group of the Like-A-Chef brand. Sales, recorded at the SKU level, contain many rows for many different cookie SKUs. The bridge table contains rows with pairs of keys. The column on the left contains the product group key, and the column on the right contains the SKU key. A query that joins the sales plan to actual sales through this bridge will naturally roll up actual sales to the same level of detail as the plan. This allows such summarization to occur on the fly using simple SQL, without the need to perform a recursive transversal of a hierarchy tree. This structure would be created in the data warehouse to aid in the delivery of combined sales and sales plan data. In this situation, building such a structure is optional. The existing relationships between Product Group, Standard Product, and Product (SKU), as depicted in the business model (see Figure 7.10), are sufficient to resolve the relationship. The advantage of this structure is that it reduces the join path required to associate the data. This may significantly reduce the time to deliver such information to the marts and other external applications.

However, one of the issues we face is that sales plan is not always by product group. In fact, a plan may be created at any level in the product hierarchy. How can a bridge be constructed so that detailed sales data can roll to the sales plan, regardless of the level of the plan? A more generic solution is in order, and the solution lies in addressing two problems: keys and tables.

The issue with keys is that you have a number of different entities: product group, brand, SKU, which all have different key formats and content. Also, because of the way the hierarchy structure is received from the source system, there is no guarantee that a business key value is unique across each entity. There is nothing, other than internal business rules, to stop a business key for a brand from being the same as a business key for a product group. In the bridge, we want one column for the parent key, and we want that key value to be unique. The solution here is to use surrogate keys. With a surrogate, all keys will have the same format, and the data warehouse load process can control the value assignment, ensuring uniqueness.

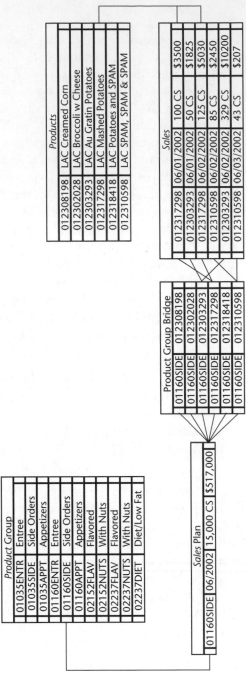

Figure 7.13   Bridging a hierarchy.

Tables are another matter. The notion that each entity must have its own table makes implementing the bridge and rolled-up reports impractical. The sales plan table would require a foreign key to each entity's table that may be the level of the plan. One would presume in such a structure that only one of the keys would be populated, say the foreign key to the brand entity if the plan is at the brand level, and the other keys would be null. If the bridge mimicked this structure, a large union query would be necessary to pull and combine plan and sales data one level at a time. The solution is to fold the hierarchical entities into the same table as the products. The hierarchy and the SKUs would share the same surrogate primary key, ensuring uniqueness. The table's business key would be expanded to include a row type code to identify SKU versus product group versus brand, so that rows can be identified, and business key values need only be unique within row type.

When entities are combined in this manner, it is important to identify those attributes that are common across entity types. Certainly, the primary key, the row type, and the business key are all attributes that apply to all rows. In addition, at least one descriptive text column should be used in common so that any query can retrieve a description of the business key regardless of the row type.

With these two issues resolved, building the bridge structure is simply a matter of creating bridge row pairs for every possible parent of a SKU. In the case, of the product hierarchy, each SKU will require five rows in this table, one for each level in the hierarchy representing the division-SKU, brand-SKU, product group-SKU, standard product-SKU and SKU-SKU relationships. The latter, often referred to as an identity relationship, covers situations where a plan is done at the SKU level, allowing a SKU-level plan to join with SKU-level sales data.

Figure 7.14 shows how this may appear in the data warehouse. Notice that the sales plan contains a single surrogate foreign key reference to the Product table. Since Product contains all the hierarchy elements, this one key is sufficient regardless of the level of the plan.

Updating the Bridge

In addition to the parent-child foreign keys, the bridge should also contain effective and expiration dates to maintain historical perspective of the relationship. In addition, a Boolean (yes/no) column should be provided to simplify isolating the most current relationship. This provides a value that can be indexed to rapidly access the current version of a relationship. It also may contain a level ID that represents the level of the parent. This value is not necessary when using the bridge in a query, but it does assist in updating the bridge. This level ID can be the level number, or better yet, a type code that identifies the parent entity. The latter is preferable for updating because this code will remain consistent even if the hierarchy structure, and the number of levels, changes.

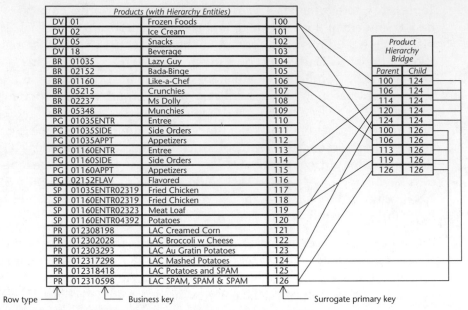

Figure 7.14 A generic bridge structure.

Updates to the bridge need to be applied from the perspective of the child key. This is because in a simple hierarchy, the child has a single ancestral line, making it a consistent key for locating parents that need to be changed. Looking at it another way, assume that there is a row in the bridge with parent, A, and child, X. A change in the hierarchy assigns child X to parent B. Unless you know the pervious parent, you would not be able to locate the A-X relationship, unless you located it using the child key. So, locating the current relationship for child X will find the A-X relationship.

Update the A-X row by setting the current indicator column to false and the expiration date to the effective date of the new relationship. Note that the primary key for this table needs to be the parent key, child key, and the effective date because it is possible that over time the same parent-child relationship may have been superseded then reinstated, resulting in multiple rows for the same parent-child relationship. Including the effective date will ensure a unique key. The next step would be to insert a new row for the B-X relationship, setting the current flag to true, the effective date to the appropriate date, and the expiration date to some large value, such as December 31, 9999.

The Customer Hierarchy

The customer hierarchy is received from the source system as a recursive tree data structure. The customer entities are received in a single feed with role

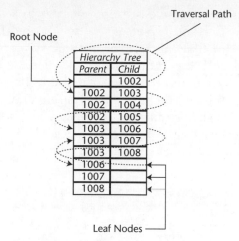

Customers		
1002	HQ	B&Q Markets
1003	PG	B&Q Nth East
1004	PG	B&Q Central
1005	PG	B&Q Sth East
1006	SO	B&Q NE Frozen
1007	SO	B&Q NE Pet
1008	SO	B&Q NE Juice
1009	SH	Allegheny Frz
1010	SH	Bronx Frz
1011	SH	Freeport Frz
1012	SH	Hartford Frz
1013	SH	Allegheny Amb
1014	SH	Bronx Amb
1015	SH	Freeport Amb
1016	SH	Hartford Amb

Figure 7.15   A simple tree data structure.

identifiers that identify Customer HQ, Planning Group, Sold-To, and Ship-To roles. Let's first take a look at the tree data structure and then examine how it is best implemented in the data warehouse.

The Recursive Hierarchy Tree

A recursive tree data structure is the most elegant and flexible data structure for storing a hierarchy. Any type of hierarchy can be stored in a recursive tree. What is more, the method to traverse the hierarchy is the same regardless of its type. But, in spite of its universal applicability, a recursive tree structure has some drawbacks when used in a data warehouse.

In its simplest form, a recursive tree data structure is a table with two columns: a parent foreign key and a child foreign key. This defines the basic parent-child relationship common to all hierarchies. Figure 7.15 shows an example of a simple recursive tree structure for the customer hierarchy shown in Figure 7.10.

The data table on the left shows how these foreign keys would be stored in the recursive tree structure. Root nodes, the topmost entities in the hierarchy, are identified by their null parent foreign key values. This is a common convention as the root node, by definition, is a node with no parent. The leaf nodes, which are nodes with no children, are represented by null child foreign key values.

To report the hierarchy structure from a recursive tree, the query must traverse the tree using a recursive algorithm. A recursive algorithm is a coded routine that calls itself. To understand what this means, imagine the hierarchy tree as a lot of trees. If you removed the top level of a hierarchy diagram, you would be left with a number of smaller, independent hierarchy diagrams. Repeated trimming of the top level creates more, smaller hierarchies, until you finally have only a collection of leaves. The recursive process operates in a similar manner. It starts at the root of the tree and traverses the tree. It does this by going to the first child and traversing that child's tree, and so on. It continues going down levels until it hits a leaf. It then returns to the immediate parent and goes to the next child for that parent and traverses that child's tree. When all the children are exhausted, it returns to the immediate parent and goes to its next child. Below is an example of such a routine. As you can see, the actual pseudocode is much smaller than the paragraph needed to describe it.

```
Traverse_Tree (node)
      If node is null then return.
    Output node.
    For each node.child {Traverse_Tree (child)}
/*For each child, traverse the child's tree. The act of a routine call-
ing itself is called recursion.*/
    return.
```

Some database systems, such as Oracle, provide a SQL extension that performs a recursive tree traversal within a SELECT statement. Alternately, some OLAP tools do recognize and work with hierarchies stored as recursive tree structures. Such a tool would be able to query directly from the structure without modification. But these solutions may present limitations or performance issues. A generic solution that works with any database or tool is to publish the hierarchy to the marts by exploding the tree. This technique will be addressed later in this chapter.

As mentioned earlier, a recursive tree structure is basically a pair of foreign key references. One key points to the parent entity, and the other points to the child entity. For this to work, both the parent and child entities must reside in the same table. If this were not the case, both the table structure and the queries to support it would be a mess. Using the customer hierarchy as an example, Figure 7.16 illustrates the situation. In the example, there are separate tables for each entity: Customer HQ, Planning Group, Sold-To Customer, and Ship-To Customer. Since any row in the tree may reference any one of the tables, eight foreign keys are required, one parent key and one child key to each table. Each relationship is optional because only one parent and one child key is populated on each row. This is a bad structure that is almost impossible to query. Furthermore, the number of foreign keys increases proportionally to the depth of the tree, making it impossible to represent a tree of unknown depth, something a properly implemented recursive tree structure is very capable of doing.

The solution to this problem is the same as that we discussed for the bridge earlier in this chapter—that is, to store the hierarchical elements in the same table as the lowest-level elements. In this case, all would be folded into a single customer table. This would require the addition of a row type column as

Hierarchy Tree							
Parent Key				Child Key			
HQ	PG	SO	SH	HQ	PG	SO	SH
				1002			
1002					1003		
1002					1004		
1002					1005		
	1003					1006	
	1003					1007	
	1003					1008	
		1006					
		1007					
		1008					

Customer Headquarter	
1002	B&Q Markets

Customer Planning Group	
1003	B&Q Nth East
1004	B&Q Central
1005	B&Q Sth East

Sold-To Customer	
1006	B&Q NE Frozen
1007	B&Q NE Pet
1008	B&Q NE Juice

Ship-To Customer	
1009	Allegheny Frz
1010	Bronx Frz
1011	Freeport Frz
1012	Hartford Frz
1013	Allegheny Amb
1014	Bronx Amb
1015	Freeport Amb
1016	Hartford Amb

Figure 7.16 A tree with separate entities.

part of the natural key for both row identification and to avoid possible duplicate keys, should a planning group or HQ code be the same. In fact, you will probably find that if your operational system uses a recursive tree structure to represent a hierarchy, the data structures in the system have already taken this into account and store all the hierarchy elements in the same table.

The challenge with a recursive tree structure is the maintenance of the hierarchical elements. It is possible that the same entity may appear in multiple hierarchies. For example, a manufacturer may have manufacturing divisions appearing in a product cost hierarchy and sales divisions appearing in a customer revenue hierarchy. In addition, financial hierarchies that include all divisions may exist. In the approach described, the hierarchy entities would coexist in the same table as the detailed entities. In this case, divisions would appear in the product table to support the product cost hierarchy, the customer table to support the customer revenue hierarchy, and the accounts table for the financial hierarchy. There are two approaches to deal with this situation. One approach is to create a table for the entity, such as a Division table, then use an insert/update trigger on the table to propagate the transaction to all tables where the same data resides. In this case, the operational interface would only maintain the single table. The other approach is to update each table individually with the same information. The trigger approach has the advantage of encapsulating all updates into a single transaction, but it does "hide" the replication from the load process. In either case, you do not need to be concerned with the hierarchies themselves. You are simply replicating information about the division to tables that need to contain it. You would always replicate all divisions to all tables. It does not matter what role a particular division plays, because the hierarchy structures would only reference those divisions necessary for its purpose. While you may be concerned that this approach causes data replication, the reality is that such situations are fairly uncommon and do not involve a lot of data. Both approaches will work and can be easy to implement. The choice is a matter of style and fitting the solution into your system environment.

Using Recursive Trees in the Data Mart

Unless your OLAP or reporting tool can work directly with recursive tree structures, it is often not feasible to deliver such recursive structures to a mart. This section will examine the issues with recursive structures as they apply to reporting, and present methods to deliver such data to the data marts.

Sorting from a Recursive Tree

There are a number of shortcomings that make a recursive tree structure unsuitable for a data mart. One shortcoming of the basic recursive tree structure is that there is no sense of sequence. Traversing the tree is simply a matter of moving from parent to child to parent, and so on. Each query to retrieve a parent's children returns them is no particular order, resulting in report sequences that may vary from run to run. SQL extensions to traverse these structures are not much help, since they return a single set of a fixed number of columns. For example, the Oracle extension returns the parent, child, and level number. This information, by itself, is not sufficient to sort the data beyond the visit sequence returned by the query. To sort the data, you have two basic options: a recursive sort or building a sort key. In a recursive sort, the process would sort a parent's children before moving down to the child and sorting the child's children. To build a sort key, you create a single string with a concatenation of sort values that follow the traversal path from the root to the leaf. The resulting string would appear similar to a directory path and file-name. Sorting on this string would produce a properly sequenced report. Presuming that the desired sort is by description, Figure 7.17 shows how that result set would look based on the customer hierarchy tree shown in Figure 7.15. Neither is possible without somebody writing code outside of SQL (or your database vendor providing such functionality).

Sorted Customer Hierarchy			
Key	Type	Description	Sort Key
1002	HQ	B&Q Markets	B&Q Markets
1004	PG	B&Q Central	B&Q Markets/B&Q Central
1003	PG	B&Q Nth East	B&Q Markets/B&Q Nth East
1006	SO	B&Q NE Frozen	B&Q Markets/B&Q Nth East/B&Q NE Frozen
1008	SO	B&Q NE Juice	B&Q Markets/B&Q Nth East/B&Q NE Juice
1007	SO	B&Q NE Pet	B&Q Markets/B&Q Nth East/B&Q NE Pet
1005	PG	B&Q Sth East	B&Q Markets/B&QSth East

Figure 7.17 A sorted hierarchy.

Exploded Customer Hierarchy										Customers		
Parent	Child	Level	Distance	Bottom	Seq	Eff Dt	Exp Dt		1002	HQ	B&Q Markets
1002	1002	1	0	N	1	...	...		1003	PG	B&Q Nth East
1002	1003	1	1	N	3	...	...		1004	PG	B&Q Central
1002	1004	1	1	N	2	...	...		1005	PG	B&Q Sth East
1002	1005	1	1	N	7	...	...		1006	SO	B&Q NE Frozen
1002	1006	1	2	Y	4	...	...		1007	SO	B&Q NE Pet
1002	1007	1	2	Y	6	...	...		1008	SO	B&Q NE Juice
1002	1008	1	2	Y	5	...	...		1009	SH	Allegheny Frz
1003	1003	2	0	N	3	...	...		1010	SH	Bronx Frz
1003	1006	2	1	Y	4	...	...		1011	SH	Freeport Frz
1003	1007	2	1	Y	6	...	...		1012	SH	Hartford Frz
1003	1008	2	1	Y	5	...	...		1013	SH	Allegheny Amb
1004	1004	2	0	N	2	...	...		1014	SH	Bronx Amb
1005	1005	2	0	N	7	...	...		1015	SH	Freeport Amb
1006	1006	3	0	Y	4	...	...		1016	SH	Hartford Amb
1007	1007	3	0	Y	6	...	...				
1008	1008	3	0	Y	5	...	...				

Figure 7.18 The exploded customer hierarchy.

Another challenge is determining which children belong to which parents (or parents to children) from anywhere in the hierarchy. In a recursive structure, it requires recursive code to travel up and down the tree to identify these relationships. Identifying a relationship between any two levels is very difficult to do in a SQL-based environment unless you can eliminate the recursive nature of the tree structure. An exploded tree structure will do just that.

Exploding the Hierarchy

A technique to deliver recursive hierarchy data to a data mart is to "explode" the recursive tree structure. Exploding is the act of traversing the recursive structure and generating a new structure that contains every possible relationship across all levels of the tree. The result is a nonrecursive table of relationship pairs. This table would also contain attributes that describe the relationship's position in the hierarchy. Figure 7.18 shows an explosion of the customer hierarchy shown in Figure 7.15.

Exploding the tree eliminates the need for recursive queries, as there are no longer self-joins to the hierarchy. Table 7.1 describes the attributes of an exploded hierarchy entity. When delivered in this form to a data mart, hierarchical reports can be generated using simple, single pass SQL queries. The additional attributes allow a query to isolate the portion of the hierarchy of interest. The result is a flexible structure that has other uses besides hierarchical reporting.

Table 7.1 Exploded Hierarchy Attributes

COLUMN	USAGE
Parent	Foreign key to the superior entity.
Child	Foreign key to the inferior entity.

(continued)

Table 7.1 *(continued)*

COLUMN	USAGE
Level	The level of the parent entity in the hierarchy. A value of 1 indicates a top, or root, node. In reporting this value can be used to indent descriptions.
Distance	The number of levels between the parent and child entity. A value of 1 indicates an immediate descendant. A value of zero indicates an identity row. The parent and child foreign keys contain the same value.
Bottom	A true/false value. If true, the child entity is a leaf. It is at the bottom of the hierarchy.
Sequence	A value used to sort the result set to produce a properly sequences hierarchical report.
Eff Dt	Effective date of the relationship.
Exp Dt	Expiration date of the relationship.

With the exception of additional attributes, this structure is almost identical to the bridge structure discussed earlier in this chapter. The difference is it includes child references at all levels, whereas the previous bridge only stored the lowest level child. Both of these tables are, in fact, bridge tables. The bridge table discussed previously could just as easily have contained rows for all relationship pairs as this table does. The difference is simply a matter of the requirements for the application. When the application uses are unknown or subject to change, storing a full picture, as shown in Figure 7.18, will cover any situation at the expense of a larger table. Even though the table is larger than the recursive tree, it is not that much larger to make its use prohibitive; in fact, it remains a fairly compact structure that provides a lot of utility.

The additional attributes in this table provide a means to represent the hierarchical nature of the data in reports. Values, such as level and distance from parent are derived in the process of traversing and exploding the tree. The sequence number can be generated if you perform a sorted traversal. Sorting the parent's children in the desired sequence before exploding the child's tree does this. If you are maintaining history, the effective and expiration dates of each relationship is also derived during explosion.

Maintaining History

Introducing time sensitivity into a recursive tree structure complicates updates and traversal of both the recursive tree and the exploded tree structures. We will examine the issues and propose techniques to deal with them.

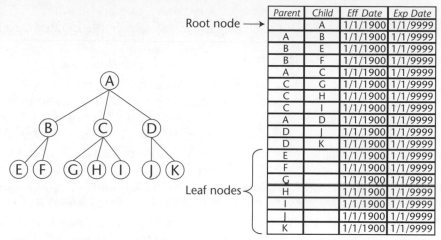

Parent	Child	Eff Date	Exp Date
	A	1/1/1900	1/1/9999
A	B	1/1/1900	1/1/9999
B	E	1/1/1900	1/1/9999
B	F	1/1/1900	1/1/9999
A	C	1/1/1900	1/1/9999
C	G	1/1/1900	1/1/9999
C	H	1/1/1900	1/1/9999
C	I	1/1/1900	1/1/9999
A	D	1/1/1900	1/1/9999
D	J	1/1/1900	1/1/9999
D	K	1/1/1900	1/1/9999
E		1/1/1900	1/1/9999
F		1/1/1900	1/1/9999
G		1/1/1900	1/1/9999
H		1/1/1900	1/1/9999
I		1/1/1900	1/1/9999
J		1/1/1900	1/1/9999
K		1/1/1900	1/1/9999

Figure 7.19   A tree and its data.

Updating the Recursive Tree

The nature of a recursive tree structure is such that for any point in time, every parent-child relationship is unique. The primary key for such a table is the combination of the parent and child foreign keys. If the structure is to be date sensitive, then effective date becomes part of the primary key. Maintaining these dates can be a challenge in a typical data warehouse environment.

More often than not, the source operational system only maintains a current view of any hierarchy. Aggravating the situation is the fact that there is seldom a record of any changes that are applied. As a result, feeds into the data warehouse are typically point-in-time snapshots of the current hierarchy structure. It is up to the load process to determine what has changed so that history can be recorded properly.

Fortunately, such differences can be detected using a basic sort/merge technique. Create a current snapshot of the tree in the data warehouse, representing the last known state of the tree, sorted by the parent key and the child key. Sort the incoming data into the same sequence. Where the keys on the incoming file match the snapshot, there is no change. If the key exists in the incoming file and not in the snapshot, it is a new relationship. If the key exists in the snapshot but not in the incoming file, it is an expired relationship. You can also accomplish the same results performing direct lookups on the existing table. However, in order to detect obsolete relationships you must query using the child key, returning its parent. If the returned parent is different from the parent in the new snapshot, the old parent relationship is deactivated and replaced by the new parent relationship. The choice of update technique will depend on the size of the hierarchy structure. The sort/merge technique tends to provide better performance for large hierarchies. Figure 7.19 shows a recursive tree and its data. Figure 7.20 shows the tree after a structural change and the data in the updated table.

Exploding a Time-Sensitive Tree

Notice in Figure 7.20, when node C was moved from its original parent A to its new parent Y, the dates for the A-C relationship and the Y-C relationship reflect the time of the change. However, the dates for children of node C did not change because those relationships did not change. But, when the tree structure is exploded, the table will contain relationships between node A and C's children as well as node Y and C's children. The dates for the A-G and Y-G relationships must take into account the dates for the A-C and Y-C relationships. As the tree is exploded to lower levels, the children must assume the time period that represents the intersection of the parent's effective dates and the child's effective dates. Figure 7.21 shows how the relationships would appear in the explosion table before and after the change.

The effective period of the relationships between node A and nodes C, G, H, and I changed to reflect the movement of node C as a child of node Y. However, notice that the relationships between node C and its children, nodes G, H, and I, have not changed. This demonstrates how compact an exploded hierarchy can be. There is no need for portions of the explosion to inherit changes that do not directly affect them.

An important point to consider when doing such an explosion is that you cannot use the dates in a join to aid in exploding the tree. You must perform a traditional traversal, using the child key to self-join to the parent key to traverse down a level. Children of this parent may only be eliminated if the child node's effective period falls out of the derived time period of the parent. Deriving time periods, checking ranges, and halting further transversal requires that such a process be implemented using a 3GL or ETL tool rather than SQL.

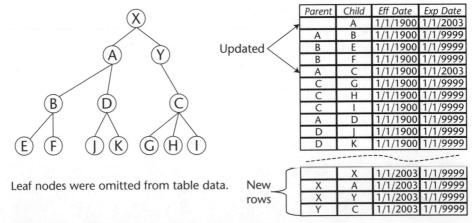

Parent	Child	Eff Date	Exp Date
	A	1/1/1900	1/1/2003
A	B	1/1/1900	1/1/9999
B	E	1/1/1900	1/1/9999
B	F	1/1/1900	1/1/9999
A	C	1/1/1900	1/1/2003
C	G	1/1/1900	1/1/9999
C	H	1/1/1900	1/1/9999
C	I	1/1/1900	1/1/9999
A	D	1/1/1900	1/1/9999
D	J	1/1/1900	1/1/9999
D	K	1/1/1900	1/1/9999
	X	1/1/2003	1/1/9999
X	A	1/1/2003	1/1/9999
X	Y	1/1/2003	1/1/9999
Y	C	1/1/2003	1/1/9999

Updated

Leaf nodes were omitted from table data. New rows

Figure 7.20 Effect of change to the tree structure.

Exploded Tree (Before)				
Parent	Child	...	Eff Dt	Exp Dt
A	C		1/1/1900	1/1/9999
A	G		1/1/1900	1/1/9999
A	H		1/1/1900	1/1/9999
A	I		1/1/1900	1/1/9999
C	G		1/1/1900	1/1/9999
C	H		1/1/1900	1/1/9999
C	I		1/1/1900	1/1/9999

Exploded Tree (After)				
Parent	Child	...	Eff Dt	Exp Dt
A	C		1/1/1900	1/1/2003
A	G		1/1/1900	1/1/2003
A	H		1/1/1900	1/1/2003
A	I		1/1/1900	1/1/2003
Y	C		1/1/2003	1/1/9999
Y	G		1/1/2003	1/1/9999
Y	H		1/1/2003	1/1/9999
Y	I		1/1/2003	1/1/9999
C	G		1/1/1900	1/1/9999
C	H		1/1/1900	1/1/9999
C	I		1/1/1900	1/1/9999

Figure 7.21   Changing a time-sensitive exploded tree.

This is not an issue if all that is required is a point-in-time snapshot of an exploded tree. In this case, it is a simple matter of restricting the self-join on rows whose effective period encompasses the desired date. So, when publishing the exploded structure to a data mart, you should target the output to suit the requirements. While it is certainly advantageous to provide a complete history of a hierarchy, it is rare the business has any use for it in typical data mart applications. What is more common is to provide the current structure and a previous structure, usually defined as the structure on a specific date, such as the end of last year. This can be handled by simply delivering two snapshot tables to the mart. The previous structure table would only need to be refreshed when the target date changed. These snapshot structures need only carry an as-of date to reflect the point in time the snapshot was created. It is well worth mentioning that the delivered snapshot would use the same surrogate key values as those stored in the source historical tree structure. Each data mart receiving such a snapshot would also receive the same referenced (dimensional) data.

Case Study: Retail Purchasing

The purchasing organization of our retailer, GOSH, is responsible for the timely purchase and supply of goods to the retail outlets. The company uses a number of avenues to accomplish this. The core organization is their internal buyers. The buyers are responsible for determining demand and stocking levels of goods in the store. They determine this by sales projections and by feedback from the stores. Each buyer is responsible for a particular group of products wholly contained within a department. Depending on the nature of the goods, there may be multiple buyers and different organizations within a department. For example, in sporting goods, buyers are organized by supplier.

In women's clothing, buyers specialize in particular types of clothes (shoes, coats, dresses, and so on).

Figure 7.22 shows the organizational chart of the purchasing group. The highest level, Purchasing Area, represents a general category of goods structured to moderate the number of departmental mangers reporting to purchasing area managers. Within a department, there may be group managers that report to the department manager depending on the overall size of the department. Below the department manager, or group manager, are the buyers who are responsible for purchasing the goods. In some cases, there are subgroup managers in areas with many products and high purchasing activity. In general, buyers are responsible for particular SKUs; however, large departments may assign regional buyers that are responsible for the same SKU's in different stores. In these situations, the Purchasing Department manager establishes the store assignments. These assignments do not relate to the store hierarchy defined by the Sales Department. In such situations, there is also a designated primary buyer who is responsible for actually purchasing the SKU from the supplier. Purchasing requests for the SKU from the other buyers are consolidated through the primary buyer. The primary buyer is always one of the regional buyers responsible for that SKU.

The purchasing organization is fluid. There are frequent changes to buyer assignments within a department. Buyers also move between subgroups, groups, departments, and purchasing areas. Buyers are interested in seeing the sales plan and sales history based on the current hierarchy. Management is also interested in examining a buyer's performance based on SKU responsibilities over time.

Analysis

The purchasing organization represents a ragged hierarchy. In this case, buyers may belong to a department, a group, or a subgroup, meaning that the depth of the hierarchy will vary depending on the department. In addition, the leaves of the hierarchy are dependent on two entities, the product (SKU) and the store. For consistency, it should be presumed that the buyer assignments are always based on SKU and store. It is simply that, in some cases, a buyer is responsible for all stores. Notice how terminology is different from that of the store hierarchy. A "department" from a store's point of view is roughly equivalent to a "purchasing area," whereas a "department" in the purchasing organization has no equivalent in a store. This is a common situation in any large organization. It is important that terminology be qualified so there is no confusion. These entities should have distinct names in the data warehouse, such as "store department" and "purchasing department."

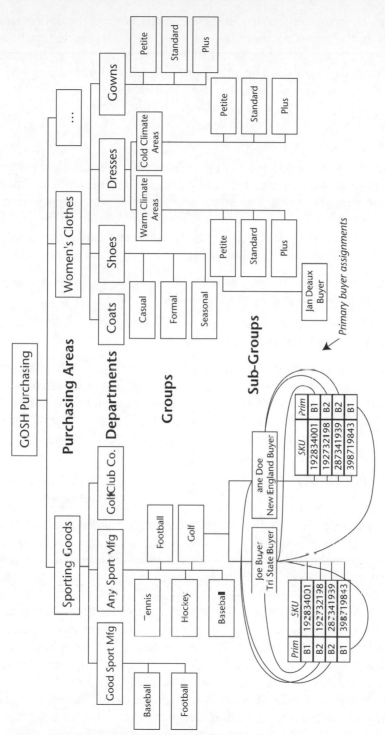

Figure 7.22 GOSH purchasing organization.

Because this is a ragged hierarchy, it is best represented in the data warehouse using a recursive tree structure. This allows for a varying hierarchy depth without affecting reporting functionality. Another advantage of the recursive tree structure is that levels can be added or removed without having an impact on existing queries. Such changes are effected by the content of the data structure rather than by the data structure itself. The hierarchy can change without a change to the model or schema. It is well suited for this type of organization. Figure 7.23 shows the business model.

The primary buyer is an independent relationship and is not a part of the purchasing hierarchy. It is based purely on SKU as the business rule is that a SKU has only one primary buyer. The buyer's product responsibility may or may not depend on the store. This requires two associative entities, Buyer Responsibility to address non-store-specific relationships, and Buyer Store Responsibility to address store-specific relationships.

There are four options as to how the associative entities in this model are physically implemented. These will be discussed in the next section.

Implementing the Business Model

Figure 7.24 shows an example of the physical structures that implements the business model. The structure has been simplified; the host of columns one would normally see in a real implementation are removed for clarity. The data shown in this figure will be used as the basis for further discussion of this hierarchy.

The Buyer Hierarchy

As the business case outlined, the depth of the hierarchy can vary depending on the department. Some departments are further subdivided, while others are not. The fact that a leaf, the buyer, may appear at different levels in the hierarchy makes the hierarchy a ragged one. The recursive tree structure will handle this without any adjustment to its treatment described in the previous section. In fact, the recursive tree structure is inherently insensitive to the existence or nonexistence of levels in the hierarchy tree. As you can see in figure 7.24, buyer key 1017, Joe Buyer, belongs to the Any Sport Golf group (key = 1011), while buyer key 1019, Jan Deaux, belongs to a subgroup, Women's Dresses Warm – Petite (key = 1015). These two relationships are enforced by the parent/child key values 1011/1017 and 1015/1019, respectively in the Buyer Hierarchy table. There is no special logic or indicators necessary to accommodate different types of relationships.

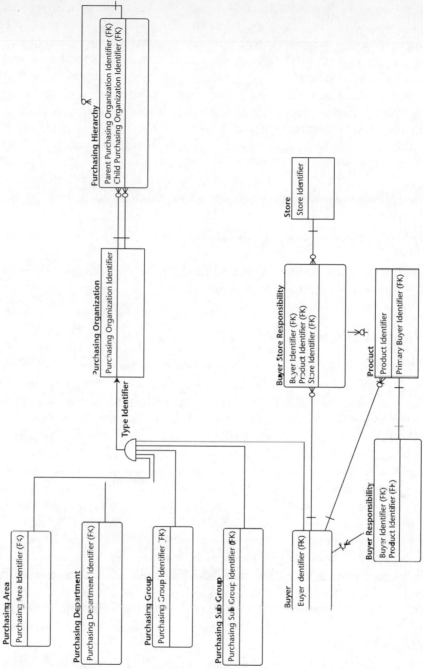

Figure 7.23   The purchasing business model.

The maintenance issues with this structure are the same as discussed in the previous case study. The basic table structure is still a relationship between parent and child nodes. At any point in time, each combination of parent and child keys will be unique. Change detection is accomplished by examining the structure from the child key's point of view, looking for children with different parents, rather than parents with different children. (See "Maintaining History," earlier in this chapter.) This hierarchy is best delivered to the data marts as an exploded tree structure as discussed in the previous case study. Delivery to other systems may require flattening the hierarchy into a 2NF structure. This is doable since the hierarchy has a maximum depth. Field values for missing hierarchy levels in the output file may need to be left blank or set to a predefined value as necessary for the target system.

Implementing Buyer Responsibility

In this section, we will examine the buyer responsibility and how it should be implemented in the model and physical database.

Flattening a Ragged Hierarchy

The delivery process may require converting a ragged hierarchy stored in a recursive tree structure into a flat 2NF representation. This is doable provided the hierarchy is of known depth. A flat 2NF structure is simply a row that contains one or more columns for each level of the hierarchy. There is one row per leaf.

The challenge when generating such a structure is to be aware that, because the structure is ragged, levels may be skipped. It is up to the process to recognize when a level is skipped and to populate the output with a value appropriate to the target system.

You can detect the level by joining to the referenced table via the foreign keys in the hierarchy tree. Type code columns in the referenced table should be available to allow you to populate the proper column in the delivered output.

When dealing with a ragged hierarchy of unknown depth, the only viable solution to creating such a structure is to deliver the hierarchy path as a single delimited text value. The generated string would have an appearance similar to a file path specification. Using the hierarchy in Figure 7.22 as an example, the string *"'GOSH Purchasing','Womens Clothes','Shoes','Formal'"* would describe the formal shoes group in the women's shoes department. If your target system can receive such a flattened hierarchy as an unknown number of columns, one trick is to use the file's column delimiter (such as a comma) as the delimiter in the string. When written to a text file, the single string will have the appearance of multiple columns to the application that reads it as a comma-delimited file.

Buyer Hierarchy	
Parent	Child
	1002
	1003
1002	1004
1002	1005
1002	1006
1003	1007
1003	1008
1003	1009
1004	1010
1005	1011
1005	1012
1009	1013
1009	1014
1013	1015
1013	1016
1011	1017
1011	1018
1015	1019
1017	
1018	
1019	

Buyer		
Key	Type	Description
1002	PA	Sporting Goods
1003	PA	Women's Clothes
1004	DP	Good Sport Mfg
1005	DP	Any Sport Mfg
1006	DP	GolfClubCo.
1007	DP	Women's Coats
1008	DP	Women's Shoes
1009	DP	Women's Dresses
1010	GR	Good Sport - Baseball
1011	GR	Any Sport Golf
1012	GR	Any Sport Hockey
1013	GR	Women's Dresses Warm
1014	GR	Women's Dresses Cold
1015	SG	WDW - Petite
1016	SG	WDW - Standard
1017	BY	Joe Buyer
1018	BY	Jane Doe
1019	BY	Jan Deaux

Buyer Responsibility		
Store	Product	Buyer
28	6102	1017
28	6103	1017
28	6104	1017
28	6105	1017
35	6102	1017
35	6103	1017
35	6104	1017
35	6105	1017
36	6102	1017
36	6103	1017
36	6104	1017
36	6105	1017
37	6102	1017
37	6103	1017
37	6104	1017
37	6105	1017

Product		
Key	SKU	Buyer
6102	192834001	1017
6103	192732198	1018
6104	287341939	1018
6105	398719843	1017

Store		
Key	ID	Name
28	012	Paramus
35	025	Queens
36	135	Plattsburgh
37	417	New Haven

Figure 7.24   Purchasing tables.

The Primary Buyer

In our business case, a relationship exists between buyers and products at two levels: The primary buyer, who does the actual purchasing, and the secondary buyers, who are responsible for determining purchasing requirements. There is always a one-to-one relationship between a SKU and the primary buyer. Since the primary buyer is wholly dependent on the SKU, the Product entity carries the foreign key to the primary buyer, as shown in Figure 7.23.

The Secondary Buyer

The secondary buyer relationships are represented by two associative entities in the business model shown in Figure 7.23. The Buyer Responsibility entity represents relationships based on buyer and product, while the Buyer Store Responsibility entity represents relationships that are based on buyer, product, and store. The sum of these two entities represents all buyer responsibility relationships.

Upon examining the model, you may notice that the relationship between Buyer, Buyer Responsibility, and Product appears to be the same one-to-many relationship as the Primary Buyer relationship between Buyer and Product. Based on the case study, it is the same relationship because the primary buyer is the responsible buyer when the relationship is not store specific. However, it only remains true if historical relationships are not being maintained. If you add effective and expiration dates to the Buyer Responsibility entity, it becomes a many-to-many relationship. When keeping history, you need to allow for the fact that organizational changes may move a product's buyer responsibility from being store nonspecific to being store specific, while at the same time the primary buyer will remain the same. Since primary buyer and responsible buyer are two different roles in the business, the model should not make assumptions in an attempt to combine the two.

For the physical implementation, Figure 7.24 shows a single Buyer Responsibility table consisting of foreign keys for buyer, product, and store. This is the result of combining the two associative entities into a single table. There are pros and cons to this approach. One problem in doing this is that non-store-specific buyer-product relationships must contain rows for every store. This creates a larger table that is more difficult to maintain. This is offset by the fact that the rows themselves are not very large.

Combining the two simplifies delivery of data that uses these relationships. If the tables were separate, delivery would require union queries to combine the two result sets. For non-store-specific relationships, the store information would be missing. This may not be tolerated by downstream systems, requiring an unrestricted join to store to create rows with store information. It is also reasonable to assume that all stores do not carry all products. Therefore implementing a delivery query that creates store information may produce results that are inconsistent with other such queries due to the need to apply business rules. These rules would have already been taken into account in the combined structure.

An alternate solution is to create and maintain both tables corresponding to the entities in the business model, and then use an internal delivery process to create a full, separate table, as shown in Figure 7.24. This is a viable solution if there are time constraints in your update process and the process to generate the combined table can be executed at a less critical time. This isolates the logic to build a combined table to a single process, easing maintenance. It also performs the process once, so it does not need to be repeated for multiple deliveries of the data.

Delivering the Buyer Responsibility Relationship

From the standpoint of the data warehouse, the buyer relationship table is a simple, effective solution that is compact and easy to maintain. From a data mart point of view, it is a very difficult structure to query. The primary problem is that the store relationship is optional. If a query needs to associate sales with the buyer hierarchy, it must first isolate the buyer using the product, store, and date recorded for the sale. To allow for buyers that are not store specific, you must perform an outer join from the sale to the buyer/product relationship table. This can lead to undesirable side effects in the result sets produced by such queries.

Exporting the Relationship

In general, when designing data marts your goal is to create structures that are easy to query and perform well. You should avoid situations that require outer joins as much as possible. In fact, if the marts are designed using dimensional models, outer joins should be unnecessary. To eliminate the need to perform outer joins, the data mart will require the use of store as a foreign key in the buyer/product relationship table. This means that every row has both a product and store key value specified. To accomplish this, the process that exports data to the data mart should generate rows for each store when the original row has no store specified.

Expanding the data to include all stores will significantly increase the number of rows being passed to the data marts. The increase is directly proportional to the number of stores. The actual volume passed to the data mart can be controlled by only passing changes since the last export. On the data mart end, such a structure will have a large number of rows, but the rows themselves would be small. This may be a manageable situation if the data mart only requires a current snapshot of the relationship.

You can use such a structure to maintain historical relationships as well, however, if reassignments occur frequently, the table could explode in size, making it burdensome to update as well as query. Alternately, you can store only the current and previous buyer in this table. The primary key of such a table would be the store and product IDs, meaning that it would have the same number of rows as the current snapshot table. The difference is that when the row is updated, the current buyer ID is moved the previous buyer column before the current buyer column is overwritten with a new value. Figure 7.25 shows how this would be accomplished.

This technique is identical to type 3 slowly changing dimensions described by Dr. Kimball[1]. But, in this case, it is applied to a bridge table rather than a dimension table. One business issue you would need to resolve would be how to deal with new rows. Do you populate both the current and previous buyers with the assigned buyer or do you set the previous buyer to a null or "unknown" value? Both ways have valid arguments, and your choice will depend on how the business wishes to see their reports.

---

[1] *The Data Warehouse Toolkit,* Second Edition. Ralph Kimball, Margy Ross, Wiley & Sons (2002)

Buyer Responsibility			
Store	Product	Buyer	Prev Buy
35	6103	1017	

Assign buyer 1018 to store 35 and Product 6103

Buyer Responsibility			
Store	Product	Buyer	Prev Buy
35	6103	1017	1017

Move the current buyer into the previous buyer column

Buyer Responsibility			
Store	Product	Buyer	Prev Buy
35	6103	1018	1017

Store the new buyer assignment

Figure 7.25 Maintaining current and previous references.

Delivering the Buyer

If the relationship table is too unwieldy for your data mart application, an alternative is to simply include the buyer's foreign key with the sales data that is being exported to the data mart. The export process would use whatever logic is necessary to locate and assign the buyer, removing that burden from the data mart queries. Aside from aiding query performance in the data marts, the storage requirements are significantly reduced. An incremental load to the data mart in this manner will store the responsible buyer at the time of the sale. Queries of past sales would not reflect new changes to the relationship structure.

If the requirement of the data mart is to reflect the current buyer structure for all sales in the timeframe of the mart, you will need to refresh all the sales data in the data mart with the most current buyer assignment. In this case, you also have the option of including the point in time buyer foreign key, allowing the data to be viewed using either the current buyer or the buyer at the time of the sale.

Refreshing a data mart may not be as onerous a task as it may first appear. How practical it is depends on factors such as the timeframe covered by the mart, the frequency of change in the buyer/product relationship, your processing window and how current the business needs such a relationship. It may be that the business only needs to see the data restructured on a weekly or monthly basis. In such cases, current sales updates to the data mart can be performed incrementally using current buyer assignments.

Case Study: The Combination Pack

The marketing group for the Lazy Guy brand has developed a new line of "meals-in-a-box." One package will contain a full meal, including appetizer and dessert, ready for the microwave. The package will contain one appetizer, one entrée, two side dishes and a Bada-Binge ice cream dessert. The company is very excited about the idea and is anxious to go forward as quickly as possible.

From a sales and inventory standpoint, each meal-in-a-box is a single SKU that is assembled by placing existing products into a box. It is sold at retail as a single consumer unit with its own UPC code.

When the idea was presented to the sales and manufacturing divisions, issues began to arise. The brand manager for Bada-Binge wanted assurances that the brand would receive the revenue for the ice cream sold in the package. Accounting wanted assurances that costs would be charged to the appropriate brands and divisions. Manufacturing pointed out that the package and labeling of the component items would be different than the normal retail product. These component products will be assigned a different SKU to distinguish them from the normal product. They will never be sold as individual products. The Logistics group requires a weight and size breakdown so that storage and transportation costs can be properly charged to the correct brand. And the Lazy Guy brand manager requires that revenue be distributed across the product groups (appetizer, entrée, and side dishes).

The marketing group and sales have countered that significant effort will be expended to launch and promote the new product. They need to see all the sales and revenue associated with it to gauge their efforts. They propose a new product group under the Lazy Guy brand to report these products.

After extensive discussion, the business agreed that everybody should get what he or she wanted. Sales of the meal-in-a-box product will be reported both as a single unit and as its components. A new product group "meal-in-a-box" will be added to the Lazy Guy brand. All meal-in-a-box SKUs will be assigned to that product group. The operational system will provide a new feed containing a single level bill of materials for each meal-in-a-box SKU. This bill of materials will only contain the SKUs of the finished goods placed in the box. Reporting would use the hierarchy assigned to the component SKUs when reporting revenue at the component level. Reports that include component level SKUs will be referred to as "exploded" sales reports.

Analysis

Initial analysis of this situation is you have a single complex ragged hierarchy as shown in Figure 7.26. This hierarchy expands the existing product hierarchy

(Figure 7.8) to include a new level, component, as well as an additional product group. Products at the component level have many parents, the product group it belongs to and the many meal-in-a-box SKUs it may be used in.

The business has decided that there will be two classes of reports from this hierarchy. "Actual" sales, which report the SKUs sold and "exploded" sales that report actual sales for unassembled products and component sales for assembled products, such as the meal-in-a-box. Actual sales reports can continue to function as they have before. The meal-in-a-box SKUs are simply new products being sold. Exploded reports require a different approach. If the product has components, it must first go down the hierarchy to its children (the components) before it can roll up to higher levels in the hierarchy. This type of hierarchy traversal would require custom query code to implement and would be very difficult, if not impossible, to implement using an off-the-shelf query tool.

The solution requires the problem be broken into smaller pieces. First, you must recognize that the hierarchy stored in the data warehouse and the hierarchy stored in the data mart are there for different reasons. The data warehouse structures should be designed to best collect and maintain the information, while the data mart structures are there to facilitate queries. Second, the grand total of an actual report will equal the grand total of an exploded report that looks at the same sales. In other words, from a reporting standpoint, the actual hierarchy and the exploded hierarchy are mutually exclusive. They are simply two different ways to look at the same thing and would never be used in combination. Third, since they are never reported together, there is no requirement to combine both structures in the data warehouse.

After breaking the problem down, it becomes apparent that the basic product hierarchy remains the same. There are some new SKUs representing the component items and new products as well as a new product group. This is all normal activity that any hierarchy structure should be able to deal with on a day-to-day basis. What has changed is that the sales data for some SKUs must be allocated to different SKUs (the components) in order to produce the exploded sales reports. We will now examine the additional elements needs in the warehouse and discuss the process required to provide exploded sales data in the data marts.

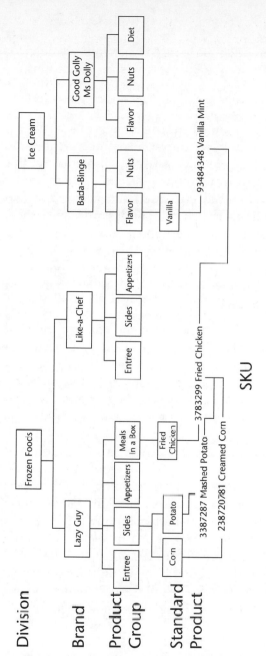

Figure 7.26 The expanded product hierarchy.

Adding a Bill of Materials

To address the allocation of a product sale to its components, we need to know what the components are and how the business wishes to account for each component's contribution to the sale. In this case, this information can be stored in a simplified bill-of-materials structure.

A normal bill of materials is maintained in a recursive tree structure. This allows for ragged hierarchies of unknown depth, a common attribute of a bill of materials. However, in this case we have a two-level hierarchy: the retail product and its components. In a recursive tree structure there are rows to identify roots (null parent keys) and leaves (null child keys). In a two-level hierarchy, all parent nodes are roots and all child nodes are leaves, there is no need to provide special identification to determine if you are at the top or bottom of the hierarchy. With root and leaf identity rows removed, there is no need for recursion since the entire hierarchy can be stored as one list of relationships. In fact, the structure needed is a bridge table rather than a recursive tree. Figure 7.27 shows this structure.

Since this table is needed to allocate revenue to the component SKUs, the bridge structure should include additional columns to store allocation factors. It will be up to the business to determine how these factors are to be calculated as well as how many factors will be required. An invoice has a lot of different components that are of interest to different areas of the company. Revenue, the number of greatest interest, would certainly be allocated in some manner. An allocation method may be to calculate a ratio of the standard price of each item against the total standard price of all items. If one item's price contributes 40 percent of the total, then its revenue allocation factor would be set to 0.40. You may also require factors to allocate costs, such as shipping charges, which may be based on the weights of each item. Of course, a quantity factor is necessary to translate the number of units sold to the corresponding number of units of the component item. With the exception of the quantity factor, the sum of each allocation factor should total to 1, representing 100 percent of the item. These allocation factors should be precalculated and stored in the bridge structure. The business may also require that these factors be recalculated periodically. To allow for this the structure should include effective and expiration dates.

Bill of Materials			
Parent	Child	% Revenue	Qty
8129	897	0.200	1
8129	12099	0.170	1
8129	30289	0.100	1
8129	80232	0.430	1
8129	90098	0.100	1

Products			
Key	Type	SKU	Description
897	PR	93484348	Vanilla Mint– MIAB 3oz
8129	PR	3783299	MIAB Fried Chicken
12099	PR	3387287	Mashed Potato – MIAB 6oz
30289	PR	238720781	Creamed Corn – MIAB 4oz
80232	PR	398429900	Fried Chicken – MIAB 3pc
90098	PR	294729047	Calamari App – MIAB

Figure 7.27   Implementing the bill of materials.

Publishing the Data

When publishing this information to the data marts, it is better to avoid the need to explode the sales data in the data mart. This adds additional calculation burden on the mart that can adversely impact query performance. If a data mart is to provide exploded numbers, the data should be exploded as part of the publication process of the data mart. If the mart requires both, two simple true/false flags can be added to the row to support both types of queries. One flag would be set to true if the row is to be included in an actual sales report, and another flag would be set true if the row is to be included in an exploded sales report.

Those SKUs that do not have components would be stored as a single row with both flags set true. The meal-in-a-box SKUs will have rows with the actual sales flag set to true and the exploded sales flag set to false. The exploded components of the meal-in-a-box SKUs would have their actual sales flag set to false and the exploded sales flag set to true. Since the product hierarchy is based on SKU, the one hierarchy can be applied to either type of report, because the SKUs are different and the allocated values are precalculated.

Transforming Structures

In the previous discussions, you saw that there is a lot of inherent flexibility in using recursive tree structures for hierarchies. Changes to the hierarchy do not require changes to the data structure, it is compact, and it is easy to record changes and easy to maintain historical perspective. However, the downside is query complexity, requiring recursive code to use the structure makes the recursive tree less suitable for the data marts From a data mart standpoint, flat hierarchy structures and bridges provide support for the needed reporting functionality without the need for special logic or recursive queries. Since it is advantageous to use a recursive structure in the data warehouse and advantageous to use flattened structures in the data marts, the data warehouse should be positioned to transform these structures when necessary.

In this section, we will examine additional techniques to transform hierarchical structures.

Making a Recursive Tree

If data is received from the source system as a flattened hierarchy, you may wish to consider storing the data in a recursive tree structure. Previously in this chapter, we showed how a 2NF flat structure can be transformed into a 3NF flat structure by appending ancestry to each business key (see Figure 7.12). Now that the data and keys are in 3NF, you can further transform it into a recursive tree structure.

Figure 7.28 shows the transformations that need to occur. The first step is to fold the hierarchy elements into a single entity table. This step is necessary so that the tree's foreign keys reference a single table. Figure 7.14 shows the products and hierarchy table with surrogate keys assigned. Once surrogate keys have been established, you build the tree by creating a series of unique parent-child relationship rows. There are a number of ways to do this, depending on the data feed you receive and the tools available to you to implement the ETL processes.

If you start with a 3NF flat hierarchy, such as the product hierarchy shown in Figure 7.12, the process should generate a row for every hierarchical entity as a child. For example, for every row in the Product Group table, create a row using the Product Group key as the child key and the Brand foreign key on the Product Group row as the parent key. Next, create root node rows using the root entity, Division. Create one row for each Division using the Division key as the child key and a null value for the parent key. The null indicates no parent, which defines a root node. The use of null may cause side effects, depending on the database system being used. Other conventions are to set the foreign key value to zero or –1 to indicate a null reference. Since the 3NF data coming in uses the business, or natural key, it is necessary to perform a lookup against the folded entity table to obtain the proper surrogate key.

When the hierarchy elements are folded into a single table, be sure to include a type identification column to distinguish between each entity. This code should be part of the natural key to this table, ensuring uniqueness between each entity type. The folded table itself should have a surrogate primary key to avoid the need for compound joins between the tree's foreign key and this table.

Flattening a Recursive Tree

While a recursive tree is preferred for the data warehouse, nonrecursive structures are better suited for the data marts. Earlier in this chapter we discussed generating a bridge table containing an explosion of the recursive tree to eliminate the need for recursion in queries. A bridge structure has the advantage of being compact, but the disadvantage of requiring additional joins to retrieve attributes relating to the entities.

When it comes to hierarchies, it is common that the only attribute a hierarchical element has is a description. When this is the case, it may be advantageous to deliver the hierarchy to the data mart as a flattened 1NF or 2NF structure. Figure 7.29 shows an example of this. The levels are spread horizontally across a row. Each leaf entity has a foreign key pointing to its hierarchy row. This type of flattening works best with balanced hierarchies; however, it can accommodate ragged hierarchies by leaving missing levels null. It is not, however, a useful technique for hierarchies of unknown depth.

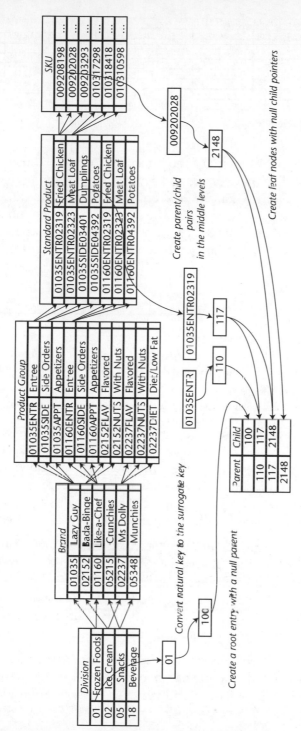

Figure 7.28   Transforming a 3NF flat hierarchy.

Flattened Product Hierarchy							
Div	Div Desciption	Brand	Brand Desc	Prd Grp	Group Desc	Std Prd	Std Prd Desc
01	Frozen Foods	035	Lazy Guy	ENTR	Entree	02319	Fried Chicken
01	Frozen Foods	035	Lazy Guy	ENTR	Entree	02323	Meat Loaf
01	Frozen Foods	035	Lazy Guy	SIDE	Side Orders	03401	Dumplings
01	Frozen Foods	035	Lazy Guy	SIDE	Side Orders	04392	Potatoes
01	Frozen Foods	160	Like-a-Chef	ENTR	Entree	02319	Fried Chicken
01	Frozen Foods	160	Like-a-Chef	ENTR	Entree	02323	Meat Loaf
01	Frozen Foods	160	Like-a-Chef	ENTR	Entree	04392	Potatoes

SKU	
009208198	...
009202028	...
009203293	...
010317298	...
010318418	...
010310598	...

Figure 7.29 A flattened recursive tree.

This example uses the product hierarchy shown in Figure 7.12. Notice when flattening the structure in this manner, we can revert to the original business key. The fact that all parts of the hierarchy exist on the same row provides context for the codes, eliminating any ambiguity. The structure only contains hierarchical elements and not SKUs. The SKU contains a foreign key that points to its hierarchy. This reduces the redundancy inherent in such a structure.

Summary

Within the data warehouse, the most useful structure for hierarchies is the recursive tree. It can be used to store any type of hierarchy. It also is very tolerant of change, requiring only data updates rather than structural schema changes. It has the disadvantage of not being fully supported in most SQL dialects, requiring external code to manipulate the structure.

Bridge structures (associative entities) can be created to provide a nonrecursive representation of the tree. These structures can be used by any SQL dialect and are the only suitable nonrecursive structure for hierarchies of unknown depth. Bridges are also useful to aggregate detailed numbers to compare to numbers specified at higher levels in the hierarchy. This type of functionality is commonly needed in applications that compare budget numbers with actual numbers.

Flattened, nonrecursive structures represent the hierarchy as a collection of independent attributes. These may be used to store hierarchies in the data warehouse, but they are best used in data marts. Flat structures are easy and efficient to query. However, they may only be used where the maximum hierarchy depth is fixed. They are also better suited for balanced rather than ragged hierarchies; however, they may be used in both cases.

Hierarchies are usually delivered to external systems or data marts in a nonrecursive form. This is primarily due to the nature of the target system. Analysis of your OLAP tools and other software will drive the presentation requirements for hierarchies to these other systems.

8

Modeling Transactions

This chapter examines the nature of business transactions, such as sales and purchases, and how to model and store them effectively within the data warehouse. We will first examine business transactions themselves. We will look at how such transactions occur and the use of this information within a data warehouse. Next, we will discuss the types of interfaces that deliver transaction data to the data warehouse. We will examine and classify the different forms such data interfaces take and the impact those forms have on the load process. We then discuss the delivery process from the data warehouse to the data marts and other analytic applications. We outline the advantages of storing the transactional data in a manner suitable for the delivery process. Finally, the case studies present specific examples to address the most common transaction interface types.

Business Transactions

Business transactions entail the activities or events of interest within the company. For a company such as GOSH, one of the most significant transactions is the sales transaction. In its simplest form, a transaction is a single activity, such as the delivery of an item to a customer in exchange for payment, as shown in Figure 8.1.

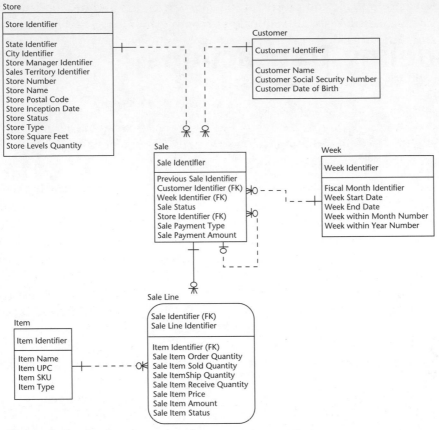

Figure 8.1 Simple sales transaction.

This sales transaction is a one-time event, and once transacted, does not change. If all transactions were like this, the warehouse design would be simplified. The transactions are often more complex because of a number of factors:

- Payment could have been made using a company credit card, and the business is interested in tracking information about the sale until the payment is actually received.

- The customer could return part or all of the purchase, and the return transaction needs to be related to the sale transaction.

- The customer paid for part of the purchase in cash and part with a credit card.

- The customer purchased a large number of items that need to be delivered over time. The transaction remains open until delivery is complete.

- The customer could log onto the company's Web site and order the item, so the transaction actually begins with the order.

Furthermore, the complexity of the data warehouse is compounded when history is tracked. We will examine these complexities in the first case study, which addresses sales data received in a snapshot interface.

Business Use of the Data Warehouse

The anticipated business use of the data warehouse is a major driver of its design. In Chapter 4, we described the first four steps of the data warehouse system modeling effort as being driven by the business needs. Let's see how they apply to the transactions.

The first step is to select the data elements of interest. In the case of the transactional data, this step is pursued in two parts. First, we must determine which states of the order are of interest to us. A data warehouse that is built for sales analysis may only be interested in completed sales, and hence may not require information from open orders. A data warehouse that is built to provide information for forecasting or logistics, on the other hand, may require open order information. Once we decide upon the states of interest, we must then examine each data element to determine the elements that are of interest. Since we're dealing with transactional data, we should be conservative, and if we are in doubt, we should generally bring the element into the data warehouse. The reason for this is that subsequent retrieval of the data may be difficult, perhaps impossible.

The second step is to ensure that we maintain the historical perspective. If we're only interested in closed sales, and a transaction can never change after it is closed, then there is no need for an additional time variant component of the key since a closed transaction can have only one occurrence. If, however, we're tracking open orders, we know that the information can change, as shown in Figure 8.2. In this case, we need to maintain a date, identifying when the change occurred, that provides us with the snapshot of the order or of the order line.

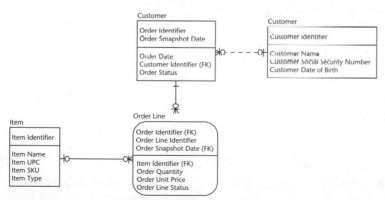

Figure 8.2 Open order over time.

In the case studies that follow, we will expand on the importance of historical perspective and what it means to the business. An important decision in your design process is how you wish to represent change. Is it simply enough to capture the new state of a transaction, or is it more important to capture the magnitude of the change? For example, if you need to answer the question, "What were my orders for the week?" what is the correct answer? It may be a simple sum of new orders received during the week, but what if a customer changed an older order during that week? Is the increase or decrease to the older order also considered an order for that week? If you need to include such changes, it cannot be easily calculated unless you store the magnitude of the change in the data warehouse. By storing the magnitude—or difference—of change rather than the current value at the time of the change, you can easily provide differences over time as well as re-create a current value snapshot for any point in time. If you only store current value snapshots, you must subtract one snapshot from the other to derive the difference. This is very difficult to do in SQL. Based on the most likely business needs, we recommend storing differences, possibly in addition to current value snapshots in the data warehouse. The case studies at the end of this chapter offer some techniques for doing this.

The third step is to add derived data. Each sales detail line may have a quantity of an item and a price for that item. The extended cost represents the product of the two. Discounts may be applied to a sale, and sometimes, they are apportioned among the various items sold. If the business rule for "net sales amount" is that it is the revenue derived from selling the item after considering discounts, and excluding taxes, then a derived field could be included in the data warehouse.

The fourth step is to ensure that we capture the appropriate level of granularity. This is the point at which we decide whether or not to actually store the transaction in the data warehouse. Storing each transaction is expensive, and it is worth doing only if transactional level information is needed for analysis. If the analysis only requires data that is summarized (daily sales of each item at each store), then the transaction-level data need not be brought into the data warehouse.

Average Lines per Transaction

The sixth data model transformation step deals with merging data in tables. This step comes into play with transactional data if the average number of lines per transaction is relatively low. Some companies may have only one or two lines per transaction. In such situations, denormalizing the header-line relationship and combining the data into a single table may enhance performance. Other companies have many lines for a typical transaction; when this happens, it is often more advantageous to maintain separate header and detail tables.

Granularity

With the decreasing cost for storing data and the increasing use of data-mining techniques, it is not uncommon to find the data warehouse capturing detailed transactional data even when its use is not eminent. We recommend that all business information in the transaction be captured in some form. This data can be stored within the data warehouse or archived in compressed flat files and stored off-line for future use.

While the former is preferable, since it provides ready access to the data, the latter is a practical consideration particularly if the quantity of data is high and its potential use is low.

Business Rules Concerning Changes

The business rules concerning changes affect the data warehouse design. The eighth data warehouse modeling step segregates data based on volatility. Let's assume that the company permits a customer to designate a different delivery point for each line in an order. Once a line is created, however, the item and its delivery point cannot be changed. (To change a delivery point, the customer must cancel the line and enter a new line.) In this example, for a line detail, the item and delivery point information is stable, and the only volatile information is the quantity. Hence, if the quantity ordered changes often until the order is finalized, the modeler should consider splitting the line detail.

Application Interfaces

In this section, we will examine the ways that transactional data is received into the data warehouse from external applications. How the data is presented to the data warehouse has an impact on how the data is processed to achieve the desired information model. Those processing requirements may also affect the model itself. The effects of the interface and process on the model are discussed in detail in the case studies that follow. But first, let us define the types of application interfaces typically encountered.

We divide the act of moving data into three parts: the interface, the load, and the data warehouse. The interface refers to all aspects of extracting data from a source system and delivering it to the data warehouse load process. It encompasses the data, its format, and the process that delivers it. Of concern in this discussion is the form of the data received. The mechanics of extracting information from the application system or delivering it to the load process is of secondary concern and not discussed in this chapter. The load refers to the processes that transform and load the data received from the interface into the data warehouse. Finally, the data warehouse refers to both the model and physical instantiation of the database.

There at two general categories of application interfaces: snapshots and delta interfaces. A snapshot interface presents the data as it exists at the time of extraction, while a delta interface contains changes to the data since the last time data was extracted. Within each of these very broad categories are a variety of subtle variations. There is also another method of data capture, the database transaction log, which provides an additional mechanism outside the business application to obtain change data. This will be discussed separately at the end of this section.

Also note in this discussion that we will not distinguish between standard application interfaces and custom interfaces. It is not uncommon, even with packaged applications, to enhance the application to produce purpose-built interfaces for the data warehouse. These interfaces still fall into one of these general categories, and once created, require the same processing a similar package interface would require. This does not mean that such efforts to build custom interfaces are not effective. On the contrary, often proper interfaces do not exist or those provided are unsuitable and would require extensive processing to produce usable data for the data warehouse. In this chapter, as we discuss each interface, we will look at the processing challenges each one entails. Sometimes, altering the interface can significantly reduce the overall time and effort to bring data into the data warehouse. As you will see in the case studies, delta (change driven) interfaces are better suited for delivering transactional information.

Snapshot Interfaces

A snapshot interface provides a picture of what the data looks like at the time it was extracted. It provides no information about what occurred in the system between the time of the last snapshot and the new one. Snapshots are commonly used for reference data, such as code description tables, and may also be used for larger datasets, such as customer or product data. They are also used to extract complex structures, such as recursive hierarchy trees, and for infrequent interfaces, such as a monthly inventory extract.

Complete Snapshot Interface

A complete snapshot interface is simply an extraction of everything that exists in a table or tables within the application database, sometimes without any discrimination as to the currency or validity of the data. This is a snapshot in its purest form.

In some cases, such as code description tables or other simple structures that do not require historical perspective, it may be appropriate to load such data en masse. However, this is usually not the case, and a process with a little more finesse is called for. There are a number of issues the load process may need to consider when processing such an interface:

Deletions.   If something is deleted in the application, how will it appear in the snapshot? Some applications set a flag indicating that the item was deleted, whereas others physically remove the row from the table. In the latter case, the load process will need to determine what is missing in the snapshot.

Changes.   Does the interface include a change timestamp? Without it, you do not know which items in the interface have changed since the last time you received it. If such knowledge is necessary for subsequent processing, you will need to implement change detection logic in your load process.

Currency.   Are records in the extract current or does the data extract include obsolete or future data? Is there sufficient information in the data to determine its state? Should such records be processed and if not, what percentage of the data falls into this category? Sometimes an interface can be significantly reduced in size by altering the application delivering the data to eliminate such items.

Current Snapshot Interface

This type of interface delivers data that represents the current active state of the data. Obsolete and deleted items do not appear in the current snapshot interface. This is often done to reduce the volume of data delivered or where obsolete data is not available from the application system.

The main difference between this and a complete snapshot is how you interpret data missing from the interface. For example, if you are receiving a current snapshot of customer data, by definition you would not receive customers who are no longer active. You would not receive information on when or why the account was closed. All you would know is the account is not "current" based on its absence from the data extract. Whereas in a complete snapshot, it means the data has been physically removed from the application system's database. One could then derive what that means to the data warehouse based on the rules imposed in the application system. Most application systems would not permit physical deletion of a customer unless the customer was entered in error or is inactive and has not transacted business for some period of time. Over that time, the warehouse would have received any changes in status that lead up to the eventual deletion. If such information is important to the data warehouse, a current snapshot interface is not an appropriate way to deliver it. You may need to use to a complete snapshot or, preferably, a delta interface.

Delta Interfaces

Delta interfaces get their name from the triangular Greek symbol that is used in mathematics to mean *change in*. Thus, a delta interface is one that provides changes to existing data. Transactional data is almost always delivered in some form of delta interface. In all cases, a delta interface is aware of the last time data was extracted. The extract will always contain what has changed since the last extract or the impact of that change.

Columnar Delta Interface

The columnar delta interface, also referred to as a change log, is the most detailed and voluminous of delta interfaces. Such an interface contains one row per column changed. The row would contain the primary key of the data that was updated, the name of the column that was changed, a timestamp for when the change occurred, and the before and after values for the column.

From the standpoint of knowing what has changed, this is by far the perfect interface. However, from a processing point of view, it is often too much of a good thing. If all you are interested in is a few columns, then dealing with such an interface can be practical. However, even when dealing with as few as 20 columns or so, developing a process can become tedious and time-consuming. Dealing with issues such as column name differences between the application and the warehouse, repetitive updating of the same row, or retaining unchanged values when creating a time variant image all add to the complexity of the process.

Row Delta Interface

A row delta interface is similar to the columnar delta interface, except that instead of one row per column, it contains a single row for all columns. In this type of interface, the row is populated with the primary key and any attribute values that have changed. Attributes that did not change would be null or contain some predefined value indicating no change. An alternate form is a transactional orientation, where the interface would contain the entire transaction document structure with only changed values being populated.

This type of interface presents processing challenges similar to those of the columnar delta interface. The data warehouse load process would be required to examine each column to determine its status and act accordingly. This type of processing is difficult to do with almost all commercially available ETL tools on the market.

Delta Snapshot Interface

The delta snapshot is a commonly used interface for reference data, such as a customer master list. The basic delta snapshot would contain a row or transaction that changed since the last extraction. It would contain the current state of all attributes without information about what, in particular, had changed.

This is the easiest of the delta interfaces to process in most cases. Since it contains both changed and unchanged attributes, creating time-variant snapshots does not require retrieval of the previous version of the row. It also does not require the process to examine each column to determine change, but rather, only those columns where such an examination is necessary. And, when such examination is necessary, there are a number of techniques discussed later in this chapter that allow it to occur efficiently with minimal development effort.

Transaction Interface

A transaction interface is special form of delta snapshot interface. A transaction interface is made up of three parts: an action that is to be performed, data that identifies the subject, and data that defines the magnitude of the change. A transaction interface is always complete and received once. This latter characteristic differentiates it from a delta snapshot. In a delta snapshot, the same instance may be received repeatedly over time as it is updated. Instances in a transaction interface are never updated.

The term should not be confused with a business transaction. While the characteristics are basically the same, the term as it is used here describes the interaction between systems. You may have an interface that provides business transactions, but such an interface may be in the form of a delta snapshot or a transaction interface. The ways that each interface is processed are significantly different.

Database Transaction Logs

Database transaction logs are another form of delta interface. They are discussed separately because the delta capture occurs outside the control of the application system. These transaction logs are maintained by the database system itself at the physical database structure level to provide restart and recovery capabilities.

The content of these logs will vary depending on the database system being used. They may take the form of any of the three delta structures discussed earlier. In row snapshot logs, it may contain row images before and after the update, depending on how the database logging options are set.

There are three main challenges when working with database logs. The first is reading the log itself. These logs use proprietary formats and the database system may not have an API that allows direct access to these structures. Even if they did, the coding effort can be significant. Often it is necessary to use third-party interfaces to access the transaction logs.

The second challenge is applying a business context to the content of the logs. The database doesn't know about the application or business logic behind an update. A database restoration does not need to interpret the data, but rather simply get the database back to the way it was prior to the failure. On the other hand, to load a data warehouse you need to apply this data in a manner that makes business sense. You are not simply replicating the operational system, but interpreting and transforming the data. To do this from a database log requires in-depth knowledge of the application system and its data structures.

The third challenge is dealing with software changes in both the application system and the database system. A new release of the database software may significantly change the format of the transaction logs. Even more difficult to deal with are updates to the application software. The vendor may implement back-end changes that they do not even mention in their release notes because the changes do not outwardly affect the way the system functions. However, the changes may have affected the schema or data content, which in turn affects the content of the database logs.

Such logs can be an effective means to obtain change data. However, proceed with caution and only if other avenues are not available to you.

Delivering Transaction Data

The primary purpose of the data warehouse is to serve as a central data repository from which data is delivered to external applications. Those applications may be data marts, data-mining systems, operational systems, or just about any other system. In general, these other systems expect to receive data in one of two ways: a point-in-time snapshot or changes since the last delivery. Point-in-time snapshots come in two flavors: a current snapshot (the point in time is now) or the state of the data at a specified time in the past. The delivery may also be further qualified, for example, by limiting it to transactions processed during a specified period.

Since most of the work for a data warehouse is to deliver snapshots or changes, it makes sense that the data structures used to store the data be optimized to do just that. This means that the data warehouse load process should perform the work necessary to transform the data so it is in a form suitable for delivery. In the case studies in this chapter, we will provide different techniques and models to transform and store the data. No one process will be optimal for every avenue of delivery. However, depending on your timeframe and budget, you may wish to combine techniques to produce a comprehensive solution. Be careful not to overdesign the warehouse. If your deliveries require current snapshots or changes and only rarely do you require a snapshot for a point in time in the past, then it makes sense to optimize the system for the first two requirements and take a processing hit when you need to address the third.

Updating Fact Tables

Fact tables in a data mart may be maintained in three ways: a complete refresh, updating rows, or inserting changes. In a complete refresh, the entire fact table is cleared and reloaded with new data. This type of process requires delivery of current information from the data warehouse, which is transformed and summarized before loading into the data mart. This technique is commonly used for smaller, highly summarized, snapshot-type fact tables.

Updating a fact table also requires delivery of current information that is transformed to conform to the grain of the fact table. The load process then updates or inserts rows as required with the new information. This technique minimizes the growth of the fact table at the cost of an inefficient load process. This is a particularly cumbersome method if fact table uses bitmap indexes for its foreign keys and your database system does not update in place. Some database systems, such as Oracle, update rows by deleting the old ones and inserting new rows. The physical movement of a row to another location in the tablespace forces an update of all the indexes. While b-tree indexes are fairly well behaved during updates, bitmap indexes are not. During updating, bitmap structures can become fragmented and grow in size. This fragmentation reduces the efficiency of the index, causing an increase in query time. A DBA is required to monitor the indexes and rebuild them periodically to maintain optimal response times.

The third technique is to simply append the differences to the fact table. This requires the data warehouse to deliver the changes in values since the last delivery. This data is then transformed to match the granularity of the fact table, and then appended to the table. This approach works best when the measures are fully additive, but may also be suitable for semiadditive measures as well. This method is, by far, the fastest way to get the data into the data mart. Row insertion can be performed using the database's bulk load utility, which can typically load very large numbers of rows in a short period of time. Some databases allow you to disable index maintenance during the load, making the load even faster. If you are using bitmap indexes, you should load with index maintenance disabled, then rebuild the indexes after the load. The result is fast load times and optimal indexes to support queries.

Case Study: Sales Order Snapshots

In this case study, we examine how to model and process a snapshot data extract. We discuss typical transformations that occur prior to loading the data into the data warehouse. We also examine three different techniques for capturing and storing historical information.

Our packaged goods manufacturer receives sales orders for processing and fulfillment. When received by the company, an order goes through a number of administrative steps before it is approved and released for shipment. On average, an order will remain open for 7 to 10 business days before it is shipped. Its actual lifespan will depend on the size, available inventory, and delivery schedule requested by the customer. During that time, changes to the content or status of the order can occur.

The order is received by the data warehouse in a delta snapshot interface. An order appears in the extract anytime something in the order changes. The order when received is a complete picture of the order at that point in time. An order transaction is made up of a number of parts:

- The order header contains customer related information about the order. It identifies the sold-to, ship-to, and bill-to customers, shipping address, the customer's PO information, and other characteristics about the order. While such an arrangement violates normalization rules, transaction data extracts are often received in a denormalized form. We will discuss this further in the next section.

- A child of the order header is one or more pricing segments. A pricing segment contains a pricing code, an amount, a quantity, and accounting information. Pricing segments at this level represent charges or credits applied to the total order. For example, shipping charges would appear here.

- Another child of the order header is one or more order lines. An order line contains a product ID (SKU), order quantity, confirmed quantity, unit price, unit of measure, weight, volume, status code, and requested delivery date as well as other characteristics.

- A child of the order line is one or more line-pricing segments. These are in the same format as the order header-pricing segments, but contain data pertaining to the line. A segment exists for the base price as well as discounts or surcharges that make up the final price. The quantity in a pricing segment may be different than the quantity on the order line because some discounts or surcharges may be limited to a fixed maximum quantity or a portion of the order quantity. The sum of all line-pricing segments and all order header-pricing segments will equal the total order value.

■ Another child of the order lines is one or more schedule lines. A schedule line contains a planned shipping date and a quantity. The schedule will contain sufficient lines to meet the order quantity. However, based on business rules, the confirmed quantity of the order line is derived from the delivery schedule the customer is willing to accept. Therefore, only the earliest schedule lines that sum to the confirmed quantity represent the actual shipping schedule. The shipping schedule is used for reporting future expected revenue.

Figure 8.3 shows the transaction structure as it is received in the interface. During the life of the order, it is possible that some portions of the order will be deleted in the operational system. The operational system will not provide any explicit indication that lines, schedule, or pricing information has been deleted. The data will simply be missing in the new snapshot. The process must be able to detect and act on such deletions.

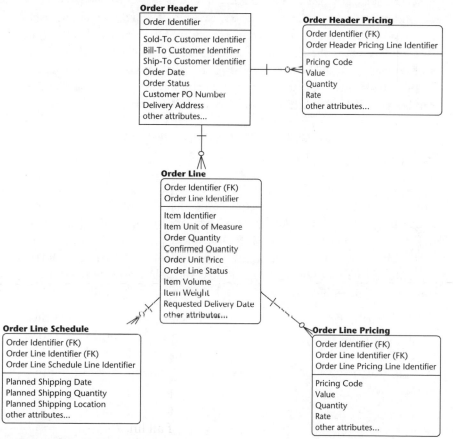

Figure 8.3 Order transaction structure.

Unit Price and Other Characteristics[1]

When delivering data to a data mart, it is important that numeric values that are used to measure the business be delivered so that they are fully additive. When dealing with sales data, it is often the case that the sales line contains a unit price along with a quantity. However, unit price is not particularly useful as a quantitative measure of the business. It cannot be summed or averaged on its own. Instead, what is needed is the extended price of the line, which can be calculated by multiplying price by quantity. This value is fully additive and may serve as a business measure. Unit price, on the other hand, is a characteristic of the sale. It most certainly useful in analysis, but in the role as a dimensional attribute rather than a measure.

Depending on your business, you may choose not to store unit price, but rather derive it from the extended value when necessary for analysis. In the retail business, this is not an issue since the unit price is always expressed in the selling unit. This is not the case with a packaged goods manufacturer, which may sell the same product in a variety of units (cases, pallets, and so on). In this case, any analysis of unit price needs to take into account the unit being sold. This analysis is simplified when the quantity and value are stored. The unit dependent value, sales quantity, would be converted and stored expressed in a standard unit, such as the base or inventory unit. Either the sales quantity or standardized quantity can simply be divided into the value to derive the unit price.

Transforming the Order

The order data extracted from the operational system is not purposely built for populating the data warehouse. It is used for a number of different purposes, providing order information to other operational systems. Thus, the data extract contains superfluous information. In addition, some of the data is not well suited for use in a data warehouse but could be used to derive more useful data. Figure 8.4 shows the business model of how the order appears in the data warehouse. Its content is based on the business rules for the organization.

This is not the final model. As you will see in subsequent sections of this case study, the final model varies depending on how you decide to collect order history. The model in Figure 8.4 represents an order at a moment in time. It is used in this discussion to identify the attributes that are maintained in the data warehouse.

1 The term "characteristic" is being used to refer to dimensional attributes as used in dimensional modeling. This is to avoid confusion with the relational modeling use of attribute, which has a more generic meaning.

A number of attributes are eliminated from the data model because they are redundant with information maintained elsewhere. Item weight and volume were removed from Order Line because those attributes are available from the Item UOM entity. The Delivery Address is removed from the Order Header because that information is carried by the Ship-To Customer role in the Customer entity. This presumes that the ship-to address cannot be overridden, which is the case in this instance. If such an address can be changed during order entry, you would need to retain that information with the order. As mentioned earlier, the data being received in such interfaces are often in a denormalized form. This normalization process should be a part of any interface analysis. Its purpose is not necessarily to change the content of the interface, but to identify what form the data warehouse model will take. Properly done, it can significantly reduce data storage requirements as well as improve the usability of the data warehouse.

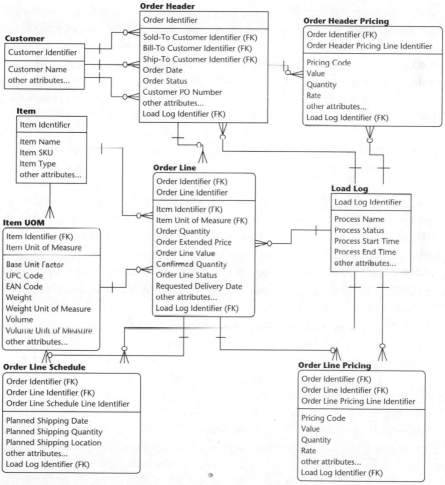

Figure 8.4 Order business model.

Units of Measure in Manufacturing and Distribution

As retail customers, we usually deal with one unit of measure, the *each*. Whether we buy a gallon of milk, a six-pack of beer or a jumbo bag of potato chips, it is still one item, an *each*. Manufacturing and distribution, on the other hand, have to deal with a multitude of units of the same item. The most common are the *each*, or consumer unit; the case; and the pallet, although there are many others, such as carton, barrel, layer, and so forth. When orders are received, the quantity may be expressed in a number of different ways. Customers may order cases, pallets, or eaches, of the same item. Within inventory, an item is tracked by its SKU. The SKU number not only identifies the item, but also identifies the unit of measure used to inventory the item. This inventory unit of measure is often referred to as the base unit of measure.

In such situations, the data warehouse needs to provide mechanisms to accommodate different units of measure for the same item. Any quantity being stored needs to be tagged with the unit of measure the quantity is expressed in. It is not enough to simply convert everything into the base unit of measure for a number of reasons. First, any such conversion creates a derived value. Changes in the conversion factor will affect the derivation. You should always store such quantities as they were entered to avoid discrepancies later. Second, you will be required to present those quantities in different units of measure, depending on the audience. Therefore, you cannot avoid unit conversions at query time.

For a particular item and unit of measure, the source system will often provide characteristics such as conversion factors, weight, dimensions, and volume. A challenge you will face is how to maintain those characteristics. To understand how the data warehouse should maintain the conversion factors and other physical characteristics, it is important to understand the SKU and its implications in inventory management. The SKU represents the physical unit maintained and counted in inventory. Everything relating to the content and physical characteristics of an item is tied to the SKU. If there is any change to the item, such as making it bigger or smaller, standard inventory practice requires that the changed item be assigned a new SKU identifier. Therefore, any changes to the physical information relating to the SKU can be considered corrections to erroneous data and not a new version of the truth. So, in general, this will not require maintaining a time-variant structure since you would want error corrections to be applied to historical data as well.

This approach, however, only applies to units of measure that are the base unit or smaller. Larger units of measure can have physical changes that do not affect inventory and do not require a new SKU. For example, an item is inventoried by the case. The SKU represents a case of the product. A pallet of the product is made up of 40 cases, made up of five layers with eight cases on a layer. Over time it has been discovered that there were a number of instances where cases

on the bottom layer were being crushed due to the weight above them. It is decided to reconfigure the pallet to four layers, each holding 32 cases. This changes the weight, dimensions, volume, and conversion factors of the pallet but does not affect the SKU itself. The change does not affect how inventory is counted, so no new SKU is created. However the old and new pallets have significance in historical reporting, so it is necessary to retain time-variant information so that pallet counts, order weights, and volumes can be properly calculated.

This necessitates a hybrid approach when applying changes to unit of measure data. Updates to base units and smaller units are applied in place without history, while updates to units larger than the base unit should be maintained as time-based variants.

Another type of transformation creates new attributes to improve the usability of the information. For example, the data extract provides the Item Unit Price. This attribute is transformed into Item Extended Price by multiplying the unit price by the ordered quantity. The extended price is a more useful value for most applications since it can be summed and averaged directly, without further manipulation in a delivery query. In fact, because of the additional utility the value provides and since no information is lost, it is common to replace the unit value with the extended value in the model. Also, since the unit price is often available in an item price table, its inclusion in the sales transaction information provides little additional value. Another transformation is the calculation of Order Line Value. In this case, it is the sum of the values received in Order Line Pricing for that line. There may be other calculations as well. There may be business rules to estimate the Gross and Net Proceeds of Sale from the Order Line Pricing information. Such calculations should take place during the load process and be placed into the data warehouse so they are readily available for delivery.

By performing such transformations up front in the load process, you eliminate the need to perform these calculations later when delivering data to the data marts or other external applications. This eliminates duplication of effort when enforcing these business rules and the possibility of different results due to misinterpretation of the rules or errors in the implementation of the delivery process transformation logic. Making the effort to calculate and store these derivations up front goes a long way toward simplifying data delivery and ensuring consistency across multiple uses of the data.

The data warehouse is required to record the change history for the order lines and pricing segments. In the remainder of this case study, we will present three techniques to maintain the current transaction state, detect deletions, and maintain a historical change log. We will evaluate each technique for its ability to accomplish these tasks as well as its utility for delivering data to downstream systems and data marts.

Technique 1: Complete Snapshot Capture

The model in Figure 8.2 shows an example of structures to support complete snapshot capture. In such a situation, a full image of the transaction Stock Keeping Unit (in this case, an order Stock Keeping Unit) is maintained for each point in time the order is received in the data warehouse. The Order Snapshot Date is part of the primary key and identifies the point in time that image is valid. Figure 8.5 shows the complete model as it applies to this case study.

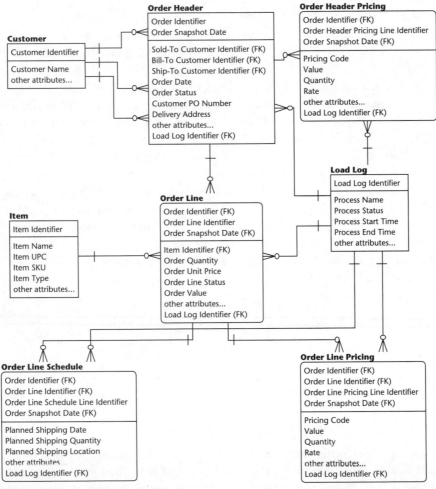

Figure 8.5   Complete snapshot history.

This approach is deceptively simple. Processing the data extract is a matter of inserting new rows with the addition of applying a snapshot date. However, collecting data in this manner has a number of drawbacks.

The first drawback concerns the fact that the tables themselves can become huge. Let's say the order quantity on one line of a 100-line order was changed. In this structure, we would store a complete image of this changed order. If order changes occur regularly over a period of time, the data volume would be many times larger than is warranted. A second drawback is that it is extremely difficult to determine the nature of the change. SQL is a very poor tool to look for differences between rows. How do you find out that the difference between the two versions of the order is that the quantity on order line 38 is 5 higher than the previous version? How do you find all changes on all orders processed in the last 5 days? The data as it exists provides no easy way to determine the magnitude or direction of change, which is critical information for business intelligence applications. A third drawback is that obtaining the current state of an order requires a complex SQL query. You need to embed a correlated subquery in the WHERE clause to obtain the maximum snapshot date for that order. Here is an example of such a query:

```
SELECT...
FROM ORDER_HEADER, ORDER_LINE
WHERE ORDER_HEADER.ORDER_SNAPSHOT_DATE = (SELECT
MAX(ORDER_SNAPSHOT_DATE) FROM ORDER_HEADER h WHERE h.ORDER_IDENTIFIER =
ORDER_HEADER.ORDER_IDENTIFIER)...
```

Implementing a Load Log

One table that is crucial to any data warehouse implementation is the Load Log table as shown in Figure 8.5. This table is invaluable for auditing and troubleshooting data warehouse loads.

The table contains one row for every load process run against the data warehouse. When a load process starts, it should create a new Load Log row with a new unique Load Log Identifier. Every row touched by the load process should be tagged with that Load Log Identifier as a foreign key on that row.

The Load Log table itself should contain whatever columns you deem as useful. It should include process start and end timestamps, completion status, names, row counts, control totals, and other information that the load process can provide.

Because every row in the data warehouse is tagged with the load number that inserted or updated it, you can easily isolate a specific load or process when problems occur. It provides the ability to reverse or correct a problem when a process aborts after database commits have already occurred. In addition, the Load Log data can be used to generate end-of-day status reports.

(continued)

> ## Implementing a Load Log *(continued)*
>
> Using this technique, the burden to determine the magnitude of change falls on the delivery process. Since SQL alone is inadequate to do this, it would require implementation of a complex transformation process to extract, massage, and deliver the data. It is far simpler to capture change as the data is received into the data warehouse, performing the transformation once, reducing the effort and time required in delivery. As you will see in the other techniques discussed in this section, the impact on the load process can be minimized.

Technique 2: Change Snapshot Capture

Storing complete copies of the order every time it changes takes up a lot of space and is inefficient. Rather than store a complete snapshot of the transaction each time it has changed, why not just store those rows where a change has occurred? In this section, we examine two methods to accomplish this. In the first method we look at the most obvious approach, expanding the foreign key relationship, and show why this can become unworkable. The second method discussed uses associative entities to resolve the many-to-many relationships that result from this technique. But first, since this technique is predicated on detecting a change to a row, let us examine how we can detect change easily.

Detecting Change

When processing the data extract, the contents of the new data is compared to the most current data loaded from the previous extract. If the data is different, a new row is inserted with the new data and the current snapshot date. But how can we tell that the data is different? The interface in this case study simply sends the entire order without any indication as to which portion of the order changed. You can always compare column-for-column between the new data and the contents of the table, but to do so involves laborious coding that does not produce a very efficient load process. A simpler, more-efficient method is to use a cyclical redundancy checksum (CRC) code (see sidebar "Using CRCs for Change Detection").

A new attribute, CRC Value, is added to each entity. This contains the CRC value calculated for the data on the row. Comparing this value with a new CRC value calculated for the incoming data allows you to determine if the data on the row has changed without requiring a column-by-column comparison. However, using a CRC value presents a very remote risk of missing an update due to a false positive result. A false positive occurs when the old and new CRC values match but the actual data is different. Using a 32-bit CRC value, the risk of a false positive is about 1 in 4 billion. If this level of error cannot be tolerated, then a column-by-column comparison is necessary.

Using CRCs for Change Detection

Cyclical redundancy checksum (CRC) algorithms are methods used to represent the content of a data stream as a single numeric value. They are used in digital networks to validate the transmission of data. When data is sent, the transmitter calculates a CRC value based on the data it sent. This value is appended to the end of the data stream. The receiver uses the same algorithm to calculate its own CRC value on the data it receives. The receiver then compares its CRC value with the value received from the sender. If the values are different, the data received was different than the data sent, so the receiver signals an error and requests retransmission. CRC calculations are sensitive to the content and position of the bytes, so any change will likely result in a different CRC value.

This same technique is useful for identifying data changes in data warehouse applications. In this case, the data stream is the collection of bytes that represent the row or record to be processed. As part of the data transformation process during the load, the record to be processed is passed to a CRC calculation function. The CRC is then passed along with the rest of the data. If the row is to be inserted into the database, the CRC is also stored in a column in the table. If the row is to be updated, the row is first read to retrieve the old CRC. If the old CRC is different than the new CRC, the data has changed and the update process can proceed. If the old and new CRC values are the same, the data has not changed and no update is necessary.

CRC algorithms come in two flavors, 16-bit and 32-bit algorithms. This indicates the size of the number being returned. A 16-bit number is capable of holding 65,536 different values, while a 32-bit number can store 4,294,967,296 values. For data warehousing applications, you should always use a 32-bit algorithm to reduce the risk of false positive results.

A false positive occurs when the CRC algorithm returns the same value even though the data is different. When you use a 16-bit algorithm, the odds of this occurring is 1 in 65,536. While this can be tolerated in some network applications, it is too high a risk for a data warehouse.

Many ETL tools provide a CRC calculation function. Also, descriptions and code for CRC algorithms can be found on the Web. Perform a search on "CRC algorithm" for additional information.

Method 1—Using Foreign Keys

Figure 8.6 shows a model using typical one-to-many relationships. Although it is not obvious at first glance, this model is significantly different from that shown in Figure 8.5.

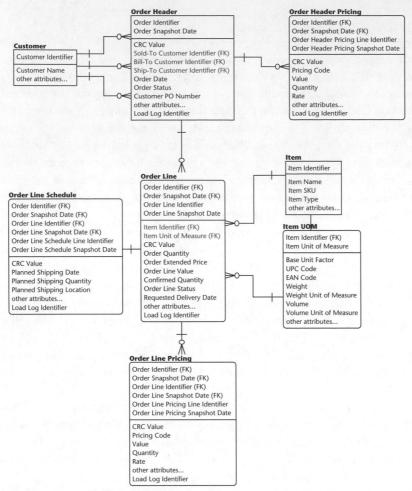

Figure 8.6 Change snapshot history.

In this model, each table has its own snapshot date as part of the primary key. Since these dates are independent of the other snapshot dates, the one-to-many relationship and foreign key inference can be misleading. For example, what if the order header changes but the order lines do not? Figure 8.7 shows an example of this problem.

On March 2, 2003, order #10023 is added to the data warehouse. The order contains four lines. The order header and order lines are added with the snapshot dates set to March 2. On March 5, a change is made to the order header. A new order header row is added and the snapshot date for that row is set to March 5, 2003. Since there was no change to the order lines, there were no new rows added to the Order Line Table.

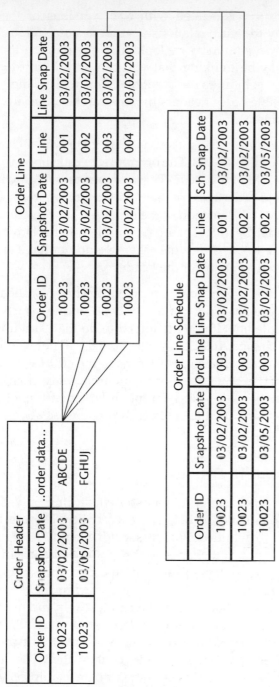

Figure 8.7 Change snapshot example.

Each order line can rightly be associated with both versions of the order header resulting in a many-to-many relationship that is not obvious in the model. What's more, how do you know by looking at the data on the order line? At this point, you may be thinking that you can add a "most current order header snapshot date" column to the order line. This will certainly allow you to identify all the possible order headers the line can be associated with. But that is not the only problem.

Carrying the scenario a bit further, let's also say that there was a change to order schedule line 002 for order line 003. The original schedule lines are in the table with snapshot dates of March 2, 2003. These reference the March 2 versions of the order header and order line. The new row, reflecting the schedule change also references the March 2 version of the order line, but references the March 5 version of the order header. There is a problem here. How do we relate the new schedule line to the order line when we do not have an order line that references the March 5 version of the header?

The short answer to this is that whenever a parent entity changes, such as the order header, you must store snapshots of all its child entities, such as the order line and order schedule line. If you are forced to do that, and it is common that the order header changes frequently, this model will not result in the kind of space savings or process efficiencies that make the effort worthwhile. A more reasonable approach is to accept that maintaining only changes will result in many-to-many relationships between the different entities. The best way to deal with many-to-many relationships is through associative entities. This brings us to method 2.

Method 2—Using Associative Entities

As the discussion with the first method demonstrated, storing only changes results in many-to-many relationships between each entity. These many-to-many relationships must be handled with associative entities. Figure 8.8 shows such a model. One significant change to the model is the use of surrogate keys for each entity. Since the primary motivation for storing only changed rows is to save space, it follows that surrogate keys are appropriate to reduce the size of the association tables and their indexes. In the model, the associative entities between the Order Header and Order Line and Order Line Pricing are what you would normally expect. However, the other two, Order Line Line Pricing and Order Line Line Schedule, contain the Order Header key as well. This is because, as we discussed in the update example shown in Figure 8.7, changes occur independently of any parent-child relationships in the data. The associative entity must maintain the proper context for each version of a row.

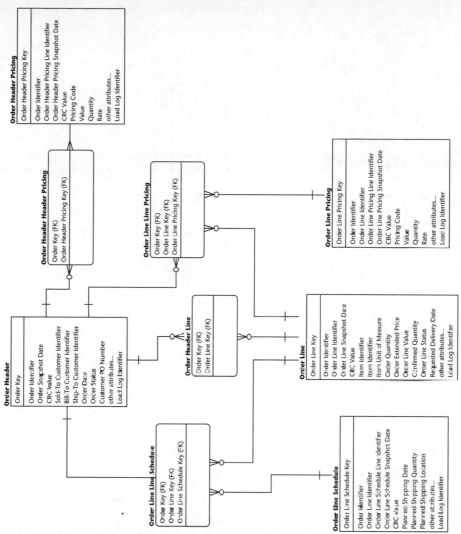

Figure 8.8 Change snapshot with associative entities.

The process to load this structure must process each transaction from the top, starting with the Order Header. The process needs to keep track of the key of the most current version of the superior entities as well as know if the entity was changed. If a superior entity was changed, rows need to be added to the associative entities for every instance of each inferior entity regardless of a change to that entity. If the superior entity did not change, a new associative entity row is necessary only when the inferior entity changes. Figure 8.9 shows the associative entity version of the update scenario shown in Figure 8.7. As you can see, the associative entities clearly record all the proper states of the transaction.

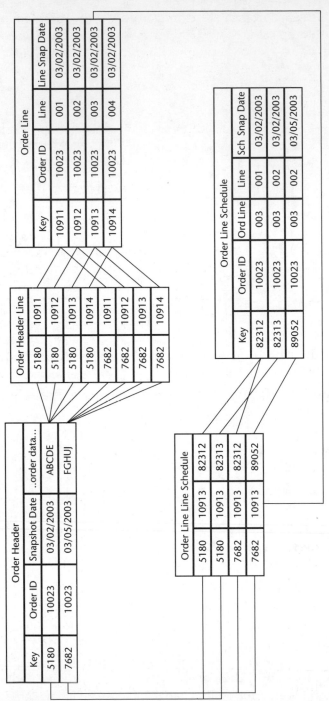

Figure 8.9 Change snapshot example using associative entities.

The first method discussed is unworkable for a number of reasons; the most basic being that there isn't enough information to resolve the true relationship between the tables. Using associative entities resolves this problem and produces the same results as in the first technique, but with a significant saving in storage space if updates are frequent and if updates typically affect a small portion of the entire transaction. However, it still presents the same issues as the previous method. Its does not provide information about the magnitude or direction of the change.

The next technique expands on this model to show how it can be enhanced to collect information about the nature of the change.

Technique 3: Change Snapshot with Delta Capture

In this section, we expand on the previous technique to address a shortcoming of the model, its inability to easily provide information of the magnitude or direction of change. When discussing the nature of change in a business transaction, it is necessary to separate the attributes in the model into two general categories. The first category is measurable attributes, or those attributes that are used to measure the magnitude of a business event. In the case of sales orders, attributes such as quantity, value, and price are measurable attributes. The other category is characteristic attributes. Characteristic attributes are those that describe the state or context of the measurable attributes. To capture the nature of change, the model must represent the different states of the order as well as the amount of change, the deltas, of the measurable attributes.

Figure 8.10 shows the model. It is an expansion of the associative entity model shown in Figure 8.8. Four new delta entities have been added to collect the changes to the measurable attributes as well as some new attributes in the existing entities to ease the load process.

The Delta entities only contain measurable attributes. They are used to collect the difference between the previous and current values for the given context. For example, the Order Line Delta entity collects changes to quantity, extended price, value, and confirmed quantity. The Order Line entity continues to maintain these attributes as well; however, in the case of Order Line, these attributes represent the current value, not the change. This changes the purpose of the snapshot entities, such as Order Line, from the previous technique. In this model, the delta entities have taken the role of tracking changes to measurable attributes. The snapshot entities are now only required to track changes to the characteristic attributes. Measurable attributes in the snapshot entities contain the last-known value for that context. New instances are not created in the snapshot entities if there is only a change in the measurable attributes. A new attribute, Current Indicator, is added to Order Line. This aids in identifying the most current version of the order line. It is a Boolean attribute whose value is true for the most current version of a line. Note that this attribute could also be used in the previous example to ease load processing and row selection.

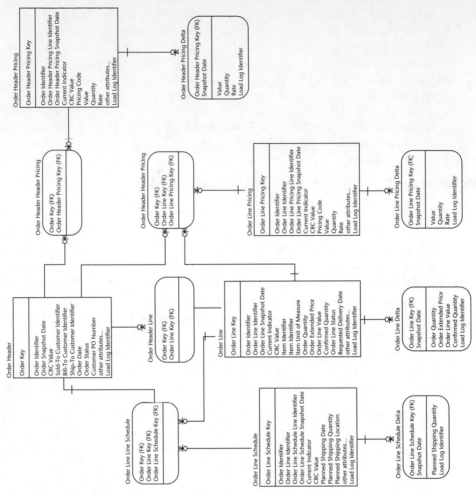

Figure 8.10 Associative entity model with delta capture.

Load Processing

When loading a database using this model, there are a number of techniques that simplify the coding and processing against this model. First is the use of the CRC Value column. In this model, snapshot tables such as Order Line are used to track changes in the characteristic columns only. This is different from the previous technique where the Order Line table is used to track changes in all columns. The delta tables, such as Order Line Delta, are tracking changes to measures. Therefore, for this approach, the CRC value should only be calculated using the characteristic columns. If the CRC value changes, you have identified a change in state, not in measurable value. This event causes the creation of a new row in the Order Line table. If the CRC value does not change, you perform an update in place, changing only the measurable value columns.

Database Triggers

Database triggers are processes written in SQL that are executed by the database system when specific events occur. These events are tied to update actions against a table. Triggers may be executed whenever a row in a table is inserted, updated, or deleted. Within a trigger, the programmer has the ability to access both the old and new values for a column. These values can be examined and manipulated, new values may be derived, and actions against other tables in the database may be affected.

The second technique is the use of the Current Indicator. When you are processing a row, such as Order Line, locate the current version using the business key (Order Identifier and Order Line Identifier) and a Current Indicator value of true. If, after comparing CRC values, the current row will be superseded, update the old row, setting the Current Indicator value to false. The superseding row is inserted with the Current Indicator set to true.

The third technique is the use of database triggers on the snapshot tables to update the delta tables. Based on the previous two techniques, there are only three possible update actions that can be implemented against the snapshot tables: inserting a new row, updating measurable columns on the current row, or setting the Current Indicator column to false. When a new row is inserted in the snapshot table, the trigger also inserts a row in the delta table, using the new values from the measurable columns. When the measurable columns are being updated, the trigger examines the old and new values to determine if there has been a change. If there has been a change, it calculates the difference by subtracting the old value from the new value and storing the differences as a new row in the delta table. If the Current Indicator is being changed from true to false, the trigger inserts a new row in the delta table with the values set to the negative of the values in the snapshot table row. This action effectively marks the point in time from which this particular state is no longer applicable. By storing the negatives of the value in the delta table, the sum of the deltas for that row become zero. We still, however, retain the last known value in the snapshot row.

What you wind up with in the delta tables is a set of differences that can be summed, showing the changes that the measurable values underwent during the life of the snapshot. You can calculate a value for any point in time by summing these differences up to the point of interest. And, with the use of the associative entities, these values are framed within the proper characteristic context.

With the data stored within the data warehouse in this manner, you can easily provide incremental deliveries to the data marts. When you need to deliver changes to a data mart since the last delivery, you use the current time and the last delivery time to qualify your query against the Snapshot Date column in the delta table. You then use the foreign key to join through to the other tables to obtain the desired characteristics. Depending on your requirements, you can reduce the size of the output by summing on the characteristics. It is typical with this type of delivery extract to limit the output to the content of one delta table. It is difficult, and not particularly useful, to combine measurable values from different levels of detail, such as order lines and order line schedules, in the same output.

This technique addresses the two key delivery needs of a data warehouse. Using the Current Indicator, it is easy to produce a current snapshot of the data, and, using the delta tables, it is easy to deliver changes since the last delivery. This structure is less than optimal for producing a point-in-time snapshot for some time in the past. This is so because the snapshot tables contain the last-known measurable values for a given state, not a history of measurable values. To obtain measurable values for a point in time, it is necessary to sum the delta rows associated with the snapshot row.

An interesting aspect of this is that, by recording the magnitude and direction of change, this model provides more information than the other models, yet it may actually require less storage space. There are fewer rows in the snapshot tables and the associative entities because new snapshot rows are only created when the characteristics change, not the measurable values. The delta rows are greater in number, but most likely much smaller than the snapshot rows. If your environment sees more changes to measurable values than changes to characteristics, you may experience some storage economy. Even if this is not the case, any increase in storage over the previous technique is not proportionally significant. If one of your primary delivery challenges is to perform incremental updates to the data marts, this structure provides a natural, efficient means to accomplish that.

Case Study: Transaction Interface

GOSH stores receive all retail sales transaction data through its cash register system. The system records the time of sale, the store, the UPC code if the item, the price and quantity purchased, and the customer's account number if the customer used an affinity card. The data also includes sales taxes collected; coupons used; a transaction total; a method of payment, including credit card or checking account number; and the amount of change given. In addition to sales transactions, returns and credits are also handled through the cash register system. The clerk can specify the nature of the return and disposition of the item when entering the credit.

In addition to tracking sales, the company wishes to monitor return rates on items. Items with high rates of return would be flagged for investigation and possibly removed from the stores. They are also interested in tracking customer purchase habits through the affinity cards. Affinity cards are credit cards issued by a bank under GOSH's name. These are different from private-label cards, such as those offered by major department stores. With a private-label card, the store is granting credit and assumes the risk. The issuing bank assumes the credit risk with affinity cards. From this arrangement, GOSH receives information about the customer, which they use in marketing efforts. Based on the customer's interests, they offer promotions and incentives to encourage additional sales.

Information is transmitted from the stores at 15-minute intervals. Data volumes vary significantly, depending on the time of day and the season. A large store can produce, at peak times, 10,000 detail lines per hour. During the heaviest times of the year, this peak rate can be sustained for 6 to 7 hours, with a total of 100,000 lines being produced during a 14-hour day. Since the sizes of the stores vary, daily volume can reach as many as 12 million lines a day across 250 stores. Overall volume averages around 800,000 lines per day over a typical year. There are 363 selling days in the year, with all stores closed on Christmas and Mother's Day.

Modeling the Transactions

Figure 8.11 shows the business model for the sales transactions. In it we capture information about the sale as well as any returns and coupons used. Return and coupon information is carried in separate sales lines, with optional foreign key references back to the sale line that was being returned or for which the coupon was used. GOSH was able to tie a return back to the original sale line by printing the sale identifier as a bar code on every receipt. When the item is returned, the receipt is scanned and the original sale identifier is sent with the return transaction. The coupon line reference is generated by the cash register system and transmitted with the transaction. However, this relationship is optional since sometimes returns are made without a receipt, and coupons are not always for a specific product purchase.

There are accommodations we may wish to make in the physical model. We may not wish to instantiate the Return Line and Coupon Line entities as tables, but instead incorporate those columns in the Sale Line table. Depending on how your database system stores null values, there may be no cost in terms of space utilization to do this. Logically, there is no difference in using the model since the return sale and coupon sale foreign key references are optional to begin with. They would continue to be optional if those columns were moved into the Sale Line table. The advantage of combining the tables is that it would speed the load process and simplify maintenance.

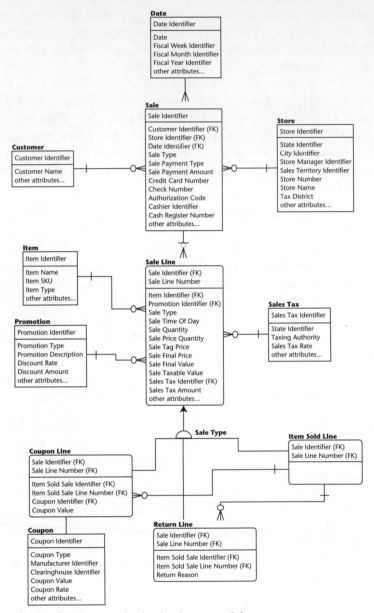

Figure 8.11 Retail sales business model.

Another point worth mentioning in the model is the collection of prices and values in the sale line. Hopefully, all these attributes are received in the data feed and are not derived. The cash register system has facilities to calculate value and tax. Often these calculations are complex, but even simple calculations may be subject to interpretation. For example, if an item is priced at 8 for $1.00 and the customer buys 7, how much is the customer charged? The answer will depend on how you round $0.875. Is the rounding method the same in the cash register system as it is in the database? Do you want to take that chance? In situations like this, it is simpler and more accurate to take the numbers the data extract gives you and not attempt to eliminate or derive data.

Processing the Transactions

The nice thing about transaction interfaces is that the content is precisely what the data warehouse needs. Every transaction represents new information that is additive to prior information. Transactions are not repeated or changed. So, aside from data validation and transformations, there isn't much to do besides insert the data into the data warehouse. The only real issue to address is how the data is delivered to the data marts. There are two general schools of though on this topic. One method is to prepare the data for delivery in the same process that prepares the data for the data warehouse, then load the data and deliver it simultaneously. The other method is to load the data warehouse and deliver the data using data warehouse queries after the load. We will discuss each method.

Simultaneous Delivery

Figure 8.12 shows the process architecture for simultaneous delivery. In this scenario, the data is transformed in the ETL process for loading into the data warehouse as well as staging for delivery of the data to the data marts or other external systems. The staging area may be nothing more than a flat file that is bulk loaded into the data mart databases.

The advantage of this method is that it shortens the time necessary to get the data into the data marts. There is no need to wait until the data has been loaded into the data warehouse before it can be loaded into the data marts. If you have a long data warehouse load process, or the processing window is so small, you may wish to consider this approach.

However, the time saving does not come without a cost. There is a disadvantage that the data warehouse and the data marts may get out of sync because of technical problems, such as hardware failures. Since no process would exist to move the data from the data warehouse to the data marts, recovery from such a situation would require processes involving the staging area. It would also require some mechanism to validate the recovery based on reconciliation with the data warehouse. So, to address these issues, you would wind up having to develop additional processes, including one to pull the data from the data warehouse, should there be a disaster or some other critical situation. You would also require putting an ongoing audit in place to detect when synchronization problems occur. We recommend against using this technique except in very rare instances.

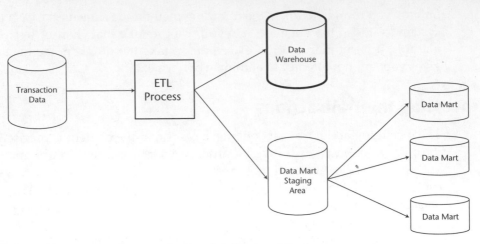

Figure 8.12 Simultaneous load and delivery architecture.

Postload Delivery

Figure 8.13 shows an example of a postload delivery process. After the data has been transformed and loaded into the data warehouse, other processes extract and deliver the data to the target data marts or external systems.

The disadvantage of this approach is the delay between receiving the data and making it available to the data marts. Such a disadvantage may be small or nonexistent if sufficient time exists in your process schedule. Among the advantages are that it is easier to control the process and ensure synchronization. The data warehouse becomes the sole source of data, assuring that all downstream systems are receiving the same information. Another advantage is it reduces development time. In the other method, it is necessary to develop redundant fail-safe processes to use the data warehouse for disaster recovery as well as put an audit mechanism in place to ensure synchronization. With this method, you need only develop a single process to deliver data from the data warehouse to the marts. The time frame of the delivery process can be a parameter or control table driven so that disaster recovery can be serviced through the same process. We recommend this approach unless time constraints absolutely require simultaneous delivery.

A transaction interface is one of the simplest interfaces to process. Transactions are received once, are fully additive, and they are not updated. Each transaction defines its own scope as well as the direction and magnitude of change. It is an ideal data extract for both the data warehouse and data marts. So ideal, in fact, that one is tempted to send the extract to both the data warehouse and the data marts at the same time. We recommend that you resist this temptation and perform all data deliveries from the data warehouse. You should consider

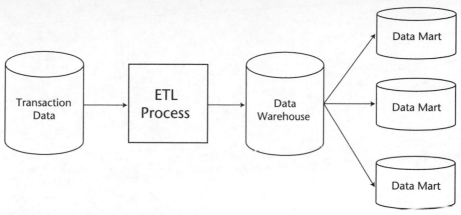

Figure 8.13 Postload delivery architecture.

simultaneous delivery only in cases where delivery time is critical. If you do, you should also invest in the proper process infrastructure to provide fallback delivery processes as well as suitable audits to ensure data consistency with the data warehouse.

Summary

There are numerous means of receiving transactional information into the data warehouse, far too many to discuss in any detail within this chapter. One of the points you should take away from this discussion is the importance of recording the magnitude and direction of change inferred in a transaction. This is an inherent nature found in some extracts while in others, considerable effort must be made to derive this information. It is that change that drives a considerable portion of business analysis. Deriving and quantifying change within the data warehouse goes a long way to supporting and simplifying that analysis.

CHAPTER 9

Data Warehouse Optimization

Optimization is a broad topic that envelops the entire data warehouse environment from source system data acquisition to final delivery to the information consumer. A data warehousing program within an organization not only needs to provide a query environment that is fast and responsive, but must also itself be fast and responsive in addressing the needs of its user community. To that end, we will not only examine aspects of creating an efficient physical database (the technology model), but also examine means to improve the development process and system models as well.

We begin with a look at the data warehouse design and development. Next, we discuss physical database techniques to improve the load and publication of data into the data warehouse and to the marts. We will also briefly examine physical database techniques for the data marts. Finally, we will discuss changes to the entity structures in the system model that can effect optimization of the physical model.

Optimizing the Development Process

The development process includes design and analysis as well as coding the load and publication applications. This section discusses both areas.

Optimizing Design and Analysis

The modeling methodology is at the core of the Corporate Information Factory. We strongly believe that following this methodology will significantly reduce the risk of rework, greatly improve overall understanding of the data warehouse content, and contribute to the overall success of the implementation. A model, after all, is nothing more than boxes and lines on paper. The effort to correct and change the model is significantly less than modifying processes and schemas developed from a faulty model. A small effort up front to get the model right goes a long way toward shortening the development process and improving the overall development experience.

Chapter 4 touches on the modeling methodology, but you might refer to Bill Inmon's *Building the Data Warehouse, Third Edition* (Wiley, 2002) for the complete data warehouse development methodology, including deliverables and explanations of why each step is needed.

Optimizing Application Development

If you are reading this book, it is safe to assume that you intend to create an enterprise data warehouse. If you follow the methodology, the effort must be viewed as a long-term program with many short-term projects incrementally expanding the overall scope of the data warehouse. This implies a commitment of manpower over the life of the program to develop, implement, and support the applications to load and deliver the data warehouse.

Labor costs are the most significant expense any organization will encounter in a data warehouse project. Using those resources effectively can reduce cost and development time. To that end, for a program of this size, you should give very serious consideration to the purchase and use of an extract, transform, and load (ETL) tool. A good ETL tool provides a development environment specifically designed to perform the types of tasks necessary to load and deliver data warehouses. Use of such a tool can dramatically decrease the application development effort over traditional coding methods using languages such as COBOL, C, Java, or SQL. Reductions in labor effort and development time of 60 percent or more are common, with 80 percent reductions in effort attainable with those experienced with the tool.

Selecting an ETL Tool

There are a number of excellent ETL products on the market today. You can find an extensive list of major and minor ETL vendors at http://www.dwinfocenter.org. When selecting such a tool, here are some points you should consider in your evaluation.

Data access. Where is your source data, and what database systems are used? Can the tool connect to and read these sources? How will such connections affect your operational system? How does the tool handle transfer of data across your network?

Throughput. Does the tool support memory caching for code and key lookups? Is the data streamed between transformations? Can the transformations execute asynchronously across multiple processors? Does the tool support parallel streams for very high data volumes?

Extensibility. Do the transformations provided with the tool perform most of the tasks you require? Can you easily code and implement custom transformation logic not covered in the tool? Is the custom logic reusable?

Real-time data acquisition. Do you require real-time or near-real-time data collection? Does the tool support it? Does the tool need to interface with messaging software?

Meta data. When you develop an ETL process, you are defining the data sources, transformations (that is, business rules), and targets for the data. There is a wealth of valuable information embedded in these processes. What facilities does the tool provide to publish the meta data for use in a meta data repository, OLAP access tools, or other forms of documentation?

The tool's development environment. Does the GUI work for your developers? How well does it integrate the various aspects of development? How does it support reuse of existing processes or modules? Does it support access control, versioning, and releases? Does it support a tiered implementation environment (that is, development, QA, and production)? Does the tool provide debug and test facilities?

Your environment. What are your expected volumes and how do you handle bulk data transfer across your network? Do you permit data streaming between applications across the network or must the data be extracted locally, compressed and then moved to the target system? If the ETL tool requires custom transformations to be written outside the tool using an API and a language such as C, do you have the staff to do such work within your control, or does it require resources outside your control? What is the project impact of using outside resources? Does the tool require its own server, or can it coexist on the data warehouse server? The latter is preferable as it reduces network impact.

Proof of concept. Is the chosen vendor willing to perform a proof of concept exercise? If you have no prior experience with the chosen tool, or even if you do, it is a good idea to engage in a proof of concept exercise prior to final purchase. The vendor will rightly insist that such an exercise be well defined and close ended. It will be up to you to develop a small scenario that encapsulates issues of most concern to you. It should be well documented with clear definition of the data source, the transformations, and the target structures. The scenario should include a clear statement of the expected outcomes and definition of a successful conclusion.

The vendor.   As with any other software purchase, you should evaluate the vendor itself. You should consider training, after sales support, commitment to product improvement, and the stability of the company.

Optimizing the Database

This section looks at techniques to optimize the physical database implementation without impacting the logical data model. There are a number of logical data model changes that are possible to optimize database performance. These changes will be discussed in the next section "Optimizing the System Model."

Since this book does not cover any specific database system in particular, the strategies and techniques discussed here are necessarily generic in their description and approach. Each database system product varies in its features and implementation approach. Some techniques may not produce the optimal results or may require some adjustment to suit the particular product. We believe what is outlined here to be generally applicable across all systems; however, you should consult with your database administrator for specific details and benefits for your environment.

We first examine techniques to optimize the data warehouse physical schema. The techniques examine options to arrange data and indexes within the database and their applicability to the data warehouse environment. Next, we examine processing techniques to improve load and publication performance.

Data Clustering

Data clustering is a technique where related rows from different tables are placed within the same disk block so that, optimally, the system retrieves all the data in a single disk read. Figure 9.1 shows an example of an invoice transaction made up of an invoice header and invoice line table. The invoice number relates the two tables. The database system attempts to place the invoice line rows in the same physical data block as the invoice header row with the same invoice ID.

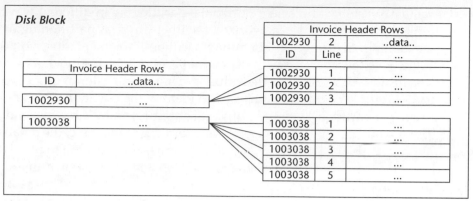

Figure 9.1 Data clustering.

When all goes well, a query that accesses a specific invoice and its lines can do so very quickly. To be effective, it requires that the data to be inserted is presented to the database in a single transaction. If not, the data block may fill with headers, leaving no room for the lines. This may cause the database to create extension blocks or split blocks impacting the insert process or defeating the query benefit of co-location. This technique also requires careful tuning based on the size and number of invoice header and line rows. Getting it wrong may result in too many reads or allocation of too much space.

This technique is geared toward random access of specific related rows. Within a data warehouse it may be useful for structures that require real-time data update, much in the same manner as a transactional system. The downside is that this technique hampers bulk data access because the data density is lower, with a table's rows spread over more disk real estate than what would be expected in a nonclustered table. A table scan, in particular, performs poorly with this structure.

Table Partitioning

Table partitioning, sometimes referred to as horizontal partitioning, is a technique to break a single table's data into multiple independent subtables based on values in one or more columns in the row. For example, a table may have a transaction date column used to partition the data by year. Transactions with dates in 2001 would be placed in a physically separate structure than transactions with dates in 2002. Another form of partitioning, vertical partitioning is a technique where the columns in a table are split into multiple tables. This type of partitioning directly affects the model and how data is accessed, whereas horizontal partitioning is transparent to the applications. We discuss vertical partitioning in the section on model optimization.

Database systems implement horizontal partitioning in different ways. These implementations can be categorized as either physical partitioning or logical partitioning. In a physical horizontal partition implementation, you define a single table that then contains a series of partition specifications. The partition specification first identifies the value, either a single column or an expression using multiple columns that is used to identify the partition. This is followed by a list of partitions with their physical attributes and the range of values that apply to that partition. When a row is inserted into the table, the database system calculates the partition value and identifies the partition to place the row. The actions are transparent to the application. Figure 9.2 shows an example of this approach.

In a logical horizontal partition implementation, you define individual tables for each "partition" you wish to create. You then create a view, using a SELECT . . . UNION statement to combine these tables into a single view. Figure 9.3 shows a data model implementing this approach to horizontal partitioning. In some implementations you cannot insert or update against the view. Instead, your application must determine the appropriate subtable to update. Enhanced forms of this method allow you to update against the view, and the database system would use WHERE clauses within the SELECT...UNION statement to determine which table is updated. This approach has an advantage in that the individual tables do not need to have the same columns. Such discrepancies can be handled within the SELECT...UNION statement.

These are two distinctly different approaches to horizontal partitioning. In the first approach, the partitions are defined in the physical schema and are fully transparent to the logical model and applications that access the database. In the second approach, you are required to define tables and a view to consolidate the tables. All tables are visible to applications. It is questionable how well the database system can take advantage of such a partitioning arrangement; therefore, further discussion in this section presumes a physical horizontal partition implementation.

Reasons for Partitioning

There are two basic reasons for partitioning tables: improve the manageability of large tables and improve query response through parallel queries of large data sets. These two motivations can result in conflicting partition designs. It is important to understand your primary motivation when developing partitioning strategies.

Manageability is the most common reason for partitioning, particularly for enterprise data warehouses in a Corporate Information Factory framework.

The reason is simple; the primary purpose of the enterprise data warehouse is to serve as a data store. It is the data marts, using dimensional models, that serve as the primary query platform. Therefore, the partitioning strategy should be targeted to improve the data storage function.

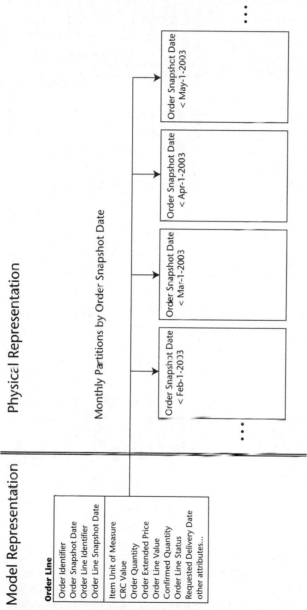

Figure 9.2   Physical partitioning.

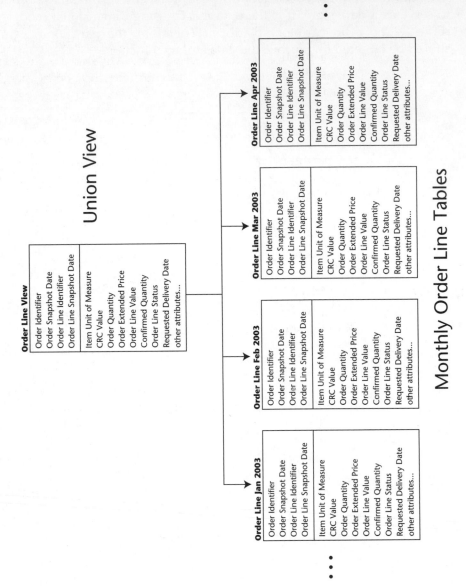

Figure 9.3 Logical partitioning.

This is not to say that query performance is not important. It is just that in this environment, it is difficult to apply partitioning strategies to obtain better performance. We see why this is so in the section "Vertical Partitioning for Performance."

Partitioning for Manageability

Partitioning is at its greatest advantage when dealing with very large tables (many millions of rows) that contain a distinguishing characteristic that is commonly used as a predicate when accessing the table. If a date, such as transaction date, is used as that predicate (the table is partitioned by that date), then partitioning can also serve to ease backup and maintenance tasks.

Dates are the most commonly used partitioning parameter. Partitioning a transaction table by date range (months, years, etc.) has a number of advantages:

- The most active partitions are easily identified. This allows you to locate the active partitions on high-availability devices. Older data can be located on slower or non-redundant storage systems to reduce costs.

- Incremental backups need only copy active partitions. Normal updates to the database will only occur in one or two partitions because such updates usually affect current data. An incremental backup need only copy those partitions that have changed. Without partitioning, the entire table is backed up even though only a small portion changed.

- Archival can be accomplished by simply moving entire partitions after the archive backup. Date-based partitions allow you to retire data after archival by simply taking the partition off line. You do not need to explicitly delete the rows.

- The sizes of the partitions are predictable. You can use historical volumes and trends to predict storage requirements for future partitions. If you used other partitioning criteria, such as ranges of customer numbers, you run the risk of some partitions growing much faster than others because some customers engage in more activity than others. With dates you can predict the high activity periods and adjust your allocations. Also, old partitions become stable and do not grow unless you load old, historical information.

In general, when partitioning by date, you should choose a time period that results in partitions of a size you are willing to work with and of a number that is not a burden to manage. This depends on your data volumes and the time span covered by the enterprise data warehouse. The most commonly used date partitioning ranges are year or month. The time it takes to backup and restore individual partitions, and the number of devices available to you to distribute the partitions across, should be the primary driver in determining the appropriate partitioning time span.

Implementing a Tiered Storage Strategy

Data warehouse managers are often at conflict between the user demands to maintain many years of historical data and the costs of doing so. As data ages, its value to the company tends to decline as well as its frequency of access. Yet, more often than not, the old data is stored on the same high-performance, high-availability hardware as the current data.

Date-based table partitioning can provide a means to resolve this conflict. By classifying the transactional data as current, old, and archive you can place the data partitions on appropriate devices. Current partitions would be those that are either frequently updated or frequently accessed. These would reside on the high-performance, high-availability hardware. Old partitions, those that are not updated and are accessed occasionally can be placed on traditional non-RAID disk devices. Device reliability is less of an issue with this type of data. Since the data is no longer updated, restoring data lost due to disk failure is a simple process.

Data that reaches the archive stage should be moved off the partition into flat files or separate tables and placed on optical or tape media for access. The old partition can then be dropped. It is important to do this because of the potential for future schema changes. If the archive data remains as a partition, schema changes to the table will affect the archived partitions as well. This can cause maintenance problems, particularly if the archive data is stored on read-only media.

Enforcing this structure is well within the control of the data warehouse manager. Quality controls in the development of the loading processes and the delivery processes can ensure that access is focused on the correct partitions. For loading, it is a matter of validating dates and generating exceptions for updates to noncurrent data. For delivery processes, policies should require that all queries to partitioned tables include predicates based on the partitioning date column.

From a query perspective, this type of partitioning strategy is neutral. It doesn't really help or hinder query performance very much. If a query selects a specific, short time span then the database would access only those partitions that fall in the time span. If the query spans multiple partitions, and the database and hardware support it, the database can access each partition in parallel to gather the result set. However, if the query does not specify a date or uses a very long time span, then the query must examine many partitions, hindering overall performance. A global index, discussed in a later section, can mitigate this.

Partitioning for Performance

Query performance is not a key issue for the data warehouse. The primary purpose of the data warehouse is to retain data and deliver data to external systems. While there may be time constraints on the delivery process, we have outlined other techniques to address this within the data model and loading process. We do not recommend partitioning strategies solely for query performance improvement because such strategies are often at odds with those to improve maintainability. We believe that improving the maintainability of the data warehouse is far more valuable to an organization.

But why do performance and maintenance requirements conflict? It is because query performance is gained by creating an environment where queries can operate against a table using multiple parallel subprocesses. It is a basic divide-and-conquer approach. Rather than have a single query execute against a table with 10 million rows, you can get the results faster if you have 10 queries executing in parallel against 10 smaller tables of 1 million rows each. Presuming, of course, that your database supports parallel queries, you have a multiprocessor server, and your disk channel bandwidth can handle the volume. To accomplish query performance improvements, you must arrange your partitions in such a way that encourages parallel access to the data.

You may be thinking that, if you create partitions by month, you can achieve maintainability and query performance improvements at the same time. Well, yes—provided your delivery queries span multiple months. However, if most of your delivery processes provide incremental data spanning a day or two, those queries will not execute in parallel because all the data is in a single partition. In general, this is acceptable for most data warehouse implementations. Those times when you need to pull a lot of data this action benefits from partitioning that was designed to improve maintainability—precisely why you should go no further.

We mean that you should not alter your partitioning strategy to improve the incremental queries. To do this, you need to implement a partitioning strategy that always results in parallel queries against partitions that have a high likelihood of containing the data you are looking for. One way to do this is to use a technique called hashing. A simple hash method is to use the remainder of some numeric value to decide which partition to place the data. Let's say you divide a table into seven partitions and use the transaction number to decide in which partition to place the data. The partitioning algorithm would take the remainder of the transaction number divided by 7 and use that value, a number ranging from 0 to 6, to select one of the seven partitions.

Using this approach, the data is spread evenly across all seven partitions. Any query for this table would execute seven parallel queries to get the data. Any query pulling even moderate amounts of data would run significantly faster than a single serial query. However, because the data is spread evenly across the partitions, you lose any maintainability advantages. When the table is updated, all partitions are affected. Incremental backups would always copy the entire table, and archiving becomes more difficult. You also cannot use the age of the data to manage data storage and disk utilization. We believe that this can be a useful technique for the data marts, but not something you would want to do in the data warehouse.

Indexing Partitioned Tables

When discussing partitioned tables, there are two general types of indexes: global indexes and local indexes. A global index is a structure that indexes all rows, regardless of the partition. A local index is a structure that indexes only rows in a specific partition. Your database may support both types or just one of the two. In most cases, where both types are available, you can use a mix of types for different indexes.

In the enterprise data warehouse, local partition indexes (shown in Figure 9.4) are the better choice. These indexes only span the data in the partition, resulting in smaller indexes. These smaller indexes are faster to maintain, rebuild, and query. This improves the performance of the data-loading functions as well as the data delivery functions. In the latter case, most data delivery queries are very time specific. Such queries can easily locate the appropriate time-based partitions and use the smaller indexes for data selection. Also, since the older partitions are stabilized, their indexes can be rebuilt once updates are no longer expected. This provides optimal performance for a long period of time.

Global indexes, shown in Figure 9.5, are a large burden on the loading process. If your data volumes are large, it is most likely you use the databases bulk data-loading facilities whenever possible. The fastest loading mechanisms allow you to bypass index maintenance during the loading, requiring you to rebuild the index after the loading is complete. Global indexes can become so large that rebuilding them may take hours. This would preclude using many of the fast loading options available through bulk loading. Without using bulk loads, the sheer size of a global index spanning many years of transaction data has a significant negative impact on the load times.

Global indexes also hamper your ability to move or remove partitions. You may have a policy in place to move data over two years old to less expensive nonredundant disk subsystems. So, periodically, you move old partitions to another device. Most database systems require you to rebuild any global indexes when a partition is moved or removed. Such a process may add many hours to the procedure, increasing the downtime of the data warehouse.

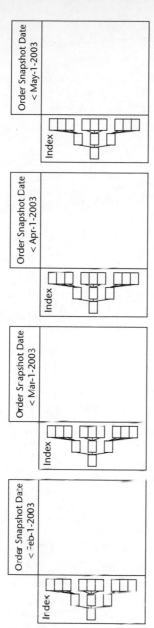

Figure 9.4 Local partition index.

Global indexes also affect your ability to take advantage of parallel queries. If global indexes exist and the database optimizer decides to use one of them, it cannot execute the query in parallel because there is only one index structure.

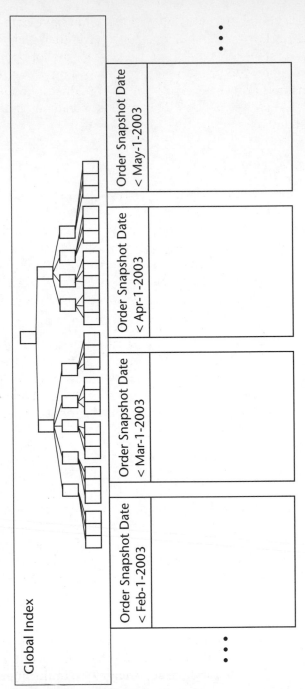

Figure 9.5 Global partition index.

This recommendation also holds true for data marts. If you have data marts that are partitioned, local indexes will usually perform better than global ones. But, there is a catch. Database systems that give you a choice do not permit the use of local indexes to support the primary key. The reasoning is simple: the database is unable to ensure enforcement of a primary key constraint if it must use multiple independent index structures. This dilemma leads us to a more controversial area, enforcing referential integrity.

Enforcing Referential Integrity

Today's relational databases support a host of features to ensure referential integrity throughout the database. These features often degrade the performance of processes that load large amounts of data into the data warehouse. This is a problem unique to data warehousing, where it is not unusual to have very large tables containing transactional data spanning many years. The overhead involved in enforcing key constraints grows as the sizes of the tables grow. We do not have the luxury of purging old data to maintain trim, efficient tables, as one does in an OLTP environment.

There is no argument that the ability to enforce referential integrity constraints within the database system is a very useful and practical feature. However, if you are faced with large tables, large data loads, and a short processing window, these features may be your downfall. We suggest that you examine the alternative of enforcing referential integrity in the loading process, rather than in the database.

You should examine your existing or planned loading processes, looking at the data validation they are already performing. Chances are, those processes are already checking foreign key values, looking for existing rows using the primary key, and doing other data validation checks. More often than not, these checks are redundant to the integrity checks in the database. Why perform them twice? A well-developed loading process can be equally adept at assuring referential integrity as database constraints. Removing those constraints opens a number of options to efficiently load large amounts of data into the data warehouse. These options can significantly reduce load times.

Why is this controversial? Those trained to design databases for OLTP systems insist that database-enforced referential integrity is the only way to go. We must agree that, for an OLTP system, they are absolutely correct. But, a data warehouse is different. In an OLTP environment, updates occur through multiple asynchronous transactions. It is critical that referential integrity checks occur within the bounds of the transaction being executed; otherwise, a check that was valid at one moment may no longer be valid the next moment due to changes made by another concurrent transaction. Timing is everything in this environment, and the only way to ensure proper checks is to handle them at the database level. A data warehouse, on the other hand, uses batch processes that load data in a controlled, serial manner. You have control over the sequencing and dependencies inherent in these processes. You can arrange the processes so that reference data is loaded first, followed by transactional data. You can use the process schedule to eliminate potential integrity conflicts.

Even in a real-time data warehouse environment, you have greater control over the flow and application of transactions than you do in an OLTP environment. You can establish priorities and queues to deal with the transactions in a manner more suitable for processing. Data-warehousing processes have a great deal more latitude because they are not constrained by the human interfaces inherent in an OLTP system.

If load times are a problem, we recommend that you consider removing some constraints from the data warehouse database. This includes primary key constraints, foreign key constraints, and unique index constraints. Examine your loading processes to see where redundancies exist and where elimination of the constraints will benefit load times. Investigate adding logic to your process to enforce a constraint that is causing performance problems in the database. For example, defining a unique primary key index on a large partitioned table requires use of a global index. Removing the primary key constraint allows use of local indexes instead.

Keys and Physical Schema

The notion of a key in a relational model is purely a logical concept. A primary key classifies one or more attributes as the unique identifier for instances of the entity. This manifests itself in the physical schema as a constraint, a rule that is enforced by the database engine. This constraint basically states that the combination of values stored in the collection of columns must be unique for the table. The database system often generates an index on these columns to assist it in enforcing the constraint. Such an index is often required and is usually referred to as the primary key index.

However, the tie between a key and an index is a marriage of convenience. There is no relationship between keys and indexes in relational modeling. Keys can exist without indexes and indexes can exist without keys. A key is a logical concept, while an index is a physical structure to aid in locating rows in a table.

The point of all this is that you do not need to create constraints, such as a primary key constraint, in the physical database to have an index or enforce primary key rules. Such a rule can be enforced externally and be aided by an index structure of your choosing. Doing so does not violate the basic concepts of relational modeling.

Index-Organized Tables

If possible, defining index-organized, also called index-clustered, tables can aid database performance. An index-organized table is one where the index and table data are maintained in the same structure. Normally, separate structures are used, with the table data residing in one data structure and one or more indexes residing in their own structures with pointers to the appropriate row in the table structure. Figure 9.6 shows an index-organized table structure.

The advantage of an index-organized structure is the database does not have to perform the extra step of reading the table data when the index entry is found. In an index-organized structure, the data is already there since it is part of the index structure.

A disadvantage of an index-organized structure is the table must only have one index, based on the primary key. You cannot define alternate indexes or inversion indexes for index-organized tables. This limits its usefulness to simple tables, such as code description tables, that do not require alternate access paths. Yet, even with this limitation, it is a useful technique, particularly when the data delivery processes include code descriptions and other reference data in its output.

Indexing Techniques

There are two basic indexing techniques that the data warehouse designer should use: binary tree (b-tree) indexing and bitmap indexing. B-tree indexing is used extensively in OLTP database design and is the best choice where query paths are known and controlled. Bitmap indexes, on the other hand, perform best in ad hoc query environments and are the index of choice for dimensional data marts. We will examine both techniques and discuss their applicability in different situations.

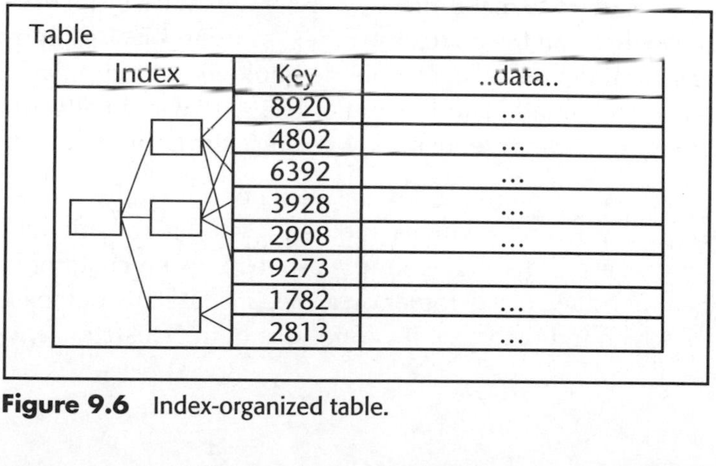

Figure 9.6 Index-organized table.

Note that different database systems provide a variety of indexing structures beyond the two mentioned here. Structures such as hash indexes or join indexes present other opportunities to improve performance in specific circumstances. We have limited the discussion to b-tree and bitmap structures as they are the most distinct in their capabilities and use.

B-Tree Indexes

Binary tree (b-tree) indexes use a recursive tree structure to store the index value and pointers to other index nodes and, in the case of a leaf node, a pointer to the data row. It is called a binary tree because each node visit requires a binary decision: Is the value on the index node less than the value I am looking for or is it larger? This test is used to choose one of two paths, provided by the "left" node and "right" node pointers, to traverse the next node. Eventually, the path leads to a leaf node that matches or does not match the value being searched for. If it does not match, the value is not found. If it does match, the database uses the leaf node pointer to retrieve the data row.

Figure 9.7 shows this basic structure. The diagram and the description represent a simplified generic structure. In reality, database systems use much more complex structures based on these principles. These structures are proprietary and have features to improve performance within the vendor's specific database environment. But, in general, they all function in a similar manner.

B-Tree Index Types

There are two general types of b-tree indexes: simple indexes and compound indexes. A simple index is an index based on a single column. A compound index is an index based on two or more columns. When designing a compound index, the column sequence is very important. The positions of columns in the index definition have the same significance as the positions of letters in an alphabetized list. The first column, as for the first letter, is the most significant and is required to make effective use of the index. If the first column is not used as a predicate in the query, the index is not usable. It is the same situation as trying to find a name in the phone book when you only know the second, third, and fourth letters of the name. The only way to effectively find all possible names is to search sequentially through the entire phone book.

So, should you avoid compound indexes? Well, no, not really. B-tree indexes cannot be used in combination with each other. If you had a table with a simple b-tree index on date and another simple b-tree index on customer number and you queried for a specific customer on a specific date, the database would have to choose which index to use. It cannot use both. This choice would be performed by the database's optimizer, and as a result it would either look at all rows for the specific date and scan for customer or look at all rows for the customer and scan for date. If, on the other hand, you defined a compound b-tree index using date and customer, it would use that index to locate the rows directly. The compound index would perform much better than either of the two simple indexes.

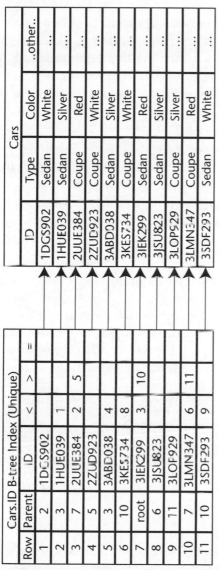

Figure 9.7 Simplified b-tree index structure.

B-Tree Index Advantages

B-tree indexes work best in a controlled environment. That is to say, you are able to anticipate how the tables will be accessed for both updates and queries. This is certainly attainable in the enterprise data warehouse as both the update and delivery processes are controlled by the data warehouse development team. Careful design of the indexes provides optimal performance with minimal overhead.

B-tree indexes are low maintenance indexes. Database vendors have gone to great lengths to optimize their index structures and algorithms to maintain balanced index trees at all times. This means that frequent updating of tables does not significantly degrade index performance. However, it is still a good idea to rebuild the indexes periodically as part of a normal maintenance cycle.

B-Tree Index Disadvantages

As mentioned earlier, b-tree indexes cannot be used in combination with each other. This means that you must create sufficient indexes to support the anticipated accesses to the table. This does not necessarily mean that you need to create a lot of indexes. For example, if you have a table that is queried by date and by customer and date, you need only create a single compound index using date and customer in that order to support both.

The significance of column order in a compound index is another disadvantage. You may be required to create multiple compound indexes or accept that some queries will require sequential scans after exhausting the usefulness of an existing index. Which way you go depends on the indexes you have and the nature of the data. If the existing index results in a scan of a few dozen rows for a particular query, it probably isn't worth the overhead to create a new index structure to overcome the scan. Keep in mind, the more index structures you create, the slower the update process becomes.

B-tree indexes tend to be large. In addition to the columns that make up the index, an index row also contains 16 to 24 additional bytes of pointer and other internal data used by the database system. Also, you need to add as much as 40 percent to the size as overhead to cover nonleaf nodes and dead space. Refer to your database system's documentation for its method of estimating index sizes.

Bitmap Indexes

Bitmap indexes are almost never seen in OLTP type databases, but are the darlings of dimensional data marts. Bitmap indexes are best used in environments whose primary purpose is to support ad hoc queries. These indexes, however, are high-maintenance structures that do not handle updating very well. Let's examine the bitmap structure to see why.

Bitmap Structure

Figure 9.8 shows a bitmap index on a table containing information about cars. The index shown is for the Color column of the table. For this example, there are only three colors: red, white, and silver. A bitmap index structure contains a series of bit vectors. There is one vector for each unique value in the column. Each vector contains one bit for each row in the table. In the example, there are three vectors for each of the three possible colors. The red vector will contain a zero for the row if the color in that row is not red. If the color in the row is red, the bit in the red vector will be set to 1.

If we were to query the table for red cars, the database would use the red color vector to locate the rows by finding all the 1 bits. This type of search is fairly fast, but it is not significantly different from, and possibly slower than, a b-tree index on the color column. The advantage of a bitmap index is that it can be used in combination with other bitmap indexes. Let's expand the example to include a bitmap index on the type of car. Figure 9.9 includes the new index. In this case, there are two car types: sedans and coupes.

Now, the user enters a query to select all cars that are coupes and are not white. With bitmap indexes, the database is able to resolve the query using the bitmap vectors and Boolean operations. It does not need to touch the data until it has isolated the rows it needs. Figure 9.10 shows how the database resolves the query. First, it takes the white vector and performs a Not operation. It takes that result and performs an And operation with the coupe vector. The result is a vector that identifies all rows containing red and silver coupes. Boolean operations against bit vectors are very fast operations for any computer. A database system can perform this selection much faster than if you had created a b-tree index on car type and color.

Cars				Color Bit Map Index		
ID	Type	Color	..other..	Silver	Red	White
1DGS902	Sedan	White	...	0	0	1
1HUE039	Sedan	Silver	...	1	0	0
2UUE384	Coupe	Red	...	0	1	0
2ZUD923	Coupe	White	...	0	0	1
3ABD038	Sedan	Silver	...	1	0	0
3KES734	Coupe	White	...	0	0	1
3IEK299	Sedan	Red	...	0	1	0
3JSU823	Sedan	Silver	...	1	0	0
3LOP929	Coupe	Silver	...	1	0	0
3LMN347	Coupe	Red	...	0	1	0
3SDF293	Sedan	White	...	0	0	1

Figure 9.8 A car color bitmap index.

Cars				Color Bit Map Index			Type Bit Map Index	
ID	Type	Color	..other..	Silver	Red	White	Sedan	Coupe
1DGS902	Sedan	White	...	0	0	1	1	0
1HUE039	Sedan	Silver	...	1	0	0	1	0
2UUE384	Coupe	Red	...	0	1	0	0	1
2ZUD923	Coupe	White	...	0	0	1	0	1
3ABD038	Sedan	Silver	...	1	0	0	1	0
3KES734	Coupe	White	...	0	0	1	0	1
3IEK299	Sedan	Red	...	0	1	0	1	0
3JSU823	Sedan	Silver	...	1	0	0	1	0
3LOP929	Coupe	Silver	...	1	0	0	0	1
3LMN347	Coupe	Red	...	0	1	0	0	1
3SDF293	Sedan	White	...	0	0	1	1	0

Figure 9.9 Adding a car type bitmap index.

Since a query can use multiple bitmap indexes, you do not need to anticipate the combination of columns that will be used in a query. Instead, you simply create bitmap indexes on most, if not all, the columns in the table. All bitmap indexes are simple, single-column indexes. You do not create, and most database systems will not allow you to create, compound bitmap indexes. Doing so does not make much sense, since using more than one column only increases the cardinality (the number of possible values) of the index, which leads to greater index sparsity. A separate bitmap index on each column is a more effective approach.

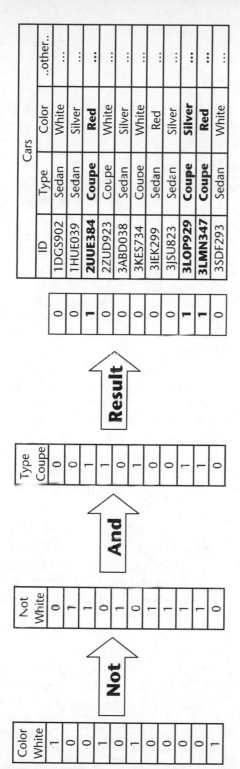

Figure 9.10 Query evaluation using bitmap indexes.

Cardinality and Bitmap Size

Older texts not directly related to data warehousing warn about creating bitmap indexes on columns with high cardinality, that is to say, columns with a large number of possible values. Sometimes they will even give a number, say 100 values, as the upper limit for bitmap indexes. These warnings are related to two issues with bitmaps, their size and their maintenance overhead. In this section, we discuss bitmap index size.

The length of a bitmap vector is directly related to the size of the table. The vector needs 1 bit to represent the row. A byte can store 8 bits. If the table contains 8 million rows, a bitmap vector will require 1 million bytes to store all the bits. If the column being indexed has a very high cardinality with 1000 different possible values, then the size of the index, with 1000 vectors, would be 1 billion bytes. One could then imagine that such a table with indexes on a dozen columns could have bitmap indexes that are many times bigger than the table itself. At least it would appear that way on paper.

In reality, these vectors are very sparse. With 1,000 possible values, a vector representing one value contains far more 0 bits than 1 bits. Knowing this, the database systems that implement bitmap indexes use data compression techniques to significantly reduce the size of these vectors. Data compression can have a dramatic effect on the actual space used to store these indexes. In actual use, a bitmap index on a 1-million-row table and a column with 30,000 different values only requires 4 MB to store the index. A comparable b-tree index requires 20 MB or more, depending on the size of the column and the overhead imposed by the database system. Compression also has a dramatic effect on the speed of these indexes. Since the compressed indexes are so small, evaluation of the indexes on even very large tables can occur entirely in memory.

Cardinality and Bitmap Maintenance

The biggest downside to bitmap indexes is that they require constant maintenance to remain compact and efficient. When a column value changes, the database must update two bitmap vectors. For the old value, it must change the 1 bit to a 0 bit. To do this it locates the vector segment of the bit, decompresses the segment, changes the bit, and compresses the segment. Chances are that the size of the segment has changed, so the system must place the segment in a new location on disk and link it back to the rest of the vector. This process is repeated for the new value. If the new value does not have a vector, a new vector is created. This new vector will contain bits for every row in the table, although initially it will be very small due to compression.

The repeated changes and creations of new vectors severely fragments the bitmap vectors. As the vectors are split into smaller and smaller segments, the compression efficiency decreases. Size increases can be dramatic, with indexes growing to 10 or 20 times normal size after updating 5 percent of a table. Furthermore, the database must piece together the segments, which are now spread across different areas of the disk in order to examine a vector. These two problems, increase in size and fragmentation, work in concert to slow down such indexes. High-cardinality indexes make the problem worse because each vector is initially very small due to its sparsity. Any change to a vector causes it to split and fragment. The only way to resolve the problem is to rebuild the index after each data load. Fortunately, this is not a big problem in a data warehouse environment. Most database systems can perform this operation quickly.

Where to Use Bitmap Indexes

Without question, bitmap indexes should be used extensively in dimensional data marts. Each fact table foreign key and some number of the dimensional attributes should be indexed in this manner. In fact, you should avoid using b-tree indexes in combination with bitmap indexes in data marts. The reason for this is to prevent the database optimizer from making a choice. If you use bitmaps exclusively, queries perform in a consistent, predictable manner. If you introduce b-tree indexes as well, you invariably run into situations where, for whatever reason, the optimizer makes the wrong choice and the query runs for a long period of time.

Use of bitmap indexes in the data warehouse depends on two factors: the use of the table and the means used to update the table. In general, bitmap indexes are not used because of the update overhead and the fact that table access is known and controlled. However, bitmap indexes may be useful for staging, or delivery preparation, tables. If these tables are exposed for end-user or application access, bitmaps may provide better performance and utility than b-tree indexes.

Conclusion

We have presented a variety of techniques to organize the data in the physical database structure to optimize performance and data management. Data clustering and index-organized tables can reduce the I/O necessary to retrieve data, provided the access to the data is known and predictable. Each technique has a significant downside if access to the data occurs in an unintended manner. Fortunately, the loading and delivery processes are controlled by the data warehouse development team. Thus, access to the data warehouse is known and predictable. With this knowledge, you should be able to apply the most appropriate technique when necessary.

Table partitioning is primarily used in a data warehouse to improve the manageability of large tables. If the partitions are based on dates, they help reduce the size of incremental backups and simplify the archival process. Date-based partitions can also be used to implement a tiered storage strategy that can significantly reduce overall disk storage costs. Date-based partitions can also provide performance improvements for queries that cover a large time span, allowing for parallel access to multiple partitions. We also reviewed partitioning strategies designed specifically for performance enhancement by forcing parallel access to partitioned data. Such strategies are best applied to data mart tables, where query performance is of primary concern.

We also examined indexing techniques and structures. For partitioned tables, local indexes provide the best combination of performance and manageability. We looked at the two most common index structures, b-tree and bitmap indexes. B-tree indexes are better suited for the data warehouse due to the frequency of updating and controlled query environment. Bitmap indexes, on the other hand, are the best choice for ad hoc query environments supported by the data marts.

Optimizing the System Model

The title for this section is in some ways an oxymoron. The system model itself is purely a logical representation, while it is the technology model that represents the physical database implementation. How does one optimize a model that is never queried? What we address in this section are changes that can improve data storage utilization and performance, which affect the entity structure itself. The types of changes discussed here do not occur "under the hood," that is, just to the physical model, but also propagate back to the system model and require changes to the processes that load and deliver data in the data warehouse. Because of the side effects of such changes, these techniques are best applied during initial database design. Making such changes after the fact to an existing data warehouse may involve a significant amount of work.

Vertical Partitioning

Vertical partitioning is a technique in which a table with a large number of columns is split into two or more tables, each with an exclusive subset of the nonkey columns. There are a number of reasons to perform such partitioning:

Performance. A smaller row takes less space. Updates and queries perform better because the database is able to buffer more rows at a time.

Change history. Some values change more frequently than others. By separating high-change-frequency and low-change-frequency columns, the storage requirements are reduced.

Large text. If the row contains large free-form text columns, you can gain significant storage and performance efficiencies by placing the large text columns in their own tables.

We now examine each of these reasons and how they can be addressed using vertical partitioning.

Vertical Partitioning for Performance

The basic premise here is that a smaller row performs better than a larger row. There is simply less data for the database to handle, allowing it to buffer more rows and reduce the amount of physical I/O. But to achieve such efficiencies you must be able to identify those columns that are most frequently delivered exclusive of the other columns in the table. Let's examine a business scenario where vertical partitioning in this manner would prove to be a useful endeavor.

During the development of the data warehouse, it was discovered that planned service level agreements would not be met. The problem had to do with the large volume of order lines being processed and the need to deliver order line data to data marts in a timely manner. Analysis of the situation determined that the data marts most important to the company and most vulnerable to service level failure only required a small number of columns from the order line table. A decision was made to create vertical partitions of the Order Line table. Figure 9.11 shows the resulting model.

The original Order Line table contained all the columns in the Order Line 1 and Order Line 2 tables. In the physical implementation, only the Order Line 1 and Order Line 2 tables are created. The Order Line 1 table contains the data needed by the critical data marts. To expedite delivery to the critical marts, the update process was split so the Order Line 1 table update occurs first. Updates to the Order Line 2 table occur later in the process schedule, removed from the critical path.

Notice that some columns appear in both tables. Of course, the primary key columns must be repeated, but there is no reason other columns should not be repeated if doing so helps achieve process efficiencies. It may be that there are some delivery processes that can function faster by avoiding a join if the Order Line 2 table contains some values from Order Line 1. The level of redundancy depends on the needs of your application.

Because the Order Line 1 table's row size is smaller than a combined row, updates to this table run faster. So do data delivery processes against this table. However, the combined updating time for both parts of the table is longer than if it was a single table. Data delivery processes also take more time, since there is now a need to perform a join, which was not necessary for a single table. But, this additional cost is acceptable if the solution enables delivery of the critical data marts within the planned service level agreements.

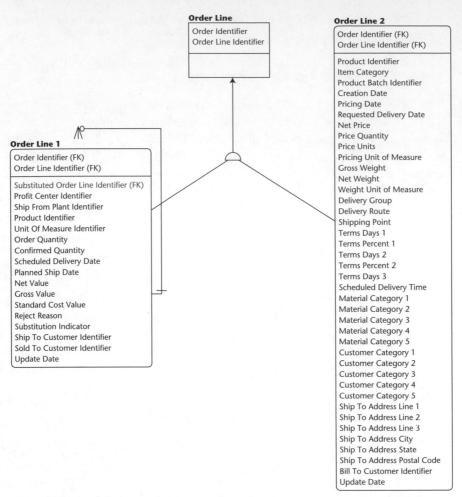

Figure 9.11 Vertical partitioning.

Vertical partitioning to improve performance is a drastic solution to a very specific problem. We recommend performance testing within your database environment to see if such a solution is of benefit to you. It is easier to quantify a vertical partitioning approach used to control change history tracking. This is discussed in the next section.

Vertical Partitioning of Change History

Given any table, there are most likely some columns that are updated more frequently than others. The most likely candidates for this approach are tables that meet the following criteria:

- You are maintaining a change history.
- Rows are updated frequently.
- Some columns are updated much more frequently than others.
- The table is large.

By keeping a change history we mean creating a new row whenever something in the current row has changed. If the row instance has a fairly long lifespan that accumulates many changes over time, you may be able to reduce the storage requirements by partitioning columns in the table based on the updating frequency. To do this, the columns in the table should be divided into at least three categories: never updated, seldom updated, and frequently updated. In general, those columns in the seldom updated category should have at least one-fifth the likelihood of being updated over the columns in the frequently updated category.

Categorizing the columns is best done using hard numbers derived from the past processing history. However, this is often not possible, so it becomes a matter of understanding the data mart applications and the business to determine where data should be placed. The objective is to reduce the space requirements for the change history by generating fewer and smaller rows. Also, other than columns such as update date or the natural key, no column should be repeated across these tables.

However, this approach does introduce some technical challenges. What was logically a single row is now broken into two or more tables with different updating frequencies. Chapter 8 covered a similar situation as it applied to transaction change capture. Both problems are logically similar and result in many-to-many relationships between the tables. This requires that you define associative tables between the partition tables to track the relationships between different versions of the partitioned rows. In this case, a single association table would suffice. Figure 9.12 shows a model depicting frequency-based partitioning of the Order Line table.

Notice that the partitioned tables have been assigned surrogate keys, and the Order Line table acts as the association table. The column Current Indicator is used to quickly locate the most current version of the line. The actual separation of columns in this manner depends on the specific application and business rules. The danger with using this approach is that changes in the application or business rules may drastically change the nature of the updates. Such changes may neutralize any storage savings attained using this approach. Furthermore, changing the classification of a column by moving it to another table is very difficult to do once data has been loaded and a history has been established.

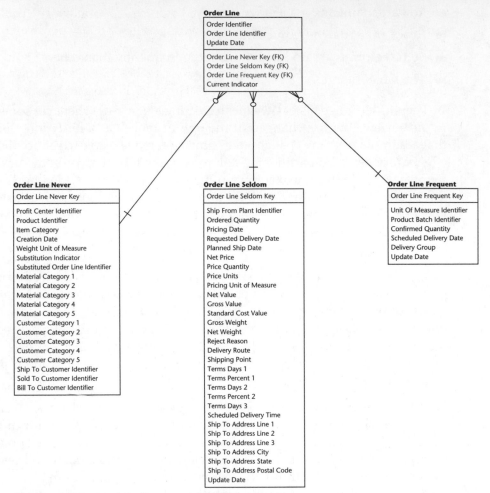

Figure 9.12 Update-frequency-based partitioning.

If storage space is at a premium, further economies can be gained by subdividing the frequency groupings by context. For example, it may make sense to split Order Line Seldom further by placing the ship to address columns into a separate table. Careful analysis of the updating patterns can determine if this is desirable.

Vertical Partitioning of Large Columns

Significant improvements in performance and space utilization can be achieved by separating large columns from the primary table. By large columns we mean free-form text fields over 100 bytes in size or large binary objects. This can include such things as comments, documents, maps, engineering drawings, photos, audio tracks, or other media. The basic idea is to move such columns out of the way so their bulk does not impede update or query performance.

The technique is simple. Create one or more additional tables to hold these fields, and place foreign keys in the primary table to reference the rows. However, before you apply this technique, you should investigate how your database stores large columns. Depending on the datatype you use, your database system may actually separate the data for you. In many cases, columns defined as BLOBs (binary large objects) or CLOBs (character large objects) are already handled as separate structures internally by the database system. Any effort spent to vertically partition such data only results in an overengineered solution. Large character columns using CHAR or VARCHAR datatypes, on the other hand, are usually stored in the same data structure as the rest of the row's columns. If these columns are seldom used in deliveries, you can improve delivery performance by moving those columns into another table structure.

Denormalization

Whereas vertical partitioning is a technique in which a table's columns are subdivided into additional tables, denormalization is a technique that adds redundant columns to tables. These seemingly opposite approaches are used to achieve processing efficiencies. In the case of denormalization, the goal is to reduce the number of joins necessary in delivery queries.

Denormalization refers to the act of reducing the normalized form of a model. Given a model in 3NF, denormalizing the model produces a model in 2NF or 1NF. As stated before in this book, a model is in 3NF if the entity's attributes are wholly dependent on the primary key. If you start with a correct 3NF model and move an attribute from an Order Header entity whose primary key is the Order Identifier and place it into the Order Line entity whose primary key is the Order Identifier and Order Line Identifier, you have denormalized the model from 3NF to 2NF. The attribute that was moved is now dependent on part of the primary key, not the whole primary key.

When properly implemented in the physical model, a denormalized model can improve data delivery performance provided that it actually eliminates joins from the query. But such performance gains can come at a significant cost to the updating process. If a denormalized column is updated, that update usually spans many rows. This can become a significant burden on the updating process. Therefore, it is important that you compare the updating and storage costs with the expected benefits to determine if denormalization is appropriate.

Subtype Clusters

Figure 9.13 shows an example of a subtype cluster. Using banking as an example, it is common to model an Account entity in this manner because of the attribute disparity between different types of accounts. Yet, it may not be optimal to implement the physical model in this manner. If the model were physically implemented as depicted, delivery queries would need to query each account type separately or perform outer joins to each subtype table and evaluate the results based on the account type. This is because the content of each of the subtype tables is mutually exclusive. An account of a particular type will only have a row in one of the subtype tables.

There are two alternative physical implementations within a data warehouse. The first is to implement a single table with all attributes and another is to implement only the subtype tables, with each table storing the supertype attributes. Let's examine each approach.

The first method is to simply define one table with all the columns. Having one table simplifies the delivery process since it does not require outer joins or forced type selection. This is a workable solution if your database system stores its rows as variable length records. If data is stored in this manner, you do not experience significant storage overhead for the null values associated with the columns for the other account types. Whereas, if the database stores rows as fixed length records, then space is allocated for all columns regardless of content. In this case, such an approach significantly increases the space requirements for the table. If you take this approach, do not attempt to consolidate different columns from different subtypes in order to reduce the number of columns. The only time when this is permissible is when the columns represent the same data. Attempting to store different data in the same column is a bad practice that goes against fundamental data modeling tenants.

The other method is to create the subtype tables only. In this case, the columns from the supertype table (Account) are added to each subtype table. This approach eliminates the join between the supertype and subtype tables, but requires a delivery process to perform a UNION query if more than one type of account is needed. This approach does not introduce any extraneous columns into the tables. Thus, this approach is more space efficient than the previous approach in databases that store fixed-length rows. It may also be more efficient for data delivery processes if those processes are subtype specific. The number of rows in a subtype table is only a portion of the entire population. Type-specific processes run faster because they deal with smaller tables than in the single-table method.

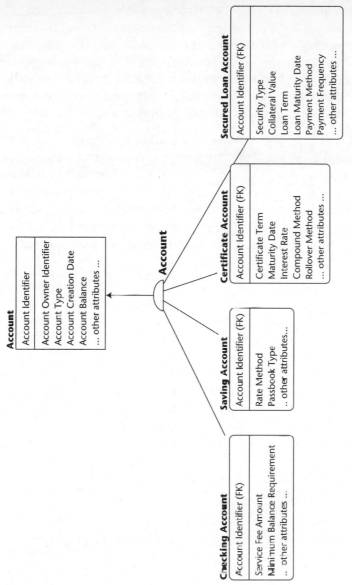

Figure 9.13 Subtype cluster model.

Summary

This chapter reviewed many techniques that can improve the performance of your data warehouse and its implementation. We made recommendations for altering or refining the system and technology data models. While we believe these recommendations are valid, we also warn that due diligence is in order. As mentioned earlier, every vendor's database system has different implementation approaches and features that may invalidate or enforce our recommendations. Other factors, such as your specific hardware environment, also play into the level of improvement or degradation such changes will impose. Unfortunately, other than placing the entire database in memory, there is no magic bullet that always ensures optimal performance.

If this is your first time at implementing a data warehouse, we recommend that, short of implementing table partitioning, you do not make assumptions about database performance issues in your design. Instead, spend some time to test scenarios or address performance problems as they occur in the development and testing phases. In most cases, such problems can be resolved with minor adjustments to the loading process or physical schema. Doing so avoids the risk of overengineering a solution to problems that may not exist.

PART THREE

Operation and Management

Once the data warehouse and its supporting models are developed, they need to be maintained and easily enhanced. This last part of the book deals with the activities that ensure that the data warehouse will continue to provide business value and appropriate service level expectations. These chapters also provide information about deployment options for companies that do not start with a clean slate, a common situation in most organizations.

In Chapter 10, we describe how the data warehouse model evolves in a changing business environment, and in Chapter 11, we explain how to maintain the different data models that support the BI environment.

Chapter 12 deals with deployment options. We recognize that most companies start out with some isolated data marts and a variety of disparate decision support systems. This chapter provides several options to bring order out of that chaos.

The last chapter compares the two leading philosophies about the design of a BI environment—the relational modeling approach presented in this book as the Corporate Information Factory and the multidimensional approach promoted by Dr. Ralph Kimball. After the two approaches are discussed, differences are explained in terms of their perspectives, data flow, implementation speed and cost, volatility, flexibility, functionality, and ongoing maintenance.

CHAPTER 10

Accommodating Business Change

Building an infrastructure to support the ongoing operation and future expansion of a data warehouse can significantly reduce the effort and resources required to keep the warehouse running smoothly. This chapter looks at the challenges faced by a data warehouse support group and presents modeling techniques to accommodate future change.

This chapter will first look at how change affects the data warehouse. We will look at why changes occur, the importance of controlling the impact of those changes, and how to field changes to the data warehouse. In the next section, we will examine how you can build flexibility in your data warehouse model so that it is more adaptable to future changes. Finally, we will look at two common and challenging business changes that affect a data warehouse: the integration of similar but disparate source systems and expanding the scope of the data warehouse.

The Changing Data Warehouse

The Greek philosopher, Heraclitus, said, "Change alone is unchanging." Even though change is inevitable, there is a natural tendency among most people to resist change. This resistance often leads to tension and friction between individuals and departments within the organization. And, although we do not like to admit it, IT organizations are commonly perceived as being resistant to change. Whether this perception is deserved or not, the data warehouse organization must overcome this perception and embrace change. After all, one of the significant values of a data warehouse is the ability it provides for the business to evaluate the effect of a change in their business. If the data warehouse is unable to change with the business, its value will diminish to the point were the data warehouse becomes irrelevant. How you, your team, and your company deal with change has a profound effect on the success of the data warehouse.

In this section, we examine data warehouse change at a high level. We look at why changes occur and their effect on the company and the data warehouse team. Later in this chapter, we dig deeper into the technical issues and techniques to create an environment that is adaptable to minimize the effect of future changes.

Reasons for Change

There are countless reasons for changes to be made to the data warehouse. While the requests for change all come from within the company, occasionally these changes are due to events occurring outside the company. Let us examine the sources of change:

Extracompany changes.   These are changes outside the direct control of the company. Changes in government regulations, consumer preference, or world events, or changes by the competition can affect the data warehouse. For example, the government may introduce a new use tax structure that would require the collection of additional demographic information about customers.

Intracompany changes.   These are changes introduced within the company. We can most certainly expect that there will be requests to expand the scope of the data warehouse. In fact, a long list of requests to add new information is a badge of honor for a data warehouse implementation. It means the company is using what is there and wants more. Other changes can come about due to new business rules and policies, operational system changes, reorganizations, acquisitions, or entries into new lines of business or markets.

Intradepartmental changes.   These are changes introduced within the IT organization. These types of changes most often deal with the technical infrastructure. Hardware changes, or changes in software or software versions, are the most common. Often these changes are transparent to the business community at large, so the business users usually perceive them as noncritical.

Intrateam changes. These are changes introduced within the data warehouse team. Bug fixes, process reengineering, and database optimizations are the most common. These often occur after experience is gained from monitoring usage patterns and the team's desire to meet service level agreements.

A final source of change worth mentioning is personnel changes. Personnel changes within the team are primarily project management issues that do not have a material effect on the content of the data warehouse. However, personnel changes within the company, particularly at the executive and upper management levels, may have a profound effect on the scope and direction of the data warehouse.

Controlling Change

While it is important to embrace change, it is equally important to control it. Staff, time, and money are all limited resources, so mechanisms need to be in place to properly manage and apply changes to the data warehouse.

There are many fine books on project management that address the issues of resource planning, prioritization, and managing expectations. We recommend the data warehouse scope and priorities be directed by a steering committee composed of upper management. This takes the data warehouse organization itself out of the political hot seat where they are responsible for determining whose requests are next in line for implementation. Such a committee, however, should not be responsible for determining schedules and load. These should be the result of negotiations with the requesting group and the data warehouse team. Also, a portion of available resources should be reserved to handle intradepartmental and intrateam changes as the need arises. Allocating only 5 to 6 hours of an 8-hour day for project work provides a reserve that allows the data warehouse team to address critical issues that are not externally perceived as important as well as to provide resources to projects that are falling behind schedule.

Another aspect of the data warehouse is data stewardship. Specific personnel within the company should be designated as the stewards of specific data within the data warehouse. The stewards of the data would be given overall responsibility for the content, definition, and access to the data. The responsibilities of the data steward include:

■ **Establish** data element definitions, specifying valid values where applicable, and notifying the data warehouse team whenever there is a change in the defined use of the data.

- **Resolve** data quality issues, including defining any transformations.
- **Establish** integration standards, such as a common coding system.
- **Control** access to the data. The data steward should be able to define where and how the data should be used and by whom. This permission can range from a blanket "everybody for anything" to requiring a review and approval by the data steward for requests for certain data elements.
- **Approve** use of the data. The data steward should review new data requests to validate how the data is to be used. This is different from controlling access. This responsibility ensures that the data requestor understands the data elements and is applying them in a manner consistent with their defined use.
- **Participate** in user acceptance testing. The data steward should always be "in the loop" on any development projects involving his or her data. The data steward should be given the opportunity to participate in a manner he or she chooses.

Within the technical environment, the data warehouse environment should be treated the same as any other production system. Sufficient change control and quality assurance procedures should be in place. If you have a source code management and versioning system, it should be integrated into your development environment. At a minimum, the creation of development and quality assurance database instances is required to support changes once the data warehouse goes into production. Figure 10.1 shows the minimal data warehouse landscape to properly support a production environment.

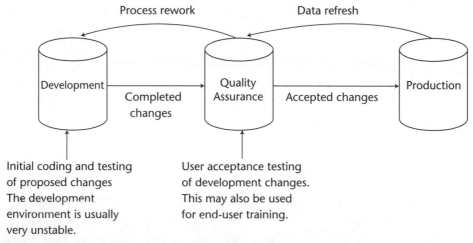

Figure 10.1 Production data warehouse landscape.

Implementing Change

The data warehouse environment cuts a wide swath though the entire company. While operational applications are usually departmentally focused, the data warehouse is the only application with an enterprise-wide scope. Because of this, any change to the data warehouse has the potential of affecting everyone in the company. Furthermore, if this is a new data warehouse implementation, you must also deal with an understandable skepticism with the numbers among the user community. With this in mind, the communication of planned changes to the user community and the involvement of those users in the validation and approval of changes are critical to maintain confidence and stability for the data warehouse.

A change requestor initiates changes. It is the responsibility of the change requestor to describe, in business terms, what the nature of the change is, how it will be used, and what the expected value to the business. The change requestor should also participate in requirements gathering, analysis, discussions with other user groups, and other activities pertinent to the requested change. The change requestor should also participate in testing and evaluating the change as discussed later in this section.

As shown in Figure 10.1, the development instance would be used by developers to code and test changes. After review, those changes should be migrated to the quality assurance instance for system and user acceptance testing. At this point, end users should be involved to evaluate and reconcile any changes to determine if they meet the end users' requirements and that they function correctly. After it has cleared this step, the changes should be applied to the production system.

Proper user acceptance testing prior to production release is critical. It creates a partnership between the data warehouse group, the data steward, and the change requestor. As a result of this partnership, these groups assume responsibility for the accuracy of the data and can then assist in mitigating issues that may arise. It is also worthwhile to emphasize at this point the importance of proper communication between the data warehouse group and the user groups. It is important that the requirement of active participation by the user community in the evaluation, testing, and reconciliation of changes be established up front, approved by the steering committee, and presented to the user groups. They need to know what is expected of them so that they can assign resources and roles to properly support the data warehouse effort.

The data warehouse team should not assume the sole responsibility for implementing change. To be successful, the need for change should come from the organization. A steering committee from the user community should establish scope and priorities. The data steward and change requestor should be actively involved in the analysis and testing phases of the project. Fostering a collaborative environment increases interest and support for the data warehouse throughout the organization.

Modeling for Business Change

Being a skeptic is an asset for a data warehouse modeler. During the analysis phase, the business users freely use the terms "never" and "always" when discussing data content and relationships. Such statements should not be taken at face value. Usually, what they are saying is "seldom" and "most of the time." In building the data model, you should evaluate the effect of this subtle change in interpretation and determine an appropriate course of action. The other aspect of anticipating change in the data model is to understand the business itself and the company's history. If the company regularly acquires or divests parts of its business, then it is reasonable to expect that behavior to continue. It is an important concern when developing the model.

In this section, we look at how to address anticipated and unknown changes in the data model. By doing so, you wind up with a more "bullet-proof" design, one capable of accepting whatever is thrown at it. This is accomplished by taking a more generic, as opposed to specific, view of the business. A paradox to this approach, which often confuses project managers, is that a generic, generalist approach to design often involves the same development effort as a more traditional specific design. Furthermore, it allows the data warehouse to gracefully handle exceptions to the business rules. These exceptions can provide invaluable information about and insight into the business processes. Rather than having the information rejected or the load process abort in the middle of the night, this information can be stored, identified, and reported to the business.

Assuming the Worst Case

When you are told that a particular scenario "never" or "always" occurs, you must approach your model as if the statement were not true. In your analysis, you need to weigh the cost and effect of this assumption and the overall viability of the data warehouse. Sometimes, it doesn't really matter if the statement is true or false, so there is no need to make accommodations in the model. In other cases, even one occurrence of something that would "never" happen can cause significant data issues.

For example, in an actual implementation sourced from a major ERP system, there was a business rule in place that order lines could not be deleted once an order was accepted. If the customer wished to change the order, the clerk was required to place a reject code on the line to logically remove the line from the order. This rule implied that as order changes were received into the data warehouse, the extract file would always contain all lines for that order. However, in this particular case, there was a back-end substitution process that modified the order after it was entered. In this instance, customers ordered generic items that were replaced with SKUs representing the actual product in different packaging. For example, the product might be in a "10% more free" package, or a package with a contest promotion, and so forth. The back-end process looked at available inventory and selected one or more of these package-specific SKUs to fulfill the order. These substitutions appeared as new lines in the order. This substitution process ran when the order was first entered, when it was changed, as well as the day prior to shipping. Each time the process ran, the substitution might occur based on available inventory. If it had originally chosen two SKUs as substitutions and later found enough inventory so that it only needed one SKU, the second SKU's line would be physically deleted from the order.

The end result was that these deleted lines went undetected in the load process. They remained in the data warehouse as unshipped lines and were reflected as unfulfilled demand in reports. The problem was soon discovered and corrected, but not without some damage to the credibility of the numbers provided by the data warehouse. Problems like this can be avoided by performing a worse case analysis of the business rule.

Relaxing the enforcement of business rules does not mean that data quality issues should be ignored. To the contrary, while you need to take business rules into account when designing the model, it is not the purpose of the data warehouse to enforce those rules. The purpose of the data warehouse is to accurately reflect what occurred in the business. Should transactions occur that violate a rule, it is the role of the warehouse to accept the data and to provide a means to report the data as required by the business.

Imposing Relationship Generalization

The subject area and business data models serve their purpose to organize and explain how components and transactions within the business relate to each other. Because such models are not specific to data warehousing, they often ignore the realities of historical perspective. This is understandable because such issues are peculiar to data warehousing, and incorporating potential historical relationships into the business data model would overcomplicate the model and would not accurately reflect how the business operates.

Figure 10.2 Document line relationships.

For example, a typical manufacturer receives orders, creates shipments, and invoices the customer. In this case, the business policy is to not create a back order when insufficient inventory exists, and every shipped line appears as a line on the invoice. Figure 10.2 shows how this would appear in the business data model.

This model does not account for events that occur during the course of business. Shipment documents may be cancelled and recreated, invoices may be reversed and reinvoiced, or shipment lines may be consolidated at the distribution center. Operationally, this model holds up because canceled or deleted documents "disappear" from the business. Shipment line consolidation occurs when the same SKU appears more than once in a shipping order. The distribution center staff simply combines the quantities and overship one of the lines. The other lines for the same SKU are not shipped, and therefore, are not invoiced.

Canceled documents, reversals, and consolidations must be maintained in the data warehouse so that these cases can be properly reported. What appear to be simple one-to-one relationships can become many-to-many relationships in the data warehouse. For example, a shipment line may have many invoice lines because of reversals and reinvoicing. Where line consolidations occur at the distribution center, the data warehouse is required to infer a relationship to those unshipped lines to properly report the order information that led to the invoice. Without such relationships, it becomes difficult to determine what really happened over the course of time.

In situations like this, you need to incorporate associative entities into the system model. Figure 10.3 shows an example of how this can be modeled. One of the challenges in applying associative entities in a case like this is controlling their use in a SQL query. Uncontrolled, such a structure could distort result sets being delivered with repeated rows. Adding some attributes, set during the load process, to the associative entity can help control how result sets are generated.

The Current Indicator attribute can be used to control the view being delivered. As documents are canceled or reversed and regenerated, this indicator would be used to identify the most recent relationship. For example, if a shipment document were canceled prior to actual shipment, the relationships for the canceled document would be set to not current. When a new shipment document was created to fulfill the order, the new relationships would be set as current. This technique allows you to maintain the old and new relationships and easily distinguish between the two. The Inferred Indicator attribute can be included to identify those relationships that were inferred by the data warehouse load process to support information requirements. For example, an invoice line may have an explicit reference back to a shipment line. The shipment line will have a reference back to an order line. Based on this, you can infer a relationship between the billing line and an order line. Deliveries exporting an operational view of the data would generally include only current relationships. However, a special-purpose data mart used to analyze the business process would be interested in all relationships.

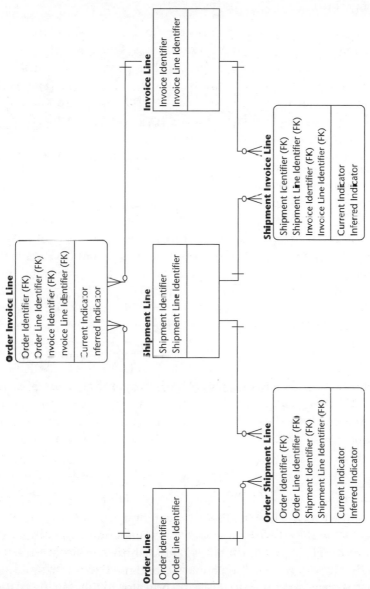

Figure 10.3 A generalized relationship.

By generalizing the relationship, we have also enabled the data warehouse to accommodate business changes without significantly affecting the model. For example, should the company decide to permit back orders, the generalized structure will support it. The nice thing about using associative entities is that they work equally well regardless of the nature of the relationship. This same structure will support one-to-one and one-to-many relationships without any problems. Using them even to represent simple relationships, leaves you in a position to support changes in the relationship as well as capture situations where the stated relationship rules have been violated.

The latter point is very important. It is not up to the data warehouse to enforce data relationships. That is up to the operational systems. In some cases, particularly when standard packages are used in the operational environment, the systems are unable to enforce all business rules. The duty of the data warehouse is to reflect what exists in the business. By generalizing those relationships, it allows the data warehouse to adapt to changing situations, including those that are unforeseen or not permitted. The downside is that the technique does increase the complexity of the model; therefore, it should be used only where justified.

Using Surrogate Keys

We have touched on surrogate keys a number of times in this book. However, their use is so critical in creating a flexible, adaptable environment, they are worth mentioning again. Why do we have keys? From a relational modeling point of view, they identify an instance of an entity. We all have names, account numbers, and other identifiers for things (entity instances) that exist in a system somewhere, so it is natural to think that our name or account number would serve as a key. From a human interface and operational system standpoint this makes sense, but does it make sense for a data warehouse?

As change is inevitable, it is also inevitable that, over time, natural key values will change. Anything can happen: Someone changes his or her name, companies merge and combine their accounts, or companies reorganize. Natural key identifiers are fragile and are often broken. So, it is inevitable that over the lifespan of the data warehouse, many natural keys will change. Surrogate keys isolate the data warehouse from these changes. It allows it to maintain referential integrity over time regardless of what occurs in the operational systems.

By separating the real world from the data warehouse's need to join tables, you have protected the data warehouse and its content from the ambiguity and changes the real world represents. Surrogate keys are simple, arbitrary unique numbers assigned to a row as the primary key. A row would also contain the necessary natural key attributes that identify the row to the outside world. During the load process, you use the natural key values to locate the row and use the surrogate primary key as the foreign key in the data you are loading.

Changing Keys

Business keys change a lot more often than we in IT care to admit. Every now and then you receive a notice in the mail from your bank, credit card company, or cable TV supplier telling you that your account number has changed. These changes are usually due to a change in the application system or a business merger. If you have been on the systems end of such changes, you can appreciate how difficult a change this can be. An enormous effort is spent ensuring that the new numbers have been assigned properly, accounts remain in balance and integrity is maintained. This is tedious, detailed work that often requires repeated reexamination.

This problem is magnified many times over in a data warehouse because the data covers a much longer time span. Questions come up about what to do with inactive accounts, how to address downtime while the tables are rekeyed, and how to ensure that the results will be correct. Furthermore, resources are often strained during such efforts, with priority being given to cleaning up current accounts and with little interest being paid to historical data. Often the data warehouse team is left (or forced) to work out a strategy to perform a partial, phased key conversion. These and other issues are mitigated or completely eliminated with surrogate keys.

When natural keys are changed, it is simply a matter of updating the columns in the table that contains those values. There is no need to change or reassign the primary key. The data warehouse keys remain stable. Foreign keys continue to reference the same row. All that changed was how we, or the operational system, reference that instance.

NOTE

Some operational systems use surrogate keys in their database schema. The data warehouse should treat these like any business key and use its own surrogate key generator. This is critical in order to maintain isolation from the operational system. If you attempt to use the surrogate keys provided by the operational system, you have essentially placed control of referential integrity in the hands of the operational system vendor. As we discussed earlier in this chapter, if you use business keys—such as customer number—instead of surrogate keys, the data warehouse is significantly impacted by business decisions that may change the keys. It is worse if you use surrogate keys provided by an operational system because you are now vulnerable to design decisions made by the vendor, which are out of your control. Any decision to upgrade software versions, change vendors, or other actions that affect that operational system may have a severe and destructive impact on the data warehouse.

This stability is critical in a data warehouse because it often stores data spanning many years and possibly decades. If you are faced with a situation where 20,000 SKUs are renumbered and you have a data warehouse with 100 million rows referencing those SKUs you will be faced with a very risky endeavor if you used the SKU as the key. How would you recover if the cross-reference data you received mistakenly translated two old SKU numbers to a single new SKU number? After the change is applied, how would you know which transactions referred to which SKUs? Sure, you can add a column to the table to store the old SKU, but do you really want to be mass-updating 100 million rows? If you used surrogate keys, all you would need to do is update the SKUs on 20,000 product rows. Primary and foreign keys would not change, and referential integrity would be ensured. The database would remain stable, and natural key changes would be reduced to simple updates.

It is important to mention that not every table requires a surrogate key. Transaction tables will not gain particular advantage since the transaction identifier does not require the same time stability as a customer identifier. Also, most tables in a normalized database structure are simple code description tables. Such tables are of less concern than the core business entity tables, such as Customer and Product. These core entities often translate directly to dimensions in the delivered data marts. Maintaining surrogate keys on these entities in the data warehouse will ensure key conformance across the data marts. This is less of an issue with code tables because the codes and their descriptions are often assimilated into existing dimensions or combined with other code values into a junk[1] dimension. Those tables that are important enough to stand alone as a dimension in a data mart should be considered as candidates for a surrogate key.

In this section, we looked at considerations that should be made in the initial design to allow for unknown or unexpected occurrences in the business. Adding a healthy dose of skepticism to an end user's use of the terms "always" and "never" can avoid potential data warehouse problems that do not manifest themselves in the operational systems. Judicious use of relationship generalization can improve the flexibility of the model and allow for an orderly detection and reporting of unusual or unexpected relationships. Finally, the use of surrogate keys for some entities enhances the stability of the database and protects it from the changing nature of business keys.

Implementing Business Change

In this section, we examine two common change scenarios and describe a course of action to adjust the data warehouse to deal with the change. In the first scenario, we will discuss how to deal with the inclusion of a new disparate

1 The term junk refers to a dimension that contains a collection of left over attributes. See *The Data Warehouse Toolkit, Second Edition* (Kimball et al, Wiley, pp 117-119).

data source for an existing subject area. In the second, we look at the impact the addition of new subject areas has on an existing data warehouse.

Integrating Subject Areas

This topic could have been given a number of different titles: "Dealing with Mergers and Acquisitions," "Integrating Legacy Data," or "Attaining a Common Enterprise View." They all represent different scenarios involving the same basic problem: You have multiple, independent application systems that do the same thing. The data warehouse is called upon to accept and integrate data from these systems.

Problems arise when you try to consolidate subject areas. Using Customers as an example, it is common for independent systems to have independent identifiers and attributes for their customers. From an enterprise perspective, though, it is necessary to view activities of a customer across these different systems regardless of how the customer is identified in those systems. The first step to a solution is to assess the situation and resolve the following business questions:

- What is a customer?
- What roles can a customer assume (Sold-to, Ship-to, Bill-to, Payer, Retail, Wholesale, and so on)?
- What do we need to know about the customer?
- How do we identify the same customer across systems?

The answers to these questions are driven by the needs of the business. From a data warehouse point of view, they present three technical challenges: standardizing attributes, inferring roles, and integrating entities. We examine how the model can be developed to address these challenges. While these model changes can be retrofitted into an existing warehouse, we recommend that, if you are developing a new data warehouse and foresee the need to perform such integration in the near future, you consider incorporating some of these modeling elements now to reduce the work in the future.

Standardizing Attributes

Standardizing attributes is a very basic problem germane to any system integration. Every system has codes and descriptions that provide information about the customer. It is necessary to standardize these codes to a common coding system if the data is to be integrated across application systems. Creating standards can be a difficult, politically charged task.

Often, coding systems are incompatible due to a different focus or level of detail embedded in the codes. For example, two divisions of a company are running the same sales order software, both maintain an Order Reason attribute. One division uses the code to track how the customer intends to use the purchase, while the other division uses the code to determine why the customer ordered from them. In the former case, the division is selling industrial equipment, while in the latter case they are selling consumer goods. Because they have different purposes—one represents intended use, while the other determines marketing effectiveness—they must be modeled as separate attributes in the data warehouse.

Problems arise when the purpose is the same but the coding is different. Using the same two divisions, both maintain a Return Reason code. The industrial equipment division maintains a long list of specific codes that identify known and potential problems with the equipment that may cause a return, while the consumer goods division contains codes relating to consumer preference, such as Wrong Color or Wrong Size. There are two avenues to address this problem. If the business wishes to analyze why goods are being returned across divisions, it is necessary for the coding to conform to a common system.

In this particular case, one would not expect any agreement between the two divisions on a common coding system. However, it is likely that agreement could be reached on common category groupings for these codes. The data warehouse load should derive this category based on the agreed-on business rule. The data warehouse should also store the original code and description to support divisional analysis. However, since there is a good chance that the same code values may be used for different purposes, the entity that stores these descriptions should include a division or source system attribute as part of its key to ensure uniqueness.

Alternately, you can store the original values in different attributes; however, this can become a problem if there are a lot of divisions with different coding systems for the same code. The database table will quickly become cluttered with columns for each version of the code, as well as innumerable reference tables for each coding scheme. When it is possible to reach agreement on a common coding system, it is a good idea to also store the original code, but not necessarily the original description. The original code would not be supplied in deliveries to external marts or systems, but rather it would be stored to allow for future changes to the transformation rules that were the result of the common code agreement. It is not unusual for such rules to change after the business has had time to use the new coding system. The data warehouse should be prepared to reassign codes based on rule changes. This is not possible unless you have the original code value.

The other side to this is a situation in which it is not possible to reach agreement. Unfortunately, this situation is probably more common than we would like. The only option you really have in this situation is to create separate attributes for each interpretation. You should then clearly document the source and meaning of these attributes, as well as when they should be used. You must also decide how to set attributes that do not apply in a particular case. You can either leave them null or set them to a default value. That choice would depend on your database system and internal policies. This situation clearly complicates the delivery process and presentation of such attributes in the data marts. End users must be made aware of the differences between the attributes and why an attribute may not have a value in some circumstances.

Inferring Roles and Integrating Entities

If you are in a situation where you need to integrate data from two different order entry systems, it is not unlikely that each would have a completely different way to handle customer roles. In one case, you may have a system that has a single customer identifier, and other information, such as shipping address, billing address, and so forth adjunct to the order being processed. In the other case, the system may have explicit unique customer identifiers for each role, such as a sold-to customer, bill-to customer, payer customer, and ship-to customer. If in both cases you are taking about the same customer, integration can be a challenge.

The first decision you face is which roles should be represented in the data warehouse. From a modeling standpoint, you should treat each role as a new instance of Customer. This offers you the greatest flexibility should new roles present themselves in the future. It also allows flexibility with the existing interfaces. In the second system mentioned, reference data for the role is explicitly created, whereas in the first system it is not. You may encounter variances in the role data for the first system in the transactions you receive. For example, a ship-to address may change. In such cases, it becomes a simple matter of creating a new Customer instance to hold the new address information.

The foreign key in the transaction determines the actual role a Customer plays. Where a role does not exist in a particular interface, a business rule should be established to determine which customer instance assumes that role. If later you need to add to the roles because of a new interface, you can apply a similar inference rule to update historical data.

This leads to a discussion on how to key the reference data. From a business view, you would require a source system identifier, the source system's entity (customer) identifier, and possibly a role identifier, to accommodate the first system mentioned. In the data warehouse, using this as a primary key for the Customer entity presents a lot of problems. First, you need to allow for consolidation of common customers. Incorporation of one system's identifier over another can make this very difficult. Second, new consolidations may occur after the fact, after the users have seen the integrated data and discover additional commonality. Third, it is a compound key that adds complexity to SQL queries and can degrade performance.

The best approach is to assign a surrogate primary key and create two associative entities, one to cross-reference the source system keys to the primary key and the other to map entity consolidations. The first cross-reference would be used during reference data updates and transaction loads to locate the surrogate key of the Customer entity. The transaction entities would use the surrogate key as the foreign key. This structure would also be used in data delivery to obtain one or more natural keys for presentation to end users.

The second cross-reference would be used to map foreign keys to the Customer entity. As customer consolidations are identified, this structure would be updated to remap existing foreign keys to the proper Customer instance. This second cross-reference allows you to perform this reassignment without having to update the foreign key values in the transaction tables. This avoids a risky and tedious update, and provides an easy way to reverse a consolidation should an error be discovered later.

Adding Subject Areas

Addition of new subject areas is a natural extension of any data warehouse effort. It is rare that a company would fund a data warehouse effort that did not provide benefit in a short period of time. This requires an iterative approach to design and implementation that limits the subject areas implemented in each phase. This development approach dictates that each subject area be developed independently. It is the addition of transactional data into the data warehouse that ties the subject areas together.

Challenges arise when the subject areas implemented are incomplete for the transactions being stored. For example, the initial phase of a project calls for implementing sales data and the scope is limited to Customer, Product, and Financial, such as profit centers, subject areas. Later, it is decided that the Purchasing Organization needs to be added and the buyers need to be tied to sales to evaluate their performance.

The basic changes necessary are to model the purchasing subject area, add foreign keys to the sales data, and modify the sales data load process. None of this is particularly difficult. The challenge is what to do with the historical sales data. This is a business decision. On one hand, the business may decide to only perform analysis on data moving forward, in which case there is nothing to worry about. On the other hand, they may decide to retroactively assign buyers for some period of time in the past. Technically, this is not difficult to do. It is simply the implementation of some business rule, based on product and time, to update the newly added buyer foreign key in the sales data. How successful this is depends on the quality of the historical data from the Purchasing area and the completeness of the business rule. Some analysis should be done to see if the effort is worthwhile. At issue is not the effort necessary to update the data, but rather whether the results are useful to the business or whether inaccuracies create misinformation that can be detrimental to the data warehouse.

In this section, we examined issues with the integration and addition of subject areas in the data warehouse. You need to be careful in the design of the data warehouse to provide avenues to perform such changes if it is reasonable to expect that such changes will occur. At the same time, you also need to be careful not to overengineer a solution that adds unnecessary complexity, increases development time, or addresses problems that may never occur. We recommend that if integration is not an issue now, but may be in the future, you use surrogate keys in the subject areas for the most important entities. This positions the database to accept new structures and business keys to accommodate such integration when the need arises.

Summary

In this chapter, we examined the causes and impact of change on the data warehouse. We looked at how you can minimize the impact of change in the model by using surrogate keys, generalizing relationships, and relaxing a strict interpretation of business rules. We also discussed some of the integration challenges faced when business changes result in additional sources of similar data.

Unless you are omniscient, you will not be able to anticipate and prepare for all future changes. We do not believe that such preparation is desirable or practical; after all, your goal is to produce a working system, not spend a lifetime designing one. However, you can achieve an environment that is change-friendly. Spending a little time up front to establish an adaptable approach can go a long way toward reducing the effort and disruption that future changes can bring.

CHAPTER 11

Maintaining the Models

As we all know, a viable data warehouse must evolve over time to meet constantly changing business needs. This evolution requires changes to the data warehouse data models, and one of the challenges facing the data warehouse team is managing the data warehouse model and keeping it synchronized with the business data model, the physical schema, and the multiple data mart models. This task is critical for ensuring that the enterprise view is maintained, yet the tool support for this effort is limited.

After explaining the challenges, this chapter describes pragmatic approaches for managing the multiple models. Special attention is given to expanding the governing business and data warehouse models to encompass other areas so that the data warehouse continues to provide the enterprise view. We then also delve into the challenges created by having multiple people maintaining the data models.

Governing Models and Their Evolution

To put the model maintenance problems in perspective, we begin by reviewing the four types of models (see Figure 11.1) that were first introduced in Chapter 2 and then describe the factors that create changes to these models.

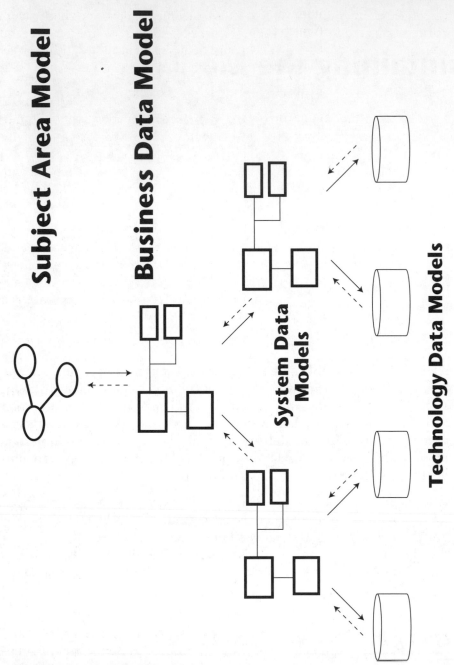

Figure 11.1 Data model types.

Subject Area Model

The subject area model depicts the major groupings of people, places, things, events, and concepts of interest, or subject areas, to the enterprise. This model provides the blueprint for each of the succeeding models. Each entity within the business data model (which is the next level model) is assigned to one, and only one, of the subject areas depicted in the subject area model. The subject area model's subject areas have mutually exclusive definitions for each of the areas.

There are three major causes for this model to be changed or augmented:

Lack of completeness.   The data warehouse is built iteratively, and most often, the supporting models are only developed to the extent required to support the piece of the data warehouse being developed at the time. It is possible that the subject area model was only partially developed and that additional subjects will need to be added when they are included in the data warehouse.

Major business change.   The subject area model contains the major subjects of interest to the enterprise. At this level, there are rarely business changes that affect this model. One exception occurs when the company enters into a new business line, either through acquisition, merger, or expansion. For example, if a retailer decides to issue credit cards, it may choose to establish a subject area for Accounts separate from the Customers subject area.

Refinement of the business data model.   The third major cause for a change to the subject area model is refinement. Unlike the lack of completeness, which entails adding subject areas, this change is created as a result of the feedback (upward arrow in Figure 11.1) from changes to the business data model. This happens when a new entity that doesn't appear to fit cleanly into any of the predefined subject areas is added to the business data model. At that point, the subject area model needs to be revised, with the revision potentially consisting merely of a definition update.

Whenever a new subject area is added or changed, its definition needs to be reviewed in the context of the existing subject areas. If the new area is found to overlap with an existing subject area, then the existing area's definition should be adjusted, and some of the entities assigned to it may need to be moved to the new area.

Business Data Model

The business data model is an abstraction or representation of the data in the given enterprise that helps people envision how information in the business relates to other information in the business—how the parts fit together. This model is not based on any organizational responsibilities, business processes, or system restrictions. It is based solely on the business rules that govern the way different entities are related to each other. The causes of change to this model are conceptually similar to the causes of changes to the subject area model:

Lack of completeness. The data warehouse is built iteratively, and unless a business data model already exists, it will typically be developed only to the extent required to support the portion of the data warehouse being developed. As new data warehouse iterations are undertaken, the business data model should be expanded to encompass those areas. In the ideal environment, the business data model is the foundation for all development activities, including new operational systems' development, and therefore, it will need to be expanded whenever there is any new systems development effort that addresses areas not previously encompassed by the model.

Business change. The business data model portrays the entities of interest and the business rules or relationships governing them. Whenever one of these changes, the business data model should be updated to reflect the change. Examples of business changes that could affect the model include:

- A change in purchasing policy from one in which an item may be purchased from many vendors to one in which an item may be purchased from only one vendor. When each vendor could be providing multiple items, this changes the relationship between vendor and item from a many-to-many relationship (which requires an associative entity) to a one-to-many relationship.

- A retailer may move into the electronic marketplace. When this happens, the concept of a store as the physical place at which purchases are made changes and the business data model must be adjusted accordingly.

- A financial institution may shift from dealing with the account holder as a single customer to a posture of recognizing each of the owners of the account as distinct customers. This, too, generates several changes in the business data model.

Refinement of a system data model. The third major cause for a change to the business data model is refinement. Figure 11.1 shows a feedback (upward) arrow from the system data model to the business data model. This feedback recognizes that there may be changes that are initiated at the system model level. This can occur when a programmer is making changes to a database based on a requested system change without consulting the business data model first. The impact on the business data model needs to be assessed and appropriate changes to that model, if any, should be made.

System Data Model

The third level of data models, or the system data model in Figure 11.1, describes the relationships among entities as they are reflected in a particular "system." In this context, "system" may mean an application system, an ERP (or other) package, a data warehouse, or a data mart. This model represents the electronic representation of the data in that system independent of the specific technology and database management system (DBMS). This model exists for each system, and while the change may be triggered by something outside the domain of a system, the only reason this model would change is if there is a need to change something in the system.

Examples of changes to our system of interest, the data warehouse, include:

Addition of new data elements.   The data warehouse should be built to include the elements that are needed to support the business intelligence requirements. Step 1 of the methodology for creating this model, described in Chapter 4, consists of selecting the data elements of interest. Over time, additional elements will be needed, and these must be added to the system data model for the warehouse. As indicated in the description of the business data model, when new data elements are added to the system model, feedback to the business data model is needed, and if those elements are assessed as being needed in that model, they must be added. Not all data element additions affect the business data model, though. The creation of derived data (Step 3 in Chapter 4) and summarized data (Step 5 in Chapter 4) don't require additions to the business data model as long as they are based on elements in that model and do not change the underlying relationships. (If they are not based on elements in the business model, those elements need to be added to the business data model.)

Granularity change.   The data warehouse granularity is dictated in Step 4 of the process described in Chapter 4. Even though the business data model may show detailed sales transaction information, a data warehouse that is built with a granularity of daily sales summaries does not include the details. If the company subsequently decides that it needs to perform shopping basket analysis and needs to include transaction-level data in the warehouse, the data warehouse system model needs to be enhanced to accommodate the new granularity level.

Physical schema adjustments.   Changes in the physical schema represented by the technology data model could also have an impact. These changes are often incorporated to improve performance and may consist of denormalizing some data to reduce the join activity needed to deliver data to the data marts. The feedback mechanism from the physical schema (technology model) to the system model, shown in Figure 11.1, dictates that the changes are reflected in that model. The base data elements should all be in the business data model, but copies of elements made to accomplish denormalization should not be represented in the business data model. That model is a pure 3NF model. If an element is added to a table to improve performance and does not actually depend on the key of that table, it cannot be included in a pure 3NF model since every element in that model needs to depend on the key, the whole key, and nothing but the key of the entity it's in.

Technology Data Model

The technology data model is a collection of the specific information being addressed by a particular system and implemented with specific technologies. All the technology used for this data store needs to be considered, including the hardware, operating system, and DBMS. Further, strategies for denormalization, views, partitions, indexing, and referential integrity are all reflected in the model. Some aspects of security are also incorporated into the model; other aspects may be considered external to the model. This model may change if anything relating to these factors changes, if there is a change in the governing system data model, or if there is a change to another technology model.

Governing system data model change. Top-down development approaches generate the system data model first and then use it to generate the technology data model. Therefore, as each new enhancement to the data warehouse is contemplated, the system data model needs to be updated. The technology model is updated to reflect those revisions.

Technical environment changes. The other major source of changes to the technology model is based on its role. This model describes the physical environment, and hence any change to this environment dictates a change to the technology data model. For example, if we migrate from one DBMS to another, the technology model is adjusted to reflect changes that are needed to meet performance objectives in the new environment.

Changes in other technology models. A technology model exists for the data warehouse and for each of the data marts. When there is a change to a data mart, changes in the data warehouse model may be dictated to satisfy performance objectives.

Synchronization Implications

Synchronization can be required due to changes in any of the models, although not all changes in one model dictate a change in another model. For example, a change in a technology model that is based on a physical constraint does not create a change in the system model; however, a change that is based on denormalizing to improve performance may create a change in the system model. Similarly, a change in the business model does not necessarily change all of the subordinate system models. Only those models that reflect information addressed by the change are affected. For example, if you add attributes to the business data model that are not within the scope of a particular operational system, its system data model remains unchanged.

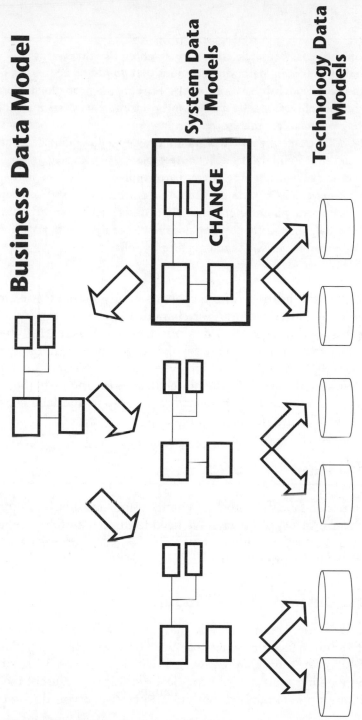

Figure 11.2 Synchronization implications.

Criticality

Model synchronization is absolutely critical for an enterprise that wants to achieve the goal of consistent data. Organizations that do not recognize the role and value of the data models in ensuring consistent data are prone to skimp in this area. The impact of skipping the model synchronization activities may not be felt initially; they will manifest themselves in a new series of silo applications that eventually will recreate the data integration problems that made data integration so difficult in the initial data warehouse project.

An effective data stewardship program and proper placement of the data management staff are extremely important. Without an effective data stewardship program, there is no focal point for quickly making decisions for synchronizing the models; if the data management group does not have the appropriate level of authority, development teams will tend to ignore its policies.

One of the hidden implications of the changes in any model (for example, a system data model) is the potential for changes required in other models of that type (that is, the other system data models). As Figure 11.2 illustrates, when there is a change in a system model, the subordinate technology models and the business data model need to be reviewed to determine the impact on them. If the change in the system data model dictates an update to the business model due to the feedback, then every other system model needs to be reviewed to determine if it needs to change.

Model Coordination

Now that we understand the types of changes and how they can affect the individual models, let's explore what we need to do to maintain synchronization among the models. We will examine the coordination for each pair of models, as shown in Figure 11.3.

Subject Area and Business Data Models

The subject area model is not generally maintained within the modeling tool itself. It is often drawn using tools such as Visio (not necessarily the data modeling version), PowerPoint, CorelDraw, or a word processor. This is because the common modeling tools do not provide a graphic to represent the subject area. Definitions are maintained within a spreadsheet or document. We describe three techniques that facilitate keeping these two models synchronized. If the modeling tool supports it, we've found the first approach is the easiest to maintain and provides the best tool for communicating with the business community.

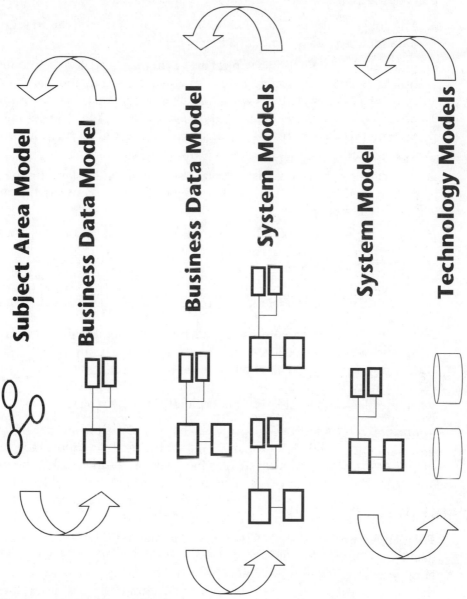

Figure 11.3 Model coordination.

Color-Coding

The recommended approach, when the modeling tool supports it, is to establish a different color for each subject area and to use that color for the background of the entities that belong in the subject area. The major advantages of this approach are:

- The subject areas are visible and do not require the modeler to segregate data into separately maintained views.

- Since all the data within a subject area is in a single color, the modeler can quickly visualize the subject areas. Further, in general, there are more relationships between entities within a subject area than between entities that are in different subject areas. With this knowledge, the modeler has useful information for organizing the business data model by grouping entities of the same color (that is, subject area) together.

- The visible subject area distinctions also help in understanding the model and in identifying the data stewards who should be contacted to help with each section.

- With a default color of white, the modeler need not be concerned with the subject area initially, but can look for white entities for subject area assignments prior to completing the work. This lets the modeler focus his or her attention on entities and attributes during model creation and ensures that the business data model remains coordinated with the subject area model.

The major disadvantage of this approach is that often the model is printed in black and white. The colors either do not appear at all or are represented as shades of gray, so the distinction between the subject areas is only visible on a color monitor or in a color print of the model. Further, if the color selected is dark, the black and white print may actually impede seeing the text.

We recommend selecting light colors whenever possible so that the printing impact is minimized. Additionally, some of the modeling tools permit adjusting other display properties, such as the thickness of the border, the font size, and type. These adjustments can be used to distinguish the subject areas without presenting any printing problems. Further, the model can be laid out so that subject areas are segregated on separate pages with a text box of the subject area name appearing on each page. Figure 11.4, first introduced in Chapter 3, shows another approach in which the subject areas were segregated on a page and the name of the subject area was inserted.

Subject Area Views

The first technique entails using the "subject area" views provided by the modeling tool and setting up a separate subject area in the modeling tool to correspond to each subject area. (This technique cannot be used if the tool does not provide the ability to divide the model into subject area views.) This technique facilitates the grouping of the data entities by subject area and the provision of views accordingly. The major advantages of this technique are:

- Each entity is assigned to a subject area and the subject area assignment is clear.

- If a particular data steward or data modeler has responsibility for a specific subject area, then all of the data for which that person is responsible is in one place.

- Information can easily be retrieved for specific subject areas.

The major disadvantage of this technique is that the subject area view is fine for developing the data model, but a single subject area rarely provides a complete picture of the business scenario. Hence, for discussion with business users, we need to create additional (for example, process-oriented) views, thereby increasing the maintenance work.

Including the Subject Area within the Entity Name

The third approach is to include the subject area name or code within the entity name. For example, if the Customers subject area is coded CU and the Products subject area is coded PR, we would have entities such as CU Customer, CU Prospect, PR Item, and PR Product Family.

The major advantages of this approach are:

- It is easy to create the initial entity name with the relationship to the subject area.

- It is independent of the data-modeling tool.

- There is no issue with respect to displaying the relationship between an entity and a subject area.

- Alphabetic lists of entities will be grouped by subject area.

The major disadvantages of this approach are:

- The entity name is awkward. With this approach, the modeler is moving away from using business-meaningful names for the entity names.

- Maintenance is more difficult. It is possible to have an entity move from one subject area to another when the subject area is refined. A refinement, for example, may change the definition of subject areas, so that with the revised definition, some of the entities previously assigned to it may need to be reassigned. With this approach, the names of the entities must change. This is a relatively minor inconvenience since it does not cascade to the system and technology models.

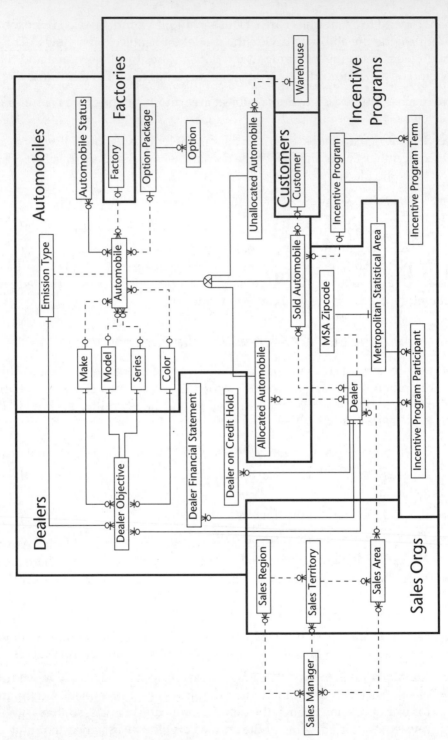

Figure 11.4 Segregating subject areas.

Associative Entities

Associative entities that resolve the many-to-many relationship between entities that reside in different subject areas do not cleanly fit into a single subject area. Because one of the uses of the subject area model is to ensure that an entity is only represented once in the business data model, a predictable process for designating the subject area for these entities is needed. Choices include basing the decision on stewardship responsibilities (our favorite) or making arbitrary choices and maintaining an inventory of these to ensure that they are not duplicated. If the first option is used, a special color can be used for these entities if desired; if the second option is used, entities could be shown in multiple subject area views, since they still would exist only once in the master model.

Business and System Data Models

The toughest relationship to maintain is that between the business data model and the system data model. This difficulty is caused by the volume of changes, the fact that these two models need to be consistent—but not necessarily identical—to each other, and the limited tool support for maintaining these relationships. Some examples of the differences include:

Differences in the attributes within an entity.   The entity within the business data model includes all of the attributes for that entity. Within each system model, only the attributes of interest to that "system" are included. In Chapter 4 (Step 1), we discussed the exclusion of attributes that are not needed in the data warehouse.

Representation over time.   The business data model is a point-in-time model that represents the current view of the data and not a series of snapshots. The data warehouse represents data over time (that is, snapshots), and its governing system model is therefore an over-time model. As we saw in Step 2 of the methodology for developing this model, there are substantial structural differences that exist in the deployment since some relationships change, for example, from one-to-many to many-to-many.

Inclusion of summarized data.   Summarized data is often included in a system model. Step 5 of our methodology described specifically how to incorporate summarized data in the data warehouse. Summarized data is inappropriate in a 3NF model such as the business data model.

These differences contribute to the difficulty of maintaining the relationships between these models. None of the data-modeling tools with which we are familiar provide an easy way to overcome these differences. The technique we recommend is that the relationship between the business data model and the system models be manually maintained. There are steps that you can take to make this job easier:

1. Develop the business data model to the extent practical for the first iteration. Be sure to include definitions for all the entities and attributes.

2. Include derived data in the business data model. The derived data represents a deviation from pure normal form. Including it within the business data model promotes consistency since we will be copying a portion of this model as a starting point for each system data model.

3. Maintain some physical storage characteristics of the attributes in the business data model. These characteristics really don't belong in the business data model since that model represents the business and not the electronic storage of the information. As you will see in a subsequent step, we use a copy of information in the business data model to generate the starting point for each system data model. Since an entity in the business data model may be replicated into multiple system data models, by storing some physical characteristics in the business data model, we promote consistency and avoid redundant entry of the physical characteristics. The physical characteristics we recommend maintaining within the business data model are the column name, nullability information, and the datatype (including the length or precision). There may be valid reasons for the nullability information and the datatype to change within a systems model, but we at least start out with a standard set. For example, the relationship between a customer and a sales transaction may be optional (null permitted) in the business data model if prospects are considered customers. If we are building a data warehouse or application system that only applies to people who actually acquired our product, the relationship is mandatory, and the foreign key cannot be null.

4. Copy the relevant portion of the business data model and use it as the starting point of the system data model. In the modeling tool, this consists of a copy-and-paste operation—not inclusion. Inclusion of entities from one model (probably represented as a view in the modeling tool) into another within the modeling tool does not create a new entity, and any changes made will be reflected back into the business data model.

5. Make appropriate adjustments to the model based on the scope of the application system or data warehouse segment. Each time an adjustment is made, think about whether or not the change has an impact on the business data model. Changes that are made to reflect history, to adjust the storage granularity, and to improve performance generally don't affect the business data model. It is possible that as the system data model is developed definitions will be revised. These changes do need to be reflected in the business data model.

6. Periodically compare the system data model to the business data model and ensure that the models are consistent with each other and that all of the differences are due to what each of the models represents.

This process requires adherence to data-modeling practices that promote model consistency. Significant effort will be required, and a natural question to ask is, "Is it worth the trouble?" Yes, it is worth the effort. Maintaining consistency between the data warehouse system model and the business data model promotes stability and supports maintenance of the business view within the data warehouse and other systems. The benefits of the business data model noted in Chapter 2 can then be realized.

Another critical advantage is that the maintenance of the relationship between the business data model and the system data model forces a degree of discipline. Project managers are often faced with database designers who like to jump directly to the physical design (or technology model) without considering any of the preceding models on which it depends. To promote adherence to these practices, the project managers must ensure that the development methodology includes this steps, that everyone who works with the model understands the steps and why they are important. Effective adherence to these practices should also be included in the job descriptions.

The forced coordination of the business and system data models and the subsequent downstream relationship between the system and technology models ensures that sound data management techniques are applied in the data warehouse development of all data stores. It promotes managing of data and information as corporate assets.

System and Technology Data Models

Most companies have only a single instance of a production database such as a data warehouse. Even companies that have multiple production versions of this database typically deploy them on the same platform and in the same database management system. This approach significantly simplifies the maintenance of the system and technology data models since we have a one-to-one relationship, as shown in Figure 11.5.

Most of the data-modeling tools maintain a "logical" and "physical" data model. While these are often presented as two separate data models, they are often actually two views of the same data model with (in some tools) an ability to include some of the entities and attributes in only one of the models. These two views correspond to the system data model and the technology data model. Without the aid of a repository, most of the tools do not enable the modeler to easily maintain separate system and technology data models. If a company has only one version of the physical data warehouse, we recommend coupling these tightly together and using the data-modeling tool to accomplish this.

The major advantage of this approach is its simplicity. We don't have to do any extra work to keep the system and technology models synchronized—the modeling tool takes care of that for us. Further, if the data-modeling tool is

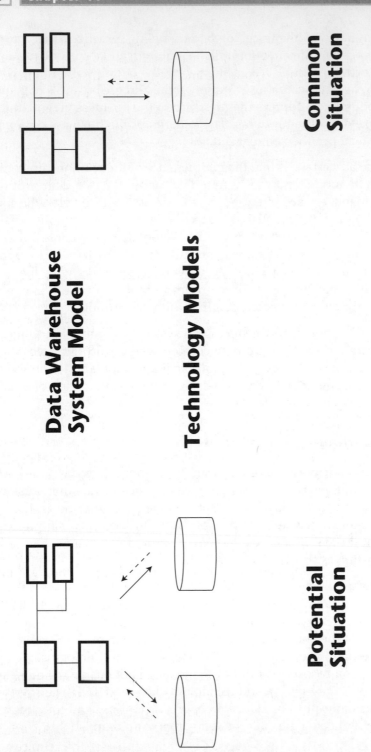

Figure 11.5   Common deployment approach.

used to generate the DDL for the database schema, the system model and the physical schema are always synchronized as well. The final technology model is dependent on the physical platform, and changes in the model are made to improve performance. The major disadvantage of this approach is that when the system and technology model are tightly linked, changes in the technology model create changes in the system model, and we lose information about which decisions concerning the model were made based on the system level constraints and which were made based on the physical deployment constraints. While this disadvantage is worth noting, we feel that a pragmatic approach is appropriate here unless the modeling tool facilitates the separate maintenance of the system and technology models.

Managing Multiple Modelers

The preceding section dealt with managing the relationships between successive pairs of data models. Another maintenance coordination we face is managing the activities of multiple modelers. The two major considerations for managing a staff of modelers are the roles and responsibilities of each person or group and the collision management facilities.

Roles and Responsibilities

Traditionally, data-modeling roles are divided between the data administration staff and the database administration staff. The data administration staff is generally responsible for the subject area model and the business data model, while the database administration staff is generally responsible for the technology model. The system model responsibility may fall in either court or may be shared. The first thing that companies must do is establish responsibilities at the group level.

Even if a single group has responsibility for a model, we have the potential of having multiple people involved. Let's examine each of the data models individually.

Subject Area Model

The subject area model is developed under the auspices of a cross-functional group of business representatives and rarely changes. While it may be under the responsibility of the data administration group, no single individual in that group should change the subject area model. Any changes to this model need to be understood and sanctioned by the data administration organization. We feel the most appropriate approach is to maintain it under the auspices of the data stewardship group (if one exists), but data administration if there is no data stewardship group. This model actually helps us in managing the development of the business data model.

Business Data Model

The business data model is the largest data model in our organization. This is true because, when completed, it encompasses the entire enterprise. A complete business data model may contain hundreds of entities and over 10,000 attributes. All entities and attributes in any of the successive models are either extracted from this model or can be derived, based on elements within this model. The most effective way to manage changes in this model is to assign prime responsibilities based on groupings of entities, some of which may be defined by virtue of the subject areas. We may, for example, have a modeler responsible for an entire subject area, such as Customers. We could also split responsibility for a subject area, with the accountability for some of the entities within a subject area being within the realm of one modeler and the accountability for other entities being within the realm of another modeler. We feel that allocating responsibility at an attribute level is inappropriate.

Very often an individual activity will impact multiple subject areas. The entity responsibilities need to be visibly published so that efforts that entail overlaps can involve the appropriate people.

Having prime responsibilities allocated does not mean that only one modeler can work within a section of the model. It means that one modeler is responsible for that section. When we undertake a data warehouse effort that encompasses several subject areas, it may not be appropriate to involve all of the responsible data analysts. Instead, a single person may be assigned to represent data administration, and that person coordinates with the modelers responsible for each section of the model.

System and Technology Data Model

We previously recommended that the data-modeling tool facilities be used to maintain synchronization between the system and technology data model. We noted that, in respect to the tool, these are in fact a single model with two views. The system and technology data models are developed within the scope of a project. The project leader needs to assign responsibilities appropriately and to ensure that the entire team understands each person's responsibility. Since all of the activities are under the realm of the project leader, the project plan can be used to aid in the coordination.

Remember that any change to the system data model needs to be considered in the business data model. The biggest challenge is not in maintaining the synchronization among the people responsible for any particular model—it is in maintaining the synchronization among the people responsible for the different (that is, business data model and system data model) models. Just as companies have procedures that require maintenance programmers to consider downstream systems in making changes, procedures are needed to require people maintaining models to consider the impact on other models. The impact of the changes was presented in Figure 11.2. An inventory of the data models and their relationships to each other should be maintained so that the affected models can be identified.

Collision Management

Collision management is the process for detecting and addressing changes to the model. The process entails providing the modeler with access to a portion of the model, making the model changes, comparing the revised model to the base model, and incorporating appropriate changes. A member of the Data Administration team is responsible for managing this process. That person must be familiar with the collision management capabilities of the tool, have data modeling skills, have strong communication and negotiation skills, and have a solid understanding of the overall business data model.

Model Access

Access to the model can be provided in one of two forms. One approach is to let the data modeler copy the entire model, and another is to let the data modeler check out a portion of the model. When the facility to check out a portion of the model exists, some tools provide options with respect to exclusivity of control. When these options are provided, the data modeler checks out the model portion and can lock this portion of the model, protecting it from changes made by any other person. Anyone else who makes a request to check out that portion of the model is informed that he or she is receiving read-only access and will not be able to save the changes. When the tool does not provide this level of protection, two people can actively make changes to the same portion of the model, and the one who gets his or her changes in first will have an easier time getting them absorbed, as described in the remainder of this section. With either approach, the data modeler has a copy of the data model that he or she can modify to reflect the necessary changes.

Modifications

Once the modeler has a copy of the portion of the data model of interest, he or she performs the modeling activities dictated by his or her responsibilities. Remember, these changes are being made to a copy of the data model—not to the base model (that is, the model from which components are extracted). When the modeler completes the work, the updates need to be migrated to the base model.

Comparison

Each data modeler is addressing his or her view of the enterprise. The full business data model has a broader perspective. The business data model represents the entire enterprise; the system data model represents the entire scope of a data warehouse or application system. It is possible for the modeler to be unaware of other aspects of the model that are affected by the changes. The collision management process identifies these impacts.

Prior to importing the changes into the base model, the base model and the changed model are compared using a technique called collision management. The technique has this name because it looks for collisions—or differences—between the two models and identifies them. The person responsible for overall model administration can review the identified collisions and indicate which ones should be absorbed into the base model. This step in the process also provides a checkpoint to ensure that the changes in the system model are appropriately reflected in the business model. Any changes that are not incorporated should be discussed with the modeler.

Incorporation

The last step in the process is incorporation of the changes. Once the person responsible for administering the base model makes the decision concerning incorporation of the changes, these are incorporated. Each modeling tool handles this process somewhat differently, but most provide for some degree of automation.

Summary

Synchronization of the various data models is critical if you are to accomplish a major goal of the data warehouse—data consistency. The business data model is used as the foundation for all subsequent models. Every data element that is eventually deployed in a database is linked back to a defined element in the business data model. This linkage ensures consistency and significantly simplifies integration and transformation activities in building the data warehouse.

The individual data models may change for a variety of reasons. Changes to the subject area model and business data model are driven primarily by business changes, and revisions to the other models are driven primarily by impacts of these changes and deployment decisions. The challenge of keeping the models synchronized is exacerbated by the absence of tools that can automate the entire process. The most difficult task is keeping the business data model synchronized with the lower-level models, but as we saw, this synchronization is at the heart of keeping the enterprise perspective.

CHAPTER 12

Deploying the Relational Solution

B y now, you should have a very good idea of what your data warehouse should look like and what its roles and functions are. This is all well and good if you are starting from scratch—no warehouse, no marts—just a clean slate from which to design and implement your business intelligence environment. That rarely happens, though.

Most of you already have some kind of BI environment started. What we find most often is a mishmash of reporting databases, hypercubes of data, and standalone and unintegrated data marts, sprinkled liberally all over the enterprise. The questions then become, "What do I do with all the stuff I already have in place? Can I ever hope to achieve this wonderful architecture laid out in this book?" The answer is yes—but it will take hard work, solid support from your IT and business communities, and a roadmap of where you want to go. You will have to work hard on garnering the internal support for this migration. We have given you the roadmap in Chapter 1. Now, all you need is a migration strategy to remove the silos of analytical capabilities and replace them with a maintainable and sustainable architecture.

This chapter discusses just that—how your company can migrate from a stovepipe environment of independent decision support applications to a coordinated central data warehouse with dependent data marts. We start with a discussion of data mart chaos and the problems that environment causes. A variety of migration methods and implementation steps are discussed next, thus giving the reader several options by which to achieve a successful and maintainable environment. The pros and cons of each method are also covered. Most of you will likely use a mixture of more than one method. The choice you make is dependent upon a variety of factors such as the business culture, political environment, technological feasibility, and costs.

Data Mart Chaos

In a naturally occurring BI environment—one in which there are no architectural constraints—the OLAP applications, reporting systems, statistical and data mining analyses, and other analytical capabilities are designed and implemented in isolation from each other. Figure 12.1 shows the appealing and deceivingly simple beginnings of this architecture. There is no doubt that it takes less time, effort, money, and resources to create a single reporting system or OLAP application without a supporting architecture than it does to create the supporting data warehouse with a dependent data mart—at least for the individual effort. In this case, Finance has requested a reporting system to examine the trend in revenues and expenses.

Let's look at the characteristics that naturally occur from this approach:

- The construction of the independent data mart must combine both data acquisition and data delivery processes into a single process. This process does all the heavy lifting of data acquisition, including the extraction, integration, cleansing, and transformation of disparate sources of data. Then, it must perform the data delivery processes of formatting the data to the appropriate design (for example, star schema, cube, flat files, and statistical sample) and then deliver the data to the mart for loading and accessing by the chosen technology.

- Since there is no repository of historical, detailed data to dip into when new elements or calculations are needed, the extraction, integration, cleansing, transformation, formatting, and ultimately delivery (ETF&D) process must go all the way back to the source systems continuously.

- If detailed data is required by the data mart—even if it is used very infrequently—then all the needed detail must be stored in the data mart. This will eventually lead to poor performance.

- Proprietary and departmentalized summarizations, aggregations, and derivations are stored in the data mart and may not require detailed meta data to describe them since they are used by a limited audience with similar or identical algorithms.

- Definitions of the key elements or attributes in the data mart are specific to the group using the data and may not require detailed meta data to describe them.

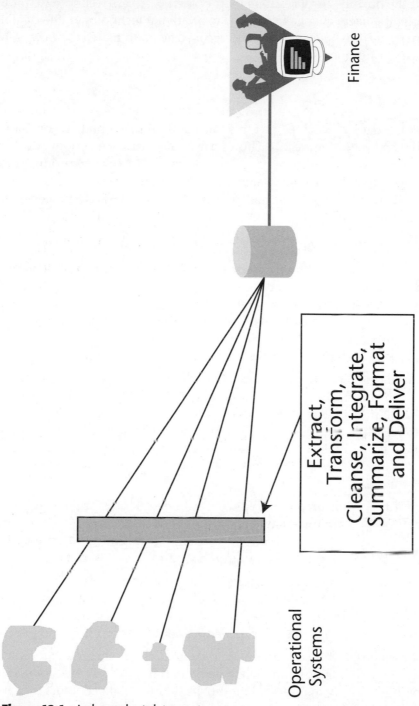

Finance

Extract,
Transform,
Cleanse, Integrate,
Summarize, Format
and Deliver

Operational
Systems

Figure 12.1   Independent data mart.

■ If the business users change their chosen BI access technology (for example, the users change from cube to relational technology), the data mart may need to be torn down and reconstructed to match the new technological requirements.

Why Is It Bad?

Now let's see what happens if this form of BI implementation continues down its natural path. Figure 12.2 shows the architecture if we now add two more departmental requests—one for Sales personnel to analyze product profitability and one for Marketing to analyze campaign revenues and costs. We see that for each data mart, a new and proprietary set of ETF&D processes must be developed.

There are some obvious problems inherent in this design including the following.

Impact on the operational systems. Since these three marts use very similar data (revenues and expenses for products under various circumstances), they are using the same operational systems as sources for their data. However, instead of going to these systems once for the detailed revenue and expense data, they are interfacing three times! This has a significant impact on the overall performance of these critical OLTP systems.

Redundant ETF&D processing. Given that they are using the same sources, this means that the ETF&D processes are basically redundant as well. The main differences in their processing are the filters in place (inclusion and exclusion of specific data), the proprietary calculations used by each department to their version of revenues and expenses, and the timing of their extracts. This leads to the spider web of ETF&D processing shown in Figure 12.2.

Redundancy in stored detailed data. As mentioned for the single data mart, each mart must have its own set of detailed data. While not identical, each of these marts will contain very similar revenue and expense transaction records, thus leading to significant duplication of data.

Inconsistent summarized, aggregated, and derived fields. Finance, Sales, and Marketing certainly do not use the same calculations in interpreting the detail data. The numbers generated from each of these data marts has little to no possibility of being reconciled without massive effort and wasted time.

Inconsistent definitions and meta data. If the implementers took the time to create definitions and meta data behind the ETF&D processes, it is highly unlikely that these definitions and meta data contents match across the various data marts. Again significant effort has been wasted in creating and recreating these important components.

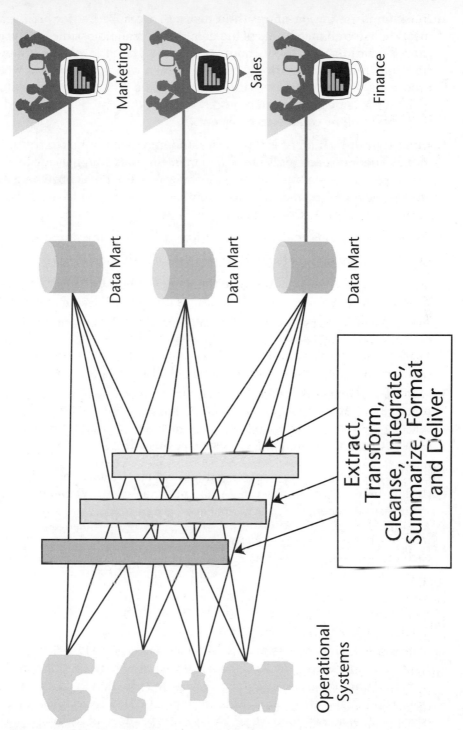

Marketing

Sales

Finance

Data Mart

Data Mart

Data Mart

Extract, Transform, Cleanse, Integrate, Summarize, Format and Deliver

Operational Systems

Figure 12.2 Naturally occurring architecture.

Inconsistent integration (if any) and history. Because the definitions and meta data do not match across the data marts, it is impossible for the data from the various operational sources to be integrated in a like manner in each data mart. Each mart will contain its own way of identifying what a product is. Therefore, there is little hope that the different implementers will have identical integration processing and, thus, all history stored in each mart will be equally inconsistent.

Significant duplication of effort. The amount of time, effort, resources, and money spent on each individual data mart may be as high as for the initial CIF implementation but it should be obvious that there is no synergy created as the next data mart is implemented. Let's list just of few of the duplicated efforts taking place:

- Source systems analyses are performed for each data mart.
- Definitions and meta data are created for each mart.
- Data hygiene is performed on the same sets of data (but not in the same fashion).

Huge impact on IT resources. The maintenance of data marts becomes nightmarish, given the spider web architecture in place. IT or the line of business IT becomes burdened with the task of trying to understand and maintain the redundant, yet inconsistent, ETF&D processes for each data mart. If a change occurs in the operational systems that affects all three marts, the change must be implemented not once but three times—each with its own set of quirks and oddities—resulting in about three times the resources needed to maintain and sustain this environment.

Because there is no synergy or integration between these independent efforts, each data mart will have about the same price tag on it. When added up, the costs of these independent data marts become significantly more than the price tag for the architected CIF approach.[1] (See Figure 12.3.) For each subsequent CIF implementation, the price tag drops substantially to the point that the overall cost of the environment is less than the cost of the individual data marts together.

Why is this true? Let's look at the reasons for the decreasing price tag for BI implementations using the architected environment:

- The most significant cost for any BI project is in the ETL design, analysis, and implementation. Because there is no synergy between the independent data mart implementations, there is no reduction in cost as more and more data marts are created. This reduction in the CIF architecture occurs because the data warehouse serves as the repository of historical and

---

1 "Data Warehouses vs. Data Marts" by Campbell (Databased Web Advisor, January 1998, page 32)

detailed data that is used over and over again for all data marts. Any data that was brought into the data warehouse for a data mart that has been deployed merely needs to be delivered to the new mart; it does not need to be recaptured from the source system. The ETL processes are performed only once rather than over and over again.

- The redundancy in definition and meta data creation is greatly reduced in the CIF architecture. Definitions and meta data are created once and simply updated with each new data mart project started. There is no "reinventing" of the wheel for each project. Issues may still arise from disparities in definitions but at least you have a sound foundation to build from.

- Finally, there is no need for each individual data mart to store the detailed data that it infrequently needs. The data is stored only once in the data warehouse and is readily accessible by the business community when needed At that point, the detail could be replicated into the data mart.

This means that by the time the third or fourth data mart is created there is a substantial amount of properly documented, integrated, and cleansed data stored in the data warehouse repository. The next data mart requirement will likely find most, if not all, of its supporting data already to go. Implementation time, effort, and cost for this data mart are significantly less than it would be for the standalone version.

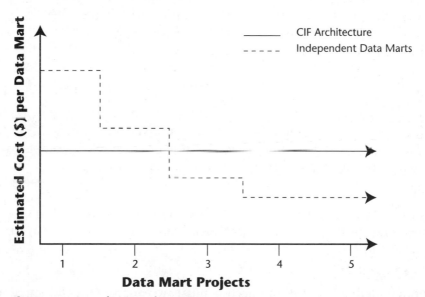

Figure 12.3 Implementation costs.

Criteria for Being In-Architecture

Having laid the foundation for the need of a CIF-like architecture for your BI environment, what then are the criteria for a project being "in-architecture," that is, the guidelines for ensuring that your projects and implementations adhere to your chosen architecture? Here is our checklist for determining whether your project is properly aligned with the architectural directions of the company:

- It is initiated and managed through a Program Management Office (PMO). The PMO is responsible for creating and maintaining the conceptual and technical architectures, establishing standards for data models, programs, and database schemas, determining which projects get funding, and resolving conflicts and issues within a project or across projects.

- It employs the standardized, interoperable, technology platforms. The technology may not be the same for each BI implementation but it should be interoperable with the existing implementations.

- It uses a standardized development methodology for BI projects. There are several books available on this subject. We suggest you adopt one of these methodologies, modify it to suit your environment, and enforce its usage for all BI projects.

- It uses standard-compliant software components for its implementation. Just as the hardware should be interoperable and standardized, so should the software components including the ETL and access software.

- It uses model-based development and starts with the business data model. Change procedures for the data models are established and socialized.

- It uses meta data- or repository-driven development practices. In particular, the ETL processing should be meta data-driven rather than hand-coded.

- It adheres to established change control and version management procedures. Because changes are inevitable, the PMO should be prepared for change by creating and enforcing formal change management or version control processes to be used by each project.

It is important to note that these architectural criteria are evolutionary; they will change as the BI environment grows and matures. However, it is also important to ensure that the architectural criteria are deliberate, consistent, and business-driven with business value concluded.

Migration to the chosen BI architecture must be planned and, ultimately, it must be based on a rigorous cost/benefit analysis. Does it make sense for a specific project to adhere to the PMO standards? The long-term costs and benefits of adhering or not adhering will make that determination. The migration process will take a long time to accomplish; furthermore, it may never be finished. As a final consideration, you should be aware that the architected applications and processes must support communication with nonarchitected systems gracefully and consistently.

With these guidelines in place, let's look at how you would get started in your migration process. Following is a high-level overview of the steps to take:

1. Develop a strategic information delivery architecture. This is the roadmap you use to determine which data marts will be converted to the architecture and in what order. The CIF is a solid, proven one that many companies have successfully implemented.

2. Obtain the buy-in for your architecture from the IT and business community sponsors.

3. Perform the appropriate cost/benefit analyses for the various conversion projects. This should include a ranking or prioritization for each project.

4. Obtain funding for the first project through the PMO.

5. Design the technical infrastructure with the PMO hardware and software standards enforced.

6. Choose the appropriate method of conversion from those in the following section. Each option may generate significant political and cultural issues.

7. Develop the project plan and scope definition, including the timeframes and milestones, and get the appropriate resources assigned.

The next section will describe in detail the different methods you can use to accomplish the migration of independent data marts into a maintainable and sustainable architecture. As with all endeavors of this sort, the business community must be behind you. It is your responsibility to constantly garner their active support of this migration.

Migrating from Data Mart Chaos

In this section, we discuss several approaches for migrating from "data mart chaos." The idea is to go from the chaos of independent data marts to the Corporate Information Factory architecture. In our experience, there are at least five different methods to achieve a migration from chaos, and it is likely that you will find yourself using components from each of these in your approach. We list them here and discuss them in detail in the following sections:

- Conform the dimensions used in the data marts.

- Create a data warehouse data model and convert each data mart model to it.

- Convert data marts to the data warehouse architecture—two paths are described.

- Build new data marts only "in-architecture"—leave old marts alone.
- Build the full architecture from one of the existing independent data marts.

Each method has its advantages and disadvantages, which you must consider before choosing one. We list these with each section as well.

Conform the Dimensions

For certain environments, one way to mitigate the inconsistency, redundancy of extractions, and chaos created by implementing independent data marts is to conform the dimensions commonly used across the various data marts. Conforming the dimensions consists of creating a single, generic dimension for each of the shared dimensions used in each mart. For example, a single product dimension would be created from all the product dimension requirements of the data marts. This unified dimension would then replace all the fractured versions of a product dimension in the data marts.

This technique is for those environments that have only multidimensional or OLAP data marts. It cannot be used if your BI environment includes a need for statistical analyses, data mining, or other nonmultidimensional technologies. Given this caveat, what is it about the multidimensional marts that allows this technique to help mitigate data mart chaos?

First, each data mart has its own set of fact and dimension tables, unique to that data mart. The dimensions consist of the constraints used in navigating the fact table and contain mostly textual elements describing the dimensions. Examples of one such dimension, the Product dimension, are shown for the Finance, Sales, and Marketing data marts described in Figure 12.4. We see that each data mart has its own way of dealing with its dimensions. Sales and Marketing have identified various attributes to include in their Product dimension. Finance does not even call the dimension Product; it uses the term Item and uses an Item identifier as the key to the dimension.

Second, the facts or measurements used in the fact table are derived from these dimensions. They form the intersection of the various dimensions at the level of detail specified by the dimensions. In other words, a measurement of revenue for a product (or item) is calculated for the intersection of the Product ID, the Store ID, Time Period, and any other desired dimensions (for example, Salesperson, Sales Region or Territory, or Campaign). Therefore, the dimensions hold the key to integration among the data marts. If the depictions of a dimension such as Product are all at the same level of detail and have the same definition and key structure, then the measurements derived from their combination should be the same across data marts. This is what is meant by conforming the dimensions.

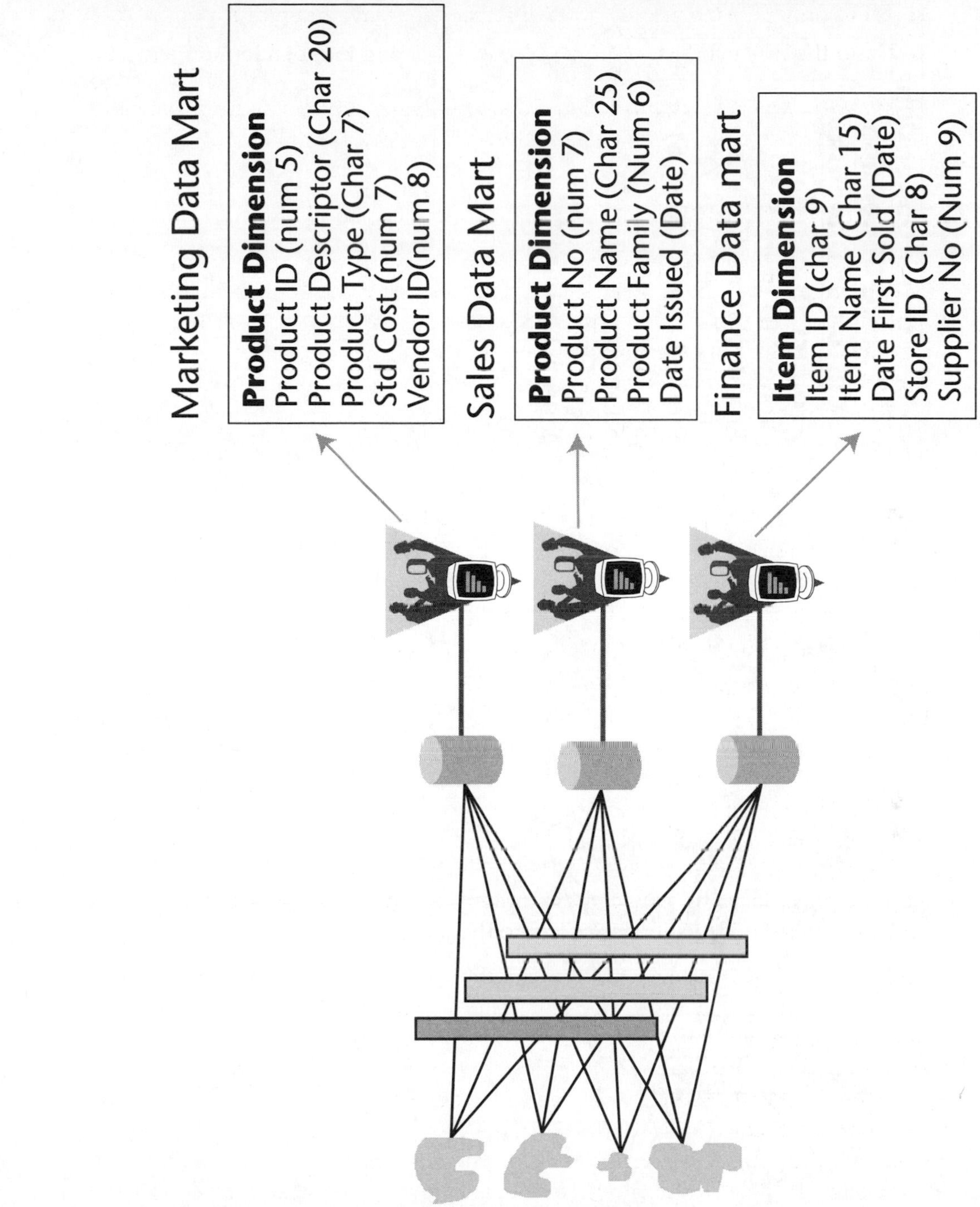

Marketing Data Mart

Product Dimension
Product ID (num 5)
Product Descriptor (Char 20)
Product Type (Char 7)
Std Cost (num 7)
Vendor ID(num 8)

Sales Data Mart

Product Dimension
Product No (num 7)
Product Name (Char 25)
Product Family (Num 6)
Date Issued (Date)

Finance Data mart

Item Dimension
Item ID (char 9)
Item Name (Char 15)
Date First Sold (Date)
Store ID (Char 8)
Supplier No (Num 9)

Figure 12.4 Each data mart has its own dimensions.

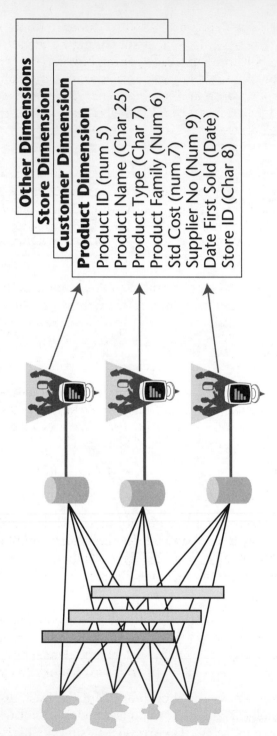

Figure 12.5 Conversion of the data marts.

The differences between the three data marts' Product dimensions are reconciled and a single Product dimension is created containing all the attributes needed by each mart. It is important to note that getting buy-in for this can be a very difficult process involving a lot of political skirmishing, difficult compromising from different departments, and resolving complicated integration issues. This process can be repeated for each dimension that is used in more than one data mart. The next dimension is examined, reconciled, and implemented in the three marts.

Once the new conformed dimensions are created, each data mart is converted to the newly created and conformed dimensions. (See Figure 12.5.) The reconciliation process can be difficult and politically ugly. You will encounter resistance to changing implemented marts to the conformed dimensions. Make sure that you have your sponsor(s) lined up and that you have done the cost/benefit analysis to defend the process.

This technique is perhaps the easiest way to mitigate at least some of the data mart chaos. It is certainly not the ideal architecture but at least it's a step in the right direction. You must continue to strive for the enterprise data warehouse creation, ultimately turning these data marts into dependent ones.

NOTE

Conformation of the dimensions will not solve the problems of redundant data acquisition processes, redundant storage of detailed data, or the impact on the source systems. It simply makes reconciliation across the data marts easier. It will also not support the data for the nonmultidimensional data marts.

Create the Data Warehouse Data Model

The next process takes conformation of the dimensions a step further. It is similar to the prior one, except that more than just the dimensions will be conformed or integrated. We will actually create the data warehouse data model as a guide for integration and conformation. Note, though, that we are still not creating a real, physical data warehouse yet.

The first step is to determine whether your organization has a business data model in existence. If so, then you should begin with that model rather than reinventing it. If it does not exist, then the business data model must be created within a well-defined scope. See Chapter 3 for the steps in creating this model.

The data warehouse or system model is then built from the business data model as described in Chapter 4. The data warehouse model is built without regard to any particular data mart; rather its purpose is to support all the data marts. We suggest that you start with one subject area (for example, Customers, Products, or Sales) and then move on to the next one.

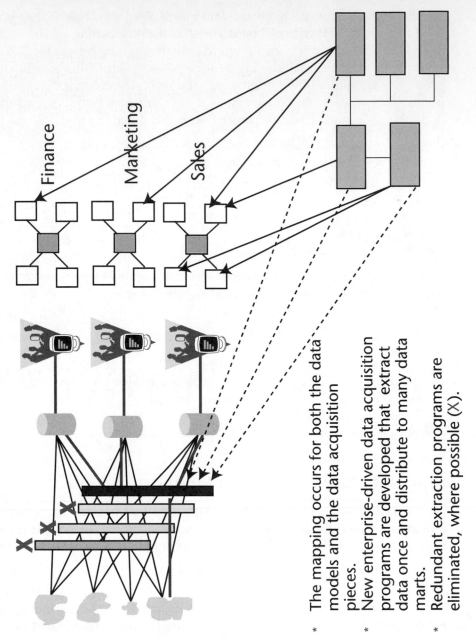

Finance

Marketing

Sales

* The mapping occurs for both the data models and the data acquisition pieces.
* New enterprise-driven data acquisition programs are developed that extract data once and distribute to many data marts.
* Redundant extraction programs are eliminated, where possible (X).

Figure 12.6 Create the data warehouse data model.

The data warehouse data model focuses on the integration of strategic data only, that is, it will use only a subset of the business data model's entities and attributes. Once a subject area is finished, you begin mapping the various data mart data models to the data warehouse one. As this process continues, you will notice that changes will occur in both data models. It is inevitable that new requirements will turn up for the warehouse data model and that the data mart models must convert to the new enterprise standards.

These standardized data model attributes are then mapped back to the data acquisition programs, the programs are rewritten and, in some cases, redundant ones are eliminated where possible. A one-to-many relationship is established for the data acquisition programs and the data marts they must load; one program may "feed" two or more marts with data. Figure 12.6 shows this process for the data acquisition process for one source system.

This process can be a time-consuming effort to retrofit into the existing data marts and to see the benefits of integration. As in the previous case, you may encounter resistance from the business community to changing their implemented marts. The good news is that, unlike the previous migration path, you have a minimal base from which to grow future data marts, you have properly documented meta data, and you have a proper data warehouse data model. The creation of this model also gives you a design from which to implement a real data warehouse—perhaps behind the scenes.

There will still be problems with maintenance because not all the duplicate data acquisition programs can be replaced until a real data warehouse exists, so you must continue to push for the implementation of the warehouse and the conversion of the data marts to dependent ones. However, at least some of the redundant data acquisition processing may be eliminated.

Create the Data Warehouse

In this migration path, we see for the first time the construction of a real, physical data warehouse and the conversion of the chaotic, independent data marts to maintainable, dependent ones. There are two paths available for you to achieve this state. In the first path, you create one subject area at a time in the new data warehouse and then convert each mart to be dependent upon that subject area in the data warehouse.

As an alternative, you can convert one entire data mart at a time to the new architecture, bringing into the warehouse all of the data needed to support that mart. This requires that the entire data model for the data mart be converted into the enterprise data warehouse data model at once. Then, the data mart is fed the data it needs from the newly constructed data warehouse. Let's look at each of these approaches in more detail.

Convert by Subject Area

This approach starts with a selection of the subject area to be converted. If the business data model exists, it should be used as the starting point for the data warehouse data model. If it does not exist, then the business data model for the chosen subject area must be created. The requirements for the individual data marts are gathered for the chosen subject area and the modeler follows the established methodology for creating the data warehouse data model. (See Chapter 4.)

The emphasis of the data warehouse system model is on the integration of the enterprise data, that is, the focus in on "Getting the data in" to a proper repository. The detailed data (the least common denominator) is modeled for the subject area, mapped to the source systems, and the data acquisition programs are developed. We recommend that you consider establishing a data stewardship program (see prior chapters for more detail on data stewardship) to help with the creation of enterprise standards for entities, attributes, definitions, as well as calculated, derived, and aggregated data.

Each data mart must be mapped to the implemented data in the data warehouse and the mart models are changed to match the enterprise nature of the data warehouse data model. Be sure to perform an analysis to ensure that the detailed data in the data warehouse will serve a solid basis for the various marts.

Data acquisition programs for the subject area create the integrated, cleansed, and transformed data, which is then loaded into the data warehouse. The data marts' schemas are recreated based on the new data model. Data delivery programs must be created to populate the data marts ("Getting information out"). For the first time, there is a true separation between data acquisition and data delivery. At the completion of this phase, the next subject area is picked and the process begins again. See Figure 12.7.

There are significant advantages to this approach. By examining the requirements of all the data marts for an entire subject area, you are far more likely to maintain an enterprise view of the data. This means that the data warehouse data model may be much more stable, and thus the data warehouse will be easier to maintain and sustain.

The disadvantage of this approach is that all of the implemented data marts as well as the reports and queries using them will have significant changes occurring to them over and over as each subject area is implemented in the data warehouse. The business community may not be very tolerant of the constant upheaval to their analytical applications.

Convert One Data Mart at a Time

A variation of the third approach is to convert the data marts, one at a time. In this approach, an entire data mart is analyzed and the business data model and data warehouse data model are created in support of this mart. This will most certainly cross multiple subject areas. In addition, the likelihood of getting a rather proprietary view of the data is high so the modeler must be very careful to develop the business and data warehouse data models so that they reflect the enterprise business rules.

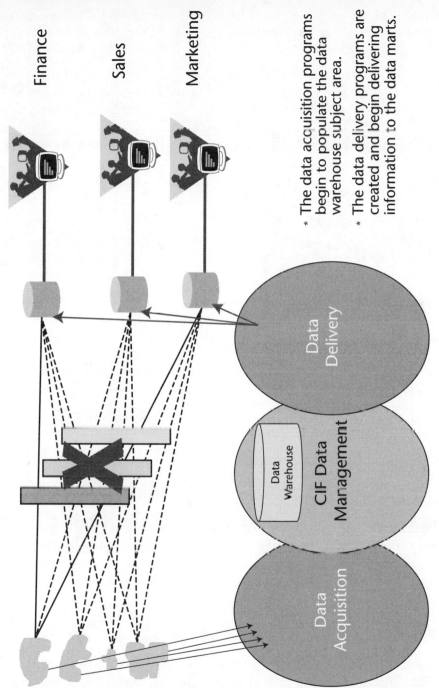

Finance

Sales

Marketing

* The data accuisition programs begin to populate the data warehouse subject area.

* The data delivery programs are created and begin delivering information to the data marts.

Data Delivery

CIF Data Management

Data Warehouse

Data Acquisition

Figure 12.7 Converting one subject area at a time (continued).

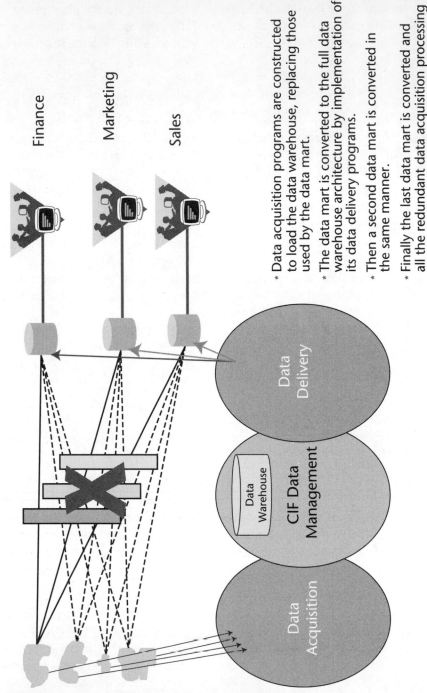

Figure 12.8 Converting one data mart at a time.

No doubt, there will be changes to the data warehouse data model (and therefore the reconstructed data mart) with every new data mart brought into the architecture. Your goal in this approach is to mitigate the changes to the converted data marts as much as possible. The entire data warehouse infrastructure must be set up from the first data mart onward. This means that the entire data delivery programs for the first data mart must be created in addition to the data acquisition programs for the data warehouse. Once the first restructured data mart is back into production, the team begins work on to the next data mart, using the same process, as shown in Figure 12.8.

As with the subject-area-oriented conversion, this process is time-consuming but well worth the effort in the long run. You will need to set expectations up front regarding the changes that may happen to the converted data marts and their models as more and more data marts are implemented. Without doubt, changes will occur as a broader enterprise focus is attained. Once again, we recommend that you establish a data stewardship function to mitigate this situation and to garner agreement and adherence to the enterprise standards for entities, attributes, definitions, and calculated, aggregated, and summarized data. With the data warehouse in place, we now have a critical mass of data that will begin to pay substantial dividends with each subsequent request for change.

Build New Data Marts Only "In-Architecture"— Leave Old Marts Alone

You may find that it is just not possible to convince the business community of the benefits of converting their independent marts into the more manageable and maintainable environment. We have run into this several times, and a curious thing happens if you use this fourth approach.

First off, you must leave the aging data marts alone. They will continue to be supported by their existing staff in their chaotic state. However, it must be mandated that all new data marts will be planned and designed using the adopted data warehouse architecture. The classical data warehouse methodology is used to create the full Corporate Information Factory architecture as described in the previous chapters, resulting in a dual environment.

The real strategy here is that we are building for the future by creating an enterprise data architecture. Each implementation of a CIF architecture component will help to better prepare the IT department for the eventual conversion or demise of the aging legacy data marts (Lega-Marts!). What we have observed at our clients in this situation is that the more success achieved with the CIF architecture, the more (often self-imposed) pressure is placed on the legacy data mart owners to convert to the architecture. Indeed, the advantages of the architecture themselves often "sell" these reluctant owners into converting to the architecture:

- It is very easy to bring in new data elements or calculated fields into existing dependent data marts since they already exist in detail form in the data warehouse.

- It is easy to switch access tools if the starting blocks of data reside in the data warehouse. It becomes a much simpler process of tearing down and rebuilding the data mart from data stored in the data warehouse repository.

- The separation of data acquisition from data delivery means that the lega-mart owners have a much simpler set of programs to maintain and sustain.

- Reconciliation is much simpler within and between the dependent data marts. This is difficult at best in the independent data mart environment.

The bottom line is that you may be pleasantly surprised to find that you win over the reluctant business community—one lega-mart at a time!

Build the Architecture from One Data Mart

Many times, we find that one data mart that is surprisingly sophisticated in terms of its focus, design, and implementation. This data mart could serve as a starting point for your enterprise data warehouse architecture. Some of the characteristics to look for in this data mart include the following:

- The data mart has nicely integrated and detailed data. The data acquisition processing includes reasonable data cleansing procedures and is well documented. It is a plus if the process is supported by an ETL tool.

- The technology is scalable and can be easily expanded to accommodate large amounts of data. The technology is not proprietary, such as some cube technologies.

- The design has a mostly enterprise-wide perspective. The implementers interviewed more than just one department or used the business data model as a starter model to get the entities, attributes, definitions, and calculations used in their data mart.

- The technology can support both a data warehouse and data mart. We recommend a standard relational database management system rather than the cube technology, which may be proprietary.

If you find such a data mart in your organization, and its owner is cooperative, you can proceed to convert it into the preferred architecture through the following four steps:

1. Begin with an analysis of the data in the chosen mart for what data belongs in the data warehouse data versus the data used in the data mart. Your job is to separate the data into the data model for the data warehouse and the data model for the data mart. We recommend that you begin by separating

detailed data from the more summarized or aggregated data as the criteria for data warehouse data as opposed to data mart data. Remember that the data warehouse model will be more normalized, and the data mart model may be a star schema, snowflake schema, token design, flat files, or other design, depending on the technology chosen for the data mart. The data warehouse data model should be based on the business data model and should have the characteristics outlined in this book.

2. Map the data warehouse data model to the source systems. You also begin the natural separation of the data acquisition and data delivery programs. It may be prudent to examine other potential data marts to see if there are other easily attainable pieces of data that will facilitate the conversion of other data marts. (By extending the design to include other data, you may get some welcomed help with some of the political problems you may encounter later—see the next section for a discussion of these.) The data acquisition programs are designed, coded, tested, and executed. You then begin loading the data warehouse.

3. Map the data mart data model to the data in the data warehouse. The data delivery programs are then designed, coded, and tested. These are much simpler than the previous programs used to create the data mart because all the heavy lifting (the extraction, integration, transformation, and cleansing) has been done by the data acquisition programs. The data delivery programs focus on the extraction of the subset of data needed by the data mart (filter), set up of the data according to the needs of the access tool (format), including the aggregation and summarization that is required, and distribute the data to the appropriate data mart (delivery).

4. Here, the data mart schema is implemented and the data delivery programs are put into production. Data begins flowing from the data warehouse into the specific data mart. It is important to note that the data warehouse and data mart may only be logically separated at this point in time. To simplify life, you may decide to co-locate both constructs in the same instance of the database. If a performance problem occurs later, you can easily separate the two components with minimal effort since the data model for the data mart and the data delivery programs are already logically separated. The last step is to decide on the next data mart to be brought into the established architecture and to repeat the process. Fortunately, the subsequent data marts will be easier to build because much of the data needed for them may already reside in the newly created data warehouse.

The advantages to this migration path are:

■ Many of the integration issues have already been decided upon. Since the data mart was created with an enterprise view maintained (mostly), the heated discussions and escalation of issues have already taken place and resolutions put into practice. You may find a few remaining issues to solve but, by and large, most should be taken care of.

- The hardware and software are acceptable for an enterprise database. The technology was chosen with growth, scalability, and performance in mind.

- The data mart was well documented through the meta data captured in the ETL tool. This makes separating the data acquisition process from the data delivery process much simpler.

As with every situation that changes the status quo, there will be challenges. Politically, you may run into difficulty in getting acceptance of this data mart as the beginnings of the enterprise data warehouse. There are several reasons for this, including:

- The data mart may be perceived as proprietary or belonging to the department or function that created this. Other departments may not feel that their particular view of the world is not well represented in this "version of the truth." Resolution may require executive intervention to assure skeptics that the resulting data warehouse can be used enterprise-wide.

- The chosen data mart may not have as much of the enterprise perspective maintained throughout as first thought. Upon analysis, you may find that it does indeed reflect the perspectives of one set of users rather than the collective view of the enterprise. Once again, data stewardship will be a useful function to mitigate or remove this challenge.

- Arguments may come up over who "owns" the data warehouse. Since the beginnings of the warehouse were created under the jurisdiction of the independent data mart, these implementers may feel that they paid for the warehouse and, therefore, it is still theirs rather than belonging to the enterprise as a whole. The enterprise may wish to "pay back" the department or function for the data warehouse part of the architecture, thus ensuring a neutral ownership.

You should be very sensitive to any or all of these problems and head them off as soon as they are discovered. Strong management support can be invaluable to you in maintaining the proper course of actions.

Choosing the Right Migration Path

As with any enterprise-wide endeavor, the politics and culture of your organization must be taken into account before making any decision about how you will migrate from data mart chaos to a sustainable and maintainable environment. You must consider the following characteristics of your company when choosing the path:

- The level of executive support for this endeavor. Are your executives on board with this migration? Do they understand and actively support you and your team?

- The willingness of the business community to "share" its data. This one factor will have a significant impact on your ability to migrate independent marts to the dependent state.

- The business community's resistance to change. Many business users are so fed up with IT constantly changing their environment that they actively campaign against any further changes to their world (especially if they control the production of their data mart).

- The stability of the overall enterprise. In today's economy, many organizations are undergoing massive changes such as mergers, acquisitions, and divestitures. In this unstable environment, it may be difficult to make any headway toward an "enterprise" view when what constitutes the very enterprise is in doubt.

Some of your best arguments will come from the reduction in costs and effort spent in maintaining a chaotic analytical environment. Never lose sight of the ultimate reason for creating a maintainable and architected environment.

Summary

This chapter has shown you five different paths to migrate from the world of independent and chaotically created data marts to one that is architected and efficient. Migration from chaos is not easy; after all, it took the organization many years to get itself into the chaotic situation. It should realize that getting out of it might also take years.

The costs and benefits of moving from chaos to an architected environment must be determined before attempting any of the paths we have discussed in this chapter. You must prove to the affected parties that migration to an architecture will be ultimately beneficial to the enterprise as a whole (and hopefully to the individuals as well). It must be shown that the final state will be worth the disruption and costs to the organization.

You may choose to use more than one of the pathways described in this chapter. Different situations call for different approaches, and no one approach will work in all situations. Carefully think through each situation, the politics involved, the support you have, and the timeframe you have for the conversion. Then examine these pathways for the one that seems best suited for that situation.

An architected approach will no doubt be the accepted one, if you do your homework. We wish you all the best in this most difficult endeavor!

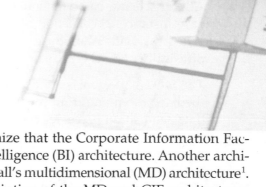

CHAPTER 13

Comparison of Data Warehouse Methodologies

I t's appropriate at this point to recognize that the Corporate Information Factory (CIF) is not the only business intelligence (BI) architecture. Another architecture worth noting is Dr. Ralph Kimball's multidimensional (MD) architecture[1]. This chapter starts with a brief description of the MD and CIF architectures and then highlights the significant similarities and differences between the two by using the criteria of scope, perspective, data flow, implementation speed and cost, volatility, complexity, and functionality.

Perhaps as a way of introducing the two architectures, we should explain that we believe that a combination of the data-modeling techniques found in the two architectural approaches works best—ERD or normalization techniques for the data warehouse and the star schema data model for multidimensional data marts. That said, it is important that BI architects study their situation, politics, and culture to determine what works best in their environment.

The Multidimensional Architecture

The MD architecture (see Figure 13.1) is based on the premise that all BI analyses have at their foundation a multidimensional design. The star schema is an elegant data model that layers multidimensional meta data over what is basically a

1 See *The Data Warehouse Lifecycle Toolkit*, Ralph Kimball et al., Wiley Publishing, Inc., 1998.

two-dimensional data store (columns and rows), making it act to the user as if it were multidimensional. The star schema gave BI a solid and much needed push into the mainstream when it first appeared. It is still one of the most popular and useful designs for usage in strategic decision-making environments.

One of the more significant differences between the MD and CIF architectures is in the definition of the data mart. For the MD architecture, the aggregated data mart star schema is approximately the same as the data mart in the CIF architecture. The atomic-level data mart star schema contains the detailed data roughly equivalent to the content in the CIF's data warehouse. However, the design of the atomic-level data marts (star schemas) is significantly different from the design of the CIF data warehouse (denormalized ERD schema). These data-modeling differences constitute the main design differences in these two architectures.

All star schema-based data marts may or may not reside within the same database instance. A collection of these schemas in a single database instance is called the Data Warehouse Bus Architecture. Unlike the CIF, a separate and physically distinct data warehouse does not exist.

The MD architecture is divided into two groups of components and processes—the back room and front room. The back room is where the data-staging and data acquisition processes take place. Mapping to the operational systems and the technical meta data surrounding these maps is also part of the back room. It is roughly equivalent to the CIF's "Getting Data In" components with some notable exceptions. One is the lack of an ERD-based data warehouse, as mentioned, and the other is the presence of atomic and aggregated star schema data marts—both discussed later in this chapter. The latter appears in both the back and front rooms.

The data-staging area contains the conformed dimensions but it is also the place where surrogate keys are generated, maps to the operational systems are kept, current loads of operational data are stored, and any atomic data not currently used in the data marts is stored. Most of the heavy lifting performed by the ETL tools occurs here as well.

The Data Warehouse Bus Architecture consists of two types of data marts:

Atomic Data Marts.   These data marts hold multidimensional data at the lowest common denominator level (lowest level of detail available throughout the environment). They may contain some aggregated data as well to improve query performance. The data is stored in a star schema data model.

Aggregated Data Marts.   These data marts contain data related to a core business process such as marketing, sales, or finance. Generally, the atomic data marts supply the data to be aggregated for these data marts but that is not mandatory. It is possible to create an aggregated data mart directly from the data-staging area. As with the atomic data marts, data is stored in the aggregated data marts in star schema designs.

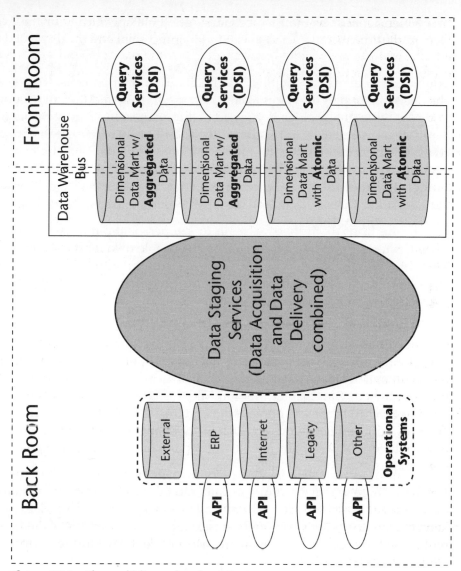

Figure 13.1 The multidimensional architecture.

Your need for both types of data marts depends on your business requirements and the performance of each of these structures in your environment. However, it is important to understand that the MD architecture starts and ends with its focus primarily on the individual business unit(s) or group of business users with a specific BI requirement. This singular focus is reflected in the structure of the data, which is optimized to accommodate that unit or group of users perfectly. No two star schemas are exactly alike—each provides an optimal way of accessing data for a specific set of requirements. As unit after unit or group after group is added to the list of BI recipients, either new star schemas must be built to accommodate them specifically or the existing design must be reconstructed to expand its functionality.

The front room is the interface for the business community. We see it as roughly equivalent to the CIF's "Getting Information Out" components. It is clear that the decision support interfaces (called Access Services) and their corresponding end user access tools belong in this part of the architecture. The two types of data marts also appear in the front room as the source of data for these interfaces and tools. The basic tenet of the front room is to mask or hide the complexity going on in the back room from the business community since it is believed by these authors that users of these components neither know nor care about the significant amount of energy, time, and resources poured into creating the back room.

It is in the front room that we begin to see personal data marts (also called "spreadmarts") popping up, as well as disposable data marts (data marts created for a specific short-lived business requirement). Care should be taken in both cases to ensure that these do not supplant or replace the real data marts; otherwise, you end up with chaos again.

The end user access tools consist of OLAP engines, reporting and querying tools, and maybe even some data-mining tools. We caution the reader here that the process of building a star schema limits the usefulness of these data marts for complete and unbiased data mining and statistical analyses, as well as for exploration analyses. (See Chapter 1 for more on this.) If the data is stored in only star schemas, then it becomes impossible to find unrelated patterns or correlations in the raw data. Because the star contains only known relationships, then patterns or correlations between unrelated data sets cannot be performed.

The front room also contains the query management and activity-monitoring services. These are very useful in maintaining the appropriate performance for each data mart installation. Query management involves services such as query retargeting, aggregate awareness, and query governing. Activity monitoring captures information about the usage of these databases to determine if performance and user support are optimal.

There are many other services embedded in the front room that we do not list here. For the full set, please refer to the books by Ralph Kimball et al. Suffice it to say that much of what is captured in the CIF Operations and Administration Service Management function is also captured in parts of this architecture as well.

Because the approach is predominately a bottom-up one, it is easy to violate the corporate or enterprise business rules when constructing the star schema. If there is no insistence that top-down design work be performed, the star schemas can easily become stovepipe implementations, lacking in the ability to link together, producing inconsistent and, perhaps worse, conflicting, intelligence across the enterprise. Strong and experienced multidimensional modelers, just like experienced ERD modelers, overcome this because their experience allows them to recognize the need to do so.

In addition, over the years, the MD approach has been modified in attempts to overcome the shortcoming of the lack of an enterprise view, by ensuring that the various data mart star schemas "conform" to some enterprise standards. Conformed dimensions are one way to overcome this shortcoming. According to Kimball et al., a conformed dimension is one that means the same thing to every possible fact table to which it can be joined. Ideally, this means that a conformed dimension is identical in every star schema that uses it. Examples of these are Customer, Product, Time, and Locations dimensions.

Another workaround the shortcoming was the creation of a data-staging area (not shown in Figure 13.1). In this data store, the designer consolidates all of a dimension's attributes into a single conformed dimension to be replicated to all the requesting star schemas. It is the responsibility of the design team to create, publish, maintain, and enforce the usage of these conformed dimensions throughout all data marts. Once consolidated, the conformed dimensions are permanently stored in the data-staging area. This retrofit of an enterprise standard mitigates the possible inconsistencies and discrepancies that occur in dimensions with no enterprise consideration. The data warehouse bus design concept was developed for this purpose.

The Corporate Information Factory Architecture

Chapter 1 discusses the functions and components associated with "getting data in" and "getting information out." Figure 13.2 is a simplified version of the CIF, showing these two functions and the components and processes involved in each.

The staging area (not shown in Figure 13.2) in the CIF includes persistent tables for storing the key conversion information and other reference tables used in the data acquisition process. Replicated operational data not yet used in the warehouse may also be stored there, waiting for integration and loading into the warehouse. The staging area may or may not be separate from the data warehouse but if it is on the same platform as the warehouse, it should be in its own database instance.

In the MD architecture, the back room is completely off-limits to the business community. Unlike the data-staging area in the back room of the MD architecture, business community access to the CIF data warehouse is discouraged, but exceptions for special exploration or one-time extraction needs are permitted. Other than security restrictions that you may want to implement, there is nothing to prevent its usage since the data is completely documented, integrated, and validated. However, the data model is complicated, and the business user must understand an ERD model and how to "walk a relational database" in order to use it.

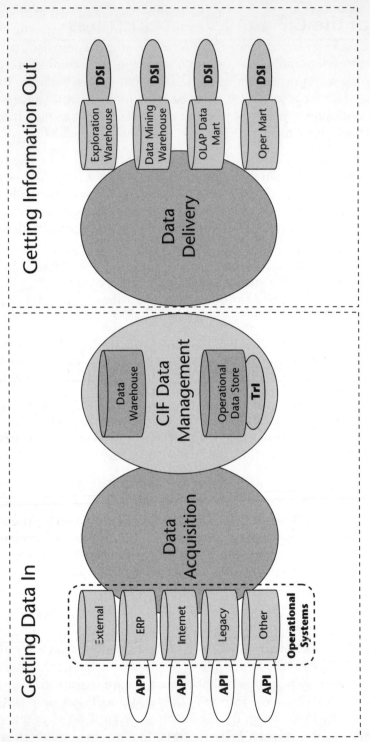

Figure 13.2 Simplified corporate information factory.

Comparison of the CIF and MD Architectures

Figure 13.3 is an adaptation of a slide from Laura Reeves of StarSoft (www.starsoftinc.com) comparing the CIF and MD architectures. The significant points in this figure are that access is generally not allowed above the diagonal line in both architectures, and there is no physical repository equivalent to the data warehouse in the MD architecture. The "data warehouse bus" shown for the MD architecture is the collection of the atomic and aggregated data marts.

Both the CIF and MD architectures have a staging area, meta data management, and sophisticated data acquisition processing. The designs of the data marts are predominantly multidimensional for both architectures, though the CIF is not limited to just this design and can support a much broader set of data mart design techniques.

What's missing in the MD architecture is a separate physical data warehouse. The "data warehouse" in this architecture as mentioned earlier is virtual and consists of the collection of all the individual data marts and their corresponding data (both atomic level and aggregated levels). The closest thing to the CIF data warehouse seems to be the "data-staging area" in the MD architecture, which, in his August 1997 *DBMS* Magazine article "A Dimensional Modeling Manifesto," Ralph Kimball states is often designed using ERD or third normal form data models.

Now, let's look more closely at the major comparison topics for the MD and CIF architectures: scope, perspective, data flow, implementation speed and cost, volatility, flexibility, functionality, and ongoing maintenance.

Scope

BI is about discovery. CIF and MD architectures both help an enterprise satisfy its basic need for more information about both itself and the environment in which it exists. CIF and MD both assume that BI requirements will emerge from business units of an organization, as well as from the organization as a whole. To illustrate how enterprise data can differ from business unit data, consider that, for a bank, "customer" might mean an individual account holder to Finance, a household of account holders to Marketing, and a non-account-holder to Customer Service. To the enterprise, "customer" means all of these and more, and distinct terms and definitions for each type of customer may be needed.

Such differences in meaning are synonymous with differences in scope. While neither of the architectures ignores enterprise scope or business unit scope, each favors one over the other. CIF places a higher priority on enterprise scope, and MD places a higher priority on business unit scope. Hence, the scope of the first few projects under the CIF architecture may be a bit larger than the scope for an MD architectural project.

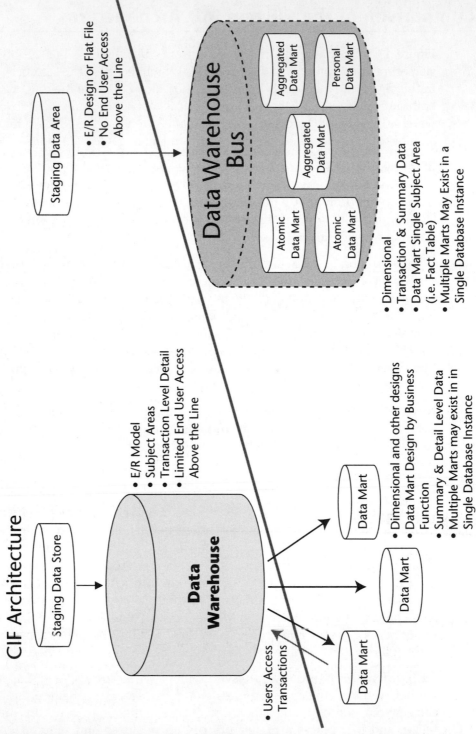

Figure 13.3 Comparison of CIF and MD architectures.

Perspective

CIF proponents frequently say that the historic problem with BI implementations is that the BI source data is difficult to locate, gather, integrate, understand, and deliver. Given an enterprise scope, they emphasize the perspective of *supplying* enterprise data. IT is often centralized and experienced at maintaining data at the enterprise level, so IT tackles the problems of supplying BI source data from an enterprise point of view. CIF proponents favor the needs of the enterprise and advocate getting the BI source data modeled for the enterprise as a prerequisite for any BI implementation. Note though, that this does not mean that the entire enterprise data must be dealt with during the first project. On the contrary, a subset of the overall enterprise's data is selected, predominantly from a subject area like Customer or Product, and the data warehouse data model and resulting database are implemented for just this small part of the overall set of enterprise data.

MD proponents frequently say the same thing about the historic problem with BI implementations. Using the same words, and given their business unit scope, they emphasize the perspective of *consuming* business unit data. Business units that consume BI data, such as Sales or Finance, are experienced with their individual needs and views. If another business unit has different needs and views, that's okay. They just don't value other business unit needs and views as much as they do their own. MD proponents favor the needs of the business unit and advocate getting the BI source data modeled for the business unit as a prerequisite for any BI implementation. It is important to note that the multidimensional modeler must strive to achieve consensus on the definition of the conformed dimensions across the enterprise, however. He or she concentrates only on those dimensions pertinent to the facts being loaded. Where a new fact is introduced that requires new dimensions not previously defined, the multidimensional modeler must again take an enterprise view and gain a consensus definition among those business areas that have some stake in that dimension.

Data Flow

To create a sustainable BI environment, one must understand the iterative nature of the projects and the relationship the ultimate environment has with the sources of data supplied to the enterprise. Like the chicken and egg paradox, BI questions create answers that create more BI questions (see Figure 13.4.). Even though BI source data starts and ends at the same places for CIF and MD, given these two architectures' unique scopes and perspectives, they view BI data flow differently. It's a matter of push versus pull. In general, the CIF approach is top-down. CIF suppliers of enterprise BI data use the business requirements to push the data from the operational systems to where it's needed. The focus is on integrating the enterprise data for usage in any data mart from the very first project.

By contrast, the MD approach is bottom-up. MD consumers of business unit BI data use the business requirements to pull the data from the operational systems to where it's needed. The focus is on getting business-unit-specific data quickly into the hands of the users with minimal regard for the overall enterprise usage until such a need is demonstrated.

CIF and MD both seek to minimize BI implementation time and cost. Both benefit greatly from a prototype of decision support interface functionality. The difference between the two in terms of implementation speed and cost involves long-term and short-term trade-offs.

Because of CIF's enterprise scope, the first CIF project will likely require more time and cost than the first MD project, due to increased overhead for making parts of the subject area and business data models as compatible across the enterprise as practically possible. CIF developers should be cautioned against both losing sight of the business unit requirements and trying to perfect the enterprise data model.

In contrast, subsequent CIF projects tend to require less time and cost than subsequent MD projects, especially for business units that utilize existing, robust subject areas. MD developers should be reminded that each subsequent MD project might include nontrivial changes to the already implemented conformed dimensions. Expediting the requirements-gathering and implementation processes may complicate the task of providing consistent and reliable data throughout the BI environment.

The detailed data generally appears once in the CIF (though some denormalization may occur for loading and data delivery performance reasons) and is readily available for any and all data marts, thus minimizing storage space requirements. This nonredundancy precludes storing data (except foreign keys) in multiple places. This feature of the data model also minimizes or may eliminate update or delete anomalies that could occur during cascading processes with redundant data content. These benefits are comprised in the MD architecture.

Volatility

The multidimensional model, especially for the aggregated data marts, is dependent on a determination of the possible questions that might be asked in order to eliminate or reduce the need to reconstruct the fact tables should new or changed dimensions be needed. If a change occurs in a business process (that is, the queries change), then the multidimensional model must be reshuffled or reconstructed. The multidimensional model can certainly be extended to accommodate *some* unexpected new data elements such as new facts (as long as they are at the same level of granularity as the rest of the fact table) and new dimensional attributes. However, at the atomic level, this can be a severe penalty. The fact tables can contain many hundreds of millions or even billions of rows, so a rebuild is not advised. Generally, a new (and mostly redundant) star schema is created when this happens.

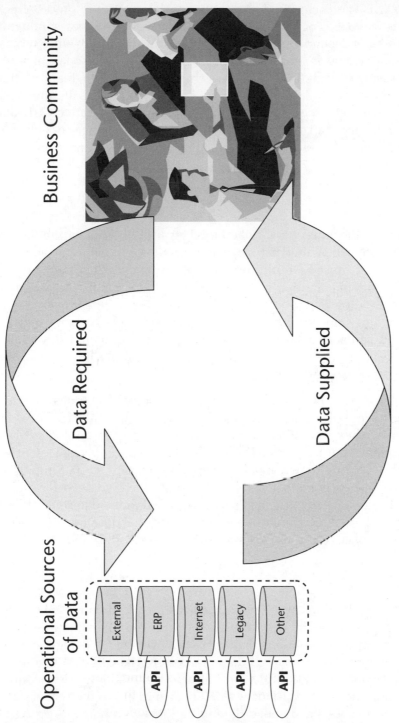

Figure 13.4 Cyclical relationship between business requirements and sources of data.

For the CIF approach, the data warehouse data model is process-free, which removes any biases or hard-coded relationships due to process influences. The data model is dependent on the enterprise's business rules—not what queries will be run against it—for its design. The data model is also far more forgiving of processing changes in the business environment due to a lack of processing bias. Because the model is not designed with any questions in mind, it can supply information for the ultimate data marts through the relatively trivial process of data delivery. If an established data mart requires changes or enhancements, it can be reasonably and quickly rebuilt from the detailed data stored in the data warehouse.

Flexibility

The MD architecture puts a stake in the ground in terms of the design of the entire BI environment. That stake is that all components (except the data-staging area) must be multidimensional in design. This might make sense from an academic standpoint; however, we find in practice that significant and useful technologies can be deployed without this stringent restriction. This is analogous to someone saying that all they have is a hammer and therefore everything must be a nail. If you design your environment using multidimensional designs, then all you will ever do are multidimensional analyses. Nothing more sophisticated or advanced.

The CIF architecture makes no such claim and, in fact, goes to extremes to include the possibility of many different forms of BI analyses. The data warehouse as we have described in this book can support technologies that are not multidimensional in nature. Technologies like memory resident BI tools are certainly not multidimensional. In fact, they require *no* data model whatsoever. Bitmapped indexes and token databases have no need for multidimensional designs. Finally, true statistical analytical tools require flat files or data sets that are not dependent upon multidimensional designs. All are supported with no caveats, biases, or false preconditioning by the CIF data warehouse.

Complexity

Complexities tend to cause fewer problems for CIF than for MD, because the architecture starts with an enterprise-focused, complex data model and then uses it in multiple situations that are usually simpler in design. In the case of creating the multidimensional data marts from the CIF data warehouse, you pull data from a more-complex, multipurpose model into a less-complex one. The data model for the CIF data warehouse minimizes the risk of data inconsistencies because the detailed data in the data warehouse is process-free. In other words, it has not been set up for a specific set of questions, functions, or processes; rather, it is able to supply data for any question or query.

For the MD approach, the multidimensional or star schema data model is easy to understand by the business community. The data model is generally less complex and resembles the way many business community members think about their data—that is, they think in terms of multiple dimensions, for example, "Give me all the sales revenues for each store, in each city and state, by market segment over the last two months." Thus, it is also easier to construct by the IT data modelers. However, given the complexity of an enterprise view of the data as you go from data mart implementation to data mart implementation, retrofitting is significantly harder to accomplish for this architecture. That is why the CIF architecture places the star schema designs in the data marts only—never in the data warehouse itself.

Functionality

The multidimensional architecture provides an ideal environment for relationally oriented multidimensional processing, ensuring good performance for complex "slice and dice," drill up, -down, and -around queries. All dimensions are equivalent to each other, meaning that all queries within the bounds of the star schema are processed with roughly the same symmetry. We recommend that it be used for the majority of CIF data mart implementations. But do remember that multidimensional modeling does not easily accommodate alternate methods of analysis such as data mining and statistical analysis.

The CIF uses a data model that is based on an ERD methodology that supports the business rules of the enterprise. This type of model is also easily enhanced or appended if need be. Attributes are placed in the data model based on their inherent properties rather than specific application requirements. This is an important differentiator in the BI world because it means that the data warehouse is positioned to support any and all forms of strategic data analyses, not just multidimensional ones. Data mining, statistical analysis, and ad hoc or exploration functionalities are supported as well as the multidimensional ones.

Ongoing Maintenance

There is an old adage: "Pay me now or pay me later." For this final discussion, that adage should be expanded to include: "But it will cost you a lot more if you pay me later." By now, you realize that the whole purpose behind the CIF is to stop the high costs of later constructions, adjustments, retrofits, and suboptimal accommodations to your BI environment. It may cost you a bit more up front, in terms of making the effort to capture an enterprise view of your company's data for your first or second BI implementation. However, BI environments build upon the past iterations and will take years to complete, if it's ever finished. Just as a sound foundation for a house takes forethought and is absolutely necessary for the longevity of the structure, regardless of the changes that occur to it over the years, a well-designed data warehouse data model will serve your enterprise for the long haul. With each iteration, the CIF as your foundation will yield tremendous paybacks in terms of:

- The end-to-end consistency and integration of your entire BI environment
- The ease with which new marts are created
- The enhancement of existing marts
- The maintenance and sustenance of the data warehouse and related data marts
- The overall satisfaction for all your business community members, including those focused on multidimensional analyses

Summary

In this chapter, we described the Multidimensional (MD) and the Corporate Information Factory (CIF) architectures in terms of their approach to the construction of the BI environment. The MD architectural approach subordinates data management to business requirements because its reason for being is to satisfy a business unit within the enterprise. On the other hand, the CIF architectural approach manages data to the subordination of the business requirements because its reason for being is to serve the entire enterprise. The similarities and differences between these two approaches stem from these fundamental differences.

As stated earlier, we find that a combination of the data-modeling techniques found in the two architectural approaches works best—ERD or normalization techniques for the data warehouse and the star schema data model for multidimensional data marts. This is the ultimate goal of the CIF and uses the strengths of one form of data modeling and combines it seamlessly with the strengths of the other. In other words, a CIF with only a data warehouse and no multidimensional marts is fairly useless and a multidimensional data-mart-only environment risks the lack of an enterprise integration and support for other forms of BI analyses. Please develop an understanding of the strengths and weaknesses of your own situation and corporation as a whole to determine how best to design the architectural components of your BI environment. We wish you continued success with your BI endeavors.

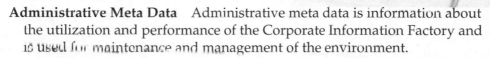

Administrative Meta Data Administrative meta data is information about the utilization and performance of the Corporate Information Factory and is used for maintenance and management of the environment.

Aggregated Data Mart An aggregated data mart is a data mart that contains data related to a core business process such as marketing, sales, and finance. Generally, the atomic data marts supply the data to be aggregated for these data marts but that is not mandatory. It is possible to create an aggregated data mart directly from the data-staging area. As with the atomic data marts, data is stored in the aggregated data marts in star schema designs.

Analytical Application An analytical application is a predesigned, ready to install, decision support application. These applications generally require some customization to fit the specific requirements of the enterprise. The source of data may be the data warehouse or the operational data store (ODS). Examples of these applications are risk analysis, scorecard applications, database marketing (CRM) analyses, vertical industry "data marts in a box," and so on.

Associative Entity An associative entity is an entity that is dependent upon two or more entities for its existence, and that records data at the point of intersection.

Atomic Data Mart   An atomic data mart is a data mart that holds multi-dimensional data at the lowest level of detail available. Atomic data marts may contain some aggregated data as well to improve query performance. The data is stored in a star schema data model.

Attribute   An attribute is the lowest level of information relating to any entity. It models a specific piece of information or a property of a specific entity. Dimensional modeling has a more restrictive definition; it refers to information that describes the characteristics of a dimension.

Attributive Entity   An attributive (or characteristic) entity is an entity whose existence depends on another entity. It is created to handle a group of data that could occur multiple times for each instance of its parent entity.

Back Room   The back room of the Multidimensional architecture developed by Ralph Kimball et al. is where the data-staging and data-acquisition processes take place. Mapping to the operational systems and the technical meta data surrounding these maps are also part of the back room.

Balanced Hierarchy   A balanced hierarchy is one in which all leafs exist at the lowest level in the hierarchy, and every parent is one level removed from the child.

Business Data Model   The business data model, sometimes known as the logical data model, describes the major things ("entities") of interest to the company and the relationships between pairs of these entities. It is an abstraction or representation of the data in a given business environment, and it provides the benefits cited for any model. It helps people envision how the information in the business relates to other information in the business ("how the parts fit together").

Business Intelligence (BI)   Business intelligence is the set of processes and data structures used to analyze data and information used in strategic decision support. The components of Business Intelligence are the data warehouse, data marts, the DSS interface and the processes to "get data in" to the data warehouse and to "get information out."

Business Management   Business management is the set of systems and data structures that allow corporations to act, in a tactical fashion, upon the intelligence obtained from the strategic decision support systems. The components of Business Management are the operational data store, the transactional interfaces, and the processes to "get data in" to the operational data store and to apply it.

Business Meta Data   Business meta data is information that provides the business context for data in the Corporate Information Factory.

Business Operations   Business operations are the family of systems (operational, reporting, and so on) from which the rest of the Corporate Information Factory inherits its characteristics.

Cardinality   Cardinality denotes the maximum number of occurrences of one entity that can be related to another entity. Usually, these are expressed as "one" or "many."

Change Data Capture   Change data capture is a technique for propagating only changes to source data through the data acquisition process.

Characteristic Entity   See Attributive Entity.

Conformed Dimension   A conformed dimension is one that is built for use by multiple data marts. Conformed dimensions promote consistency by enabling multiple data marts to share the same reference and hierarchy information.

Corporate Information Factory (CIF)   The Corporate Information Factory is a logical architecture whose purpose is to deliver business intelligence and business management capabilities driven by data provided from business operations.

Data Acquisition   Data acquisition is the set of processes that captures, integrates, transforms, cleanses, reengineers, and loads source data into the data warehouse and operational data store.

Data Delivery   Data delivery is the set of processes that enables end users or their supporting IS groups to build and manage views of the data warehouse within their data marts. It involves a three-step process consisting of filtering, formatting, and delivering data from the data warehouse to the data marts. It may include customized summarizations or derivations.

Data Mart   The data mart is customized and/or summarized data that is derived from the data warehouse and tailored to support the specific analytical requirements of a given business unit or business function. It utilizes a common enterprise view of strategic data and provides business units with more flexibility, control, and responsibility. The data mart may or may not be on the same server or location as the data warehouse.

Data-Mining Warehouse   The data-mining (or statistical) warehouse is a specialized data mart designed to give researchers and analysts the ability to delve into the relationships of data and events without having preconceived notions of those relationships. It provides good response times for people to perform queries and apply mining and statistical algorithms to data, without having to worry about disabling the production data warehouse or receiving biased data such as that contained in multidimensional designs.

Data Model   A data model is an abstraction or representation of the data in a given environment. It is a collection and subsequent verification and communication method for fully documenting the data requirements used in the creation of accurate, effective, and efficient physical databases. The data model consists of entities, attributes, and relationships.

Data Stewardship   Data stewardship is the function that is largely responsible for managing data as an enterprise asset. The data steward is responsible for ensuring that the data provided by the Corporate Information Factory is based on an enterprise view. An individual, a committee, or both may perform data stewardship.

Data Warehouse (DW)   The data warehouse is a subject-oriented, integrated, time-variant, nonvolatile collection of data used to support the strategic decision-making process for the enterprise. It is the central point of data integration for business intelligence and is the source of data for the data marts, delivering a common view of enterprise data.

Data Warehouse Bus   The data warehouse bus is a collection of star-schema-based data marts in a single database instance.

Data Warehouse Data Model   The data warehouse data model is the "system" model for the data warehouse that is created by transforming the business data model into one that is suitable for the data warehouse.

Decision Support Interface (DSI)   The decision support interface is an easy-to-use, intuitively simple tool that allows the end user to distill information from data. The DSI enables analytical activities and provides the flexibility to match a tool to a task. DSI activities include data mining, OLAP or multidimensional analysis, querying, and reporting.

Delta   During data extraction, the delta is the change in the data from the previous time it was extracted to the present extraction. Recognizing only changed data decreases the amount of data that needs to be processed during data acquisition. See also Change Data Capture.

Dependent Data Mart   A dependent data mart is one that is fully derived from the data warehouse.

Derived Field   A derived field is an element that is calculated (or derived) based on other data elements. Its storage in the data warehouse promotes business consistency and improves delivery performance.

Dimension Table   A dimension table is a set of reference tables that provides the basis for constraining and grouping queries for information in a fact table within a dimensional model. The key of the dimension table is typically part of the concatenated key of the fact table, and the dimension table contains descriptive and hierarchical information.

Dimensional Model   A dimensional model is a form of data modeling that packages data according to specific business queries and processes. The goals are business user understandability and multidimensional query performance.

Element   See Attribute.

Entity   An entity is a person, place, thing, concept, or event in which the enterprise has both the interest and capability to capture and store information. An entity is unique within the business data model.

Entity-Relationship (ER) Diagram (ERD)   The ERD is a proven and reliable data-modeling approach with straightforward rules of construction. The normalization rules yield a stable, consistent data model that upholds the policies and rules of engagement established by the enterprise. The resulting database schema is the most efficient in terms of storage and data loading as well.

Enterprise Data Management   Enterprise data management is the set of processes that manage data within and across the data warehouse and operational data store. It includes processes for backup and recovery, partitioning, creating standard summarizations and aggregations, and archival and retrieval of data to and from alternative storage.

Executive Information System (EIS)   An executive information system is a set of applications that is designed to provide business executives with access to information. Early executive information systems often failed because they lacked a robust supporting architecture.

Exploration Warehouse   The exploration warehouse is a data mart that is built to provide exploratory or true ad hoc navigation through data. This data mart provides a safe haven that provides reasonable response time for users with unstructured, unpredictable queries. Most of these data marts are temporary in nature. New technologies have greatly improved the ability to explore data or to create a prototype quickly and efficiently

External Data   External data is any data outside the normal data collected through an enterprise's internal applications. There can be any number of sources of external data such as demographic, credit, competitor, and financial information. Generally, external data is purchased by the enterprise from a vendor of such information.

Fact   A business metric or measure stored in a fact table (see Measure).

Fact Table   A fact table is the table within a dimensional model that contains the measures and metrics of interest.

First Normal Form Model   The first normal form (1NF) of the data model requires that all attributes in the entity be dependent on the key. This requires two conditions — that every entity has a primary key that uniquely identifies it and that the entity contains no repeating or multivalued groups. Each attribute is at its lowest level of detail and has a unique meaning and name.

Fiscal Calendar   A fiscal calendar is a calendar used to define the accounting cycle. The fiscal calendar describes when accounting periods begin and end.

Flattened Tree Hierarchy   A flattened tree hierarchy is a simple structure that arranges the hierarchical elements horizontally, in different columns, rather than rows.

Foreign Key   A foreign key is an attribute that is inherited because of a parent-child relationship between a pair of entities. The foreign key in the child entity is the primary key in the parent entity and links the two entities together. If the relationship is identifying, then the foreign key is part of the primary key of the child attribute.

Front Room   The front room is the interface for the business community as described in the Multidimensional Architecture developed by Ralph Kimball et al. It is clear that the decision support interfaces (called Access Services) and their corresponding end-user access tools belong in this part of the architecture.

Fundamental Entity   A fundamental entity is an entity that is not dependent on any other entity.

Getting Data In   Getting data in refers to the set of activities that captures data from the operational systems and then migrates it to the data warehouse and operational data store.

Getting Information Out   Getting information out refers to the set of activities that delivers information from the data warehouse or operational data store and makes it accessible to the end users.

Granularity Level   Granularity level is the level of detail of the data in a data warehouse or data mart.

Hierarchy   A hierarchy, sometimes called a tree, is a special type of a "parent-child" relationship. In a hierarchy, a child represents a lower level of detail, or granularity, of the parent. This creates a sense of ownership or control that the superior entity (parent) has over the inferior one (child).

Hierarchy Depth   The maximum number of levels in a hierarchy.

Identifying Relationship   An identifying relationship is a parent-child relationship in which the child entity's existence is dependent on the existence of the parent. The primary key of the parent entity is inherited as a foreign key within the child entity and is also part of its primary key.

Independent Data Mart   An independent data mart is a data mart that contains at least some data that is not derived through the data warehouse.

Information Feedback   Information feedback is the set of processes that transmit the intelligence gained through usage of the Corporate Information Factory to appropriate data stores.

Information Workshop   The information workshop is the set of tools available to business users to help them use the resources of the Corporate Information Factory. The information workshop typically provides a way to organize and categorize the data and other resources in the CIF, so that users can find and use those resources. This is the mechanism that promotes the sharing and reuse of analysis across the organization.

Intersection Entity   See Associative Entity.

Inversion Index   An inversion index is an index that permits duplicate key values.

Junk Dimension   A junk dimension is a dimension table that is a collection of "left over" attributes.

Key Performance Indicator (KPI)   A key performance indicator is a metric that provides business users with an indication of the current and historical performance of an aspect of the business.

Leaf Node   A node that is at the lowest level of a hierarchy.

Library and Tool Box   The library and tool box are components of the Information Workshop and consist of the collection of meta data that provides information to effectively use and administer the Corporate Information Factory. The library provides the medium from which knowledge is enriched. The tool box is a vehicle for organizing, locating, and accessing capabilities.

Measure   A measure is a dimensional modeling term that refers to values, usually numeric, that measure some aspect of the business. Measures reside in fact tables. The dimensional terms *measure* and *attribute*, taken together, are equivalent to the relational modeling use of the term attribute.

Meta Data   Meta dta is informational the glue that holds the Corporate Information Factory together. It supplies definitions for data, the calculations used, information about where the data came from (what source systems), what was done to it (transformations, cleansing routines, integration algorithms, etc.), who is using it, when they use it, what the quality metrics are for various pieces of data, and so on. (See also Administrative Meta Data, Business Meta Data, and Technical Meta Data.)

Modality   See Optionality.

Multidimensional Architecture   The Multidimensional Architecture is an architecture for business intelligence that is based on the premise that all BI analyses have at their foundation a multidimensional data design. It is divided into two major groups of components — the back room, where the data staging and acquisition take place, and the front room, which provides the interface for the business community and the corresponding end-user access tools.

Multidimensional Data Mart   The multidimensional data mart is a data mart that is designed to support generalized multidimensional analysis, using Online Analytical Processing (OLAP) software tools. The data mart is designed using the star schema technique or proprietary 'hypercube" technology.

Node   A member of a hierarchy.

Nonidentifying Relationship   A nonidentifying relationship is one in which the primary key of the parent entity becomes a nonkey attribute of the child entity. An example of this type of relationship is a recursive relationship, that is, a situation in which an entity is related to itself.

Normalization   Normalization is a method for ensuring that the data model meets the objectives of accuracy, consistency, simplicity, nonredundancy, and stability. It is a physical database design technique that applies mathematical rules to the relational data model to identify and reduce insertion, updating, or deletion anomalies.

OLAP Data Mart   See Multidimensional Data Mart.

On Line Analytical Processing (OLAP)   Online Analytical Processing is a term coined by E.F. Codd that refers to any software that permits interactive data analysis through a human-computer interface. It is commonly used to label a category of software technology that enables analysts, managers, and executives to perform ad hoc data access and analysis based on its dimensionality. This form of multidimensional analysis provides business insight through fast, consistent, interactive access to a wide variety of possible views of information. However, the term itself does not imply the use of multidimensional analysis or structures.

Operational Data Store (ODS)   The operational data store is a subject-oriented, integrated, current, volatile collection of data used to support the operational and tactical decision-making process for the enterprise. It is the central point of data integration for business management, delivering a common view of enterprise data.

Operational Systems   Operational systems are the internal and external core systems that run the day-to-day business operations. They are accessed through application program interfaces (APIs) and are the source of data for the data warehouse and operational data store.

Operations and Administration   Operations and administration refers to the set of activities required to ensure smooth daily operations, to ensure that resources are optimized, and to ensure that growth is managed. This consists of enterprise data management, systems management, data acquisition management, service management, and change management.

Optionality   Optionality is an indication whether an entity occurrence must participate in a relationship. This characteristic tells you the minimum number (zero or optional) of occurrences in the relationship.

Primary Entity   See Fundamental Entity.

Primary Key   A primary key uniquely identifies the entity and is used in the physical database to locate a specific row for storage or access.

Ragged Hierarchy   A ragged hierarchy is a hierarchy of varying depth.

Referential Integrity Referential integrity is the facility of a database management system to ensure the validity of a predefined foreign key relationship.

Relational Model The relational model is a form of data model in which data is packaged according to business rules and data relationships, regardless of how the data will be used in processes, in as nonredundant a fashion as possible. Normalization rules are used to create this form of model.

Relationship A relationship documents the business rule associating two entities. The relationship is used to describe how the two entities are naturally linked to each other.

Root Node A node that is at the highest level of a hierarchy.

Second Normal Form Model The second normal form (2NF) requires that all attributes be dependent on the whole key. To attain 2NF, the entity must be in 1NF and every nonprimary attribute must be dependent on the entire primary key for its existence. 2NF further reduces possible redundancy in the data model by removing attributes that are dependent on part of the key and placing them in their own entity.

Snapshot A snapshot is a view of information at a particular point in time.

Staging Area The staging area is where data from the operational systems is first brought together. It is an informally designed and maintained grouping of data that may or may not have persistence beyond the load process.

Star Schema A star schema is a dimensional data model implemented on a relational database.

Statistical Applications Statistical applications are set up to perform complex, difficult statistical analyses such as exception, means, average, and pattern analyses. The Data Warehouse is the source of data for these analyses. These applications analyze massive amounts of detailed data and require a reasonably performing environment.

Statistical Warehouse See Data-Mining Warehouse.

Stock Keeping Unit (SKU) A stock keeping unit is a component identifier used to keep track of an item when maintaining inventory. It is the smallest unit handled within the warehouse or storeroom. This term is also used interchangeably to refer to the item identifier for that unit.

Strategy A strategy is a plan or method for achieving a specific goal.

Subject Area A subject area is a major grouping of items, concepts, people, events, and places of interest to the enterprise. These things of interest are eventually depicted in entities. The typical enterprise has between 15 and 25 subject areas.

Subject Area Model   The subject area model groups the major categories of data for the enterprise. It provides a valuable communication tool and also helps in organizing the business data model.

Subject Matter Expert (SME)   The subject matter expert is the business representative with the required understanding of the existing business environments and of the requirements.

Subject Orientation   Subject orientation is a property of the data warehouse and operational data store that orients data around major data subjects such as customer, product, transaction, and so on.

Subtype Entity   A subtype entity is a logical division or category of a parent (supertype) entity. The subtypes always inherit the characteristics or attributes and relationships of the parent entity.

Surrogate Key   A surrogate key is a substitute key that is usually an arbitrary numeric value assigned by the load process or the database system. The advantage of the surrogate key is that it can be structured so that it is always unique throughout the span of integration for the data warehouse.

System Data Model   A system data model is a collection of the information being addressed by a specific system or function such as a billing system, data warehouse, or data mart. The system model is an electronic representation of the information needed by that system. It is independent of any specific technology or DBMS environment.

Systems Management   Systems management is the set of processes for maintaining the core technology on which the data, software, and tools operate.

Tactical Analysis   Tactical analysis consists of the ability to act upon strategic analyses in an immediate fashion. For example, the decision to stop a campaign in mid-execution is based on the intelligence garnered from past campaigns or recent history of activities in the current campaign (cannibalism or incorrect audience targeted).

Technical Data Model   The technology data model is a collection of the specific information being addressed by a particular system and implemented on a specific platform.

Technical Meta Data   Technical meta data is information that provides the details of how and where data was physically acquired, stored and distributed in the Corporate Information Factory.

Technical Sponsor   The technical sponsor is responsible for garnering business support and for obtaining the needed technical personnel and funding.

Technology Data Model   The technology data model is the technology dependent model of the data needed to support a particular system.

Thin Client Architecture   Thin client architecture is a technological topology in which the user's terminal requires minimal processing and storage capabilities. Most of these capabilities reside on a server.

Third Normal Form Data Model   The third normal form (3NF) requires that all attributes be dependent on nothing but the key. To attain 3NF, the entity must be in 2NF, and the nonkey fields must be dependent on only the primary key, and not on any other attribute in the entity, for their existence. This removes any transitive dependencies in which the nonkey attributes depend on not only the primary key but also on other nonkey attributes.

Transactional Interface (TrI)   The transactional interface is an easy-to-use and intuitively simple interface that allows the end user to request and employ business management capabilities. It accesses and manipulates data from the operational data store.

Tree   See Hierarchy.

Universal Product Code (UPC)   The Universal Product Code is a standard code used to identify retail products. It is commonly seen as a printed bar code on a retail package. It is primarily used in North, Central, and South America. Other parts of the world have similar coding systems.

Workbench   The workbench is a strategic mechanism for automating the integration of capabilities and knowledge into the business process.

Adelman, Sid. *Impossible Data Warehouse Situations*. Boston, MA: Addison-Wesley Professional, 2002.

Adelman, Sid and Moss, Larissa T. *Data Warehouse Project Management*. Boston, MA: Addison Wesley, 2000.

Berry, Michael J. A. and Linoff, Gordon. *Data Mining Techniques*. New York, NY: Wiley Publishing, Inc., 1997.

Berry, Michael J. A. and Linoff, Gordon. *Mastering Data Mining*. New York, NY: Wiley Publishing, Inc., 2000.

English, Larry P. *Improving Data Warehouse and Business Information Quality*. New York, NY: Wiley Publishing, Inc., 1999.

Feldman, Candace and von Halle, Barbara. *Handbook of Relational Database Design*. Reading, MA: Addison-Wesley Longman, 1989.

Hoberman, Steve. *Data Modeler's Handbook*. New York, NY: Wiley Publishing, Inc., 2000.

Imhoff, Claudia, Loftis, Lisa, and Geiger, Jonathan G. *Building the Customer Centric Enterprise: Data Warehousing Techniques for Supporting Customer Relationship Management*. New York, NY: Wiley Publishing, Inc. 2002.

Inmon, W. H. *Building the Data Warehouse, Second Edition*. New York, NY: Wiley Publishing, Inc., 1996.

Inmon, W. H. *Building the Operational Data Store, Second Edition*. New York, NY: Wiley Publishing, Inc., 1999.

Inmon, W. H., Imhoff, Claudia, and Sousa, Ryan. *Corporate Information Factory*. New York, NY: Wiley Publishing, Inc., 1998.

Inmon, W. H., Imhoff, Claudia, and Terdeman, Robert. *Exploration Warehousing*. New York, NY: Wiley Publishing, Inc., 2000.

Inmon, W. H., Rudin, Ken, Buss, Christopher K., and Sousa, Ryan. *Data Warehouse Performance*. New York, NY: Wiley Publishing, Inc., 1999.

Inmon, W. H., Terdeman, R. H., Norris-Montanari, Joyce, and Meers, Dan. *Data Warehousing for e-Business*. New York, NY: Wiley Publishing, Inc. 2002.

Inmon, W. H., Welch, J. D., and Glassey, Katherine L. *Managing the Data Warehouse*. New York, NY: Wiley Publishing, Inc., 1997.

Inmon, W. H., Zachman, John A., and Geiger, Jonathan G. *Data Stores Data Warehousing and the Zachman Framework: Managing Enterprise Knowledge*. New York, NY: McGraw-Hill, 1997.

Kachur, Richard. *Data Warehouse Management Handbook*. Paramus, NJ: Prentice Hall, 2000.

Kaplan, Robert S. and Norton, David P. *The Balanced Scorecard: Translating Strategy into Action*. Boston, MA: Harvard Business Press,1996.

Kimball, Ralph and Merz, Richard. *The Data Webhouse Toolkit*. New York, NY: Wiley Publishing, Inc. 2000.

Kimball, Ralph, Reeves, Laura, Ross, Margy, and Thornthwaite, Warren. *The Data Warehouse Lifecycle Toolkit: Expert Methods for Designing, Developing, and Deploying Data Warehouses*. New York, NY: Wiley Publishing, Inc. 1998.

Kimball, Ralph and Ross, Margy. *The Data Warehouse Toolkit: The Complete Guide to Dimensional Modeling*, 2nd Edition. New York, NY: Wiley Publishing, Inc. 2002.

Marco, David. *Building and Managing the Meta Data Repository*. New York, NY: Wiley Publishing, Inc., 2000.

Moore, Geoffrey A. *Crossing the Chasm*. New York, NY: Harper, 1991.

Moore, Geoffrey A. *Inside the Tornado*. New York, NY: Harper, 1995.

Moore, Geoffrey A. *Living on the Fault Line*. New York, NY: Harper, 2000.

Silverston, Len. *The Data Model Resource Book,*. Volumes 1 & 2, New York, NY: Wiley Publishing, Inc., 2001.

von Halle, Barbara. *Business Rules Applied*. New York, NY: Wiley Publishing, Inc., 2002.